Haunted Britain

Manchester University Press

Cultural History of Modern War
Series editors

Ana Carden-Coyne, Peter Gatrell, Max Jones, Penny Summerfield and Bertrand Taithe

Already published

Carol Acton and Jane Potter   *Working in a world of hurt: Trauma and resilience in the narratives of medical personnel in warzones*

Michael Brown, Anna Maria Barry and Joanne Begiato (eds)   *Martial masculinities: Experiencing and imagining the military in the long nineteenth century*

Quintin Colville and James Davey (eds)   *A new naval history*

James E. Connolly   *The experience of occupation in the Nord, 1914–18: Living with the enemy in First World War France*

Lindsey Dodd   *French children under the Allied bombs, 1940–45: An oral history*

Peter Gatrell and Liubov Zhvanko (eds)   *Europe on the move: Refugees in the era of the Great War*

Julie Gottlieb, Daniel Hucker, and Richard Toye (eds)   *The Munich Crisis, politics and the people: International, transnational and comparative perspectives*

Jessica Hammett   *Creating the people's war: Civil defence communities in Second World War Britain*

Grace Huxford   *The Korean War in Britain: Citizenship, selfhood and forgetting*

Linda Maynard   *Brothers in the Great War: Siblings, masculinity and emotions*

Duy Lap Nguyen   *The unimagined community: Imperialism and culture in South Vietnam*

Lucy Noakes   *Dying for the nation: Death, grief and bereavement in Second World War Britain*

Juliette Pattinson, Arthur McIvor and Linsey Robb   *Men in reserve: British civilian masculinities in the Second World War*

Beatriz Pichel   *Picturing the Western Front: Photography, practices and experiences in First World War France*

Michael Roper   *Afterlives of war: A descendants' history*

Spyros Tsoutsoumpis   *A history of the Greek resistance in the Second World War: The people's armies*

Centre for the Cultural History of War

https://www.alc.manchester.ac.uk/history/research/centres/cultural-history-of-war//

Haunted Britain

Spiritualism, psychical research and the Great War

Kyle Falcon

MANCHESTER UNIVERSITY PRESS

Copyright © Kyle Falcon 2023

The right of Kyle Falcon to be identified as the author of this work has been asserted by them in accordance with the Copyright, Designs and Patents Act 1988.

Published by Manchester University Press
Oxford Road, Manchester M13 9PL

www.manchesteruniversitypress.co.uk

British Library Cataloguing-in-Publication Data
A catalogue record for this book is available from the British Library

ISBN 978 1 5261 6497 1 hardback
ISBN 978 1 5261 9495 4 paperback

First published 2023
Paperback published 2026

The publisher has no responsibility for the persistence or accuracy of URLs for any external or third-party internet websites referred to in this book, and does not guarantee that any content on such websites is, or will remain, accurate or appropriate.

EU authorised representative for GPSR:
Easy Access System Europe – Mustamäe tee 50, 10621 Tallinn, Estonia
gpsr.requests@easproject.com

Typeset by Deanta Global Publishing Services, Chennai, India

For Lennox

Contents

List of figures	*Page* viii
Acknowledgements	xi
Abbreviations	xv
Introduction	1
1 Prophecies of war and peace: spiritualism and the new millennium	32
2 A psychic laboratory: numinous experiences and spiritualism on the Great War's battlefields	80
3 A war of sensation: telepathy, crisis apparitions and the moment of death on the home front	127
4 Living with the ghosts of war: death and mourning in the séance room	166
5 The army of the living dead: spirit photography and the public denial of death	210
Conclusion	252
Bibliography	283
Index	311

Figures

0.1 Geographical distribution of London's professional mediums, 1916. Data compiled from *Light*'s supplements and constructed using Google Maps — *page* 10

0.2 Spirit photograph. Ada Deane, 'Mrs. Ada E. Deane's Psychic Photographs, 1920–23, No. 2'. Spirit photographs, Warrick collection: Mrs Deane's photographs, Cambridge University Library, Department of Manuscripts, from the collections of the Society for Psychical Research, 54/2, 62. Reproduced by kind permission of the Syndics of Cambridge University Library — 13

1.1 David Gow, editor of *Light* from 1914 to 1931. Photo by Dora Head, *Psychic Science* 3, no. 6 (October 1927) — 42

1.2 Google Ngram search for the terms 'spiritualism' and 'psychical research' in British English books between 1850 and 2000. Google Books Ngram Viewer — 50

2.1 The trench newspaper *G.O.C.B. Chronicle* pokes fun at soldiers' superstitions. W. Heath Robinson, 'Touching Wood When Threatened with Trouble', *G.O.C.B. Chronicle* 2, no. 1 (1 February 1918) — 88

2.2 Segment of Harold Earith's attestation paper. Canadian Expeditionary Force Personnel File, Library and Archives Canada — 108

2.3 Cover art of Rosa Stuart's *Dreams and Visions of the War* (London: C. Arthur Pearson Ltd., 1917) — 114

Figures ix

4.1 Photograph of Nea Walker taken by Ada Deane in 1923. Mrs Gladys Osborne Leonard Papers, Cambridge University Library, Department of Manuscripts, from the collections of the Society for Psychical Research, 34/24/22. Reproduced by kind permission of the Syndics of Cambridge University Library 171

4.2 Nea Walker's original shorthand notes of a séance conducted on 7 May 1927. Nea Walker, 'NW Leonard 7 May 27', Mrs Gladys Osborne Leonard Papers, Cambridge University Library, Department of Manuscripts, from the collections of the Society for Psychical Research, 34/25/6. Reproduced by kind permission of the Syndics of Cambridge University Library 173

5.1 The first of two spirit photographs showing identical extras at different sittings. Ada Deane, 'Mrs. Ada E. Deane's Psychic Photographs, 1920–23, No. 2'. Spirit photographs, Warrick collection: Mrs Deane's photographs, Cambridge University Library, Department of Manuscripts, from the collections of the Society for Psychical Research, 54/2, 43. Reproduced by kind permission of the Syndics of Cambridge University Library 217

5.2 The second of two spirit photographs showing identical extras at different sittings. Ada Deane, 'Mrs. Ada E. Deane's Psychic Photographs, 1920–23, No. 1', 54/1, 11. Reproduced by kind permission of the Syndics of Cambridge University Library 218

5.3 The first of two spirit photographs by Ada Deane with unidentified sitters. Ada Deane, 'Mrs. Ada E. Deane's Psychic Photographs, 1920–23, No. 4'. Spirit photographs, Warrick collection: Mrs Deane's photographs, Cambridge University Library, Department of Manuscripts, from the collections of the Society for Psychical Research, 54/4, 67. Reproduced by kind permission of the Syndics of Cambridge University Library 223

5.4	The second of two spirit photographs by Ada Deane with unidentified sitters. Ada Deane, 'Mrs. Ada E. Deane's Psychic Photographs, 1920–23, No. 4'. Spirit photographs, Warrick collection: Mrs Deane's photographs, Cambridge University Library, Department of Manuscripts, from the collections of the Society for Psychical Research, 54/4, 83. Reproduced by kind permission of the Syndics of Cambridge University Library	224
6.1	Google Ngram search for 'supernormal' and 'paranormal' in British English books, 1880–2000. Google Books Ngram Viewer	260
6.2	Google Ngram search for 'psychical research' and 'parapsychology' in British English books, 1880–2000. Google Books Ngram Viewer	261
6.3	Google Ngram search for 'psychical research' and 'parapsychology' in American English books, 1880–2000. Google Books Ngram Viewer	262

Acknowledgements

The origins of this book can be traced to an undergraduate seminar in North Bay, Ontario, in the fall of 2008. We were reading with interest Will R. Bird's *Ghosts Have Warm Hands*, in which the author claimed to have been rescued from certain death by the ghost of his brother, Steve. Something about that ghostly encounter gnawed away at me. In fact, it is safe to say that Steve's ghost has haunted me ever since. It wasn't because I didn't believe in ghosts (I don't, by the way) or that I thought Bird may be lying about what happened to him (who can really be sure?). It wasn't even that I found it weird that ghosts were reported on the Western Front (I certainly did). What I couldn't quite shake was this sense that the ghost story did not seem to fit the broader narrative that Will Bird was trying to tell. *Ghosts Have Warm Hands* is a surprisingly realistic account of the Great War. Steve's ghost simply did not belong there. It was only in 2014 that my suspicions were confirmed after the republication of Bird's original 1930 memoir, *And We Go On*, by David Williams. This memoir was not a realist account. Bird's war was a magical one involving premonitions, psychics and spirits. At the time of the book's re-release, I was exploring the role of spiritualism during the Great War. *And We Go On* seemed to bring together many of the questions and themes that I had been mulling over. Bird was writing in a particular context, where discussions about the magical and supernatural were dominated by debates about spiritualism and psychical research, and were utilised in the interwar period to try and redeem the war. *Haunted Britain* fleshes out for the first time the culture that Bird was responding to: what I identify as the supernormal interpretation of the Great War.

This book is therefore the final product of a journey that began about fourteen years ago. Over that time I have accrued the help and guidance of too many people to adequately offer thanks in these short pages. But I will try my best. First to my family. When I first told my parents that I wanted to study history for a living, they offered nothing but support. Like many others who find themselves gravitated towards the history of the world wars, I grew up hearing stories about my great-grandfather Andrew Campbell Marshall who fought for the British in the First World War only to meet an untimely death in the Scottish coal mines, as well as his daughter Helen Fulton Brown Falcon (née Marshall) and my grandfather George Anthony Falcon, both of whom served for the Canadians in the Second. Although these memories passed from our family's lived experience in 2005, they have proved a constant source of interest and inspiration. But it is my parents, sisters, in-laws and loving wife who I am most thankful for in supporting me through the years. My parents are and will always remain my biggest fans and I hope they can take pride in this work as if it were their own.

Thank you to the faculty and students at Wilfrid Laurier University who assisted in the early stages of this project. Peter Farrugia, Sofie Lachapelle and Roger Sarty were always eager to read my work and provided invaluable guidance and recommendations. Jay Winter's feedback was particularly valuable and his work served as an early inspiration for this project. Current and former Tri-University faculty and staff offered their support whenever it was needed, including Terry Copp, Mary Chatkiris, Adam Crerar, Colleen Ginn, Mark Humphries, Linda Mahood, Amy Milne-Smith, Susan Neylan, Eva Plach, Edmund Pries, David Smith, Heather Vogel and Cindi Wieg. Special thanks to the faculty at Nipissing University who encouraged me to pursue graduate school, particularly Hilary Earl and Stephen Connor, and who I am honoured to now call friends. Fellow Laurier graduate students and alumni served as early unofficial editors. Thank you to Alec Mavaara, Brittany Dunn, Lyndsay Rosenthal, Eric Story and Carla-Jean Stokes. These brilliant scholars, instructors and friends have inspired me to be a better historian, thinker and writer.

The research for this book was possible thanks to generous financial support provided by the Social Sciences and Humanities

Research Council of Canada (SSHRC), the Tri-University Program, the History Department and the Faculty of Postdoctoral and Graduate Studies at Wilfrid Laurier University. The Laurier Centre for Military Strategic and Disarmament Studies (now the Laurier Centre for the Study of Canada) was always very good to me, providing not just financial support but also emotional support and a much-needed distraction from the loneliness of academic research and writing (special thanks to Matt Baker and Kevin Spooner). The staffs at the Imperial War Museum, Senate House Library, Library of Congress, British Library, Cambridge University Library and Society for Psychical Research were very generous in their assistance. Jake and Meagan Crawford provided me with a place to stay and a friendly face across the pond, while Raluca Oprean photographed documents for hours on my behalf during the COVID-19 pandemic.

Portions of this book were also written while serving as an AMS Healthcare Postdoctoral Fellow at the University of Western Ontario. Thank you to Jonathan Vance and Heidi van Galen, AMS Healthcare and Research Nova Scotia. Alison Abra from St John's College, University of Manitoba, Mark Connelly from the University of Kent, Janet Watson from the University of Connecticut and Sarah Wearne all provided helpful feedback, insights or examples that were incorporated into this book. Thank you to the team at Manchester University Press, including Paul Clarke, Humairaa Dudhwala and Jen Mellor. My editor Meredith Carroll was nothing but patient and accommodating as I slowly worked on the final version of this book.

As I embarked on this journey our family experienced its own great losses. To my cousin Clint Vandenberg and my Aunt Carol Duncan, we love you and miss you and your absence has made it difficult to look upon some of the hundred-year-old stories contained in this book with the disinterested eyes of a historian. In the final months of this book's completion, my wife and I were blessed with our first born. To my son Lennox, your arrival in my life has taught me more about the people covered in this book than the dozen or so years of research that came before. I cannot read Herbert Asquith's gripping sorrow over the death of his son Raymond the same way ever again. This book is dedicated to you. To Sadie and Bagheera, you helped in ways you could never know. And finally to my wife

Jillian. There are simply no words that are adequate to express my gratitude. You have been with me from the very beginning and saw it through with me to the end. You have shared in my highs and deepest lows. I could not ask for a more loving and supportive partner. Thank you for making this possible.

Abbreviations

ASC	Army Service Corps
ASPR	American Society for Psychical Research
BCPS	British College of Psychic Science
CEF	Canadian Expeditionary Force
CUL	Cambridge University Library
CWGC	Commonwealth War Graves Commission
ESP	Extra-sensory perception
GWCSL	Great World Christian Spiritualist League
IWGC	Imperial War Graves Commission
IWM	Imperial War Museum
JSPR	*Journal of the Society for Psychical Research*
KJV	King James Version
LAC	Library and Archives Canada
LNU	League of Nations Union
LSA	London Spiritualist Alliance
NCB	Northern Cyclist Battalion
PSPR	*Proceedings of the Society for Psychical Research*
RAMC	Royal Army Medical Corps
RFA	Royal Field Artillery
RFC	Royal Flying Corps
SHL	Senate House Library
SNU	Spiritualist National Union
SPR	Society for Psychical Research
SSSP	Society for the Study of Supernormal Pictures

Introduction

The ghosts of the Great War haunted Siegfried Sassoon. One night, while convalescing in Fourth London General Hospital, Sassoon witnessed the floor become 'littered with parcels of dead flesh and bones'. Their faces glared at the ceiling or the floor while they clutched their necks or bellies. '[A] livid grinning face with bristly moustache peers at me over the edge of my bed', he writes, 'the hands clutching my sheets'. When Sassoon awoke the next morning, the animated corpses had vanished, and he could find no bloodstains on his bed sheets. By contrast, in his novel, *Memoirs of an Infantry Officer* (1930), Sassoon's protagonist George Sherston first arrives at the Western Front in 1915 believing that the dead were 'gloriously happy' in the afterlife.[1] Compared with the romantic ghosts of Sherston's imagination, Sassoon's trauma encapsulates the disillusionment of Britain's youth in the furnace of industrial warfare. The veteran and journalist Charles Edward Montague captured these feelings in his 1922 book, *Disenchantment*. 'All mortal things are subject to decay', he declares. As the old generation of 'pre-war virilists' dies out, a new voice emerges in their place. 'For them Bellona has not the mystical charm', explains Montague. The soldiers of the Great War 'have seen the trenches full of gassed men, and the queue of their friends at the brothel-door in Bethune. At the heart of the magical rose was seated an earwig.'[2]

The visceral disenchantment expressed by Montague remains a powerful myth in the Great War's cultural legacy. According to popular conceptions, Britons greeted the war with enthusiasm. After rushing to enlist, soldiers discovered the horrific realities of trench warfare. The flower of Britain's youth was led to the slaughter by incompetent generals and an ignorant home front. Those who survived were mentally scarred and left disillusioned about the war's purpose. A generation was lost in body or mind.³ The literary scholar Paul Fussell famously argued in the 1970s that British writers such as Sassoon and his contemporaries Wilfred Owen and Robert Graves exposed as farcical the high diction of religion and patriotism. The use of romantic language to glorify war, he argued, is now indistinguishable from satire within our 'modern memory'.⁴ The disenchantment of the Great War poets is well known, but perhaps lesser known is that during the war, Sassoon's mother tried to contact the spirit of her son, Hamo Sassoon, that Robert Graves claimed to see the ghost of a comrade on the battlefield, and that Wilfred Owen's brother, Harold, witnessed an apparition of Wilfred halfway around the world at the moment of his death.⁵ They were not alone. In the aftermath of the Great War, Britons read prophecies about the coming new millennium, experimented with séances and claimed to see the ghosts of their loved ones in dreams and in photographs. Reports of premonitions and visions of angels on the Great War's battlefields were widespread. Some soldiers attributed their survival to angelic, psychic or spiritual forces. Why have the traumatic memories of the war been so enduring amidst this much broader haunted landscape?

Supernatural stories set in the Great War have long represented a curiosity for historians. What were ghosts, angels, psychics and miracles doing amongst tanks, artillery, gas, machine guns, submarines and aeroplanes? Paul Fussell, for example, asks how 'a plethora of very un-modern superstitions, talismans, wonders, miracles, relics, legends and rumours' could coexist amidst 'a war representing a triumph of modern industrialism, materialism, and mechanism'.⁶ Jay Winter introduces his study on spiritualism with the proclamation that 'the Great War, the most "modern" of wars, triggered an avalanche of the "unmodern"'.⁷ Contemporaries did not view the lines between the modern and unmodern to be so self-evident. Beginning in the second half of the nineteenth century, renowned European and American thinkers endorsed, or considered seriously, the possibility of psychic and spiritual phenomena such as telepathy and the possibility of communicating with the dead, including the winner of the Nobel Prize in Physiology or Medicine, Charles Richet; the 'father of American psychology', William James; the discoverer of the element thallium, Sir William Crookes; and the co-discoverer of natural selection, Sir Alfred Russel Wallace. The classical scholar and amateur psychologist Frederic Myers's ambitious *Human Personality and its Survival of Bodily Death* drew upon the new psychological sciences to create an anti-materialist science that unified telepathy, spiritualism, hysteria and a host of other phenomena into what he called the 'supernormal': 'a faculty or phenomenon which goes beyond the level of ordinary experience, in the direction of evolution, or as pertaining to a transcendental world'.[8] Such phenomena, Myers believed, were not beyond the confines of scientific investigation even if they existed in a state beyond ordinary matter. Myers's ideas influenced spiritualism's leading proponents during the Great War, including the physicist Sir Oliver Lodge and the author Sir Arthur Conan Doyle. Lodge publicly advocated for a spiritual synthesis with modern science well into the 1930s while Conan Doyle's missionary zeal threatened the authority of the churches.[9]

The intersection of science and the supernatural in modern Europe and North America has led historians of magic to question Max Weber's famous dictum in 1918 that 'intellectual rationalization' and 'scientifically oriented technology' led to the 'disenchantment of the world'.[10] Despite Montague's association of a magical disenchantment with a postwar nihilism, historians have tended to view them in isolation, using supernatural stories of the Great War to discredit the narrative of disillusionment on the one hand or a modern secular disenchantment on the other, but not both.[11] *Haunted Britain* reconsiders enchantment, broadly understood, using war-related abnormal experiences in the context of late nineteenth- and early twentieth-century attempts to unify science and the supernatural, in order to provide a new cultural and emotional history of the Great War. It argues that the war ushered in a wave of culturally specific 'supernormal' experiences, practices and theories that were used to navigate and reconcile various modern intellectual, cultural and emotional anxieties that culminated in the cataclysm of the Great War. As grieving families and fighting soldiers across the British Empire searched for some meaning behind the upheavals brought on by modern industrial warfare, they found within the language of spiritualism and psychical research a means to navigate their grief and redeem the bloodshed. They did so by seeking an end to intellectual, social and military conflict through a single unified theological and scientific philosophy emanating from soldiers' spirits. This project to build a heaven on earth using the ghosts of the Great War contrasts sharply with the disenchantment that now typifies not only the cultural legacy of the war but also modernity itself.

Myth, memory and the sacred in Modern Britain

This book tells the story of the rise and fall of the supernormal explanation of the Great War from three main perspectives. First, it positions wartime spiritualism and psychical research within a broader turn to the sacred and the perseverance of supernatural beliefs in modern Britain. Following the latest findings in the history of magic and science, it argues that far from representing a relic of unmodern beliefs and practices, the spiritualist and psychical research movements were well adapted to modern needs. Historians, for example, used to believe that spiritualists and psychical researchers were simply reacting to a Victorian crisis of faith. According to Janet Oppenheim, figures such as Lodge and Myers embraced 'pseudoscience' because they wanted 'to believe in *something*'. They found within spiritualism and psychical research a 'refuge from bleak mechanism, emptiness, and despair'.[12] Attempts to unify science and religion were therefore a temporary diversion in the face of modern scientific progress.

With the exception of popular science writers, scholars of magic have now long since debunked this simplistic narrative of scientific progress. Magic, alchemy, miracles and the occult flourished during and after the Age of the Enlightenment, including among some of those figures widely seen as responsible for bringing about revolutions in science.[13] Witchcraft, for example, retained an important place in European and North American culture for centuries after its alleged decline in the mid-eighteenth century. In the United States, more people were killed as witches *after* the Salem witch trials than before or during.[14] The historian Thomas Water has found that between 1866 and 1899, British newspapers reported 462 outbreaks of witchcraft.[15] And in the late 1940s and early 1950s, West Germany experienced an explosion of witchcraft accusations, reports of miracle cures and demands for wonder doctors at the very same time that it was undergoing a postwar economic miracle.[16]

The continued relevance of magical beliefs amidst modern material and scientific progress should not be confused with the stubborn resistance of unenlightened superstitions, but instead understood as evidence of the highly elastic nature of supernatural beliefs, which often change, adapt and even originate *sui generis* alongside advances in modern technology and science. Monica Black's study on postwar Germany, for example, has convincingly shown that while witchcraft may be a universal phenomenon, reported across time and place, it is also culturally specific. After the fall of the Third Reich, witchcraft accusations were fuelled by distrust in one's neighbours as power and property (previously confiscated during the years of persecution) once again changed hands.[17] In late nineteenth-century Britain, philosophies and concepts that have since become symbolic of the disenchanted modern world inspired an 'Occult revival'. For example, *fin-de-siècle* occultists such as the infamous Aleister Crowley practised a ritual magic and advanced a spiritual agenda, while engaging with mainstream psychology and modern artistic movements.[18] Occultists' concept of an 'occluded self' held that a probing of the subjectivity and multiplicity of consciousness offered a gateway to the spirit. Their ideas were similar to the philosophies of the British avant-garde and surrealists who were exploring the 'mysterious inner world of the self' through art, drama and literature, and whose members would go on to artistically express their feelings of postwar disillusionment in the interwar period.[19] William James's division of the self into separate 'streams of consciousness' impacted modern psychologists, his fellow psychical researchers, occultist movements and modernist novelists such as the disillusioned Virginia Woolf and the psychical enthusiast May Sinclair.[20]

In light of scientific developments, it is easy to forget that the boundaries separating mainstream and fringe sciences are not always clear. Even Darwinism was initially considered a marginal science, and scientists have accused contemporary disciplines such as evolutionary psychology of being fundamentally unscientific.[21] In hindsight, we are also likely to underestimate the ways in which the occult seemed plausible in context. William Crookes's curiosity for hidden forces led him to séances as well as the discovery of thallium in 1861.[22] The engineer Cromwell Fleetwood Varley had to overcome concerns of fraud and disbelief as he advocated for both spiritualism and telegraphy, believing that the successful laying of the Atlantic telegraph cable in 1866 made a compelling case for spiritualism's veracity.[23] Lodge's ethereal theories placed him at the forefront of *fin-de-siècle* physics as well as psychical research. When explaining telepathy, he and his fellow physicists such as Sir William F. Barrett drew upon metaphors from the physical sciences such as induction, sympathetic resonance, X-rays, telegraphy and the telephone.[24] Lodge had even achieved wireless transmission with Hertzian waves before Marconi.[25] If invisible forces could be manipulated to transcend geographical space, how big of a leap was it to wonder if thoughts were waves, or if the distance between life and death was merely a communication problem?[26] One American spiritualist wrote that she first encountered the spirit of her son killed in the Great War through wireless telegraphy.[27]

The psychological sciences also skirted neat boundaries between science and the supernatural. It has been argued that modernism was responsible for psychoanalysis, yet some of the most consequential figures in dynamic psychiatry engaged with psychical research.[28] The founding of the Society for Psychical Research (SPR) in 1882 is often portrayed as a direct response to spiritualism's popularity, but others have linked its genesis to an alternative interpretation of various anomalous phenomena emerging at the forefront of the new sciences of the mind.[29] How else do we explain the SPR's prestigious membership, which included Pierre Janet, Charles Richet, Hippolyte Bernheim, Cesare Lombroso, Sigmund Freud and William James, or the fact that psychical researchers were the first to introduce British readers to psychoanalysis?

As in the sciences, spiritualists and psychical researchers also relied on the power of demonstration, legitimising and expressing their beliefs through observation gathered in séances, instead of faith or scripture. Conjurers took to the stage to reveal spiritualists as frauds, but some mediums such as Daniel Dunglas Home evaded exposure, leaving behind a repertoire of inexplicable feats that perplexed honest observers. Notable scientists such as Crookes and Lodge meticulously studied séances and ruled out trickery. Given the importance of empirical authority in Victorian and Edwardian Britain, the historian Peter Lamont has argued that spiritualism was about a 'crisis of evidence' not just a 'crisis of faith' and part of a general culture of proof.³⁰ Indeed, some saw spiritualism as a complement to their Christian faith, not a substitution.

The spiritual frameworks available to the Great War's belligerent nations were diverse. Spiritualism was but one player amidst a broad turn to the sacred and supernatural within Britain. Just as scholars of magic and science have challenged the myth of disenchantment, so too have historians of the Great War convincingly argued against the notion that the war experience was profane.³¹ The cultures that went to war in 1914 were religious and continued to be so afterwards. It is true that by the outbreak of the war, church attendance was in decline.³² But church affiliation in Britain was still significant.³³ Christian culture remained relevant to British national identity, including in schools, government and the arts, and through important life rituals such as baptism, marriage and funerals. Sunday school was especially popular in Britain, with over 70 per cent of five- to fourteen-year-olds enrolled in the first decade of the twentieth century.³⁴ Clergymen identified the existence of a 'diffusive Christianity', defined as 'a general belief in God, a conviction that this God was both just and benevolent ... a certain confidence that "good people" would be taken care of in the life to come, and a belief that the Bible was a uniquely worthwhile book'.³⁵

Civilian soldiers transferred a diffusive Christianity to the battlefields where the conditions of modern warfare often encouraged an experimentation and reliance on magical and psychic practices.³⁶ Chaplains observed that a 'wind-up' or 'emergency religion' was quite common, characterised by a demand for religious services prior to offensives as well as resorting to prayer in moments of peril.³⁷ To be sure, the soldiers' lack of reverence for theological details and institutional nuance offended some chaplains. Soldiers tended to treat Bibles like 'a bag of charms' and Catholic emblems were popular amongst Protestant troops.³⁸ Despite these observations, wind-up religion also signified to chaplains that British soldiers were not atheists. As a report on the religious beliefs of British soldiers observed, 'It means that in presence of the most terrific display of material force that human history has ever seen men believe that there is an Unseen Power ... However brief and transient, it is an implicit repudiation of that material view of life.'³⁹ A lack of organised religious observance was therefore countered by other supernatural beliefs.

The continued relevance of Christianity was also evident on the home front during the war as public figures such as Lloyd George, Horatio Bottomley and even H. G. Wells fused patriotic and Christian notions of sacrifice to exalt the soldier as a Christ-like figure and to justify the moral righteousness of the cause.[40] Official forms of remembrance incorporated Bible verses such as 'Their Name Liveth Forever More', which is engraved on the Stone of Remembrance found at every Commonwealth War Graves Commission (CWGC) cemetery today.[41] Christian themes were also used to produce impressive works of art, as in Stanley Spencer's *The Resurrection of the Soldiers* (1928–32).[42] As Jay Winter observes, modernism made for great literature that has survived in our cultural memory, but it could not offer solace in the face of grief or imbue sacrifice with meaning.[43] Regardless of the extent of orthodox religious belief, Christianity provided readily available symbols and language that were used to justify, understand and commemorate the war. So widespread was the appeal to the sacred on fighting nations' home fronts and battlefields that one scholar has even gone so far as to refer to the Great War as a 'holy war' akin to the Crusades and the Wars of Religion.[44] While others have been more careful in their language, it is clear that 'For the generation that fought the First World War religious belief and practice were still almost everywhere normal rather than exceptional.'[45]

Haunted Britain contributes to the historiographies of the history of magic and science and the religious history of the Great War by identifying where and how the cultures of spiritualism and psychical research could be mobilised to enchant modernity's most disenchanting experience: the slaughter wrought by industrial war. Like many of their fellow British citizens, spiritualists tended to believe in the righteousness of the war and the moral superiority of the Empire. They hoped that the war would end war, that death was not the end of the spirit and that sacrifice for the nation could bring redemption. These views were grounded in idealised and Christian concepts, but spiritualists were not blind to the implications of rationality and science, nor to industrial warfare's destructive capacity and the challenges that it posed to traditional romantic views of combat. As Oliver Lodge wrote in 1918,

Introduction 9

> No longer can we sing of arms wielded by heroic men: armaments are now physical and chemical, the outcome of prostituted science. Complex machinery, against which human flesh is battered and helpless, flames for inflicting torment, poisonous gases in which no living creature can breathe – these diabolical engines are able to overcome and almost to annihilate heroism.[46]

The brutal physical effects unleashed by materialist science necessitated a supernormal approach to exalt the British soldier. Heroes would have to be made, not on the battlefields of this world, but in the spiritual realm of the other. What if the spirits of dead soldiers could reconcile science and religion? As an elastic form of spirituality, spiritualism adapted more familiar religious beliefs to the demands of the modern world, including in the realm of warfare. The new cosmology that spiritualists constructed in the Great War's aftermath allowed fragments of the old to survive the slaughter on the Somme and Passchendaele as well as the disillusionment of the 1930s.

Who were the spiritualists? Class and gender

The second major aim of this book is to demonstrate how spiritualism and psychical research attended to certain social and cultural anxieties amidst Britain's privileged classes. Although spiritualism and psychical research were particularly attractive to the elite and middle class, for reasons we shall soon see, there were working-class spiritualists. Spiritualism's dissent from orthodoxy could appeal to those within the lower classes who believed in the supernatural but who were otherwise unsympathetic to clerical religion. For example, James J. Morse was the son of a publican, was orphaned by the age of ten and worked as a messenger, sailor and waiter in a public house. Morse could not reconcile his social upbringing with the teachings of orthodox Christianity.[47] 'My reason revolted against the dogmas of eternal torment hereafter, and also against the doctrines of original sin', he recalled, adding, 'Heaven was impossible to me, it seemed; and Hell was too awful to think of. What if there was another life?'[48] Morse was introduced to the spiritualist movement through the Unitarian Reverend J. P. Hopps and found in spiritualism a democratic religion 'freed from class restraints'.[49] He would later serve as the editor of *The Two Worlds*, a penny weekly whose socially progressive spiritualism appealed to those active in working-class reform until his death in 1919.[50]

It is difficult to know how prevalent the movement remained amongst the working classes, especially after the war. The historian Logie Barrow, for example, argues that, beginning in the 1880s, middle- and upper-class spiritualism became far more influential, and plebeian spiritualism declined before the Great War.[51] A geographical survey of mediums operating in London in 1916 appears to confirm Barrow's conclusion, showing a clear concentration of spiritualist services in the West End of London (see Figure 0.1). The wealthy's greater access to leisure time and income meant that

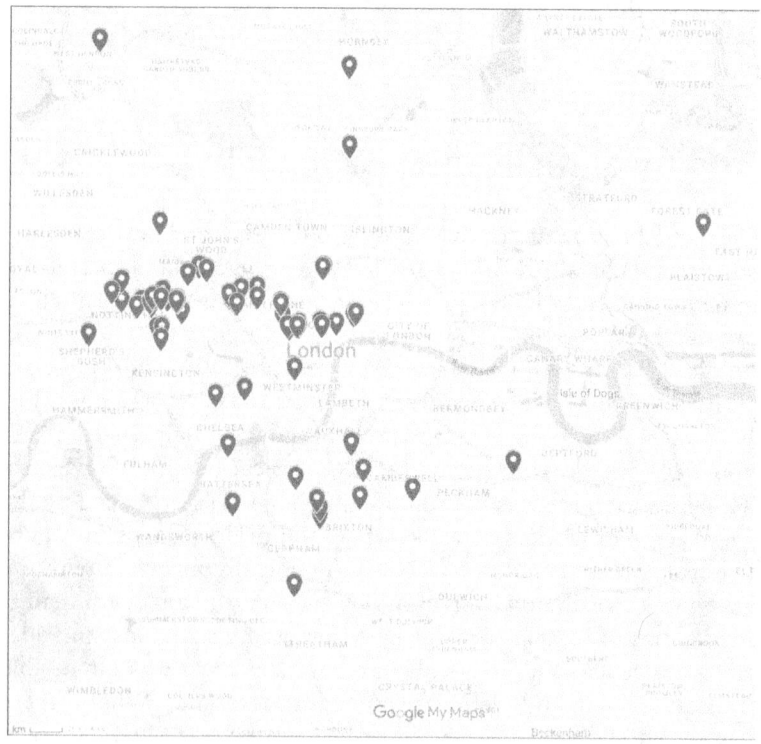

Figure 0.1 Geographical distribution of London's professional mediums, 1916.

they were more active in the movement, creating societies and journals that offered an exchange of ideas and ready volunteers for the cause.[52] The psychical researcher J. G. Piddington, for example, was a lead researcher on some of the SPR's most time-consuming investigations. He was also the inheritor of his grandfather's prosperous silver importing company. Nevertheless, spiritualism never entirely shed its links to social reformist movements, such as socialism, pacifism and feminism. Instead, elements of this history would exert influence on Britain's social and cultural elite who were looking to reconcile the contradictory and lofty ideals that initially negotiated their consent to fight during the tumultuous decades of the 1920s and 1930s. They looked towards spiritual reform from above rather than political or social reform from below – a heaven on earth moulded in their own image to solve class inequality in the 1920s and the threat of another international conflict in the 1930s.

For women, spiritualism could provide an opportunity to transgress gender norms in Victorian and Edwardian Britain. Not only could they obtain spiritual authority, but through trance, they could adopt different personalities, including a more promiscuous or masculine femininity.[53] It was women who tended to be mediums and men who usually served as the researchers. Medium advertisements in the spiritualist journal *Light* show a clear gender disparity. Between January 1914 and December 1916, of the 124 mediums whose genders can be identified, 101 were women.[54] There were exceptions of course. Peter J. Vango and Alfred Vout Peters were well-known mediums during the early twentieth century, but they tended to be viewed as feminine. Vango for example, masqueraded as a woman known as 'Sunflower' while in trance.[55] Women such as Eleanor Sidgwick (the sister of British Prime Minister Arthur Balfour) and Liz Lind Af Hageby also held leadership positions in the SPR and the London Spiritualist Alliance (LSA), respectively.[56] But overall, women were believed to be the ideal candidates for mediumship because of their supposed sensitivity and passivity.

By the interwar period, the stakes of spiritualism had grown so great that male psychical researchers exerted disturbing levels of control over the reputations and bodies of women mediums. It was men who led the physical and controlled experiments that characterised many scientific investigations into mediumship in the 1920s and 1930s, and this often involved a probing of the feminine body to eliminate trickery. Men also acted as talent managers for popular mediums and held them to high feminine standards to avoid any undo offence.[57] This retreat from more liberal to conservative attitudes towards gender mirrored the broader trend in British society. The war may have offered women new opportunities, including as spiritual authorities tending to the bereaved masses. But these opportunities were only fleeting, and spiritualism could just as easily create significant restraints on acceptable feminine behaviour, especially regarding expressions of grief. Whereas masculine ghosts could once offer Victorian women liberation, during and after the Great War, the soldier spirit was used to sustain and reinforce traditional gender roles and dynamics.

The gender dynamics of interwar spiritualism reveal an exerted effort amongst the powerful to sustain prewar norms. While the mass death of the Great War did not spare any demographic, the war disproportionately targeted Britain's elite, and it is striking how many séance attendees were parents. As David Cannadine observes, the Great War occurred at a moment when other factors were fuelling a positive trend in life expectancy. More families at the turn of the century could expect their children to survive to adulthood.[58] In 1870, the death rate for English and Welsh males ages five to nine was 8.9, and for ages ten to fourteen, 4.5. In 1900 those numbers declined by approximately half, to 4.2 and 2.3, respectively.[59] Michael Roper suggests that because infant mortality rates remained high in the late nineteenth century, parents were particularly attached to those children who made it past these dangerous early years.[60] Oliver Lodge had twelve children and Conan Doyle had five, all of whom lived to adulthood. Raymond Lodge and Kingsley Conan Doyle were the first of their children to die, both in the war.

The war also disrupted these communities' traditional mourning practices. The Imperial War Graves Commission (IWGC) decreed an 'equality of treatment'. All of Britain's dead were to be memorialised in the same fashion regardless of their rank or social background. Those who could afford to repatriate their dead or erect expensive custom gravesites were not given the opportunity.

Britons were not only denied a local gravesite, but many were also deprived of a body. By the end of the war, over 900,000 men from the British Empire had been killed and only about half of these

Figure 0.2 A solitary male takes a spirit photo with the spirit photographer Ada Deane.

bodies were ever identified. Unidentified remains were buried with the epitaph 'Known Unto God' and the names of hundreds of thousands of missing soldiers were etched in stone on monuments across the former battlefields.[61] Those on the home front compensated for the lack of a physical gravesite by erecting local monuments. The Cenotaph and the Tomb of the Unknown Warrior served as universal gravesites.[62] In the interwar period, Britons and Dominion subjects also conducted pilgrimages to France.[63] The absence of a grave or body deprived the privileged classes of adequate mourning rituals at a time when they were unaccustomed to the death of their adult children. A century removed from the conflict, it is easy to forget that the war was not just a learning curve for military tacticians and strategists but also for civilians attempting to commemorate the dead.[64] Spiritualism must be understood as an experimental alternative to traditional death rituals within a particular segment of British society experiencing the shock of mass death. Although new to many, it had established an infrastructure within British society and had already piqued the interests of high-profile figures who offered a gateway into the movement.

The war's disproportionate death toll and the Pyrrhic victory that followed therefore resulted in a cultural anxiety amongst a particular class that contributed to the search for cosmic, rather than earthly solutions. It is this demographic that best exemplifies the myth of the lost generation.[65] The future was supposed to belong to the children of the elite.[66] Herbert Asquith lamented after the death of his first son Raymond, 'the war has sucked up so much of what was so loveable and full of promise ... Whatever pride I had in the past and whatever hope I had for the future – by much the largest part was invested in him. Now all that is gone.'[67] Rudyard Kipling, like others, struggled over feelings of guilt after having sent his only child to die in war under patriotic notions. This 'unnatural selection', as Oliver Lodge referred to it, encouraged a significant segment of British society to conduct séances where the afterlife was not only 'proven' but transmissions of power and culture were sustained.[68] In the spiritualist afterlife, the dead had a future in which they progressed to greater states of spiritual awareness and assisted in the diffusion of a psychic knowledge designed to unite science and religion, end human conflict and redeem the bloodshed. This project to build a heaven on earth between 1914 and 1939 in remembrance of the fallen is the ghost story of the Great War that emerges from a study of the intersections of science, the supernatural and the war's cultural legacy.

Psychical research, emotions and war

Finally, *Haunted Britain* offers a new emotional history of the war by arguing that the psychical researcher's model of the mind offers an undervalued repository of historically specific emotional experiences. There is no attempt here to retroactively diagnose our subjects. George M. Johnson's book on mysticism and the Great War, for example, compellingly makes the case that spiritualism was a form of therapeutics in an age before psychoanalysis. But rather than truly meeting his subjects on their own terms, Johnson instead chooses to psychoanalyse them using concepts that emerged after the war. Although making for some interesting insights, his approach occasionally leads to reductionism, in which Oliver Lodge's interest in spiritualism is attributed to neglectful parents and the bullying he experienced as a child.[69]

This book instead attempts to appreciate how specific assumptions about unconscious phenomena may have shaped Britons' emotional lives. Historians of medicine and emotions have convincingly shown that certain mental illnesses, such as hysteria, fugue and multiple personalities are transient – appearing, disappearing and even reappearing in a specific time and place.[70] As the philosopher of science Ian Hacking observes, 'whatever ailed these patients … the manifestations, the marks of their illness, were entirely socially conditioned'. Hysteria and fugue, for example, were gender and class specific. The former was predominantly a feminine disorder while men of the lower classes tended to experience the latter.[71] In an era before mainstream psychoanalysis, nineteenth- and early twentieth-century mental disorders, including hysteria, shell shock and neurasthenia, unconsciously manifested physical symptoms to elicit sympathy and attention from physicians.[72] As Hacking notes, the dynamic between practitioner and patient allows for 'making up people', where the assumptions, ideas and expectations of the diagnostician shape and are shaped by the behaviour of the patient.[73] Since all of these factors can vary according to culture and time, historians have cautioned against equating mental phenomena such as shell shock and posttraumatic stress disorder (PTSD).[74] Multiple personalities thrived in nineteenth-century France under Jean-Martin Charcot's concept of hysteria and his use of hypnotism, which divided patients into their normal waking consciousness and hysterical and somnambulist selves. After Charcot's death, hysteria and multiple personalities declined. The latter was revived in the United States as ideas about child abuse and trauma changed and therapists began recovering dormant memories through hypnotism.[75]

In nineteenth- and early twentieth-century Britain, multiple personalities were intimately bound with spiritualism, where the personality of the medium was distinguished by a spirit control under trance.[76] The first generation of the SPR was influenced by evidence collected from Charcot's patients in France, dictating the form that trance mediumship took and how it was interpreted in the early twentieth century as spiritualism became more prominent in psychical research circles. The connections between mediumship and dissociative personality disorders blur any easy distinctions between reality, fraud and self-deception while highlighting the importance of cultural conditions. The case of William Stainton Moses illustrates the point. Moses was an Anglican vicar who turned to spiritualism and founded the LSA. He amassed a significant following as an eccentric trance medium and produced countless spirit scripts. Moses also experienced a lifetime of mental and somatic ailments, including depression, nervous breakdowns, congestion of the liver, catarrh bronchitis, whooping cough, throat infections, suppressed gout, neuralgic pains and Bright's disease. If we try to retroactively diagnose Moses, we discover that he was suffering from many ailments. The only coherent classifications are historical ones, such as neurasthenia. Not surprisingly, some psychical researchers wondered if his mediumship was pathological.[77] If not for Moses's social standing, gender and the context of spiritualism, he could have easily been diagnosed with hysteria.

The point is not that psychological disorders are not real or that comparisons cannot be drawn, but that the historical context matters to the types of people that can exist as well as their accompanying experiences. The patients of Charcot (and John Elliotson in the case of mesmerism) are prime examples of the elaborate types of people that can be created under certain assumptions and practices.[78] The same is true for human emotions, whose meanings and expressions are historically specific.[79] Over the last few decades, neuroscientists have argued for the importance of elasticity over biological determinism, further expanding the possibilities of the human condition that have interested historians of emotions. It is not just the ways that emotions are coded, controlled and expressed that can differ, although this is certainly important, but also the ways in which they are experienced.[80] Phenomena surrounding spiritualism and telepathy such as necromancy, mind-to-mind communications and apparitions have been reported across time and cultures but the concepts themselves were historically conditioned and they were used to not only explain a set of emotional experiences but also affected behaviours. We cannot access the subjective emotional states of historical subjects, but we can appreciate that supernormal phenomena are part of a specific emotional history.

The term supernormal, then, connotes a cluster of practices, assumptions, questions, hypotheses, theories, language and concepts that surrounded debates about spiritualism and psychical research between the period of roughly 1870 to 1939, and which were used to explain and navigate a variety of wartime emotions. Historians have used psychoanalytical frameworks to understand the emotional relationships between mothers and sons at war, and even spiritualists themselves. Even though many psychoanalytical theories have fallen out of favour in the scientific community, such approaches have been justified given the cultural importance of psychoanalysis in the modern West and for their value in illuminating the emotional world of historical subjects.[81] Why not a history that incorporates the psychical research model of mind and matter? If we are to better appreciate the war generation on their own terms and open new emotional histories of the conflict, we should take seriously the idea that the pages of spiritualist and psychical research sources tell us something real – and hopefully new – about how people felt and experienced the war, regardless of what we think about their scientific validity.

How the Great War haunted the British Empire

It is the most famous supernatural tale to emerge out of the Great War. Sometime in the fall of 1914, a woman identified only as 'Miss M.' met two officers claiming to have witnessed angelic intervention in Mons. According to one of these men, the incident occurred when advancing German cavalry cornered the outnumbered British Expeditionary Force (BEF). Turning around to face their foe, and 'expecting nothing but instant death', they 'saw between them, and the enemy a whole troop of angels'.[82] The Germans and their horses dispersed in terror, giving the British soldiers a chance to reach safety. This story of divine intervention at Mons exploded into the public consciousness after it was published in a parish magazine in the spring of 1915. A war-weary nation saw in the spectacular tale proof that the Allies were on the side of angels.[83]

Some historians have viewed the Angels of Mons as clear evidence of the supposed credulity that accompanied Britain's introduction to twentieth-century warfare. Despite the fact that the BEF had just engaged in its first battle in an industrial urban area and witnessed the first incident of direct combat between aircraft, 'Mons seemed not a curtain-raiser to a new kind of war but a battle in the best traditional manner ... the established virtues of individual courage and discipline and self-sacrifice and team spirit held firm.'[84] The Angels of Mons therefore typifies the early prominence of romantic images of war – the same ones that seduced the fictional George Sherston. Today, they appear as mere artefacts of a past that was extinguished in the trenches.

What happens when we consider the story from other perspectives offered at the time? For example, when it became clear that the Angels of Mons originated from Arthur Machen's 1914 fictional short story, 'The Bowmen', published in September 1914, the popular writer Harold Begbie proposed that Machen unconsciously drew his inspiration for the story from telepathic impressions sent from soldiers who witnessed angelic intervention in Mons.[85] In doing so, Begbie argued for the case of angels by incorporating popular supernormal concepts that had originated within psychical research communities in the late nineteenth century. 'Telepathy ... is a fact of the physical world', Begbie stated, claiming, 'no man of science would dispute' the possibility that Machen's story was telepathically inspired.[86] A tale of modern warfare, interpreted by some as a relic of a more unenlightened and romantic past, was reconceived in the language of science even while it retained its supernatural motifs.

Begbie was exaggerating about telepathy's intellectual acceptance, but how he chose to frame the Angels of Mons is a reminder that supernormal interpretations exerted significant influence in legitimising discussions about the supernatural in modern Britain, and that this same framework could also be leveraged to exalt the righteousness of the war. Historians such as Trevor Wilson have noted that it is 'unusual to associate supernatural warriors with a struggle conducted among slagheaps and factories'. But why? The subsequent displacement of the war's sacred elements by the profane tells us more about our contemporary image of the war than it does about those who experienced its carnage. Spiritualist and psychical experiences may now appear naïve given their association with the enchanted elements of modernity and the redemptive significance they placed upon the war's meaning, but they once influenced a segment of British society. The following chapters seek to demonstrate that there was nothing usual about angels amongst slag heaps and factories while answering why they appear so out of place today.

Chapter 1 offers a new history of spiritualism from the 1870s to 1939, noting the prevalence of a faith in progress, millenarian thinking and pacifist sympathies.[87] It uses spiritualist and occultist prophecies to better understand the hopes and visions of the future that existed in the minds and imaginations of the British people.

The idea that Britons suffered from a widespread disenchantment after 1918 necessarily implies that they were previously enchanted by patriotic and spiritual sentiments. Like any historical myth, there is an element of truth to this story. Britons, including the spiritualists among them, entered the twentieth century with optimism, believing in the forward march of modern industrial progress, even as the potential for social and intellectual unrest simmered below the surface. The war in turn was greeted with a level of assurance, if not enthusiasm. The validity of the struggle was made clear in Britain's eyes as Germany invaded Belgium and reports of atrocities reached home. While various social groups negotiated their consent with the promise of a greater future, existing spiritualists and psychical researchers comforted themselves with the assurance that peace would bring about a great spiritual awakening that would render war and materialism obsolete. Beginning in 1916, as Britain's elite witnessed a diminishing return on their sacrifice, they turned to the renewed public interest in spiritualism as validation of prewar prophecies: the tragedy of the death toll would bring countless numbers into the séance room where proof of the afterlife could be witnessed. Spiritualism was a cross-cultural phenomenon, but it was this school of thought, born out of their war experiences, that would emerge as uniquely British. The outbreak of the Second World War caused a crisis of faith and legitimacy within the spiritualist movement and foreshadowed how spiritualism in the era of the Great War would be remembered in hindsight.

Chapter 2 shifts attention to the battlefields, contradicting the idea that combat service was a profane experience or that enchantment occurred only on the home front. The arbitrary and anonymous nature of death from artillery shells kindled a culture of 'superstition', including premonitions, apparitions and miraculous survivals. These experiences were collected and shared by chaplains and were circulated in the spiritualist and psychic press on the home front to confirm the sacred meaning and significance of the war. The battlefield was a unique psychic laboratory, and the soldier was its scientist.

Chapter 2 expands the geographical reach of this study, examining British spiritualism as a transatlantic phenomenon, and the BEF more broadly to include Dominion soldiers who were exposed to Britain's spiritualist movement while on leave in England or through Conan Doyle's lectures abroad during the interwar period.[88] Wracked with guilt over having survived the war while his closest friends perished, the Canadian soldier Will R. Bird turned to the supernormal in 1930 to come to terms with his survival and to challenge the profanity of modernist writers such as Sassoon and Graves. By 1968, the legacy of the war had clearly changed, as most of these incidents were removed from his revised memoir to better fit the conventional narratives of lions led by donkeys.[89]

Britain's haunted landscape was therefore malleable. As memories changed, so too did the ghosts of war. Fortunately, dedicated researchers were intent on collecting experiences occurring on the fringes. While the psychotherapeutics of W. H. R. Rivers and his contemporaries recorded the traumatic memories and nightmares of the shell shocked, psychical researchers collected a vast catalogue of crisis apparitions – the vision of someone's ghost at the moment of their death – across the British Empire. Chapter 3 demonstrates how the trauma of death enveloped a British diaspora united in thought and feeling, providing a valuable window into the emotional lives of Britons at war. The supernormal paradigm interpreted these apparitions as telepathic messages, allowing those on the home front to frame their emotions as objects of scientific knowledge and providing an outlet for their grief amongst the near universalism of death in Britain. Transcendental and subjective experiences were validated as 'real' and the soldiers were agents of a psychic revelation confirming the uniqueness and importance of their individuality.

Introduction 21

It is in the séance, however, that we find the spectres of the Great War in full form. In darkened rooms across Britain, what were mere glimpses or dreams became fully fledged spirits capable of conversing with the living and helping them navigate through a postwar world. Chapter 4 uses documents discovered in the archives of the SPR to help illuminate the social function that spiritualism played for British families as their once-promising youth were eviscerated and lost forever on the battlefields.[90] Deep in the pages of psychical research reports we find the traces of their memories, as they roamed the British landscape in the thoughts and lived experiences of the bereaved. As this generation of parents, siblings and wives passed away or moved on, so too did their ghosts.

If séance transcripts provide faint traces of these feelings, the medium of spirit photography put them on full display, as explored in Chapter 5. The photograph was a material and visual object that provided evidence that the spirits were 'here'. This overlapped with public commemorations. The two minutes of silence was a public communion with the dead, and Britons often expressed feeling their presence at public commemorations. Mediums took advantage of these contexts to convince Britons of the authenticity of spiritualism and presented spirit photographs of the war dead hovering around the Cenotaph. The presence of unrecognised spirit faces in these photographs also represented, in physical form, the haunting presence of the war's missing. Spirit photographs circulated throughout Britain as believers looked to reunite unidentified spirits with their loved ones and prove spiritualism in the process. The twin aims of photographing the dead and spreading spiritualism to greater segments of the British public led to a fatal miscalculation when spiritualists published their Cenotaph spirit photographs in the popular press. Attempts to break into the mainstream occurred in the context of a 'crisis of confidence' in the 1920s.[91] Universal male franchise, women's suffrage and a new class consciousness resulted in social mobility that upset neat boundaries and traditional power structures. The public was on guard when it came to potential frauds and war profiteers, and the old prewar elites who led the spiritualist movement underestimated the intelligence and skills of working-class spirit photographers. The more spiritualists moved into the mainstream, they found themselves accused of desecrating the sacred memory of the dead and the legitimacy of their 'other world' in disarray. Attempts to stave off disenchantment had their bounds. Spirit photography more than any other form of spiritualism pushes the limits of credulity and presents unambiguous evidence of fraud. Its rise and fall is also the story of the crowning disenchantment that is the fact of death. The spiritualist project to redeem the war had clearly failed by the early 1930s even if spiritualists were unable to fully come to terms with this reality.

On 26 August 1918, a British woman named Elsi Walker (we will meet her again later) was communicating with the spirit of her sweetheart, Second Lieutenant Wilfrid Wayte. Elsi had been attending séances so frequently since Wilfrid's death in October 1917 that she was growing concerned about the effect this would have on her health. In typical Wilfrid fashion, his spirit was reassuring. Elsi need not worry, he explained, because so many had passed over recently that the war had brought the two worlds together in a way that was not possible before. 'There are so many passing over', his spirit explained, 'and so we live nearer the earth plane than we otherwise should'. Because of this, he informed her, a 'great psychic movement [is] coming, you can feel it already'.[92] Spiritualism offered a language to explain the haunting presence of the British Empire's 900,000 war dead, and the simultaneous presence and absence of the approximately 450,000 missing bodies. Battlefields, dreams, homes and memorials became what Celtic tradition refers to as 'thin places', where a site invokes a 'sense of the thinness of the veil which separates this world from the next'.[93] For the historian, the culturally specific language of the supernormal offers a unique window into this emotional history with implications for how we understand the cultural legacy of the war. Those feelings of being haunted were reconfigured into a language that retained an enchanted world, where the soldier's sacrifice was affirmed and the existence of the afterlife empirically proven. The further removed we are from these events, the less potent and familiar that language becomes. This book reconstructs the ghosts that haunted Britons after 1914.

Notes

1 Siegfried Sassoon, *Memoirs of an Infantry Officer* (London: Faber & Faber, 1997), p. 86 (original published in 1930); Mark Dollar, 'Ghost

Imagery in the War Poems of Siegfried Sassoon', *War, Literature & the Arts*, 16:1–2 (2004), 236, 241.

2 Charles Edward Montague, *Disenchantment* (New York: Brentano's Publishers, 1922), pp. 277–8.

3 For the history of this myth see Dan Todman, *The Great War: Myth and Memory* (London: Hambledon & London, 2005).

4 Paul Fussell, *The Great War and Modern Memory* (Oxford: Oxford University Press, 2000).

5 Sassoon had a poor opinion of spiritualism, writing in his diary in January 1917: 'A bitter attack on O. Lodge's spook book in the Daily Mail – Stuff like "Raymond" repels me utterly. Having discovered the fatuity of it in my own case, and watched that pathetic, foolish, clinging to the dead which goes on among so many women – who – (like my own mother) – having nothing else to distract their minds from war and wretchedness' (Siegfried Sassoon, journal entry 23 January 1917, Cambridge Digital Library, MS Add. 9852/1/8, https://cudl.lib.cam.ac.uk/view/MS-ADD-09852-00001-00008/66, last accessed June 2020).

6 Fussell, *The Great War and Modern Memory*, p. 115.

7 Jay Winter, *Sites of Memory, Sites of Mourning: The Great War in European Cultural History* Canto Edition (Cambridge: Cambridge University Press, 1998), p. 54.

8 Frederic W. H. Myers, *Human Personality and its Survival of Bodily Death*, Volume I (London: Longmans, Green and Co., 1903), p. xxii.

9 See Peter J. Bowler, *Reconciling Science and Religion: The Debate in Early-Twentieth-Century Britain* (Chicago, IL: University of Chicago Press, 2001), pp. 89–101, and *Science for All: The Popularization of Science in Early Twentieth-Century Britain* (Chicago, IL: University of Chicago Press, 2009), pp. 23–4.

10 Max Weber, 'Science as Vocation', in David Owen and Tracy B. Strong (eds), *The Vocation Lectures*, trans. Rodney Livingstone (Indianapolis, IN: Hackett Publishing Company, 2004), pp. 1–31.

11 For an example of the former see Winter, *Sites of Memory, Sites of Mourning*, pp. 54–77, and for the latter see Owen Davies, *A Supernatural War: Magic, Divination and Faith during the First World War* (Oxford: Oxford University Press, 2018), p. 232. As Davies concludes, 'the First World War and its legacy confirmed that the supernatural was profoundly modern'.

12 Janet Oppenheim, *The Other World: Spiritualism and Psychical Research in England, 1850–1914* (Cambridge: Cambridge University Press, 1988), p. 4.

13 For a historical take on this argument see the classic work by Keith Thomas, *Religion and the Decline of Magic: Studies in Popular Beliefs*

in Sixteenth- and Seventeenth-Century England (London: Weidenfeld & Nicolson, 1971), pp. 767–800. The revaluation of Weber and Thomas has grown considerably in recent decades. For a selection of this scholarship see John V. Fleming, *The Dark Side of the Enlightenment: Wizards, Alchemists and Spiritual Seekers in the Age of Reason* (New York: W. W. Norton and Company, 2013); Michael Hunter, *The Decline of Magic: Britain in the Age of Enlightenment* (New Haven, CT and London: Yale University Press, 2020); Owen Davies, *Witchcraft, Magic and Culture, 1736–1951* (Manchester: Manchester University Press, 1999); Alex Owen, *The Place of Enchantment: British Occultism and the Culture of the Modern* (Chicago, IL: University of Chicago Press, 2004); Jason A. Josephson-Storm, *The Myth of Disenchantment: Magic, Modernity, and the Birth of the Human Sciences* (Chicago, IL: University of Chicago Press, 2017); Richard Noakes, *Physics and Psychics: The Occult and the Sciences in Modern Britain* (Cambridge: Cambridge University Press, 2019); Mark Morrison, *Modern Alchemy: Occultism and the Emergence of Atomic Theory* (Oxford: Oxford University Press, 2007). For an historiographical overview see Peter Marshall, 'Disenchantment and Re-Enchantment in Europe, 1240–1920', *Historical Journal*, 54:2 (2011), 599–606.

14 See Owen Davies, *America Bewitched: The Story of Witchcraft after Salem* (Oxford: Oxford University Press, 2013).

15 Thomas Waters, *Cursed Britain: A History of Witchcraft and Black Magic in Modern Times* (New Haven, CT and London: Yale University Press, 2019), pp. 78, 195–8.

16 See Monica Black, *A Demon Haunted Land: Witches, Wonder Doctors, and the Ghosts of the Past in Post-WWII Germany* (New York: Metropolitan Books, 2020).

17 *Ibid.*, pp. 7–10.

18 Owen, *The Place of Enchantment*, pp. 7–15.

19 *Ibid.*, pp. 118–19. For a survey of avant-garde artists and the First World War see Richard Cork, *A Bitter Truth: Avant-Garde Art and the Great War* (New Haven, CT: Yale University Press, 1994).

20 See Robert Humphrey, *Stream of Consciousness in the Modern Novel* (Berkeley and Los Angeles, CA and London: University of California Press, 1954) and George M. Johnson, *Mourning and Mysticism in First World War Literature and Beyond: Grappling with Ghosts* (New York: Palgrave Macmillan, 2015), pp. 153–86.

21 Sherrie Lynne Lyons, *Species, Serpents, Spirits, and Skulls: Science at the Margins in the Victorian Age* (New York: State University of New York Press, 2009), pp. 147–204.

22 Oppenheim, *The Other World*, pp. 352–4, 377–86.

23 Richard Noakes, 'Telegraphy Is an Occult Art: Cromwell Fleetwood Varley and the Diffusion of Electricity to the Other World', *The British Journal of the History of Science*, 32:4 (1999), 423. For more on the link between technology and spiritualism see Noakes, 'Thoughts and Spirits by Wireless: Imagining and Building Psychic Telegraphs in America and Britain, circa 1900–1930', *History and Technology*, 32:2 (2016), 137–58; Jeremy Stolow, 'Wired Religion: Spiritualism and Telegraphic Globalization in the Nineteenth Century', in Stephen Streeter et al. (eds), *Empires and Autonomy: Moments in the History of Globalization* (Vancouver, BC: University of British Columbia Press, 2009), p. 89.

24 For the role of physics in shaping the concept of telepathy, see Roger Luckhurst, *The Invention of Telepathy, 1870–1901* (Oxford: Oxford University Press, 2002), pp. 75–91.

25 Oppenheim, *The Other World*, p. 379.

26 For more on nineteenth-century theories that thoughts could behave like waves or vibrations along the ether, see Noakes, *Physics and Psychics*, p. 171.

27 Grace Duffie-Boylan (originally published anonymously), *Thy Son Liveth: Messages from a Soldier to His Mother* (Boston, MA: Little, Brown & Company, 1918), pp. 2, 10–11.

28 For the relationship between modernism and psychoanalysis see Eli Zaretsky, *Secrets of the Soul: A Social and Cultural History of Psychoanalysis* (New York: Alfred A. Knopf, 2004).

29 See, in particular, Courtenay Raia, *The New Prometheans: Faith, Science and the Supernatural Mind in the Victorian Fin De Siècle* (Chicago, IL: University of Chicago Press, 2019) and Alan Gauld, *The Founders of Psychical Research* (New York: Schocken Books, 1968).

30 See Peter Lamont, 'Spiritualism and a Mid-Victorian Crisis of Evidence', *The Historical Journal*, 47:4 (2004), 897–920 and *Extraordinary Beliefs: A Historical Approach to a Psychological Problem* (Cambridge: Cambridge University Press, 2013).

31 For France see Annette Becker, *War and Faith: The Religious Imagination in France, 1914–1930*, trans. Helen McPhail (Oxford and New York: Berg Publishers, 1998). For Britain see Jason Schweitzer, *The Cross and the Trenches: Religious Faith and Doubt among British and American Great War Soldiers* (London: Praeger, 2003); Michael Snape, *God and the British Soldier: Religion and the British Army in the First and Second World Wars* (New York: Routledge, 2005); Adrian Gregory, *The Last Great War: British Society and the First World War* (Cambridge: Cambridge University Press, 2008), pp. 152–86; Edward Madigan, *Faith under Fire: Anglican Army Chaplains and the Great*

War (London: Palgrave Macmillan, 2011). For the United States see Schweitzer, *The Cross and the Trenches*; Jonathan H. Ebel, *Faith in the Fight: Religion and the American Soldier in the Great War* (Princeton, NJ: Princeton University Press, 2010). For surveys see Philip Jenkins, *The Great and Holy War: How World War I Became a Religious Crusade* (San Francisco, CA: Harper One, 2014); Adrian Gregory, 'Beliefs and Religion', in Jay Winter (ed.), *The Cambridge History of the First World War Volume 3: Civil Society* (Cambridge: Cambridge University Press, 2014), pp. 418–44 and Davies, *A Supernatural War*.

32 For example, between 1886 and 1902, church attendance amongst Anglicans and nonconformists in London declined by 20.2 per cent in Kennington, 29.8 per cent in Norwood and 37.4 per cent in Brixton. See Jeffrey Cox, *The English Churches in a Secular Society: Lambeth, 1870–1930* (New York and Oxford: Oxford University Press, 1982), p. 284.

33 Callum Brown, *The Death of Christian Britain: Understanding Secularisation 1800–2000* (New York: Routledge, 2001), pp. 12–13, 161–9. Robert Currie, Alan Gilbert and Lee Hursley measured affiliation through electoral rolls, communicants, baptisms and marriages. Using this data, Brown has concluded that overall church membership in Britain was 19.3 per cent in 1910 declining to only 19.1 in 1920 and falling to 18.1 in 1930. Other statistics show only modest declines after the war or even increases (as in the case of baptism rates in the Church of England). For example, Easter Day communicants in the Church of England declined an average of only 0.26 per cent each year between 1903 and 1956, contrasted with an average loss of 1.3 per year between 1956 and 1984 (the trends for the Church of Scotland were similar). According to the data of Currie et al., in 1914, 1919 and 1924, approximately 76 per cent of all marriages were religiously solemnised in England and Wales, declining to approximately 74 per cent and 72 per cent in 1929 and 1934, respectively. See Currie et al., *Churches and Churchgoers: Patterns of Church Growth in the British Isles since 1700* (Oxford: Clarendon Press, 1977), pp. 223–33.

34 *Ibid.*, p. 167.

35 Cox, *The English Churches in a Secular Society*, pp. 93–4. The Bishop of Rochester coined the term 'diffusive Christianity' in 1903.

36 Snape, *God and the British Soldier*, pp. 22–8.

37 *Ibid.*, pp. 45–57; Schweitzer, *The Cross in the Trenches*, pp. 187–92; Madigan, *Faith under Fire*, pp. 183–96. The *Army and Religion* report noted an 'almost universal resort to prayer in time of danger': David Cairns (ed.), *The Army and Religion: An Enquiry and Its Bearing upon the Religious Life of the Nation* (London: Macmillan & Co., 1919), pp. 74, 166–8.

38 Imperial War Museum (hereafter IWM), Private Papers of Reverend M. A. Bere, Documents.12105, letter from Montague Acland Bere, 14 January 1918, in Rennie Bere (his son) (ed.), 'Letters from an Army Chaplain in World War I', 1978, p. 140.
39 Cairns, *The Army and Religion*, p. 8.
40 Gregory, *The Last Great War*, p. 153.
41 Ecclesiastes 44:14 (King James Version) (hereafter KJV).
42 Winter, *Sites of Memory, Sites of Mourning*, pp. 167–71.
43 *Ibid.*, pp. 54–5.
44 Jenkins, *The Great and Holy War*, p. 3.
45 Gregory, 'Beliefs and Religion', pp. 418, 442. Gregory notes that religious beliefs and practices were most crucial in making sense of the war, rather than as a primal cause of the war or a determining source of public support for the conflict.
46 Sir Oliver Lodge, *Christopher: A Study in Human Personality* (London and New York: Cassell and Company, 1918), p. 3.
47 James J. Morse, *Leaves from My Life: A Narrative of Personal Experiences* (London: James Burn, 1877), pp. 1–15.
48 Quoted in Logie Barrow, *Independent Spirits: Spiritualism and English Plebeians, 1850–1910* (London and New York: Routledge & Kegan Paul, 1986), p. 127.
49 *Ibid.*, p. 131.
50 Oppenheim, *The Other World*, pp. 39–47; Barrow, *Independent Spirits*, p. 272.
51 Barrow, *Independent Spirits*, pp. 271–80.
52 Oppenheim, *The Other World*, pp. 28–39.
53 Alex Owen, *The Darkened Room: Women, Power, and Spiritualism in Late Victorian England* (Chicago, IL: University of Chicago Press, 2004), pp. 2–18.
54 This sample was tallied from *Light*'s advertisements between 3 January 1914 and 30 December 1916. It should be noted that there is a risk of double counting since some mediums may have married between 1914 and 1916. However, even if we only count those who identified as 'Mrs' in their advertisements (and this would certainly overestimate the risk of double counting), we are still left with a significant gender disparity; a ratio of over two to one (forty-nine women and twenty-three men).
55 Walter Wynn, *Rupert Lives!* (London: Kingsley Press, 1919), p. 170.
56 Eleanor Sidgwick is the most notable exception. She was one of the SPR's founding members and was influential in shaping the society in the early twentieth century. As Alan Gauld described her reputation, 'she required the prestige of an almost legendary figure' (Gauld, *The Founders of Psychical Research*, pp. 337–9).

57 Jenny Hazelgrove, *Spiritualism and British Society between the Wars* (Manchester: Manchester University Press, 2000), pp. 66–96; Beth Robertson, *Science of the Séance: Transnational Network and Gendered Bodies in the Study of Psychic Phenomena, 1918–40* (Vancouver, BC: University of British Columbia Press, 2016), pp. 10–17, 33–48.
58 David Cannadine, 'War and Death, Grief and Mourning in Modern Britain', in Joachim Whaley (ed.), *Mirrors of Mortality: Studies in the Social History of Death* (London: Europa Publications, 1981), p. 193; Pat Jalland, *Death in War and Peace: A History of Loss and Grief in England, 1914–1970* (Oxford: Oxford University Press, 2010), pp. 1–11.
59 B. R. Mitchell and Phyllis Deane, *Abstract of British Historical Statistics* (Cambridge: Cambridge University Press, 1962), pp. 38–9.
60 Michael Roper, *The Secret Battle: Emotional Survival in the Great War* (Manchester and New York: Manchester University Press, 2009), p. 89.
61 Thomas Lacqueur, *The Work of the Dead: A Cultural History of Mortal Remains* (Princeton, NJ and Oxford: Princeton University Press, 2015), pp. 447–88.
62 Winter, *Sites of Memory, Sites of Mourning*, pp. 102–5. See also Adrian Gregory, *The Silence of Memory: Armistice Day, 1919–1946* (London: Bloomsbury, 1994).
63 See David W. Lloyd, *Battlefield Tourism: Pilgrimage and the Commemoration of the Great War in Britain, Australia and Canada* (Oxford: A&C Black, 1998).
64 Drew Gilpin Faust's work on death and the American Civil War has shown the effects that mass death in war has on mourning cultures. See Drew Gilpin Faust, *This Republic of Suffering: Death and the American Civil War* (New York: Alfred A. Knopf, 2008).
65 Jay Winter, *The Great War and the British People* (London: Macmillan, 1985), pp. 92–9.
66 Trevor Wilson, *The Myriad Faces of War: Britain and the Great War, 1914–1918* (Cambridge: Polity Press, 1986), pp. 758–61.
67 Quoted in Gregory, *The Silence of Memory*, p. 22.
68 Lodge, *Christopher*, p. 2. Thank you to Jay Winter for this observation.
69 Johnson, *Mourning and Mysticism*, pp. 23–4.
70 Ian Hacking, *Mad Travellers: Reflections on the Reality of Transient Mental Illness* (Charlottesville, VA and London: University Press of Virginia, 1998), p. 13; Ian Hacking, *Historical Ontology* (Cambridge, MA: Harvard University Press, 2002), pp. 48–9, 108–10.
71 Hacking, *Mad Travellers*, pp. 12–13.
72 Edward Shorter, *From Paralysis to Fatigue: A History of Psychosomatic Illness in the Modern Era* (New York: The Free Press, 1992), pp. 1–24; Peter Leese, *Shell Shock: Traumatic Neurosis and the British Soldiers of*

the First World War (London: Palgrave Macmillan, 2002), p. 2; Mark Humphries, *A Weary Road: Shell Shock in the Canadian Expeditionary Force, 1914–1918* (Toronto, ON: University of Toronto Press, 2018), pp. 14–20.

73 Ian Hacking, *Rewriting the Soul: Multiple Personality and the Sciences of Memory* (Princeton, NJ: Princeton University Press, 1995), pp. 6, 21.

74 See for example Ben Shepherd, *A War of Nerves: Soldiers and Psychiatrists in the Twentieth Century* (Boston, MA: Harvard University Press, 2003) and Edgar Jones and Simon Wessley, *Shell Shock to PTSD: Military Psychiatry from 1900 to the Gulf War* (Hove and New York: Psychology Press, 2005).

75 The frequency of abuse discovered through recovered memories resulted in the 'memory wars' of the 1990s. Rumours regarding satanic cults abusing children spread across the United States. Family members accused of child abuse mobilised to defend themselves against 'false memory syndrome'. See Hacking, *Rewriting the Soul*, pp. 113–27 and Alison Winter, *Memory: Fragments of a Modern History* (Chicago, IL: University of Chicago Press, 2012), pp. 225–56.

76 Hacking, *Rewriting the Soul*, pp. 115, 135–6.

77 Oppenheim, *The Other World*, pp. 78–9, 411, fns. 48, 50.

78 See for example, John Miller, 'Going Unconscious', in R. B. Silvers (ed.), *Hidden Histories of Science* (New York: New York Review, 1995), pp. 1–37.

79 The literature on the history of emotions is extensive. For introductory analysis see Rob Boddice, *The History of Emotions* (Manchester: Manchester University Press, 2018) and *A History of Feelings* (Chicago, IL: University of Chicago Press, 2018); Barbara Rosenwein and Riccardo Cristiani, *What Is the History of Emotions?* (Cambridge: Polity, 2018); Jan Pampler, *The History of Emotions* (Oxford: Oxford University Press, 2015). For an overview on the history of emotions as it relates to the study of war see Lucy Noakes, *Dying for the Nation: Death, Grief and Bereavement in Second World War Britain* (Manchester: Manchester University Press, 2020), pp. 9–15.

80 Rob Boddice, 'The History of Emotions', in Sasha Handley, Rohan McWilliam and Lucy Noakes (eds), *New Directions in Cultural and Social History* (London and New York: Bloomsbury, 2018), pp. 45–64.

81 For psychoanalysis as it relates to emotions during the First World War see Roper, *The Secret Battle*, pp. 15, 26. For spiritualism see Johnson, *Mourning and Mysticism* as well as Claudie Massicotte, *Trance Speakers: Femininity and Authorship in Spiritual Séances, 1850–1930* (Montreal and Kingston, QC: McGill-Queen's University Press, 2017), pp. 42–66.

82 Quoted in David Clarke, *The Angel of Mons: Phantom Soldiers and Ghostly Guardians* (Chichester: John Wiley & Sons, 2004), pp. 119–20.
83 *Ibid.*, pp. 119–24.
84 Wilson, *The Myriad Faces of War*, pp. 42–3.
85 Clarke, *Angel of Mons*, p. 161; Arthur Machen, *The Bowmen and Other Legends of the War* (London: G. P. Putnam's Sons, 1915).
86 Harold Begbie, *On the Side of Angels: A Reply to Arthur Machen* (London: Hodder and Stoughton, 1915), pp. 19–26.
87 Scholarly works on spiritualism, psychical research and British society have tended to focus exclusively on either the nineteenth century or twentieth century. For the nineteenth century see Oppenheim, *The Other World*; Owen, *The Darkened Room*; and Raia, *The New Prometheans*. Oppenheim for example, ends her analysis in 1914 on the grounds that the context of spiritualism and motivations changed with the outbreak of the Great War. Those related to the twentieth century have offered only brief analyses of the war years. For example, see Hazelgrove, *Spiritualism and British Society between the Wars*, pp. 13–52. A notable exception is George Nelson's survey of British spiritualism. Like Hazelgrove, however, he devotes only limited time to the war and much of his book is now outdated given the amount of research that has been conducted in the last few decades. For his discussions on the war see George Nelson, *Spiritualism and Society* (London: Routledge & Kegan Paul, 1969), pp. 153–68.
88 Furthermore, it must be remembered that the Canadian Expeditionary Force (the CEF) was a very British institution (half of its members were born outside of Canada and many in the UK). They shared nearly identical military cultures during the war and many English Canadians considered themselves British.
89 For the original memoir see Will R. Bird, *And We Go On: A Memoir of the Great War*, ed. David Williams (Montreal and Kingston, QC: McGill-Queen's University Press, 2014). For his second memoir see Will R. Bird, *Ghosts Have Warm Hands* (Ottawa, ON: CEF Books, 1968).
90 Johnson's book includes spiritualist figures such as Arthur Conan Doyle and Oliver Lodge under the general term 'mysticism', but differs from this study by including non-spiritualists. He also takes a different approach, interpreting the subjects from a literary and psycho-biographical perspective, psychoanalysing these figures' writings through attachment theory and object relation theory. See Johnson, *Mourning and Mysticism*.
91 Matt Houlbrook, *The Prince of Tricksters: The Incredible True Story of Netley Lucas, Gentleman Crook* (Chicago, IL: University of Chicago Press, 2016), pp. 5–6.

92 Cambridge University Library (hereafter CUL), Department of Manuscripts, Society for Psychical Research Archives (hereafter MS SPR), Leonard Papers, 34/25/20, Elsi Walker, Leonard Sitting, 26 August 1918, p. 10b.
93 Ian Bradley quoted in Laura Béres, 'A Thin Place: Narratives of Space and Place, Celtic Spirituality and Meaning', *Journal of Religion and Spirituality in Social Work*, 31 (2012), 398–9.

1

Prophecies of war and peace: spiritualism and the new millennium

On 24 September 1938, Edith Gibbes sat down with British medium Geraldine Cummins to communicate with the spirit of her brother, Frank Gibbes. The session was underscored by a sense of urgency as the crisis over the Sudetenland threatened to embroil Europe in another war. Only days earlier, Chamberlain had flown to Munich with the intention to secure peace. Once Cummins entered into a trance, she received the following reassuring message:

> I am working harder than ever for peace ... Great Britain is not going to be involved in a great European War. I am aware ... to most people it seems inevitable. But here [in the spirit world] the enemy is breaking ... This will shortly react on Europe. Chamberlain ... is to be the peacemaker, he won't fail.[1]

Chamberlain returned from Germany six days later and made his famous proclamation 'Peace for our time'. It seemed that the spirits were correct.

Between 1938 and 1939, Gibbes and Cummins regularly looked to the spirits to predict the future. All sessions reiterated the same central message: no war.[2] In July 1939, Cummins reported, 'Hitler and Mussolini have been making very complete preparation for war ... But it is the greatest bluff of all. *They won't fight ... Remember, no war!*'[3] Two months later Hitler invaded Poland and Britain declared war on Germany. Edith Gibbes was devastated. 'Geraldine Cummins's work on prevision lay in ruins', she stated, 'it was a stupefying realisation'.[4] Cummins's failure was not an isolated case. The medium Gladys Osborne Leonard, made famous for her role in Oliver Lodge's *Raymond*, admitted that she was confident no war would erupt in 1939. 'The messages that came through at various sittings were all unanimous in declaring that there would be no war', she recalled in 1942.[5] As late as 18 August 1939, *The Two Worlds* declared, 'Spiritualists are in a large measure fully convinced there will be No Great War. This fact has been given from our platforms during the last twelve months by scores of mediums.'[6]

The shock of war in 1939 resulted in a flurry of correspondence in the pages of spiritualist and psychic journals. For two consecutive issues, the journal *Light* had to include an extended letters-to-the-editor section entirely devoted to the 'Prophecies That Failed'. Many more letters on the subject were never published.[7] Fears began to spread of a mass exodus from the movement. Ivy Uttley, a recent convert to spiritualism from Halifax, West Yorkshire, wrote to the editor of the *Psychic News* that 'if the spirit-guides are not to be trusted on such a major issue, then it seems that the bottom is knocked out of the whole subject'. Louis S. Vernon from Salford was blunter: 'What about your idiotic vapouring to the effect that the spirit world says, "There will be no war"?'[8] Spiritualist leaders were under pressure to provide an explanation. Medium Estelle Roberts thought that human free will absolved the spirit guides of blame. War and peace were the products of the living, not the guides, she argued.[9] Frank Blake, the president of the Spiritualist National Union (SNU), reiterated his faith in the spirit guides and prophecy in general, claiming that some mediums predicted inevitable war but did not receive the same attention in the press. As for those who had incorrectly prophesied peace, he reminded readers that the guides used to be human and were therefore fallible.[10]

Not all defended the error. The Roman Catholic priest and sympathiser of psychical research, Herbert Thurston, wrote that the failure of the prophecies represented an 'outstanding set-back which our journals are unable to dispute or ignore'.[11] Some saw it as a sign that spiritualists had become too reliant on prevision and needed to return to their roots. One reader of *Light* pleaded with her fellow spiritualists to 'renounce fortune telling' while an editorial in the *Two Worlds* similarly stated that 'Spiritualism does not rest upon the ability of spirits to anticipate events, but to prove their identity.'[12] With that fact in mind, the medium Horace Leaf focused on the task ahead. 'Very soon', he wrote, 'people will be seeking for the comfort which Spiritualism can give'. After all, 'the ability to do this made Spiritualism the most effective comforter during the world-war, and it can be so again'.[13]

How was it that a series of predictions had suddenly threatened the validity of the spiritualist movement that had existed since the 1850s? Contrary to some spiritualists' objections, divination was nothing new to the movement. It was as old as spiritualism itself. Nor had false prophets ever stood in the way of spiritualists' beliefs in the past. Failure could be excused; old but more accurate prophecies could be unearthed and new ones received. The crisis that emerged in 1939 was significant not simply because spiritualism had potentially been exposed by false predictions but because the outbreak of war was objectionable in a way that it had not been in 1914.

Unlike in 1939, spiritualists greeted the Great War as a necessary crusade. Those attracted to spiritualism tended to embrace a teleological worldview that reflected a broader culture of progress and British imperial exceptionalism. Although the outbreak of war in 1914 contradicted progress, it did not temper utopian expectations. Instead, the war was understood to be a cataclysmic event that would destroy materialism and usher in a new millennium of spiritual advancement and universal brotherhood. Even when the war entered a far bloodier phase in 1916, the mounting casualties only fortified hopes that a new spiritual age was dawning as Britons flocked to séances and spiritualism's public profile grew. New political, intellectual and social crises in the interwar period challenged these expectations but the firm belief that the sacrifices had not been in vain was channelled into a pacifism that ended in the ill-fated optimistic peace predictions of Cummins and other mediums. After the suffering and sacrifices of the previous conflict, progress and war became more difficult to reconcile. A Second World War was not only an affront to the sacrifices of the First but also unthinkable according to spiritualist views.

Spiritualism and the new millennium

Two kinds of prophecies proliferated in occult circles at the turn of the century. Both were a form of millennialism, defined as the 'belief in an imminent transition to a collective salvation, in which the faithful will experience well-being and the unpleasant limitations of the human condition will be eliminated'.[14] Millennial ideas have traditionally been associated with Christianity, specifically the Book of Revelation in which God's kingdom on earth is said to last 1,000 years after the second coming of Christ. Utopias, on the contrary, come more gradually and are the product of humanity's actions instead of divine intervention. Examples of utopian projects include nineteenth-century socialist movements, such as Owenism, and the pacifist movements of the interwar period.[15] Millennialist and utopian sentiments can sometimes overlap and so some scholars have distinguished between *progressive millennialism*, in which a gradual improvement of the world is achieved through human cooperation with a divine source, and *catastrophic millennialism*, in which the new millennium is brought about by a great calamity.[16] Spiritualists engaged mostly in the progressive variety but urgent or volatile social conditions, like war, made the catastrophic form more appealing.

Although rooted in early Christendom, the millennial tradition has managed to survive because of, not despite, modernity since it offers the precedent and possibility of a rapid alteration of the social order. The shocking fall of the French monarchy in 1789, for example, launched the prophetic movements of Richard Brothers and his successor Joanna Southcott in Britain. Brothers prophesied that the millennium would come in 1795, that the English would be defeated in the war against France and that George III would be overthrown.[17] Brothers's following triggered concerns from the government, who were worried that prophetic elements were to blame for the French Revolution.[18] The rapidity of industrialisation and scientific advancement in the second half of the nineteenth century further entrenched expectations that the future would be radically different from the past. While the 1763 book *The Reign of George VI, 1900–1924* depicted twentieth-century warfare according to the conventional methods, tactics and technology of the late eighteenth century, the famous 1871 short story 'The Battle of Dorking' envisioned the Germans using a secret weapon to successfully launch an invasion on the once impenetrable English coast.[19] Tales of future wars and the genre of science fiction came of age as new technologies expanded future possibilities of combat. Most notably, H. G. Wells imagined how inventions such as the aeroplane and submarine and discoveries such as dynamite and X-rays would change human conflict in the future.[20]

The term *prophecy* also carries two meanings. Originally, a prophet was someone who simply spoke or communicated 'the words of God', but it has since become synonymous with divination.[21] The date of the impending millennium is often hidden and revealed by divine or occult sources and believers look for signs, omens, visions or sacred texts to anticipate its arrival.[22] By their very nature, spiritualism and modern occult movements such as Theosophy were intimately bound with prophecy in the traditional sense. Spiritualism mediums were the source and vehicle for otherworldly revelations of a historical, theological and scientific nature. Theosophists claimed to have access to a divine wisdom at the heart of the world's religions that had been revealed to their leader, Madame Blavatsky, by a group of Mahatmas from the East.[23] Other modern occultist groups, such as the Hermetic Order of the Golden Dawn, attempted to use consciousness to explore hidden divine realities.[24] It was not a far leap from such activities to divination.

Prophets claim to be the recipients of an external knowledge but their utterances tell us far more about the past than the future. Late nineteenth- and early twentieth-century prophets operated against a backdrop of intellectual and social change that caused Europeans to renegotiate their relationships with themselves, the world and the cosmos. Over the long nineteenth century, new discoveries in the emerging fields of geology, biology, biblical criticism and anthropology increasingly challenged traditional Christian interpretations and understandings of history. In 1830, Charles Lyell's *The Principles of Geology* offered a natural history of the earth that was gradual and which operated according to unchanging universal laws. Whereas fossils were once used as evidence for the Biblical flood, Charles Darwin offered a reading of the fossil record to argue for natural selection as a universal mechanism for evolution.[25] Empire introduced Britons to greater expanses of nature and Indigenous populations that stimulated an interest in the history of civilisation and comparative religions. The anthropologist Edward Tylor pioneered the use of cross-cultural studies and argued that religion emerged out of 'primitive' peoples' attempts to explain the curiosities of the natural world. According to Tylor, these animist beliefs were rendered obsolete by science and he criticised spiritualism and Theosophy as the unhealthy survival of primitive superstitions.[26]

The cultural modernism that would become fashionable after the war originated at the *fin de siècle* and built upon scientific and artistic trends that challenged Enlightenment ideals of a clockwork-mechanistic universe and rational mind. The Michelson-Morley experiment of 1887 failed to identify an ether, which by all rights, should have presented itself. Continental-European neurologists argued that the irrational unconscious governed all human passions, not just those of hysterics. Artists turned away from realism and instead depicted the inner world of emotions while musical works such as Stravinsky's *The Rite of Spring* rejected traditional rhythm and tonality to depict 'primitive' impulses. Social movements such as the rise of socialism, communism, suffragism, anarchism and national syndicalism threatened traditional relationships between the genders and the classes, disrupting industry and occasionally leading to violence as on 13 November 1887 (Bloody Sunday).[27] The nature of modern industrial life, disappointments over the British performance in the Boer War and conditions such as neurasthenia spread fears of masculine degeneracy.[28] In such an environment, catastrophic millennialism found favour amongst some spiritualists and occultists who sensed that Europe was on the brink of a clean break from the past or in need of rejuvenation. Blavatsky predicted the coming of a great 'World Teacher' and a new spiritual age in the twentieth century. Some occultists became convinced in the 1890s that an apocalyptic conflict between good and evil was imminent.[29] Similarly, the spiritualist William Stainton Moses received prophesies that the world was on the verge of Armageddon and the Second Coming of Christ.[30]

The significance of intellectual and cultural modernism nevertheless remained limited to an elite few. The works of Einstein and Freud were still in their infancy, especially in Britain where physicists found insufficient reason to abandon the ether and where psychoanalysis was slow to take hold. Fears of a socialist revolution dissipated.[31] Discourses surrounding human history continued to emphasise the language of gradual progress rather than revolution. Half a century after Darwin's *Origin of Species*, proclamations about the death of God proved premature. Natural selection may have implied purposeless evolution initiated by chance, but most Britons were not prepared to embrace a meaningless universe. Religious sentiments dominated discussions about evolution as proponents pointed to the fossil record to argue that the development of life on earth was preordained. Darwin and his theories remained contested even amongst his fiercest supporters, leading one historian to argue that if there was a biological revolution in the late nineteenth century, it was a 'non-Darwinian revolution'.[32] Comparative religious studies inspired Tylor's secular animism but they also stimulated the religious imaginations of occultists and spiritualists who incorporated Eastern ideas and practices such as reincarnation and trance, and who argued that their philosophies represented the true source of all the world's religions.[33] Nor were Britons eager to accept cultural relativism in the context of European Imperialism. Whig historians such as Thomas Babington Macaulay and Henry Buckle contended that Europe's transition from 'primitive' beginnings to the age of the modern state was an inevitable march towards progress, in which Britain held a special destiny.[34]

Western narratives of human history likewise incorporated Eastern religious concepts of a cyclical cosmos. For example, if history was progressive why did past great civilisations like the Roman Empire decline? Thomas Arnold argued that each great civilisation contributed to the development of humanity before it reached a point of stagnation and decline, but was followed by a period of renewal. Charles Kingsley contented that such cycles were the unfolding of God's plan. According to these histories, the Greeks had contributed to intellect, the Romans to law and Christianity and the Teutonic people to liberty by initiating the downfall of Roman corruption and tyranny.[35]

Nineteenth-century theories regarding natural and human history therefore retained Christian concepts of a purposeful history with a beginning and an end while using modern language, selective scientific evidence and Eastern philosophies. The cultural changes that drove Victorians to believe in progress were similar to those that brought many towards the new occultism and spiritualism: both served the purpose of mediating between the old and the new.[36] Not surprisingly, evolutionary progress proved popular amongst spiritualists and occultists. Blavatsky believed that seven root races had contributed to the development of human history, each rising and falling upon the backs of the previous dominant race.[37] Alfred

Russel Wallace was an ardent spiritualist who eventually rejected natural selection as the complete answer to the problem of human evolution. Wallace had spent a significant amount of time living with various indigenous populations and he observed that they displayed many of the same mental faculties as 'civilised' humans, including artistry, mathematical reasoning and morality.[38] Wallace believed these traits had no purpose in a 'primitive' lifestyle and so concluded that natural selection was inadequate to explain their origins. He proposed that they had been placed there for future use by 'a superior intelligence' that 'guided the development of man in a definite direction, and for a special purpose'.[39] For Blavatsky and Wallace, discoveries within Theosophy and psychical research had revealed similar latent abilities and signalled greater evolutionary advancement in the future.[40] Spiritualists and occultists may have acknowledged that Eastern and Indigenous populations shared a universal spirituality with the West but they also contended that it was they who had tapped into its true potential thanks to the gifts of science.

A faith in progress, an interest in the preternatural potentials of human evolution and a self-conscious awareness of living in a moment of profound change led some spiritualists and psychical researchers down strange paths. In 1913, Gerald Balfour, former Conservative MP, SPR president, and brother of former British Prime Minister Arthur Balfour, conceived a child out of wedlock with the medium Winifred Coombe Tennant. It was no ordinary child, however, as the pair believed him to be the messiah. Born to a Welsh mother and English naval officer, Winifred had entered the British cultural and social elite through her marriage with Charles Coombe Tennant, a wealthy Welsh lawyer and businessman twenty years her senior. Through Charles, Winifred rubbed shoulders with Henry James, Rudyard Kipling, Cecil Rhodes and eventually Charles's brother-in-law, Frederic Myers. After the death of her infant daughter Daphne, Winifred developed her own mediumship.[41] Known by the pseudonym, Mrs Willett, her scripts became an integral part of the SPR's cross-correspondence, a series of unrelated scripts from multiple mediums shared across a community of psychical researchers. These scripts, often presented in the form of literary and classical allusions, were unintelligible on their own, but taken as a whole, were said to reveal coherent messages. Winifred soon caught the attention of Oliver Lodge, Gerald Balfour and Eleanor Sidgwick who believed she was of great significance to the future of psychical research. According to their interpretations, and Winifred's growing convictions, the spirits of psychical researchers Frederic Myers, Henry Sidgwick and Edmund Gurney were using Daphne as a sort of bridge that would help the first generation of the SPR finish its work from the other side.[42]

In the fall of 1910, 'the Plan' for Winifred emerged. After expressing his love for her, the spirit of Edmund Gurney asked her to bear his child. The child, according to Myers's spirit, was to 'be a great incarnation of Divine Effulgence'. As Winifred wrote in her diary:

> If ever another child is born ... he claims beforehand that its birth has long been planned, planned in the highest quarters, to an extent which makes it difficult to exaggerate; he anticipates that it will possess a remarkable personality – a genius in fact of high order – and will prove to be the greatest of his psychic works, to which all else has been leading up. Edmund Gurney definitely stated that the child on its psychic side would be effectively his.[43]

How was this divinely ordained child to be conceived? Would his biological father be Charles, or was it to be a miraculous conception? The answer was unclear. Then in the summer of 1911 Winifred and Gerald Balfour began an affair. As the two fell deeply in love, they became convinced that they were destined to conceive the child that was prophesied. On 9 April 1913, Winifred gave birth to Augustus Henry Coombe-Tennant. Henry was to be the messiah that would bring about an era of world peace and social justice.[44]

Conducted in secret, and known only to a handful of the SPR's members, 'the Plan' contains many of the millennial elements that would soon occur on a far grander scale within the world of spiritualism and psychical research: the belief that the tragic death of youth carried a purpose, that the children of Britain's elite were destined to save the world and that salvation would come not from the actions of humanity but through the spirits. However, as the historian Murphy Temple observes, the outbreak of war a year after Henry's birth seems to have tempered the messianic expectations that had been placed on the child. After all, how could an infant save humanity from the slaughter currently raging across the channel? Instead, Winifred would lose her first son, Christopher, on the battlefields of Ypres, his death drawing her closer to spiritualism and then to pacifism and political activism.[45] British spiritualists' and psychical researchers' hope for a new messiah would have to be rewoven out of this bloodshed, but the promise of a new millennium would continue to exert significance within these communities.

Prophecies of war: spiritualism and the outbreak of the Great War

When war with Germany was declared in 1914, prominent British spiritualists and psychical researchers publicly voiced their support. A consensus emerged about the war's causes from a spiritual perspective, the righteousness of Britain's intervention, the worthiness of the sacrifice and expectations of what would follow the peace.

The cause of the war was identified as materialism. Under the editorship of the Scottish-born poet, David Gow, *Light* advanced this opinion in a series of editorials between August and September 1914. According to *Light*, the conviction that earthly existence was the only life motivated some to seek 'the "best" out of the world *now*', leading to the abuse of industrial progress for the accumulation of wealth and territorial expansion, inflaming nationalism and stimulating the building of armaments.[46] Germany was identified as the ultimate manifestation of this materialism run amok. *Light* singled out 'one nation' for bringing Europe into conflict, 'under the great illusion of materialism'.[47] Britain's official justification for war, the violation of Belgian neutrality, was used as evidence of the link between materialism and Prussian militarism. The contrast between Britain's commitment to the Treaty of London and Germany's dismissal of it as merely a 'scrap of paper' signalled that Germany was only concerned with material benefits while the British were governed by higher convictions.[48] Oliver Lodge believed that the war was a contest between two ideals. On the British side was the ideal of 'a commonwealth of nations ... all working together and contributing each her quota for the good of humanity and the progress of the world'. On the German side, however, was 'the Prussian ideal of a single glorified state, dominating all others ... imposing its customs, its learning and its culture on all the rest of the world'.[49]

Figure 1.1 David Gow, editor of *Light* from 1914 to 1931.

Reports of German atrocities in Belgium only reaffirmed the righteousness of the cause. Under the editorship of the medium James J. Morse, *The Two Worlds* condemned the slaughter of innocent civilians and proclaimed, 'No other war has been so clearly justifiable as the one now engaging Britain and her allies. It is a terrible battle of the forces of humanity and inhumanity.'[50] William Barrett warned in his interview with *Light* that 'the German Emperor and the Prussian military caste around him ... "wish to domineer over others and at length over all"'.[51] Lodge made clear that a German victory would threaten progress. German aggression was part of a broader rot within German culture that had corrupted 'their science as well as their politics and philosophy'. Atrocities in Belgium and Einstein's rejection of the ether were both natural outcomes of Germany's brute materialism.[52] 'The war must go on', the psychical researcher William Usborne Moore explained, 'until Germany ceased to exist as an empire'.[53]

Not everyone agreed. There were debates in the spiritualist press about whether the spirits' or humanity's own actions initiated the war; if the belief in a brotherhood of man was compatible with support for the war; and whether it was ethical to kill fellow Christians or pray for victory. James L. Macbeth Bain, the honorary president of the Brighton Spiritual Mission, wrote to *Light* that if Britain had led by example and disarmed, other European nations would have followed and war would have been avoided.[54] This extreme pacifist stance was grossly unpopular in Britain and the amount of critical letters sent to *Light* in response was so numerous that Gow had to stop publishing them.[55] In *The Two Worlds*, pacifists such as the medium William Henry Evans had greater representation but the reaction was equally critical.[56] Fred Warburton of the 1/7th West Yorkshire Regiment explained that he had been a spiritualist for eleven years and had 'no qualms of conscience, as I think it is every man's duty to be here'.[57] A sergeant in the Royal Army Medical Corps (RAMC) branded a conscientious objector a 'traitor' and warned that he could not expect 'much comfort from his angel friends when he gets into a military prison'.[58] Others found a middle ground by arguing that Germany needed to be defeated while also offering prayers for all soldiers regardless of nationality.[59] J. T. Dillsen explained that he had enlisted to protect liberalism, democracy and freedom but believed that all 'militarism, whether in Germany, Britain, or anywhere else, is bad'. Dillsen asked readers of *The Two Worlds* to 'pray also for those we hurt'.[60] If pacifism remained popular in spiritualist circles in 1914, it tended to be of this more moderate variety, where it was acknowledged that some responsibility rested with everyone in Europe who embraced materialism and militarism but that the German state represented these traits in a most dangerous form. Even Evans agreed that the Kaiser was 'the incarnation of materialism'.[61]

It was not only in their pacifism that spiritualists made compromises. In order to justify their faith in progress, spiritualists turned to cyclical historical models. *Light* claimed that the conflict was a signal from 'the great Intelligence' that the time had come to purge the world of the evils of materialism.[62] Militarism was likened to a vestigial organ that had evolved for a specific purpose in early history but which was now obsolete and even harmful. Industrial progress was never intended to be a tool of militaries but to provide societies with the leisure time necessary for spiritual development.[63] When 'militarism, materialism, despotism ... rear their heads amongst us in this twentieth-century', *Light* stated, 'they appear in an atmosphere that is not only fatal to their growth, but *rapidly* fatal'.[64] This 'relic of an old dark past' had to be destroyed, it was reasoned, so 'that the way may be made clear for better things'.[65] George F. Berry, who would later serve as president of the SNU between 1920 and 1922 argued that, historically, war destroyed 'mental attitudes that have served their full purpose and continue to exist longer as only hindrances to the new and higher modes of thought'. The current conflict was part of a cycle whereby the conditions of war and peace worked towards 'the final perfection of the universe'.[66] The German state represented a materialistic philosophy that encouraged militarism and despotism and repressed spiritual development. If Germany was defeated, humanity could advance the 'the clock of progress'.[67] War was to be endured with the promise of a better, more spiritual world on the horizon.

The British Empire's united front demonstrated the benefits of war and an indication of what might follow peace. *Light* argued that 'the unexpected psychological change in Ireland' and the 'surprising splendour of Indian and Colonial unity' were indicative of the spiritual progress characteristic of the British people.[68] *The Two Worlds* was optimistic about the future of socially progressive spiritualism, noting, 'at first sight it would seem that human brotherhood was the very antithesis of human warfare. Yet the two are closer than may seem.' The journal pointed to the cessation of party and class conflict and government interventions in food, railways and finance. Britain was 'nearer a humanitarian socialism now than ever before', and these changes were only possible because of the war. 'How absurd, then, is it to feel that this union will end when the needs that called it out pass away?', one editorial asked.[69]

In reality, spiritualists were rewriting history. The responses leading up to and after the declaration of war varied and included protest, anger, anxiety, fear, relief, acceptance, enthusiasm and indifference, sometimes with more than one of these emotions expressed by the same individual.[70] In the days preceding the start of the conflict, most within the Labour party denounced the prospect of war. On 2 August, Labour led an anti-war rally in Trafalgar Square. In the following weeks, with a few exceptions (party leader Ramsay MacDonald resigned), Labour acquiesced to support the war. In October, the party issued a manifesto stating, 'the German military caste were determined on war if the rest of Europe could not be cowed into submission by other means ... the victory of Germany would mean the death of democracy in Europe'.[71] The same was the case for many dissenting churches. Between 1902 and 1907, more members of the Primitive Methodists had been imprisoned for passive resistance than any other group. During the war, 150,000 of its members joined the forces. In January 1914, the Baptist Reverend John Clifford promised the coming of a new era of brotherhood and the consignment of militarism to 'the dark ages'. He denounced war as 'anti-Christian' but supported the British war effort as necessary for progress.[72] Other pacifists like H. G. Wells argued that the horror of modern war would shock humanity into abolishing conflict, thus popularising the phrase 'the war that will end all war'.

Spiritualists followed a similar pattern. In the week before war, *Light* advocated for peace. 'It will be a sad commentary on Christendom and Civilisation if they can provide no other way', an editorial noted, warning that 'if the worst happens' the world would pay 'a price that need never have been paid'.[73] A week later *Light* claimed that the war 'had to come'.[74] Initially, *The Two Worlds* feared that war would 'put the clock of progress back for half a century' and cause unjust suffering to the poor and working class. A month later the journal was proclaiming that 'the passing awful drama is part of the solution of the world's problems, and a help towards the ultimate erection of the city of Divine Humanity'.[75] If spiritualists were nonconformists, they, like many others, conformed in 1914.

It is also inaccurate to believe that ethnic and class conflict suddenly vanished once war was declared. The strikes in South Wales and the Clyde in 1915 and the Irish rebellion in 1916 made this clear. But where public enthusiasm during August 1914 did exist, it could produce a moment of euphoria in which the elimination of social conflicts seemed like a reality.[76] The illusion of unity offered a glimpse of a possible utopia and indicated that a sudden transformation of society was possible. The Theosophist C. W. Leadbeater, for example, observed that the regenerative power of war would reward the enormity of Britain's sacrifice, arguing that those interfering with spiritual progress would be destroyed while the self-sacrifice of Britain's men 'raised themselves greatly in the scale of humanity'. Only a great war allowed 'for so splendid an outburst from so many simultaneously', he proclaimed.[77] The war could accomplish in a short time the otherwise slow and difficult progress necessary to prepare for the arrival of the Great Teacher. The ground was ripe for catastrophic millennialism.

Indeed, the opening months of the war led to a prophetic revival.[78] In 1916, the Belgian writer Maurice Maeterlinck counted eighty-three prophesies alleged to have predicted the outbreak of the war.[79] Most were said to have come from eighteenth- or nineteenth-century sources. Renowned seers, new and old, were reported to have predicted the events of the war, including Nostradamus and Joanna Southcott, while the French prophet Madame de Thebes became an international celebrity.[80] But one of the most discussed of 1914 came from an unknown monk named Johannes. He was alleged to have predicted the coming of the antichrist who would launch a war that 'massacres priests, monks, women, children and old people'. Once the war was over, it would usher in 'an era of peace and prosperity ... for all the universe'.[81] Others predicted the rise and fall of the Prussian Empire, culminating in a great war and French revenge for 1871. Rumours circulated that Prussian heads of state had long received fortunes that predicted the downfall of Prussia in the early twentieth century but had sought war anyway, attempting to defy spiritual laws. These stories confirmed the arrogance of the Kaiser and the notion that his materialistic worldview would lead to his inevitable defeat.[82] The consensus of these prophecies was summarised by *Light* when it reported on the Theosophist Alfred Percy Sinnett's prediction, first made in 1911: 'It is almost needless to say that the prophecy foreshadows the victory of the Allies, [and] the downfall of the German Empire ... The prophets are all at one on this point.'[83] In the early months of the war, it was easy for spiritualists to confirm their support for the conflict.

It would be disingenuous to claim that war prophecies were accepted wholeheartedly. As the historian of magic Owen Davies observes, their proliferation is more likely explained by the press taking advantage of the demand for reassuring news and entertainment in wartime. Since none of these forecasts accurately predicted the end of the war, some were bound to take notice of the litany of false predictions.[84] The typically more cautious SPR was particularly scathing, calling them 'irresponsible, unauthenticated, unverifiable ... anonymous hearsay', and observing that the evidence was 'so bad that it did not seem to warrant further investigation'.[85] On the other end of this spectrum were those, like one frequent correspondent of *Light* who professed to have found great comfort in the prophecies' 'composite picture', believing in 1916 that they were in the process of fulfilment.[86]

In the middle were those like David Gow who acknowledged that prophecies were of a 'precarious nature' but believed that foresight was possible.[87] Prophecy was framed in terms similar to predictions of world events by relevant authorities. While the latter looked at issues such as politics, economics and military matters, the prophet was channelling an esoteric perspective. *Light* argued in 1914 and 1916 that prophecies could be useful when they agreed with 'the natural order of things'.[88] This statement reflected the social function that prophecy served in 1914, which was to fill the fissure between the expectation of progress and the outbreak of war. When conflict with Germany was possible but uncertain, it was something to be avoided, but when war was declared, it was destiny. In fact, it was precisely because the British market had already been saturated with tales and predictions of future wars from both natural and supernatural sources prior to 1914 that the public was so receptive to wartime prognostications.[89] The consensus that emerged from this subsequent foray into divination simply reaffirmed nationalistic sentiments that the war was purposeful, that Britain's military efforts were just and that a great new age was on the horizon. As Lodge wrote in 1915, 'Seers and sensitives have known intuitively that great events were being foreshadowed, they felt the coming of the present time, and have heralded the advent of a new era.'[90] But as victory remained elusive and Kitchener's citizen army entered the battlefields, the ensuing slaughter of Britain's youth was no longer an abstract possibility but a reality many had to endure, including Lodge himself as his youngest son Raymond was killed in September 1915. As Britons realised the magnitude of their commitment and the diminishing returns of victory, they found themselves having to reconcile personal loss with their lofty ideals and expectations. Spiritualism's rise in popularity, it turned out, would help reaffirm the prophets, providing comfort during the war's darkest moments.

The spiritual harvest: Conan Doyle's new revelation

The Great War had a noticeable effect on British spiritualism, but the extent of that influence is difficult to measure. It is often taken for granted that the spiritualist movement grew on account of the war but Gerald O'Hara's study of a spiritualist society in York actually revealed a decline in members during and after the war. Using the society's minute books, he finds that it admitted 107 new full members between 1908 and 1918, but only thirty-five over the next ten years. How representative this was of the national context is unknown. O'Hara observes that applications did not significantly decrease in the 1920s, suggesting that amongst this particular society at least, membership remained consistent and closely guarded.[91] Owen Davies uses the observation that SNU census numbers showed an increase of only thirteen societies between 1914 and 1916 to question spiritualism's wartime growth. However, when dealing with the tribulations of grief that spiritualism attended to, even the year 1918 (let alone 1916 before Third Ypres and the German spring offensive) is an arbitrary endpoint.[92] The outbreak of war would have also disrupted organised spiritualism. An SNU report on societies in northern England noted that the mobilisation of so many men within the working class was thinning the ranks of the societies. As *The Two Worlds* reported, the six societies in Northumberland and Shildon were suffering 'from the depletion of their ranks through enlistments and attendant causes'.[93] The number of spiritualist societies in Britain did increase dramatically after the war. According to the SNU censuses, in 1913 there were 141 spiritualist societies belonging to the union. By 1922 this number rose to 332 and by 1938 there were 530 with a membership total of 13,617. After including those churches and societies belonging to the rival Greater World Christian Spiritualist League (GWCSL), there were 1,058 societies and 30,000 members, and this does not include unaffiliated organisations and home circles.[94] The SPR's membership likewise increased, peaking at 1,305 in 1920.[95]

The reliability of spiritualist census numbers has been questioned. One critic, for example, argued that census data indicated that American societies were deliberately inflating their membership numbers during and after the war.[96] But there are other indications that public interest in spiritualism grew on account of the war. Most important was the advocacy of Oliver Lodge and Arthur Conan Doyle. Lodge's 1916 book *Raymond* made the case for survival after death through séance communications allegedly from Raymond's spirit. The book was a success, going through a dozen reprints by 1919 and inspiring a wave of war-themed publications reporting spirit communications from fallen soldiers, including the 'sequel' to *Raymond*, *Christopher*, Eliza Kelway-Bamber's *Claude's Book* and Wesley Tudor Pole's *Private Dowding*, among many others.[97] By the end of the war, there were more books being published on spiritualism than since the movement's previous peak in the 1870s.[98] Demand for mediums followed. Between 1914 and 1916, the number of medium advertisements in *Light* increased by 29.9 per cent, suggesting that more mediums could consistently afford the four shillings for a standard one-inch advertisement.[99] The demand was enough for the Roman Catholic Church and the Anglican Church to cede to public pressure and officially respond to spiritualism in 1917 and 1920, respectively.

In the midst of this surge in public interest, a new school of thought emerged regarding the war's place and purpose in the history of human spirituality, and its most public advocate was Arthur Conan Doyle. In explaining Conan Doyle's conversion to spiritualism, both too much and too little emphasis can be placed upon his own personal losses. It is true that two of his nephews were killed in the war and that his son Kingsley and his brother died of influenza while serving in 1918 and 1919, respectively.[100] But Conan Doyle had already declared himself a spiritualist in 1916.[101] It would nevertheless be ill-advised to discount how much the war haunted Conan Doyle personally, especially when we consider the amount of energy that he devoted to spreading and defending the spiritualist movement in the 1920s. In the last decade of his life, he published dozens of books and articles on spiritualism and delivered lectures to much fanfare and criticism across the United Kingdom, Canada,

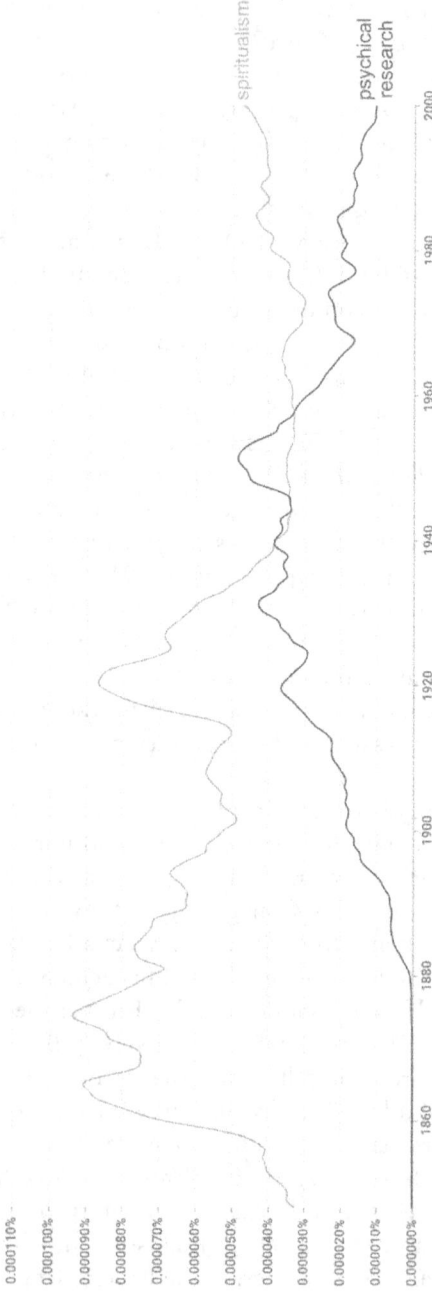

Figure 1.2 Google Ngram for the terms 'spiritualism' and 'psychical research' in British English books between 1850 and 2000.

Australia and the United States. He also found himself at the centre of several embarrassing public feuds over spiritualism's veracity that threatened his reputation.[102] If we are sometimes too quick to assume that interwar spiritualists were suffering from a 'will to believe', Conan Doyle reminds us not to abandon this explanation entirely.

Part of Conan Doyle's credulity – and he was credulous – stemmed from his conviction that the evidence in favour of spiritualism was now so strong that it was time to move from a period of 'investigation' to one of 'religious construction' – to use psychical research to answer existential questions relevant to humanity's fate.[103] On the one hand, he derided faith as a 'dark age' mentality and affirmed that a purposeful universe and the survival of human personality after death were now established scientific facts. On the other hand, he believed that spiritualism was not just scientific but also religious, confirming old revelations such as the existence of a soul, heaven and purgatory, as well as the dangers of sin. It provided corrections and additions such as the possibility of communication, the evolution of the spirit and the similarities between the worlds of the living and 'dead'. Conan Doyle argued that a spiritualist worldview had the greatest potential to bring about social and intellectual unity because it was compatible with all religions and modern science. As 'the great unifying force', spiritualism could end the sort of ideological conflicts that made war possible.[104]

Conan Doyle's scientific language, his Christian spiritualism and his belief that psychic and spiritualist phenomena were the core of all religions were not unique. What was original in his approach was that, rather than representing an awkward appendage to decades of spiritualist thought, war was integral to his spiritualist eschatology.[105] The suffering left in its wake, not the defeat of Germany, was essential to the unfolding of human history towards its divine ends. The war necessitated an introspection of the soul that would lead humanity towards what he believed was 'the greatest religious event since the death of Christ'.[106] Conan Doyle used his own journey as an example. Already a reformed materialist, he admitted that if it were not for the war he would have remained a sympathetic but only occasional student of spiritualism and psychical research.[107] The death of so many youths and the agony of grieving mothers unaware of the fate of their sons caused him to seek messages from beyond, where he found 'a call of hope and of guidance in the human race at the time of its deepest affliction'.[108] How many others had similar experiences? As he wrote, 'A future spiritual harvest will surely rise from the days in which we live' since 'the seeds of truth' are planted when the 'human soul is ploughed and harrowed by suffering'.[109]

Like his fictional creation, Sherlock Holmes, Conan Doyle used deduction to arrive at this conclusion. 'We, who have borne the pains, shall also learn the lesson which they were intended to convey', he stated, because 'if we do not learn it and proclaim it, then when can it ever be learned and proclaimed?' In other words, if the experiences of the war could not affect radical changes to the soul, progress was impossible, 'since there can never again be such a spiritual ploughing and harrowing and preparation for the seed'. Since spiritualism was a proven fact, the purposeless laws of materialism did not govern the universe. The war was not a random but unique event meant to 'shake mankind loose' from trivial material obsessions, such as militarism and religious conflict, and push progress forward.[110] Within the séance, the spirits of dead soldiers were delivering a 'vital message' capable of revealing the purpose of the Great War, which, if heeded, would redeem their sacrifice.

Conan Doyle arrived at an opportune moment for spiritualists. The war's increasing casualty list, its personal toll, and the declining confidence in victory seemed to have tempered glorifications of death in war and the crusading mentality against Germany. In 1914 for example, it was possible for mediums to proclaim that death in war was a beautiful 'remission of sin':

> War is the sole means to rid the earth of such a generation rooted in iniquity and hide-bound by misconceptions ... these derelicts of a false civilisation ... and misapplied sciences are, through the dread disciplines of disaster, destruction and death, purged of their ignoble natures, leaving all that is still noble and worthy of preservation to survive the suffering ... the dissolution of the body. Thus purified in the fiery crucible of Supreme Justice, the regenerated and emancipated spirit starts on the upward path, and with enlightened eyes and softened heart becomes the angel guardian of his loved ones still struggling on the earth-plane. Had he died ... with all his wickedness unpurged ... he would have sunk to the lowest spheres of the netherworlds and ages of slow and painful expiation would be needed to

bring him to the point attained by a death inspired by nobility of motive and self-sacrifice.[111]

After 1915, such pronouncements would have offered little comfort to the bereaved, especially as it became clear that the war was wiping out the children of Britain's social and cultural elite, not just the degenerate or wicked.

During the war's latter years, we see Conan Doyle's influence within séances and spiritualist periodicals. For example, Ellen Mary Little, who lost her son Rolf in the war, was informed that young men were offered as a sacrifice because their deaths were so tragic as to necessitate a search for meaning. If God had chosen the sick and elderly, there would be no 'incentive ... to find them, to reach them'.[112] The war was compared to Noah's flood and the end of war. 'God works in different ways', she was told, 'He came in the flood, and there was no flood again. Then He came in this war, but He won't allow another war.'[113] Also like Conan Doyle, Little interpreted the war as a spiritual revelation of Christ-like proportions. In a séance in January 1918, she was told,

> The war is a kind of sacrifice ... it's like the Christ sacrifice over again ... instead of the spirit coming into one body. It's operating through thousands of bodies – giving them powers to make again the supreme sacrifice. The spirit that made the sacrifice of Jesus has helped these young men to make the sacrifice.

Little was so moved by the message that she was convinced knowledge of the second coming had to be shared with the public.[114]

Unlike in 1914, mediums could now point to a coming spiritualist revolution as a real possibility. The medium Mrs T. P. Hands summarised this new view in May 1917:

> We in the Spirit World can see very clearly that this war ... is the beginning of the end of materialism. The hard, stony crust of materialism is already cracked, and soon will split asunder. Then will come the awakening, and in the awakening the presence in the Spirit World of so many who have been suddenly taken from the earth life will play a large part. The fact that so many families have been compelled to part with their loved ones will help very greatly to lift the people out of materialism ... Every son, husband, brother and sweetheart brought into spirit life means another link between your world and ours, and almost every home now has a link in our world.

> It is sometimes necessary that at least one should be taken from your surroundings to link your home with this world. Until such a link is formed, many homes completely ignore the existence of a Spirit World. And seeing the work to be done in the cause of Truth, shall it be said that these heroes of the war have 'died' for nought?[115]

The second coming of Christ was the thinning of the veil between the spiritual and physical worlds that was being achieved in séance rooms across the country, and which was initiated by the death of so many promising young men.

Spiritualists drew upon past prophecies that predicted a spiritualist revival in this manner, allowing them to stand out above the crowded and varied occultist prophecies of 1914. Introducing Conan Doyle's book *The New Revelation* was a prophecy from the famous medium Leonora Piper, allegedly delivered at the end of the nineteenth century:

> Before the clear revelation of spirit communication there will be a terrible war in different parts of the world. The entire world must be purified and cleansed before mortal can see, through his spiritual vision, his friends on this side and it will take just this line of action to bring about a state of perfection.[116]

The millennialist currents that had existed within psychical research prior to the war also found new moral urgency. Lodge became more invested in the spiritualist hypothesis and turned away from messianic children to the spirit of his son for answers. As Raymond Lodge communicated to his father,

> with me through you, [we] can break away the dam ... For God's sake father do it. Because if only you knew, and could only see what I see: ... the boys on our side shut out, you would throw the whole strength of yourself into this work ... from [my] death, which is only one of thousands ... the work which [I] enlisted for ... By passing away, many hundreds will benefit.[117]

Lodge's work in psychical research was now directly linked to the sacrifice of his son. Spiritualists' hopes that materialism was nearing its end or that the war would usher in a new age had not been shattered by attrition, just reinterpreted. Various millennialist strands now fell into line. The soldiers were the prophets of a spiritualist science and theological knowledge that had the potential to unify the world's philosophical systems and end both intellectual and physical conflict. Entire segments of the British population could now find an answer to why their children were being slaughtered. The message that they received leading into the 1920s was that the war had served a devastating yet significant purpose. But it could not be repeated.

False dawns: spiritualism in the 1920s

If spiritualism's rise in the interwar period is only a myth, it was certainly one its adherents believed or at the very least perpetuated. Numerous societies boasted about rising membership numbers in the early 1920s. Gow proclaimed in January 1920 that before the war, 'Spiritualism was little more than a matter of hearsay and vague rumour', but had since become socially significant. He claimed that the SNU had a membership of 30,000, 1,500 of which belonged to the LSA.[118] In 1923, he asserted that *Light*'s subscriptions had more than doubled over the previous year.[119] The Manchester Central National Spiritualist Church claimed to have 5,000 members and 20,000 'sympathizers'.[120] Mary A. Stair, the Honorary Secretary of the Fund of Benevolence (a fundraiser for the SNU) believed there were 500,000 spiritualists in the United Kingdom.[121] Stair was no doubt exaggerating but the LSA and other spiritualist organisations had to invest to expand their infrastructure in the early 1920s to accommodate a real growth in interest since the war.[122]

Spiritualists were not the only ones who observed that the movement was growing. There was an above-average prosecution rate of fortune tellers in 1921, 1924, 1927, 1928 and 1931, and as a result, some mediums, like Annie Brittain, found themselves in the crosshairs.[123] The Anglican Church was forced to revisit the issue again in 1936 when it launched an official committee to investigate the compatibility (or lack thereof) between the Church and the doctrines of spiritualism. The conclusions were mixed but seven out of the ten members agreed that there were probably cases where communications came from discarnate spirits and that 'representatives of the Church should keep in touch with groups of intelligent persons who believe in Spiritualism'.[124]

The Anglican Church even reformed some of its doctrines during the interwar period in response to those abandoning the pews for séances. The Church was certainly ill-equipped to deal with the war. The spiritualist Mabel St. Clair Stobart noted that *The Book of Common Prayer*, which had not been changed since the seventeenth century, was joyless and pessimistic. Doctrines such as original sin and eternal punishment were off-putting in times of war and the concept of the Communion of Saints was confusing. In 1914, it was not even customary for Anglicans to give prayers to the dead.[125] After the war, however, while not downplaying the importance of faith over demonstrable facts, Anglican concepts of the afterlife grew more open to the idea that the spirit progressed and evolved. Heaven became more democratic. The Church likewise acknowledged spiritualism as a form of Communion with the Saints.[126] British spiritualism was not only projecting confidence but was also drawing backlash or accommodation from church and state.

Spiritualists saw in the rising popularity of the movement what they believed to be the realisation of the promised spiritual age. In January 1920, the psychical researcher Stanley De Brath observed, 'A general impression prevails that we stand on the threshold of a new order of things. Some deduce this from spiritual assurances that it is so; some from Biblical prophecy ... some again, from the general movement of public opinion and a vague feeling that such a cataclysm as the world-war must necessarily be a new point of departure.'[127] In an editorial in May 1919, *The Two Worlds* referred to spiritualism's newfound popularity as a 'flood, bearing away on its rushing tide a materialistic science and outworn philosophy ... the resistless flood rolls on across the world of an awakening humanity'.[128] Social unrest in Britain during demobilisation challenged these hopes almost immediately. In 1919, soldiers revolted in Kinmel, race riots broke out across Britain, police went on strike and guerrilla warfare continued in Ireland.[129] *Light* dismissed these incidents as 'the growing pains of progress', in which a new state of affairs had resulted in a reactionary current that concealed the long-term trend.[130] At the beginning of 1920, the journal was prepared to write materialism's obituary and believed that 'the great wave of psychic activity' was foreshadowing 'the dawn of a new age'.[131] In retrospect, 1920 was proclaimed to be 'a year of spiritual awakening'.[132] *The Two Worlds* acknowledged the 'wave of crimes of violence and lack of moral restraint' across the country that the war had created, but there was also optimism that 'the horrors of the past have surely awakened us'. Spiritualists were called upon to move forward with determination and create a world 'as good a heaven as any other'.[133]

A sense of impatience with progress is evident as early as 1921. As Oliver Lodge noted, continued political, social and intellectual conflict had given the impression that the spiritual revolution was moving too slowly. He informed spiritualists that progress was too comprehensive to occur so quickly and he still foresaw a brighter future forged by a spiritualist revival.[134] 'We live in important times', he wrote to Arthur Conan Doyle in 1922, 'and there is evidently a serious effort being made by higher powers to bring about a better state of things and to reconcile and regenerate the nations. The operation will be slow, but I think sure.'[135] *The Two Worlds* reminded readers that, contrary to the traditional religious ideals that divine revelation was 'final, unalterable and infallible', it was in reality 'one of growth and evolution' which needed to be constructed carefully through the imperfect means of mediumship.[136]

It was not until 1923 that spiritualists were seriously conflicted by reality. In that year, the atheist Bolsheviks had proved victorious in a bloody civil war, fascists had taken power in Italy, Germany was experiencing social and economic crises in the face of hyperinflation and Britain was at war in Ireland. Intellectually, the works of Einstein and Heisenberg had initiated what Thomas Kuhn later identified as a 'paradigm shift'.[137] In May 1919, Arthur Stanley Eddington provided one of the first experimental confirmations of relativity and Einstein's theories became popular in English culture.[138] Lodge's spiritualist science remained devoted to the ether, moving him further away from a new generation of cutting-edge physics. The catastrophic millennial prophecies of the war now appeared absurd. In September 1923, *Light* criticised as sensational the 'weird' prophecies and occult apocalyptic theories that they had once promoted in 1914, and lamented how easily spiritualism could become the 'hunting grounds of many superstitious fancies'. Readers were advised to avoid the temptation of miraculous intervention. 'There are no short cuts to the Millennium', the journal stated.[139]

Some psychical researchers began to look back to the historical record to reassess the veracity of pre-war prophecies. In the early 1920s, J. G. Piddington conducted an exhaustive cross-correspondence study of 3,000 automatic writing scripts produced by six spiritualists prior to the outbreak of the war.[140] Piddington observed that the mediums in question had clearly prophesied a coming war followed by utopia. For example, on 1 December 1913, the medium Mrs King received the message 'Let not your heart be troubled. Out of great tribulation cometh great peace, for when the waters have been troubled an angel stilleth them.' And on 25 April 1914, she heard, 'This cry … is the cry of the world now, it is the dark moment before the new light.'[141] Piddington did not believe these messages necessarily warranted a supernormal source since others had predicted a war through normal means.[142] Instead, their value needed to be judged according to their outcomes. A realised utopia was so improbable that one could not predict this future by chance. 'The history of mankind is largely a history of wars', Piddington observed, 'but the history of mankind contains no instance of the realization of a Utopia'.[143] If the prophecies proved accurate, it suggested that spiritualist beings had foreseen the future. 'If in the time to come the world shows no improvement', however, or 'only some moderate degree of improvement', then 'the forecast is false'.[144]

Piddington objected to the idea that the prophecies were referring to a gradual evolution of progress since it was obvious to him that they predicted an immediate transformation. As he argued, 'nothing short of a very thorough-going and lasting change for the better in international and social conditions could be held to fulfill them'.[145] Nevertheless, Oliver Lodge described the prophecies uncovered by Piddington as 'hopeful … in what seems to me a striking and encouraging manner', suggesting that he still found it possible that their visions could be realised through gradual progress.[146] Either way, by 1923 spiritualists were forced to confront the possibility that the millennial prophecies of the war might not be realised.

Spiritualists' responses to these false dawns varied but there was still optimism about ending war. In this effort, they joined the political idealism and the pacifist movement in Britain that had grown confident in the League of Nations' ability to disarm nations and deter threats without force.[147] The League of Nations Union (LNU), which advocated for disarmament and international peace, had a membership of over 400,000 in 1931.[148] One of its founding members, Gilbert Murray, advocated that the League of Nations could create an international order of national cooperation in which armies and navies would gradually become obsolete.[149] Murray was also interested in psychical research and conducted his own personal experiments with telepathy.[150] The link was not accidental. Telepathy's promise to unite distant minds promised sympathetic, not just scientific, progress.[151] William F. Barrett, for example, believed that by 'involuntarily sharing in one another's pleasures and pains', telepathy would help make 'the brotherhood of the race' not 'a strenuous effort but a reality of all'.[152]

Other members of the LNU, such as Lord Robert Cecil, advocated for a spiritual basis upon which to bring peace to Europe. As the historian Helen McCarthy argues, after the Great War, 'a large section of religious opinion widened the search for salvation to the international sphere, where it came to pin its hopes upon the League as a unifying cause for believers of all denominations and sects'.[153] Spiritualists were one such body that hoped to use politics to realise spiritual aims. A 'Brotherhood of Man' was one of the seven principles first adopted by Emma Hardinge Britten in the late nineteenth century and it was included in the SNU's new constitution by George F. Berry in 1921. The proclamation that all of humanity was of the same brotherhood, regardless of race or creed, was not in itself pacifist, as the case of the Great War demonstrates, but 'Brotherhood of Man' was often used as the justification for the abolition of war, and the constitution was part of an effort to organise and unite spiritualists as a more influential political body.[154]

Prevention of war instead of the expectation of peace became an important aspect of spiritualism, and pacifism intensified in the movement in the 1920s.[155] In 1922, the psychical researcher Stanley De Brath pleaded with readers of *Light* to cease expecting peace through divine intervention. The old religions had failed to prevent war because they had placed too much emphasis on an intervening God and failed to accept the universal spiritual laws of evolution and progress. Spiritualism, on the contrary, was concerned with understanding and working with these laws.[156] Spiritualists like De Brath were not content with assuming that war would simply end, and called upon spiritualists to be more politically active in pacifist unions.[157] At an Armistice Day ceremony in 1924, Conan Doyle and other leadership figures called upon spiritualists to support the League of Nations as the best opportunity to realise spiritualists' goals on a political level.[158]

Although catastrophic millennialism gave way to an acceptance of gradual progress, others grew more pessimistic. Between 1922 and 1926, Conan Doyle received prophecies from his wife's mediumship of coming natural and world disasters.[159] In a 1922 letter to Lodge, he reiterated his conviction that the aim of spiritualism was 'to warn the human race and that sooner or later it should be done … We may get much direct signs that the warning will carry conviction.'[160] Messages in Conan Doyle's séances from the 1920s were filled with dire warnings. In March 1923, the control known as 'Pheneas' was quoted as stating, 'I fear the world is hopeless. Even after the fearful war, humanity is no better.'[161] Since the Great War had failed to achieve a modicum of utopia, only a true apocalypse could create the kind of radical change necessary to construct 'a new world … built upon real Christianity'. In February 1926, Conan Doyle was instructed to 'be prepared' for a signal so that he could 'pass the knowledge on and so save those who should be saved', and to 'pray for all those who are about to perish in ignorance'.[162]

In a posthumously published article, Conan Doyle pieced together these messages and laid out his new apocalyptic vision. It would begin with a series of natural disasters that would cause 'worldwide havoc' and send entire countries like Italy into the sea. These geological events would cause social unrest, leading to revolutions and eventually ending with human extinction. The destruction of civilisation would result in 'a complete rending of the veil' bringing the spirit face to face with matter. Only those who 'were working with the spiritual' would be elected to pass over before the veil was closed. The entire history of spiritualism, he reasoned, showed that it had been intended to prepare humanity for this final revelation.[163]

Conan Doyle's last words on spiritualism were far less optimistic than what he had publicly proclaimed between 1916 and 1924. The shift in attitudes reflected not only the continued political and social turbulence in Europe but also high-profile and embarrassing public exposures of spirit photographers and mediums in 1924 and 1925 (more on that later). But instead of abandoning his utopian dreams entirely, Conan Doyle simply modified his visions of the future while retaining the meaning behind the war's sacrifices. The soldiers were prophets who had given those corrupted by materialism, such as

Conan Doyle himself, a chance at redemption and resurrection. The millennium was now for a worthy few – those who had responded to their vital message versus those who did not.

Prophecies of peace: the 1930s

Conan Doyle passed away in 1930 disillusioned and defeated, but spiritualism continued to attract an audience amidst new crises. In the 1930s, international developments such as the rise of Hitler, the Abyssinia crisis, the Spanish Civil War and the reoccupation of the Rhineland forced Britons to confront the possibility of another conflict. By 1933, the League of Nations and the World Disarmament Conference had failed. Spiritualists responded to the collapse of practical political solutions like many other pacifists, with desperate pleas for peace.[164] For many spiritualists in the 1930s, war could no longer be redeemed. In part, this was driven by fears of industrial warfare but also the need to ensure that the sacrifices of the Great War had not been in vain and that humanity was not regressing back into destruction. Despite the turmoil, Britons weathered the storm and confidence in continued peace, aligned with a notion of history as purposeful and progressive, set the stage for the no-war predictions of 1939.

The disillusionment narrative that dominated popular myths of the First World War gained significant traction during the 'war book boom' of 1929. That year saw the publication of Siegfried Sassoon's *Memoirs of a Fox-Hunting Man* and Robert Graves's *Goodbye to All That*. The tales recounted in these books were more reflective of the late 1920s than the war experience themselves. Graves's writings, for example, disagree with his opinions and attitudes expressed during the war and they fit a narrative that was acceptable only in the late 1920s once the lofty ideals of the Great War had failed to materialise.[165] Not surprisingly, the trend was evident in the spiritualist movement as well. In 1933, George F. Berry questioned the motivations of the politicians who had led Britain into war. 'Did they really have the welfare of the community at heart', he asked, 'and would any similar sacrifice in the near or distant future accomplish results which the statesmen assure us we fought for 15 years ago?'[166] Remember, that in 1914, Berry greeted the Great War as part of a cycle of destruction and rejuvenation. Similarly, in 1936, the Scottish poet and spiritualist Charles Richard Cammell remembered a world in ruins in the 1920s, not one on the brink of spiritual revival. 'Disastrous as was the physical condition in which mankind found itself', he stated, 'the spiritual condition was yet worse'.[167]

The war books boom and the international threats of the 1930s transformed public commemorations into 'an object lesson in peace'.[168] Cammell's otherwise cynicism about the war was used to highlight the stakes of another conflict. As he asked rhetorically, 'was all this ... measureless sum of progress achieved ... for ... self-destruction?' Rejecting this notion, he explained that life was constantly evolving 'towards higher planes of mind and ultimately spirit'. He concluded with the reassurance that 'a vision of Utopia' was not just 'a poet's dream' but the limitless potential of the spirit.[169] Despite the occasional pessimism, most public spiritualists in the 1930s retained the faith. During a Manchester Armistice Day ceremony in 1930, the spiritualist J. Cuming Walters reassured his audience that the law of progress was real, attested to by multitudes of spirits, including those who had passed on in the Great War. 'No matter what shattering forces may be at work', he explained, 'restitution is all part of one vast plan founded upon the eternal principle of progress'.[170] Foreshadowing the crisis of 1939, he pointed out that if this were not the case then the faith of spiritualists would become a 'mockery' and it would have all been in 'jest'.[171] The medium Horace Leaf likewise believed that 'Nationalism, [is] perhaps in its final struggle for survival', and so long as the world embraced spiritualist principles 'we shall be on the way to Utopia'.[172] Such statements attest to spiritualists' steadfast belief that the deaths of millions of young men must have served some sort of cosmic purpose. They continued to find a receptive audience as Britons faced the prospect of another major war.

As desperation took hold, the ghosts of the Great War were resurrected to remind the British people of the cost and meaning of the sacrifice. In 1933, the Manchester Central Spiritualist Church held an Armistice Day ceremony in which the keynote address was given by a soldier's spirit:

> I was one of those who trod the mud of Flanders ... The clouds of war and suspicion are gathering all around you, and there is a vast host of us who are afraid that the peace we died for is not a lasting

one. War is futile and it is blasphemy to associate the name of God with it. We urge you to pray that all men will realize its futility.

The anonymous soldier-spirit proposed hosting the World Disarmament Conference in the cemeteries of Flanders to remind the nations of the 'terrors of war'.[173]

Others attempted to rouse the movement into action. A reader of *The Two Worlds* wanted to organise a 'Spiritualist Anti-War League' in 1933.[174] One frequent correspondent called upon spiritualists to make a firm commitment to peace in the event that war did erupt. 'What line of action would you, as a Spiritualist, maintain, supposing war were declared to-morrow?' he asked.[175] For one respondent, the future of the movement was tied to its stance on war: if it could not commit to pacifism now it would not survive another conflict.[176] In a reversal of 1914, spiritualists now subscribed to a philosophy in which conscientious objection, not sacrifice in war, was the adaptation necessary for spiritual survival.[177] As Cammell noted, 'If war ever had its uses, that day is gone.'[178] It was becoming increasingly difficult for spiritualists to reconcile warfare with progress.

When spiritualists did try and contemplate what would happen if another war erupted, their prognostications were dire. At an Armistice Day ceremony in 1933, the popular trance-lecturer Louisa Ann Meurig-Morris's control, 'Power', believed that another war was possible but that it would be so destructive as to bring forth the apocalypse.[179] 'It would be the last great event that we in this world would understand as war', she explained, leading to a 'rending of the veil ... after which war would have completely passed away from the earth and the human spirit achieved its liberation'.[180] This was similar to Conan Doyle's visions of the apocalypse, but most spiritualists, it seems, had since rejected the idea. In fact, Meurig-Morris (or 'Power') thought this scenario was unlikely. The Great War 'had done its work in preparing the way for a final world peace', she explained, and 'the sacrifices made had not been in vain'.[181] Meurig-Morris was optimistic a year later that humanity would continue to progress, unite science and religion and end materialism.[182]

The prevailing optimism behind the no-war prophecies of 1939 must also be viewed while considering the obvious terror that the possibility of war generated in interwar Britain. The Great War had introduced Britons to the destructive power of industrial warfare, including the prospects of aerial bombardment, a fear exacerbated by the bombing of Guernica in 1937. Books such as *The Black Death*, *The Poison War* and *Invasion from the Air* imagined planes dropping bombs filled with poisonous gas on London.[183] When war with Germany became a reality instead of a fantasy in 1939, hundreds of thousands of Britons migrated away from the cities, carried gas masks for themselves and their children and huddled in underground public shelters.[184] In September 1940, approximately 400,000 cats and dogs were euthanised by their owners to spare them death from the skies or from starvation.[185] Mediums in the 1930s attempted to allay these concerns with peace predictions. As Cummins stated, 'put the idea of bombs dropping on … England out of your head. It is not going to happen.' Gibbes chose to publish Cummins's work on foresight so as to 'give reassurance as regards the possibility of war'.[186]

Geraldine Cummins's personal history is also revealing. She was the fifth daughter of Jane and Dr Ashley Cummins, a physician and Professor of Medicine at the National University of Ireland. She began her career as a playwright and became interested in spiritualism during the Great War after psychic experiences related to the deaths of two of her brothers in combat.[187] It was around this time that she first experimented with an Ouija board at the home of the medium Hester Dowden.[188] Her status rose within the spiritualist ranks with a series of books called *The Scripts of Cleophas*, reported to be from St Paul and other Apostles, which were meant to facilitate a restructuring of Christianity. Two other books in the 1930s, *The Road to Immortality* and *Beyond Human Personality*, were presented as additions to Frederic Myers's life work as received through automatic writing. Cummins received the support of Oliver Lodge, who noticed that the contents of these scripts were similar to conversations he had with Myers before his death.[189]

Cummins proposed that the entire order and purpose of the universe came into view as the soul evolved to greater states of awareness in the spirit world. Gradually, 'the subconscious mind of the whole race' – what she labelled 'the Great Memory' – came into view, revealing all that was, is and will be. Human history, from beginning to end, existed in the ether according to the 'imagination of God'. Future events had already happened, but humanity was not conscious of them, since living beings existed in an imperfect terrestrial consciousness.[190] This was a common argument made by spiritualists and occultists of the interwar period who attempted to understand prevision. Influenced by J. W. Dunne's popular book *An Experiment with Time*, as well as certain implications from Einstein's general relativity, some spiritualists and psychical researchers contested that the division of time into past, present and future was a construction of humanity's limited physical senses.[191] Spirits, however, could see further on this plane and so reveal the future.

When Cummins looked upon that 'Great Memory', what did she see? How did the previous war and the possibility of another conflict square with her understandings and expectations of spiritual evolution? Given the volatile nature of the inter-war period, one might wonder what role another war could play in the unfolding of progress. Messages glorifying soldiers' deaths as part of materialism's destruction or a great war as a sacrifice to usher in a spiritualist revival could not be delivered with the same honest expectations and hopes in 1939 as they had in previous decades. As one who personally experienced loss in the Great War, she had further incentive to desire peace. Nor were her audiences eager to accept prophecies of doom. When Meurig-Morris had suggested it as a possibility in 1933, her spirit guide 'Power' tread carefully around the topic. As David Gow noted in his report to *The Two Worlds*, '[Power] saying that which he felt might offend, but speaking his honest thought, he indicated the possibility of another war'.[192] Another war was simply unimaginable for most. According to George Lethem, the new editor of *Light* in 1939, the 'universal fear of war' present in Europe 'was the great factor swaying the pendulum towards peace' and was a 'truer indication of what the future holds'. Governments and the people of the world 'have a war memory', he explained, which served as 'a great corrective ... We are too near to the misery and suffering of the last war to engage lightly and casually in another.'[193] The sacrifices of the soldiers had at least conditioned humanity to view war as something to be avoided at all costs. The war's destructive legacy was logically a force for peace.

As tensions with Germany escalated, the ghosts of the Great War continued to haunt Britain, crying out to be remembered. Claire Sheridan was introduced to spiritualism after her husband was killed on the Western Front.[194] In February 1939, she related an experience at a church in London where she encountered the spirits of soldiers killed in France. They had instructed her to send the following message:

> Our UNITED Spirit of Sacrifice forms a MASS MOVEMENT of great force, bringing pressure to bear upon the earth. People *must* know, *must* understand, that war is useless ... *Tell them*, TELL THEM, TELL THEM!

'Yes, I'll tell them', she responded, 'but WILL THEY LISTEN?'[195] Seven months later Britain was embroiled in another conflict with Germany. In the 1920s, the idea that Sheridan's husband had died to bring about a great spiritual revolution may have offered her solace. By the 1930s, such beliefs may have appeared naïve, but she could still cling to the idea that the spectre of millions dead loomed too large over Europe to prevent another conflict. Now that too was farcical. What then did her husband die for? Where would spiritualism go from here?

Conclusion

The outbreak of the Second World War led to a massive decline in organised spiritualism.[196] In 1941, the number of spiritualist societies and churches affiliated with the SNU decreased by 172 and the number of members, by 3,778.[197] It would be a mistake to assume that spiritualists suddenly stopped believing and abandoned the movement on account of the Second World War. Psychological studies have shown that when prophecies fail, adherents often hold steadfast to their beliefs and rationalise the failures away.[198] It is probable that the crisis was enough to cause disillusionment and disaffection amongst some believers. The medium William Henry Evans stated that, prior to the declaration of war, he had 'heard some say: "If war comes I will never believe in Spiritualism again"'.[199] It is more likely, though, that the threat of aerial bombardment and the subsequent Blitz made it too difficult to congregate with other spiritualists. Communities were literally upended by mass internal migrations, blackouts and bombings. The immediate outbreak of war in 1939 was also followed by some expressing hope that it could bring some benefits to the movement's numbers as in the previous conflict and create new public figures like Conan Doyle and Oliver Lodge.[200] In fact, the SNU did see a recovery, as its numbers peaked in the 1950s, but by 1959 the SNU had lost forty-two churches and over 3,300 members.[201] Another major war brought the bereaved back into the séance room; they just did not stay long.

Many also abandoned their pacifist principles.[202] This is hardly surprising given the unpopularity of these views once Britain was subjected to the threat of Nazi invasion.[203] The SNU officially endorsed the war under the conviction that universal brotherhood required the protection of smaller states from Hitler's aggression.[204] But something had changed. Pacifism was much more significant than it had been in 1914. When William Henry Evans once again penned a criticism of the British war effort, it was met mostly with approval from readers, not criticism.[205]

The decline in spiritualism's relevancy was a slower burn than the 1941 census numbers would suggest, but there is a history of spiritualism that is specific to the era of the Great War. Spiritualists' visions of the future show a clear convergence between the belief in an enchanted world, an idealist understanding of the war's purpose and the ultimate instability of these worldviews as the passage of time altered Britain's memories of the conflict. That trend only intensified in the following decades. After the Second World War, the Holocaust, the nuclear arms race and the Vietnam War, the 'war to end all wars' appears as naïve as the belief that salvation and revelation would come from the séance.

Notes

1 CUL MS SPR, Prediction Files, Prediction File 9, 'Message Received through Miss Cummins for Predictions Re. War', September 1938.
2 For a comprehensive inventory of these messages see Geraldine Cummins and E. B. Gibbes, *No War: The Coming European Crisis* (London: Goodmount Press, 1939).
3 'Remember, No War!', *Light*, 59:3057 (1939), 521.
4 E. B. Gibbes, 'After-Thoughts on Peace Prediction Failure', *Light*, 59:3063 (1939), 601.
5 Gladys Osborne Leonard, *Brief Darkness* (London: Cassell, 1942), pp. 28–9.

6 'World Peace Not to Be Broken! Will There Be a World Peace Pact?', *The Two Worlds*, 52:2699 (1939), 514.
7 'As We See It: Facing War Conditions', *Light*, 59:3061 (1939), 582; 'What Our Readers Are Saying', *Light*, 59:3062 (1939), 596.
8 'Dear Sir ...', *Psychic News*, 381 (1939), 11.
9 'Let the People Judge: What "Red Cloud" Said before the War', *Prediction* (10 November 1939), p. 447.
10 Frank T. Blake, 'Prophecies', *The Two Worlds*, 52:1708 (1939), 641, 646.
11 Herbert Thurston, 'Spiritualists and Their "No War" Predictions', *The Tablet* (16 September 1939), p. 357.
12 Ethel Corkey, 'What Our Readers Are Saying: The Spiritual Is What Matters', *Light*, 59:3063 (1939), 607; 'Those Spirit Prophecies', *The Two Worlds*, 52:2703 (1939), 584.
13 Horace Leaf, 'Spirits, the War and a Call', *The Two Worlds*, 52:2703 (1939), 580; Horace Leaf, 'Prophecies, the War, and a Call', *Light*, 3061:59 (1939), 579.
14 Catherine Wessinger (ed.), *The Oxford Handbook of Millennialism* (Oxford: Oxford University Press, 2011), p. 720.
15 For interwar utopian visions see Jay Winter, *Dreams of Peace and Freedom: Utopian Moments in the Twentieth Century* (New Haven, CT: Yale University Press, 2006), pp. 48–98.
16 Catherine Wessinger, 'Millennialism with and without the Mayhem', in Thomas Robbins and Susan J. Palmer (eds), *Millennium, Messiahs, and Mayhem: Contemporary Apocalyptic Movements* (New York: Routledge, 1997), pp. 47–59, and W. Michael Ashcraft, 'Progressive Millennialism', in Wessinger (ed.), *The Oxford Handbook of Millennialism*, pp. 44–65.
17 J. F. C. Harrison, *The Second Coming: Popular Millenarianism, 1780–1850* (New Brunswick, NJ: Rutgers University Press, 1979), pp. xv–xvi.
18 *Ibid.*, pp. 57–134.
19 I. F. Clarke, *Voices Prophesying War: Future Wars, 1763–3749* (Oxford: Oxford University Press, 1992), pp. 5–6.
20 *Ibid.*, pp. 6–8, 29–43.
21 Rhodri R. Hayward, 'From the Millennial Future to the Unconscious Past: The Transformation of Prophecy in Early Twentieth-Century Britain', in Bertrand Taithe and Tim Thornton (eds), *Prophecy: The Power of Inspired Language in History, 1300–2000* (Phoenix Mill: Sutton Publishing, 1997), pp. 161, 171–3.
22 Harrison, *The Second Coming*, pp. xv–xvi, 7–9, 39, 86–134.
23 See K. Paul Johnson, *The Masters Revealed: Madame Blavatsky and the Myth of the Great White Lodge* (New York: State University of New

York Press, 1994) and Bruce F. Campbell, *Ancient Wisdom Revived: A History of the Theosophical Movement* (Berkeley, CA: University of California Press, 1980).
24 Alex Owen, *The Place of Enchantment: British Occultism and the Culture of the Modern* (Chicago, IL: University of Chicago Press, 2004), p. 122.
25 Lynne Lyons, *Species, Serpents, Spirits, and Skulls: Science at the Margins in the Victorian Age* (New York: State University of New York Press, 2009), pp. 24–34.
26 Marjorie Wheeler-Barclay, *The Science of Religion in Britain, 1860–1915* (Charlottesville, VA: University of Virginia Press, 2010), pp. 71–93.
27 For the link between modernism and the Great War see Modris Eksteins, *Rites of Spring: The Great War and the Birth of the Modern Age* (Boston, MA: Houghton Mifflin, 1989).
28 Jessica Meyer, *Men of War: Masculinity and the First World War in Britain* (New York: Palgrave Macmillan, 2009), p. 3; Daniel Pick, *Faces of Degeneration: A European Disorder, c. 1848–c.1918* (Cambridge: Cambridge University Press, 1989).
29 Owen, *The Place of Enchantment*, pp. 7–8, 222.
30 'Records of Private Séances from Notes Taken at the Time of Each Sitting. No. LX. From the Records of Mrs. S', *Light*, 13:662 (1893), 436; William Stainton Moses, *More Spirit Teachings through the Mediumship of William Stainton Moses* (London: L. N. Fowler, n.d., likely 1892), pp. 30–5, 75–7.
31 For the classic discussion on this topic, see Ross McKibbin, 'Why Was There No Marxism in Britain?' in his *The Ideologies of Class: Social Relations in Britain 1880–1950* (Oxford: Clarendon Press, 1994), pp. 1–41.
32 See Peter J. Bowler, *The Non-Darwinian Revolution: Reinterpreting A Historical Myth* (Baltimore, MD: Johns Hopkins University Press, 1988).
33 Jason A. Josephson-Storm, *The Myth of Disenchantment: Magic, Modernity, and the Birth of the Human Sciences* (Chicago, IL: University of Chicago Press, 2017), pp. 98–101.
34 Casper Sylvest, *British Liberal Internationalism, 1880–1930: Making Progress?* (Manchester: Manchester University Press, 2009), pp. 151, 178–80; Peter J. Bowler, *The Invention of Progress: The Victorians and the Past* (Oxford: Basil Blackwell, 1989), pp. 1–14, 20–39.
35 Bowler, *The Invention of Progress*, pp. 48–59.
36 *Ibid.*, pp. 1–14.
37 Campbell, *Ancient Wisdom Revived*, pp. 44–5, 64–5.
38 Lyons, *Species, Serpents, Spirits, and Skulls*, pp. 112, 118.

39 Alfred Russel Wallace, *Contributions to the Theory of Natural Selection: A Series of Essays* (London: Macmillan, 1870), p. 359.
40 Janet Oppenheim, *The Other World: Spiritualism and Psychical Research in England, 1850–1914* (Cambridge: Cambridge University Press, 1988), pp. 296–325.
41 For more on Winifred's life and her relationship with Gerald Balfour, see Murphy Temple, '"Death, Where Is Thy Sting?" British Spiritualism and the First World War', unpublished PhD dissertation (Stanford University, 2020), pp. 155–224. Thank you to the author for providing a version of this dissertation.
42 Peter Lord (ed.), *Between Two Worlds: The Diary of Winifred Coombe Tennant* (Aberystwyth: The National Library of Wales, 2011), p. 23.
43 *Ibid*., pp. 60–1.
44 *Ibid*.
45 Temple, 'Death, Where Is Thy Sting?', p. 190.
46 'Inner Aspects of the Great War', *Light*, 34:1754 (1914), 402; 'The Breaking of Chains', *Light*, 34:1757 (1914), 438; 'The Victims of the Machine', *Light*, 34:1759 (1914), 462.
47 'The Victims of the Machine', 462.
48 H. Ernest Hunt, '"A Scrap of Paper": Material Might Versus Spiritual Law', *Light*, 34:1757 (1914), 436.
49 Oliver Lodge, *The War and After: Short Chapters on Subjects of Serious Practical Import for the Average Citizen from A. D. 1915 Onwards* (New York: George H. Doran Company, 1915), p. 48.
50 'Frightfulness', *The Two Worlds*, 27:1404 (1914), 502.
51 William F. Barrett, 'War in Its Psychical and Religious Aspects', *Light*, 34:1763 (1914), 507.
52 Lodge, *The War and After*, p. 93.
53 'Interview with Vice-Admiral Usborne Moore', *Light*, 34:1762 (1914), 499.
54 James L. Macbeth Bain, 'Letters to the Editor: Is War Ever Justifiable', *Light*, 34:1757 (1914), 443–4.
55 'Is War Ever Justifiable? Some Correspondence and a Conclusion', *Light*, 34:1760 (1914), 472.
56 W. H. Evans, 'Spiritualism and the Peace Ideal', *The Two Worlds*, 27:1411 (1914), 581–2. The letters to the editor section two weeks later was entirely devoted to Evans's critics. See 'The Open Court', *The Two Worlds*, 27:1413 (1914), 606–8.
57 'Our Soldier Readers', *The Two Worlds*, 28:1458 (1915), 530–1.
58 'The Roll of Honour', *The Two Worlds*, 29:1491 (1916), 272.
59 E. A. W., 'Letters to the Editor: The Compensation of Calamity', *Light*, 34:1757 (1914), 443.

60 J. T. Dillsen, 'Experiences and Reflections by a Soldier', *The Two Worlds*, 28:1443 (1915), 344–5.
61 W. H. Evans, 'An Open Letter to Spiritualists', *The Two Worlds*, 27:1399 (1914), 438.
62 'Notes by the Way', *Light*, 34:1754 (1914), 397.
63 'The Victims of the Machine', 462.
64 'The Judgement of Folly', *Light*, 34:1758 (1914), 450.
65 'A World Tragedy: The Larger View', *Light*, 34:1753 (1914), 390.
66 George F. Berry, '"Beyond These Voices": Peaceful Thoughts for Troubled Times', *Light*, 34:1758 (1914), 453.
67 'Notes by the Way', 397.
68 'Psychology and War', *Light*, 34:1767 (1914), 510–11.
69 'The War and the Spirits', *The Two Worlds*, 27:1397 (1914), 418.
70 Adrian Gregory, *The Last Great War: British Society and the First World War* (Cambridge: Cambridge University Press, 2008), pp. 9–39.
71 Quoted in John N. Horne, *Labour at War: France and Britain, 1914–1918* (Oxford: Oxford University Press, 1991), pp. 44–5. See also Trevor Wilson, *The Myriad Faces of War: Britain and the Great War, 1914–1918* (Cambridge: Polity Press, 1986), pp. 26–31 and David Swift, *For Class and Country: The Patriotic Left and the First World War* (Liverpool: Liverpool University Press, 2017), pp. 24–55.
72 Alan Wilkinson, *Dissent or Conform: War, Peace and the English Churches 1900–1945* (London: SCM Press, 1986), pp. 23–9.
73 'Notes by the Way', *Light*, 34:1752 (1914), 373.
74 'A World Tragedy: The Larger View', 390.
75 'A Horrible Calamity', *The Two Worlds*, 27:1396 (1914), 406; 'Long Views Are Needed', *The Two Worlds*, 27:1401 (1914), 466.
76 Eric J. Leed, *No Man's Land: Combat and Identity in World War I* (Cambridge: Cambridge University Press, 1979), pp. 39–72.
77 C. W. Leadbeater, *An Occult View of the War* (Los Angeles, CA: Theosophical Publishing House, 1917), pp. 23–4.
78 These prophecies were collected for publication by Ralph Shirley, the editor of the *Occult Review*. See Ralph Shirley, *Prophecies and Omens of the Great War* (London: William Rider & Son, 1914). They also appear alongside further prophecies discovered or made between 1914 and 1916 in Countess Zalinski, *Noted Prophecies, Prediction, Omens, and Legends Concerning the Great War and the Changes to Follow* (Chicago, IL: Yogi Publishing, 1917). See also Herbert Thurston, *The War and the Prophets: Notes on Certain Popular Predictions Current in This Later Age* (London: Burns & Oats, 1915).
79 Maurice Maeterlinck, *The Wrack of the Storm*, trans. Alexander Teixeira de Mattos (New York: Dodd, Mead and Company, 1916), pp. 243–56.

80 Owen Davies, *A Supernatural War: Magic, Divination, and Faith during the First World War* (Oxford: Oxford University Press, 2018), pp. 16–53; Thurston, *The War and the Prophets*, pp. 114–16, 164–6; Rene Kollar, *Searching for Raymond: Anglicanism, Spiritualism, and Bereavement between the Two World Wars* (Lanham, MD: Lexington Books, 2000), pp. 78–9.

81 'The Prophecy of the Monk Johannes: A Marvelous Prediction – If Authentic', *Light*, 34:1762 (1914), 497–8; 'Kaiser and Antichrist', *The Two Worlds*, 27:1413 (1914), 605.

82 'Notes from Abroad: The Prophecy of Mayence and the Kaiser', *Light*, 34:1763 (1914), 513; F. C. S. Schiller, 'War Prophecies', *JSPR* 17:330 (1916), 185–92.

83 'Prophecies of the War', *Light*, 34:1757 (1914), 485.

84 Davies, *A Supernatural War*, pp. 39, 52–3.

85 Schiller, 'War Prophecies', 186.

86 N. G. S., 'The Prophets and the War: Predictions in Process of Testing', *Light*, 36:1857 (1916), 262.

87 'When Will the War End', *Light*, 34:1755 (1914), 410.

88 'Notes by the Way', *Light*, 34:1755 (1914), 409; 'The End of the War: A Daring Forecast', *Light*, 34:1757 (1914), 441; 'War Prophecy: Some Reflections', *Light*, 36:1864 (1916), 316.

89 Davies, *A Supernatural War*, p. 16.

90 Lodge, *The War and After*, p. 244.

91 Gerald O'Hara, *Dead Men's Embers* (York: Saturday Night Press, 2006), pp. 224–30, 300–3.

92 Davies, *A Supernatural War*, p. 76.

93 See 'News and Notes from the North', *The Two Worlds*, 29:1475 (1916), 91.

94 Membership numbers were not collected until 1928. By 1932 the number of members had declined but without statistics from the pre-war and onward, the relative significance of this decrease is unknown. Some scholars have repeated Geoffrey Nelson's estimate of 240,000 British spiritualists, but there are reasons to be cautious with this number. Nelson doubles the 30,000 spiritualists from official societies to 60,000 to accommodate non-constituted churches. He then multiplies this number by four to include those who attended churches, but who were not members of a society, resulting in an estimate of 240,000. But why he chooses a multiple by four is never justified. See Geoffrey K. Nelson, *Spiritualism and Society* (London: Routledge & Kegan Paul, 1969), pp. 153–68, 285.

95 Richard Noakes, *Physics and Psychics: The Occult and the Sciences in Modern Britain* (Cambridge: Cambridge University Press, 2019), p. 320.

96 Davies, *A Supernatural War*, p. 76.
97 Ellen Little, the author of *Grenadier Rolf*, noted that she was inspired to try spiritualism after reading *Raymond* and was introduced to mediums through Oliver Lodge. See Ellen Little (published anonymously), *Grenadier Rolf* (London: Kingsley Press, 1920), p. 33. Lodge also provided the preface for *Claude's Book*. See L. Kelway-Bamber, *Claude's Book* (London: Psychic Book Club, 1919), pp. ix–xi. Walter Wynn (a subject of Chapter 4) likewise listed Lodge as an influence and corresponded with him on several occasions. See Walter Wynn, *Rupert Lives!* (London: Kingsley Press, 1919), pp. 22, 37–8, 153–4. In addition to the works of Little, Kelway-Bamber, Wynn and Duffie-Boylan (already cited in note 27 in the Introduction), see L. Kelway-Bamber, *Claude's Second Book* (London: Methuen & Co., 1919), Olive Charlotte Blyth Pixley, *Listening In: A Record of a Singular Experience* (London: Psychic Bookshop and Library, 1928), Oliver Lodge, *Christopher: A Study in Human Personality* (London: Cassel and Company, 1918), Wesley Tudor Pole, *Private Dowding* (London: John M. Watkins, 1918), J. S. M. Ward, *Gone West: Three Narratives of After-Death Experiences* (London: William Rider & Son, 1920) and the sequel, *A Subaltern in Spirit Land: A Sequel to 'Gone West'* (London: William Rider & Son, 1920).
98 Using the British Library Integrated Catalogue, Vanessa Chambers found that the number of books and pamphlets with 'spiritualism' in its title rose from one in 1914 to approximately fourteen in 1918 and peaked at about thirty-three in 1920 (Vanessa Chambers, 'Fighting Chance: War, Popular Belief and British Society, 1900–1951', unpublished PhD dissertation (Institute for Historical Research, University of London, 2007), pp. 110–11). A Google Ngram search reveals that the number of books containing the word 'spiritualism' rose in 1915, peaked in 1920 and 1921 and steadily declined to a low point in 1941. Richard Noakes likewise identifies a significant increase in books and articles related to psychical research and spiritualism in the JISC Library Hub Discover, ProQuest digital library, British Periodicals Collections I–III and the British Newspapers Archive during this time (Noakes, *Physics and Psychics*, p. 284, fn. 18).
99 These numbers were collected by counting the weekly ads in each number of *Light* from 3 January 1914 to 30 December 1916. Only the advertisements of individual mediums were included. A few issues are missing from bound copies of *Light* and so these numbers are only approximate. Despite the advertisements' importance for revenue, they were removed in 1917 out of concerns for spiritualism's integrity and reputation.

100 Roger Straughan, 'Sir Arthur Conan Doyle: The St. Paul of Spiritualism', in Christopher M. Moreman (ed.), *The Spiritualist Movement: Speaking with the Dead in America and around the World, Volume 1: American Origins and Global Proliferation* (Santa Barbara, CA: Praeger, 2013), pp. 116–27.
101 Arthur Conan Doyle, 'A New Revelation: Spiritualism and Religion', *Light*, 36:1869 (1916), 357–8.
102 In 1923, Conan Doyle boasted that his lectures at Carnegie Hall sold out all nine times between 1922 and 1923. See 'The Observatory', *Light*, 43:2224 (1923), 537. He also claimed to Oliver Lodge that his lectures at Queen's Hall in 1925 had an average attendance of 2,000. See CUL, MS SPR, Sir Oliver Lodge Papers (hereafter MS SPR35), 456, Letter from Arthur Conan Doyle to Oliver Lodge, 25 February 1924, p. 1. For more on his public feuds see Chapter 5.
103 Arthur Conan Doyle, *The New Revelation* (London: George H. Doran Company, 1918), p. 95.
104 *Ibid.*, pp. 48–62.
105 Sofia French, 'British Spiritualism and the Experience of War', in Moreman (ed.), *The Spiritualist Movement, Volume 3* (Santa Barbara, CA: Praeger, 2013), p. 197.
106 Conan Doyle, *The New Revelation*, p. 95.
107 *Ibid.*, p. 38.
108 *Ibid.*, p. 89.
109 *Ibid.*, pp. 58–9.
110 Arthur Conan Doyle, *The Vital Message* (London: George H. Doran Company, 1919), pp. 11–15.
111 'The Crucible of War', *Light*, 35:1777 (1915), 50.
112 Little, *Grenadier Rolf*, pp. 159–60.
113 *Ibid.*, p. 40.
114 CUL, MS SPR34/22/14, Letter from Ellen Little to Helen Salter, 26 November 1918.
115 Mrs T. P. Hands, 'Observations on the War from the Spirit World', *The Two Worlds*, 30:1547 (1917), 213.
116 Conan Doyle, *The New Revelation*. The prophecy was first published in *Light* by 'Notes by the Way', *Light*, 34:1750 (1914), 349.
117 Oliver Lodge, *Raymond: Or Life and Death* (New York: George H. Doran Company, 1916), p. 182.
118 David Gow, 'Spiritualism: Its Position and Its Prospects', *The Quest*, 11:2 (1920), 254–7.
119 '1923: Our Outlook', *Light*, 43:2191 (1923), 8.
120 'The Observatory: Light on Things in General', *Light*, 43:2205 (1923), 233.

121 'Fund of Benevolence: 16th Annual Appeal', *Light*, 43:2231 (1928), 648.
122 Gow told *The Quest* that one of the biggest challenges facing British spiritualism in the 1920s was to meet the new demand (Gow, 'Spiritualism', 254–7). In 1922, 1923 and 1924, the LSA looked to expand its offices to accommodate its burgeoning membership and associates. See Dawson Rogers, 'The London Spiritualist Alliance, LTD', *Light*, 42:2155 (1922), 264; 'The Observatory: Light on Things in General', *Light*, 43:2242 (1923), 823; and 'The Memorial Endowment Fund', *Light*, 44:2281 (1924), 621.
123 Chambers, 'Fighting Chance', pp. 224–34; Davies, *A Supernatural War*, pp. 124–5.
124 Kollar, *Searching for Raymond*, pp. 157–64.
125 Ibid., pp. 17, 23–4.
126 Georgina Byrne, *Modern Spiritualism and the Church of England, 1850–1939* (Woodbridge: The Boydell Press, 2010), p. 220.
127 S. De Brath, 'The New Era', *Light*, 40:2034 (1920), 21.
128 'The Flood', *The Two Worlds*, 32:1642 (1919), 140.
129 See Jacqueline Jenkinson, *Black 1919: Riots, Racism and Resistance in Imperial Britain* (Liverpool: Liverpool University Press, 2009), Andrew Rothstein's *The Soldiers' Strikes of 1919* (London and Basingstoke: Macmillan Press, 1980) and J. Putkowski, *The Kinmel Park Riots 1919* (Hawarden: Flintshire Historical Society, 1989).
130 'The Growing Pains of Progress', *Light*, 39:2021 (1919), 316.
131 '1919–1920: The Passing of Modern Materialism', *Light*, 40:2034 (1920), 4; 'The Outlook: A Survey and a Summary', *Light*, 40:2035 (1920), 12.
132 'At the Year's End', *Light*, 41:2086 (1921), 8.
133 'The Dawn of Peace', *The Two Worlds*, 32:1651 (1919), 246.
134 '1921. From Our Leaders to Our Readers: Messages of Hope and Courage in the New Year', *Light*, 41:2086 (1921), 4–5.
135 CUL, MS SPR35/429, Letter from Oliver Lodge to Arthur Conan Doyle, 26 September 1922.
136 'Progressive Revelation', *The Two Worlds*, 34:1752 (1921), 270.
137 See Thomas S. Kuhn, *The Structure of Scientific Revolutions* (Chicago, IL: University of Chicago Press, 1970).
138 See Katy Price, *Loving Faster Than Light: Romance and Readers in Einstein's Universe* (Chicago, IL: University of Chicago Press, 2012).
139 'The "Crisis": Some Thoughts on Spiritual Evolution', *Light*, 43:2229 (1923), 616.
140 J. G. Piddington, 'Forecasts in Scripts Concerning the War', *Proceedings of the Society for Psychical Research* (hereafter *PSPR*), 33:87 (1923), 442.

141 *Ibid.*, 526–7. The ambiguity of these messages is apparent to present-day observers, but using cross-correspondence, Piddington based his opinion on a meticulous analysis of the scripts' literary and biblical allusions, which he believed formed a coherent message out of otherwise cryptic language.

142 For examples see Francis Delaisi, *A Prophecy Fulfilled: The Present War Predicted in 1911* (Omaha, NB: Swartz Printing Co., 1916) and Lewis Einstein, *A Prophecy of the War (1913–1914)* (New York: Columbia University Press, 1918).

143 Piddington, 'Forecasts in Scripts Concerning the War', 603.

144 *Ibid.*, 597–8.

145 *Ibid.*, 597–605.

146 CUL, MS SPR35/429, Letter from Oliver Lodge to Arthur Conan Doyle, 26 September 1922.

147 Martin Ceadel, *Pacifism in Britain, 1914–1945: The Defining of a Faith* (Oxford: Clarendon Press, 1980), p. 62.

148 *Ibid.*, p. 317.

149 Martin Ceadal, 'Gilbert Murray and International Politics', in Christopher Stray (ed.), *Gilbert Murray Reassessed: Hellenism, Theatre, and International Politics* (Oxford: Oxford University Press, 2007), pp. 233–6.

150 N. J. Lowe, 'Gilbert Murray and Psychic Research', in Stray (ed.), *Murray Reassessed*, pp. 349–70.

151 See Jay Winter, 'From Sympathy to Empathy: Trajectories of Rights in the Twentieth Century', in Aleida Assmann and Ines Detmers (eds), *Empathy and Its Limits* (London: Palgrave Macmillan, 2016), pp. 110–14.

152 William F. Barrett, *On the Threshold of a New World of Thought: An Examination of the Phenomena of Spiritualism* (London: Kegan Paul, Trench, Trübner and Co., 1908), p. 99.

153 Helen McCarthy, *The British People and the League of Nations: Democracy, Citizenship and Internationalism, c. 1918–1945* (Manchester: Manchester University Press, 2011), p. 79.

154 'Discussion', *The Two Worlds*, 34:1750 (1921), 244.

155 'The Great Commemoration: A Memorable Meeting at the Queen's Hall', *Light*, 43:2236 (1923), 724.

156 See his series of articles in *Light*. Stanley De Brath, 'Spiritualism and War', *Light*, 42:2182 (1922), 695; *Light*, 42:2183 (1922), 710; *Light*, 42:2184 (1922), 732; *Light*, 42:2185 (1922), 749; *Light*, 42:2186 (1922), 764; *Light*, 42:2187 (1922), 774; *Light*, 42:2188 (1922), 790.

157 'Spiritualism and the League of Nations', *Light*, 43:2227 (1923), 581.

158 'The Great Commemoration: A Memorable Meeting at the Queen's Hall', *Light*, 43:2236 (1923), 724.

159 Ruth Brandon, *The Spiritualists: The Passion for the Occult in the Nineteenth and Twentieth Centuries* (New York: Alfred A. Knopf, 1983), pp. 226–7; CUL, MS SPR35/446, Letter from Oliver Lodge to Arthur Conan Doyle, 23 July 1924, pp. 1–2; Arthur Conan Doyle, 'How the World Will End: A Strange Prophecy and A Description of the "Last Day"', *Sunday Express* (20 July 1930), p. 10.
160 CUL, MS SPR35/441, Letter from Arthur Conan Doyle to Oliver Lodge, December 1922.
161 Arthur Conan Doyle, *Pheneas Speaks: Direct Spirit Communications in the Family Circle* (London: The Psychic Press and Bookshop, 1927), p. 60.
162 British Library, Western Manuscripts (hereafter BL WM), Add MS 88924/4/14, Arthur Conan Doyle, 'Reports on Séances: 1896–1930', n.d., pp. 25–7.
163 Conan Doyle, 'How the World Will End', p. 10.
164 Ceadel, *Pacifism in Britain*, pp. 123–4.
165 Janet S. K. Watson, *Fighting Different Wars: Experience, Memory, and the First World War in Britain* (Cambridge: Cambridge University Press, 2007), pp. 219–31.
166 'Spiritualism and the Crisis', *The Two Worlds*, 46:2401 (1933), 926.
167 C. R. Cammell, 'Peril Which Threatens Humanity: Spiritual Revival the Only Way to Salvation', *Light*, 46:2877 (1936), 129–31.
168 Gregory, *The Silence of Memory: Armistice Day, 1919–1946* (London: Bloomsbury, 1994), p. 122; Mark Connelly, *The Great War, Memory and Ritual: Commemoration in the City and East London, 1916–1939* (Suffolk: The Boydell Press, 2002), p. 177.
169 Cammell, 'Peril Which Threatens Humanity', 129–31.
170 J. Cumin Walters, 'Spiritualism and War', *The Two Worlds*, 43:2243 (1930), 472–3.
171 *Ibid.*
172 Horace Leaf, 'Spiritualism and World Federation', *The Two Worlds*, 47:2411 (1934), 91.
173 'A Spirit on Disarmament: The Conferences Should Meet in Flanders', *The Two Worlds*, 46:2399 (1939), 891.
174 S. A. W. L., 'A League of Peace', *The Two Worlds*, 46:2364 (1933), 215.
175 Observer, 'Impending Danger! Do Spiritualists Stand Prepared?', *The Two Worlds*, 46:2374 (1933), 405.
176 H. C. Vernon, 'Spiritualists and War', *The Two Worlds*, 46:2375 (1933), 423.
177 These were the views of the theologian and pacifist Canon Charles Raven (Ceadel, *Pacifism in Britain*, p. 165).
178 Cammell, 'Peril Which Threatens Humanity', 131.
179 David Gow, '"Power" on the Final World-Peace: Armistice Celebrations at the Aeolian Hall', *The Two Worlds*, 46:2399 (1933), 390.

180 *Ibid.*
181 *Ibid.*
182 James Leigh, 'How the Provinces Will Hear "Power"', *The Two Worlds*, 47:2411 (1934), 90.
183 Clarke, *Voices Prophesying War*, p. 159; Lawrence Freedman, *The Future of War: A History* (New York: Public Affairs, 2017), p. 57.
184 Alan Allport, *Britain at Bay: The Epic Story of the Second World War, 1938–1941* (New York: Alfred A. Knopf, 2020), pp. 359–60; Susan Grayzel, *At Home and Under Fire: Air Raids and Culture in Britain from the Great War to the Blitz* (Cambridge: Cambridge University Press, 2012), pp. 224, 285.
185 See Hilda Kean, *The Great Cat and Dog Massacre: The Real Story of World War II's Unknown Tragedy* (Chicago, IL: University of Chicago Press, 2017).
186 Cummins and Gibbes, *No War*, pp. 5, 30.
187 Geraldine Cummins, *Unseen Adventures: An Autobiography Covering Thirty Years of Work in Psychical Research* (London: Rider, 1951), pp. 27–9.
188 Alexander G. Gonzalez, *Irish Women Writers: An A-to-Z Guide* (Westport, CT: Greenwood Publishing Group, 2006), pp. 76–7.
189 Geraldine Cummins, *The Road to Immortality: Being a Description of the Afterlife Purporting to Be Communicated by the Late F. W. H. Myers* (London: Ivor Nicholson and Watson, 1933), p. 7.
190 *Ibid.*, pp. 105–6.
191 J. W. Dunne, *An Experiment in Time* (New York: Macmillan, 1927).
192 Gow, '"Power" on the Final World-Peace', 390.
193 'As We See It: New Year Good Wishes', *Light*, 59:2 (1939), 8.
194 Jenny Hazelgrove, *Spiritualism and British Society between the Wars* (Manchester: Manchester University Press, 2000), pp. 70–1.
195 Clare Sheridan, 'Soldiers of St. Martin's: Visions and Voices Seen and Heard in the Crypt and in the Church', *Light*, 59:3031 (1939), 92–3.
196 Nelson, *Spiritualism and Society*, pp. 162–72; Hazelgrove, *Spiritualism and British Society between the Wars*, pp. 270–3; Chambers, 'Fighting Chance', pp. 143–5; French, 'British Spiritualism and the Experience of War', pp. 200–1.
197 Nelson, *Spiritualism and Society*, p. 285.
198 The classic work on this topic is Leon Festinger, Henry Riecken and Stanley Schachter, *When Prophecy Fails: A Social and Psychological Study of a Modern Group That Predicted the Destruction of the World* (Minneapolis, MN: University of Minnesota Press, 1956).
199 W. H. Evans, 'Peace Prophecies That Failed', *Light*, 59:3060 (1939), 568.

200 'Londoner's Log', *The Two Worlds*, 52:2705 (1939), 607.
201 The SNU had more members in the early 1950s than at any other time since it began keeping records. Since the GWCSL did not keep track of its numbers, it is unknown if this was a matter of shifting allegiances or already existing churches becoming affiliated with the SNU. The SNU also did not keep records for the years before 1928, making it impossible to know if there were more or less members immediately after the Great War (Nelson, *Spiritualism and Society*, pp. 153–72, 285).
202 Nelson, *Spiritualism and Society*, pp. 153–5.
203 Ceadel, *Pacifism in Britain*, p. 69.
204 Frank T. Blake and Ernest A. Keeling, 'Spiritualists and the War: Manifesto by the Council of the Spiritualists' National Union', *The Two Worlds*, 52:2710 (1939), 665.
205 W. H. Evans, 'Spiritualism and War', *The Two Worlds*, 52:2707 (1939), 636 and *The Two Worlds*, 52:2709 (1939), 660. For response from readers see 'Mrs. Evans and War', *The Two Worlds*, 52:2709 (1939), 661.

2

A psychic laboratory: numinous experiences and spiritualism on the Great War's battlefields

One night in the trenches surrounding Vimy Ridge, a newly arrived private asked his sergeant 'Where is the war?' The sergeant directed him to a firestep, and as he overlooked the parapet into no man's land, he could see a corpse so rotted away that it was impossible to tell if it was once a German or a Canadian soldier. The startled private asked the sergeant how long he had been in the trenches. 'Sixteen months', he responded. 'Sixteen months!' the private exclaimed, 'I guess I don't need to worry yet. We've all got the same chances don't we?' Canadian soldier Will "Bill" R. Bird observed what happened next: a 'chance bullet had come from some distant point, skimming the bags, missing the wire, and the burly sergeant, and dropping, with the trajectory of a spent missile, just enough to strike the temple of the boy who had been two hours in the line'.[1] Apparently, nobody's chances were the same on the Western Front. Bird was luckier. He had served with the 42nd Battalion in the Canadian Expeditionary Force (CEF) for two years, surviving battles at Passchendaele, Amiens, Arras, Cambrai and Mons between 1917 and 1918. By the end of the war, nearly all of his original comrades and his brother were dead.

In his 1930 memoir, *And We Go On*, Bill Bird offers an unusual explanation for why he survived over other soldiers of equal capability. It all began in 1915 when he and his younger brother Steve enlisted in the war, or at least tried to enlist. While Steve was posted overseas with the 25th Canadian Infantry Battalion, Bill was denied service on account of his poor teeth. The Bird brothers would have to part ways for now, with hopes of meeting again either on the fields of France and Belgium or back home in Nova Scotia. Either way, Steve had no intentions of saying goodbye for good. 'If there's anything I can do for you, let me know', he told his brother, 'and if I don't come back maybe I'll find a way to come sometime and whisper in your ear'. Steve went missing and was presumed killed in October 1915, though his body was never found. His ghost, however, did much more than whisper. In April 1917, not long after the Canadian Corps captured Vimy Ridge, Bill returned from sick leave. As he wandered the front that now bore the scars of the recent struggle, he found shelter with two other men. Around midnight he was awoken 'by a tug at my arm'. It was Steve. 'I could see him plainly', he wrote, 'see the mud on his puttees and knees. He jerked a thumb towards the ruined houses and motioned for me to go there.' By the time Bill emerged, Steve was well ahead of him and although he tried to keep pace, the elusive figure faded from view. After waiting for ten minutes, hoping that Steve would return, Bill eventually drifted asleep. Later that morning he discovered that a shell had exploded above his shelter and killed the other two soldiers inside. 'All that day I thought of how I had been saved', he recalled, 'and I resolved that if ever again I saw Steve I would do exactly as he motioned'.[2]

And We Go On is unlike any other war memoir. The great poets and writers of the era were just as interested as Bird was in charting the 'psychic condition' of the soldier, using the medium to communicate the disorienting or traumatic experiences of trench warfare. Supernatural tales of divine intervention on the battlefield also captivated the British imagination in 1915 in the various tales and rumours that collectively came to be known as the Angels of Mons. What makes Bird's work unique is that he locates firmly within the environment of the Western Front the potential transcendental properties of the mind that interested psychical researchers and spiritualists of the time. The Angels of Mons was an awkward blend of Victorian Romanticism, medieval chivalry, Christian symbolism and modern industrial warfare. The experiences on the Somme and Passchendaele in turn exposed the profanity of trench warfare. The artist Paul Nash wrote to his wife shortly after the Battle of Passchendaele that 'Evil and the incarnate fiend alone can be master of this war, and no glimmer of God's hand is seen anywhere … It is unspeakable, godless, hopeless.'[3] Bird offers us an alternative view, one where the very properties and conditions of trench warfare lifted a psychological veil to a host of extraordinary experiences in 'which all natural explanations failed, and no supernatural explanations were established'.[4] Contrary to Nash, he explained,

> Never on earth was there a like place where a man's support ... was his faith in some mighty Power ... Unconsciously there were born faiths that carried men through critical moments, and tortured minds grasped at fantasies that served in place of more solid creeds ... It drew from even dulled and uncouth natures a perception that was attributed to the mystic and supernal. Men glimpsed, or thought they glimpsed, that grim crossroads we all must pass. It was as if for them a voice had spoken, a hand beckoned them on.[5]

These two soldiers had two very different judgements about the place of the numinous on the mud-, blood- and iron-soaked fields of Passchendaele.

Few soldiers possessed the cocksureness of their convictions or the artistic and literary gifts of Nash and Bird, but many could relate to the psychological profile that *And We Go On* portrays. On the Great War's battlefields, where randomness reigned, soldiers professed to have uncanny, psychic or miraculous experiences. Many naturally gravitated towards and experimented with the magical and the sacred for protection, often without regard for consistency or doctrinal coherency. Because spiritualists and psychical researchers cast such a broad net in terms of religious denominations and the types of phenomena that were possible, advocates were able to amass a host of evidence from the field to support their beliefs about the war's purpose. In their eyes, the frontlines of the Great War were a psychic laboratory, where an approximation with death brought soldiers into unprecedented contact with psychic phenomena and spiritual revelations. In 1930, at the height of interwar spiritualism, Will R. Bird could profit from and articulate this view as an authentic soldier experience. Gradually, his memoir was lost, replaced by a much more conventional set of war experiences in 1968. Bird's experiences, as well as the reasons for his changing attitudes, are part of the rise and fall of the supernormal interpretation of the Great War.

'Rolling the bones' on the Great War's battlefields

In February 1917, Miller, 'the brave guy', and some men from the 11th Canadian Infantry Brigade were playing craps at the front when 'a shell came over and killed one of them'. Miller, 'wanted to keep on rolling the bones', explained one soldier, 'but all the others ... were too scared, so we had to quit'.[6] The fear felt by these reluctant soldiers is understandable, since their vulnerable position had just been fatally exposed. Or, what if this was not their main concern? What if they were afraid that the game of craps was somehow determining the trajectory of the shells? This story from the Brigade's trench newspaper, *The Shell Hole Advance*, skilfully uses an event that may or may not have happened to satirically comment on something genuine about the soldiers' experience. On the Western Front, life and death were a crapshoot, the caprice of a shell no different than the roll of a die.[7] A shell could fall from the sky at a moment's notice and kill some but leave others unscathed while a bullet could ricochet and suddenly strike an unsuspecting target. In coming to terms with the nature of death at the front, soldiers turned to a host of explanations that ranged from the rational to the fantastical.

The soldiers of the Great War lived and died underneath a rain of firepower. It is estimated that by the end of the war, the Germans alone had fired 222 million rounds of artillery.[8] Not surprisingly, artillery and mortar shells were the most lethal weapons of the war, responsible for nearly two-thirds of British Army casualties.[9] In between the lulls in the fighting, each side used mortars, grenades and snipers to keep the enemy in their trenches. War was depersonalised, with danger mostly coming from a distance. It was possible for a British soldier to spend his entire war without ever seeing a German.[10]

As European armies adjusted to using indirect artillery fire, the accuracy of these weapons was poor and shellfire was targeted indiscriminately. Those on the receiving end relied on visual and audible cues, as well as good luck, to try and anticipate where a shell would land.[11] Soldiers often retraced the seemingly inconsequential decisions that made the difference between life and death. Some noticed the irony of this randomness. During the Battle of the Somme, Garnette Durham from Gloucester was almost killed while moving ammunition to the front on a narrow path. When he came across a Canadian 43rd Highlander, the latter moved out of the way and into the mud. 'Just as he did', Durham wrote, 'a shell took him fairly between the shoulders'. The Highlander's decision to politely free the path had unexpectedly sealed his fate, since 'if he had not moved out I must have done so and would have got that same one to myself'.[12] In August 1916, when Arthur Jordens of the Saskatchewan Regiment witnessed another soldier get hit in 'the same place where I was standing a second before', he dismissed the incident with a joke. 'But never mind', he wrote, 'they say the first seven years are the worst; better times afterward'.[13] Others thanked God. In the summer of 1918, Lance Corporal Talbot G. Mohan of the 1st Battalion Wiltshire Regiment was returning to the line from headquarters when he saw his comrades signalling to duck and crawl. Once he arrived, he learnt that only a moment before, another man had taken the exact same path and was shot by a sniper. On contemplation, this devout soldier believed that God, not his vigilant comrades, was responsible for his survival.[14]

Durham, Jordens and Mohan could not have anticipated or consciously controlled the outcome of their particular situations; they were all lucky. It was in this environment that soldiers gravitated towards superstitions. One of the most famous was the so-called 'three on a match'. The rule had it that you would never use the same match to light three cigarettes because that was all the time a sniper needed to find his target and fire the fatal shot.[15] There is an impression of common sense here since light could indeed draw the attention of the enemy, but the ritual was irrational in practice. As one private observed in 1916, 'Hundreds of times I have seen two cigarettes lit up and then the match solemnly blown out lest it should light the third; but if there are four cigarettes to light there is no objection!'[16] Bert Ferns with the 2/6th Battalion Lancashire Fusiliers recalled, 'nobody wanted to be the third member lighting' a cigarette, and after the second, they would just 'put the light out and move on and light from another match'. Members of his battalion also refrained from wishing anyone good luck 'because we used to feel ... we were putting the Hoodoo on them'.[17] George Peake with 1/8th Lancashire Fusiliers remembered that numerous soldiers refused to fill out page thirteen of their wills.[18]

Soldiers carried lucky objects, including charms, trinkets, dolls, pieces of rubble and jewellery. Four-leaf clovers, swastikas and mascots were particularly popular amongst the British.[19] In November 1916, four months into the Battle of the Somme, the journalist Michael MacDonagh commented on 'the enormously increased demand for ... charms and amulets'. These included the 'touchwood' or 'fumsup' charms, which were little wooden figures with 'odd sparkling eyes as if always on alert to avert danger', and with metal legs and arms that could be 'lifted to touch the head'.[20] One of the most successful sellers of these wooden 'little gods' in Britain, Henry Brandon, sold tens of thousands to soldiers and their relatives. Brandon's success prompted other British jewellers to enter the trade.[21] Even people could become lucky charms. If a soldier tended to experience more close calls than others, some might find him to be naturally lucky. This was the case with James Storey Wray from Durham who, while serving at Gallipoli and then on the Western Front, earned the nickname 'Lucky Jim' and 'Lucky Durham'.[22] Soldiers were also reported to have gravitated towards chaplains during a shelling under the impression that they might be divinely protected.[23]

The idea that the sacred could offer protection even to the non-religious was reflected in the popular use of Bibles. Stories proliferated of soldiers being saved from certain death thanks to the presence of a Bible in their breast pockets. One Captain in the Coldstream Guards, for example, reported that a shell fragment would have pierced his heart had it not been for his Bible. Miraculously, 'the missle [sic] had stopped at the ninety-first Psalm'.[24] The significance of the ninety-first Psalm had to do with its reputation amongst soldiers as the 'bomb proof Psalm'.[25] As verse seven states in the King James Bible, 'A thousand shall fall at thy side, and ten thousand at thy right hand; but it shall not come nigh thee.'[26] Catholicism's association with the miraculous also led some Protestant soldiers to take their chances with Catholic emblems.[27] A 1919 report found that 'the carrying of medals, rosaries and the like, has become very general in the Army, and is by no means confined to Catholics'.[28]

An interest in religious symbols reflected the soldiers' exposure to diffusive Christianity but it was also mirrored in their environment. On the Western Front, crucifixes and statues of the Virgin Mary peppered the French landscape and by sheer weight of numbers frequently remained intact amongst the rubble. While travelling to the Somme in the spring of 1916, Gunner George Smedley observed 'Christ on the cross, at nearly every village we pass through'.[29] J. Anderson Johnston of the 13th Battalion Rifle Brigade was moving through a ruined French village when 'I looked up and saw that we were passing under the statue of the Madonna, that with outstretched arms hung over us head downward, holding the Infant

Christ to us as if imploring our aid'.[30] These were unfamiliar sites for the predominantly Protestant citizen soldier. Most famously in Albert, a statue of the Virgin Mary dangled by a thread atop the cathedral, and as myth had it, would topple at the end of the war. It greeted units as they entered the Somme for the first time in the fall of 1916 and became a tourist attraction, even finding its way onto postcards. Curious soldiers made sketches of it in their diaries or in letters home.[31] It is not hard to understand why the image resonated with soldiers. Despite months of bloodshed on the Somme, victory remained stubbornly out of reach while life and death were often a matter of inches.[32]

For the more theologically minded, religious symbols in the landscape were not mere curiosities but a testament to Christianity's central truth. Despite the material destruction, Christ's sacrifice remained. As the Reverend David Railton explained, 'Only ... the official recognized outward seat of religion ... is all of a heap, the Saviour is always there.'[33] God was speaking to him through the rubble of war. In the battlefields of Mesopotamia, soldiers encountered sites of Biblical importance, and in some cases followed in Christ's footsteps. While on leave, soldiers like Private Walter Charles Culliford were able to visit the Church of the Holy Sepulchre, the Golden Gate, Gethsemane, the Garden Tomb and the Gates of the Old City Jerusalem. While fighting in Egypt, he described how his geographical proximity to Biblical events made him feel 'verily in the presence of God'.[34]

Not everyone interpreted incidents of 'miraculous' survival or Christian symbolism so seriously. Trench warfare could just as easily expose the absurdity of such beliefs. Charms did not stop people from dying and many soldiers surely recognised this fact. Chaplains found damaged Bibles amongst the dead that had failed to prevent bullets from piercing the flesh.[35] Nor should we assume that the use of lucky objects always indicated an endorsement of their protective abilities. That some were gifts or souvenirs highlights their personal and sentimental value.[36] As a member of the 45th Artillery Brigade observed, 'the waiting and praying women of the homelands are eager to send something "lucky to their fighting menfolk"'.[37] Satirical pieces in trench newspapers took aim at soldiers' superstitions. The trench newspaper of the Canadian 7th Battalion, *The Listening Post*, included a piece about Private Freeman, who went to a fortune teller while on leave. The 'gypsy' informed him that he was in love with two women but he would 'only marry one of em', once the war was over. 'So you see', the author wrote, 'it's worth 15 shillings to know you are shrapnel proof'.[38] A driver in the Motor Transport of the Army Service Corps (ASC) observed that 'Everything in some form or other, colour included, can be construed into good luck or bad luck.' He singled out the colour green as particularly known for bringing bad luck. As the author joked, 'It is ... a bad omen to be run over by a sage green Packard lorry on a Friday, after Pay.'[39]

For all its randomness, death and survival on the Great War's battlefields could nevertheless be explained on rational grounds. For one, the weaponry really could be inaccurate. Captain Walter Douglas Darling from Folkestone recognised this and explained to his sweetheart that he did not fear machine guns because 'from experience I know its limitation'.[40] Bombs could be dodged and experienced soldiers might be more likely to survive certain situations over new arrivals. Some rituals may have emerged from legitimate, although skewed, observations of the soldier's environment.[41] For example, many noted an association between a fear of death and leave.[42] Joseph Murray explained that this was because death after leave was an extremely common experience in his regiment. 'It was recognized that people went on leave that they didn't last five minutes when they got back', he recalled. One of his pals was dreading leave for this reason. Sure enough, he was killed on his first trip back into the frontlines while moving through a communication trench.[43] In contemplating the reasons for this association, Joseph Pickard wondered if it was because those returning from leave were too relaxed or had lost their concentration. This seems possible, but then consider Pickard's subsequent irrational behaviour. While on leave, Pickard refused to take a photograph with his mother because 'we used to say, you get a photograph taken and you come back' to the front and get killed.[44] Another British battalion found that soldiers who brought a German helmet back home were killed by a sniper after returning from leave, prompting the battalion to refrain from taking any more trophies.[45] The belief that a soldier's third leave would be his last seems reasonable given that a soldier serving long enough to qualify for three leaves was more likely to finally find himself as a casualty. However, refusing

Figure 2.1 The trench newspaper *G.O.C.B. Chronicle* pokes fun at soldiers' superstitions.

to take a third leave in response, as was reported in some cases, is not a rational reaction as it only increases the time and opportunities for injury or death to occur.[46] Instead, it is more likely that this superstition, along with the three on a match, was part of a general tendency amongst soldiers to pattern random experiences into 'threes' while others sought to identify arbitrary associations to explain why equally capable soldiers died after a leave over others (i.e. by possessing a German helmet or getting their photograph taken).[47]

The more time soldiers spent at the front, the more they were able to adapt, and many claimed to develop an instinct that allowed them to identify the warning signs of impending danger and discern the trajectories of various German shells.[48] Mohan observed that 'after experience one got to know instinctively whether a shell was going to fall near enough to do any harm'. The louder the noise of an approaching shell, the closer it would drop and thus 'less warning and ... less time to dodge it'.[49] Even practical skills, however, could manifest in pseudo-magical terms. One chaplain, for example, met a musician who claimed an almost superhuman ability to detect and predict shells thanks to his musical skills. It is unclear exactly how reliable shell instincts were. A missile's course could depend on many factors, including weather conditions, and weaponry evolved over the course of the war.[50] Some shells were notorious for their lack of warning. The shells of the German 77 mm field guns were nicknamed 'whizz-bangs' because by the time their whistling sound could be heard it was too late, and all one could do was jump for cover and hope for the best.[51] The same was true of those mortar bombs known as 'the silent Percy' and 'the silent Susan'.[52] On one occasion, Harry Lawrence Adams was almost killed by such a shell. He happened to 'suddenly notice' an incoming mortar bomb and, as he took cover, it 'burst in the very spot where I was resting'. Although some soldiers might interpret this as instinctual or even pure luck, Adams saw it as a sign 'of the protecting care of God ... in opening my eyes to the danger', since 'it is very seldom that these ... can be observed'.[53]

Charles Carrington was sceptical of a shell instinct since their sounds and trajectories varied too significantly. He never got used to shellfire and by the time of Third Ypres, he had developed a nervous disorder, in which he imagined the shells had an intelligence of their own. 'The shells are more deliberate and accurate than could be possible', he wrote, 'they seem to have a volition of their own and to wander malevolently until they see a target on which to pounce'. Carrington developed an irrational pattern of behaviour, as if he had discovered an occult knowledge unique to the front. As he explained, 'you think of absurd omens and fetishes to ward off the shell you hear coming. A strong inward feeling compels you to sit in a certain position, to touch a particular object, to whistle so many bars of a tune silently between your teeth. If you complete the charm in time you are safe.'[54] Carrington and others could reflect on the absurdity of such endeavours after the fact. But in the uncertainty of the moment, rituals and charms were a low-cost and potentially high-reward option when practical solutions were limited.

In April 1917, on the frontlines of Vimy Ridge, at around the same time and place that Steve's ghost saved Bill Bird, a group of soldiers decided to flip a coin to see who would sleep outside and who would have to sleep in the tunnels. Three won the coin toss only to be killed by a shell. One of them was 'blown to pieces'.[55] A soldier's life could literally depend upon the flip of a coin or the roll of a die. Maybe the men from the 11th Canadian Infantry Brigade really did believe their fates were determined by a game of craps. The Great War's battlefields were a consistent confrontation with the vagaries of chance, a collision between an agent of warfare and the vast impersonal complex systems that ruled his fate. In some sense, Bird's miraculous survival was just another case of a soldier who was saved from certain death by pure dumb luck. It was in the meaning that a soldier ascribed to such incidents that he could harness an illusion of control. Some were semi-rational reflections of the environment while others entered the domain of the fantastical; many more blurred the lines between the two or combined them without regard for contradictions. Soldiers could reflect on the absurdity of superstitions, but what if the absurd really did seem to lead to survival? What happened to soldiers' belief systems when certain designs or patterns took shape? One's faith in some higher power or occult knowledge could become more pronounced. Some soldiers learned to express the environment of the Great War in these ways precisely because it gave randomness a coherent design that was responsive to some agency. They ascribed to impersonal machine warfare a numinous order that revealed itself through firepower.

Tracing the hand of God: fatalism, premonitions and providence

Sometime after Bill Bird first arrived in France, his comrade Freddy was sleeping in a tent behind the lines when he suddenly awoke. 'I tell you I saw everything plainer than day', he stated, 'it was like a woman in white and it ... pointed at you, you and you'.[56] Freddy identified six men in the tent: Herman, Ira, Melville, Arthur, Sam and Mickey, and then added, 'and I know ... I am going to get mine'. Bird thought about the incident as he fell asleep. 'Was there anything in dreams?' he wondered, and 'why had he seemed so certain?'[57] The first of these men to be killed was Arthur. On the night of 24 March 1917 in the Vimy sector, Bird, Arthur and a group of reserves were called to the frontlines to dig a new communication trench when they came under heavy fire.[58] Arthur collapsed to the ground. When Bird asked him if he was hit, he just shook his head no and stated ominously 'Freddy was right'. Arthur was shot in the head later that morning. 'A chill crept over me', wrote Bird, 'how had he known?' Freddy was later killed in the attack on Vimy Ridge and when Herman was killed, Ira became anxious. After surviving a close call with a shell, he developed a crippling fear about Freddy's prophecy and disobeyed orders to return to his post.[59] Ira, Melville and Sam were killed simultaneously by the sweep of a German machine gun at Passchendaele and Mickey died in Bird's arms shortly thereafter.[60]

Bird claimed to be free from nervous tension. He did not believe this was due to his courage but stemmed instead from his faith in Steve's guidance:

> Each night when I slept I dreamt of Steve, saw him clearly, and when awake, in the trenches at night, out on listening posts, felt him near. In some definable way I depended on him. Ever since he had guided me in from that foggy unknown stretch at the back of Vimy I would go anywhere in no man's land. I knew, with a – fanatical, if you like – faith, that a similar touch would lead me straight where I should go. In the trenches, on posts, in any place, I was always watching for him, waiting for him, trying to sense him near me, and in the doing I missed the ... easy fears that seized the unoccupied mind.[61]

Bird's experiences filled him with the assurance that his near misses were not the sign of death knocking but proof of his brother's protection. In the cases of Freddy's premonitions and Bird's survival, the soldier's fate was understood in terms of greater significance than the random firing of shells and bullets. Both Ira and Bird 'glimpsed' a higher order through death and survival. Their experiences also imply a link between psychic activity and psychological stability. With Ira, premonitions were associated with nervous collapse resulting in death, but with Bird, a sort of telepathic communion with his brother led to a confidence that allowed him to transverse the same gloomy fate. Bird's book captures not just the pull between fatalism and agency that was well established in the soldiers' culture, but also that between the psychical and psychological. *And We Go On* presents evidence of a supernormal culture on the Great War's battlefields.

When confronted with death at the front, many soldiers appeared to gravitate towards fatalism. According to the *Army and Religion* report, it was 'widely prevalent' amongst the BEF.[62] As one YMCA worker observed, 'most of the men are fatalists ... in so far as they believe that if it is their fate to get shot they will be shot'.[63] If fatalism was as prevalent as chaplains feared, it would have altered soldiers' behaviours, leading them to take absurd risks or abstain from practices that would increase their chances of survival. It is possible that some soldiers became convinced of their invulnerability. Rifleman Johnston recalled that one of his comrades, 'a queer fellow ... who had roamed the world and seen strange happenings', was 'indifferent to danger' and 'had a fondness for prowling about the trenches at all hours of the night'.[64] The Reverend Kenneth Best met one soldier who took 'a perverse delight' in near misses; 'the closer the better'.[65] Similar to Bird's ghostly courage, some soldiers acted recklessly or committed acts of bravery because they claimed to have a 'guardian angel' at the front. The Reverend Monty Acland Bere met a soldier in a CCS in the spring of 1917 who claimed to have encountered a mysterious companion when he was caught in a shell hole overnight. The figure placed his hand on his head and reappeared whenever he was under fire to protect him. The soldier had accomplished impressive feats, defending a position by himself for twenty-four hours after twenty-one of his comrades had been wounded or killed.[66] The case is similar to the American soldier Elmer Harden who had a guardian angel in the trenches that he named 'Chance'. When Chance was present, he protected Harden, allowing him to perform dangerous acts of bravery, but when he was gone, Harden experienced fear.[67]

Chaplains either misunderstood or took too seriously soldiers' expressions of fatalism, which the soldiers often contradicted, sometimes in the same sentence. For example, upon receiving news that he would go over the top during the first day of the Somme, Cyril T. Newman wrote in his diary that 'I am feeling a little unsettled but ... I am trusting in God, my Rock and my Fortress, in Jesus my Redeemer, to give me Grace sufficient to do my duty well, and to meet whatever God wills.'[68] Writing again three days later, he was thankful that God had seen him through it safely. 'Shell fire, of an intensity never before known, was all around me', he wrote, 'but God was with me and brought me out unscathed. Glory be to His Holy Name. Render thanks and praise to Him for His Faithfulness.'[69] Newman was prepared to accept whatever the outcome, but having survived, he understood that his faith in God had been rewarded with divine protection.

It is more likely that expressions of fatalism were used to fend off any serious contemplation of death and to momentarily accept the powerlessness of one's situation. The prospect of death was hard to escape at the front, but to think too deeply about mortality was distressing.[70] During Third Ypres, John Mellor Poucher echoed this view in his diary, noting that 'one thinks and thinks and seems dazed. Seems like a nightmare – a Hell – one don't think about it too much or too long or they would be crazy.' When new recruits were conducting their first sentry duty, Johnston found himself having trouble sleeping, worrying whether or not they could be trusted. 'However, I soon began to take a fatalistic view of the matter', he wrote, 'and comforted myself many times by repeating "What is to be, will be", and many other trite remarks which, if they did no harm, certainly got me into an easier frame of mind'. Johnston chose to trust 'Providence that I might not wake up some night to find the Germans at our throats'.[71] Fatalism was simply a psychological defence mechanism. As Mohan explained, 'the constant apprehension of what the future will bring often leads to utter indifference'.[72] Rather than reflect on the possibility of death, many conceded, 'what is to be will be'.

Just as there were those rare soldiers who became convinced of their invulnerability, so too were there those like Bird's comrades, who became convinced of their inevitable death. In November 1917, Harry Lawrence Adams underwent a period of deep despair and was convinced that he would be killed on a specific date. Under the conditions of war, this seemed like a welcome escape, as he 'longed to leave this lower sphere and be forever with Him, which in that solemn moment seemed indeed to be far better'. After engaging in prayer with his friend Frank, the two men concluded that Adams was being tempted by the devil. He endured through this test of faith and as time passed it was clear that 'it is not the Lord's will, however, to take me home then'.[73] Pessimistic premonitions could therefore depend upon shifting moods. In Adams's case, the passage of time corresponded with a growing belief that his fate was to survive the war.

Chaplains were not wrong in identifying a fatalistic culture in the trenches; they just overestimated its significance and tended to dismiss beliefs or practices that were offensive to their theological preferences as superstitious. Some chaplains, for example, were sceptical of fatalism because it implied predetermination instead of free will, but like Newman or Adams, they could contradictorily preach about putting one's fate in God's hand, attribute a soldier's death to 'God's will' or even dabble in premonitions themselves.[74] It is also true that soldiers like Ira and Adams could be nihilistic about their fates, which, combined with a lack of expression of faith in God, could have contributed to chaplains' perceptions of a prevalent and harmful fatalism within the BEF.

The idea that someone's fate may be predetermined – or even just a simple interest in whose name was to be on the next bullet or shell – contributed to a culture of foresight. Premonitions were the most common psychical phenomena reported by soldiers, and examples can be found across the ranks. Private Alfred McLelland Burrage did not consider himself psychic but did experience 'a moment of prescience' in Ypres. While resting on the duckboards, his platoon commander passed by and smiled in his direction. 'As he smiled', Burrage recalled, 'I saw Death looking at me out of his eyes, and I knew that his number was up ... He was killed in the first few minutes of the attack.'[75] While commanding the 1st Canadian Division at Passchendaele, Lieutenant-General Cameron MacDonell was with General Herbert Plumer when he thought he heard a voice state, 'Ronald Morrison has been killed'. MacDonell reportedly turned to Plumer, 'Did you hear that, Sir?' Plumer was perplexed, as he had not heard anything. MacDonell later learned that a shell had fatally hit Morrison.[76]

Some managed to convince themselves that they were indeed psychic after experimenting with foresight. One private recalled that a comrade accurately predicted on two consecutive occasions who was next to be killed in his unit. He earned the nickname 'Hoodoo Bill' and was asked by the men to reveal who was next. He refused to engage in further prognostication and became so anxious that according to one soldier 'his nerves got the better of him' and he was taken out of the line.[77] In the masculine culture of the trenches, such sensitive soldiers were often associated with hysteria and psychotic collapse. Private Burrage was thankful he was not altogether psychic because those who were appeared to become unstable. As he wrote, it 'must be highly painful always to be aware of the unpleasant things that are about to happen'.[78] Premonitions were just another way in which soldiers contemplated death in the arbitrary environment of the Great War, but that also meant that they could be ill-adapted for survival at the front.

When premonitions came true they could confirm the existence of a higher order, but one must wonder how many were never realised. The trench newspaper of the 32nd Division, *The Switchboard*, included the story of an English officer who shared his presentments of death with an Irish servant. The latter replied, 'Thim presentimints [sic] are frauds. A cousin of mine had one once ... He felt sure he'd be killed out in Egypt, so he divided his savings between his sweetheart and his bosom chum, and went out to be shot. But niver [sic] a scratch did he get.' The servant's cousin returned home to find that his friend and sweetheart had disappeared with the money.[79] False premonitions were not just the work of trench satirists. Mohan recalled the story of Theo from Basingstoke who had a 'very morose and pessimistic nature, which was a source of great amusement'. Theo predicted that he, Mohan and another soldier named Tommy would 'all be dead in six months'. When the six months passed, Mohan and Tommy 'asked him what he had to say for his prophecy ... he told us that we had been granted an extension of life indefinitely!'[80] Not only did Mohan interpret his own war experiences through the lens of divine providence but his close comrade Freddie also successfully predicted his own death. The difference was, however, that the latter had arrived at his presentments through prayer. The fact that Mohan distinguished Freddie's faith from Theo's eccentric prognostications is one example of how supernatural beliefs could be divided into the religious and heterodox, but it also shows how they could be 'tamed' or better understood through a belief in some sort of higher power.

The use of prayer was also practised along the spectrum of religious beliefs.[81] Chaplains observed that a 'wind-up' religion was quite common, characterised by a demand for religious services prior to offensives and resorting to prayer in moments of peril.[82] For example, in September 1916, Railton gave last communion to officers in the trenches just before they died in battle.[83] On the Somme, the Reverend M. P. G. Leonard conducted a baptism for a soldier a few miles behind the lines in a gun pit. That evening the battalion went into action.[84] Men also prayed in the trenches while under shellfire and before battles. On the eve of landing at Gallipoli, Sydney Loosley of the ASC prayed for 'God to care for and watch over us having full faith that if He willed it His power and strength was greater than any shot or shell'.[85] Prayer was also observed amongst the otherwise non-religious. Burrage was raised as a Roman Catholic but had stopped practising because 'he couldn't quite believe in it'. During the war, however, 'I couldn't quite disbelieve, and if it were all true I realised that things might be very awkward for me if I happened to die in that state of mind'.[86] If soldiers were not likely to spend time contemplating the possibility of death, engagement with religion tended to be in the moment.[87]

Similar to premonitions, prayers could be used as evidence for a higher order and encourage further reliance on the supernatural. C. R. T. Evans believed that his family's prayers had saved his life. In December 1916, he wrote to his family that he found 'great comfort' in knowing 'that you were all praying for me'. His brushes with death confirmed their spiritual support. As Evans explained, 'proof of it seemed to come to me when a bullet from a sniper whistled just between Turner and me, he was only about a foot in front of me and didn't touch either of us'.[88] When under shellfire in the trenches, Evans once again turned to prayer and claimed to have experienced a miracle:

> I ... could hear them getting closer and closer. It was then that something like a miracle happened. A thought came into my mind which seemed to fill my very soul. 'It's all right, they are praying for me

at home.' Then the explosions passed further away and eventually stopped for a time. With that Turner came back to where I was and said: 'Did you see those three?' ... When I asked him what three, he said he had watched three shells in succession fall within a few yards of us and *none of them had exploded!*[89]

Evans professed, 'this hourly contact with danger has brought back a great faith in me'. Although he qualified he was 'not becoming a religious maniac', his war experiences had revealed 'a great truth about which the world is rather lax!'[90] For Evans, trench warfare was a confirmation of the supernatural that was not possible in modern civilised life. Prayer in moments of danger offered the experimental conduit to this revelation.

Life and death at the front were chaotic, and the explanations and practices that soldiers invoked could be inconsistent and contradictory. It was the written word, the art of memoir, that allowed soldiers who survived the war to piece their experiences together into a larger portrait that explained why some soldiers had gone west but others had not. Postwar memoirs by Christian soldiers like Mohan and Adams were able to look back and 'trace the Hand of God', attributing their survival to providence.[91] Like most soldiers, Adams and Mohan experienced close shaves, lucky breaks and fortunate circumstances. Two months before the end of the war, Adams was moving through a communication trench when a shell burst between him and another soldier, wounding the latter and a nearby sergeant. Adams's helmet was blown down the trench about six yards, but he was left untouched. He contemplated why he had survived but was left to marvel at God's will. 'It is beyond my comprehension', he wrote, so he promised to engage in 'daily prayer that the life so wonderfully preserved may be lived to His honour and glory'.[92] It is possible that Adams suffered from survivor's guilt, which he was able to cope with by making good on a promise to praise God's mercies. Devoid of religious frameworks, ghosts appear in Sassoon's writings to haunt him for having survived. 'They look at me reproachfully', he explains, 'because I am so lucky, with my safe wound, and the warm kindly immunity of the hospital'.[93] Mohan wrote his memoir in 1919 with the aim of proving God's existence. As he stated, 'the age of miracles is not past', as his experiences 'provided ample opportunities ... for proving this'.[94] Mohan hoped that if his writing helped even one person learn the truth of God's mercies and the importance of faith, 'then it will not have been written in vain'.⁹⁵ In framing their experiences as providential, Adams and Mohan could come to terms with their survival and redeem the deaths of their comrades.

On 28 October 1917, South African soldier William Brett St Leger had a peculiar dream. 'I dreamed last night that I had met an ensign of this regiment who told me that he knew that he would survive the winter, but that he would be killed in the Spring.' Then he saw how it would happen. The battalion was holding the line in front of a ruined village when the Germans attacked, reaching the British trenches and killing almost every man, including the ensign. 'Then from the air above the village', he wrote, 'the spirits of the officers and men of the regiment who had been killed both in battle and before swept down through the ruins of the village into the old trenches and drove the Germans out'. Amongst the spirits was Leger himself. 'I suddenly realised that I was the ensign', and when he awoke, St Leger thought to himself, that he 'was going to be killed next Spring'.⁹⁶

St Leger had been in the trenches since September 1916 and had witnessed the death or maiming of his original comrades. During Third Ypres, his battalion had lost approximately 300 men and nineteen officers in two great pushes on 31 July and 9 October. Amongst those killed was St Leger's closest friend Denis Bertram Sydney Buxton (the son of Sydney Charles Buxton, the Governor General of South Africa). St Leger learned of the news when he returned from leave the day after on 10 October. Wracked with guilt, St Leger fell into despair. 'When I went up the line the other day I felt that I wouldn't mind a bit if I did not return. I wanted to be with him again ... and all the other good fellows who have gone.' His despair was muted only by his faith. 'But I believe that everyone comes into this world for two purposes', he went on. First, 'to do a certain work' and second 'to fit himself for a better existence'. Once these two things were achieved, he reasoned, then 'he is taken away by God to enjoy his rest'. In the meantime, St Leger took comfort in the belief that 'Denis ... and all those others are happy together – supremely happy, and much happier than I ever was when I was with Denis. And they are waiting for me to join them.' St Leger wondered 'when I shall have fulfilled my parts'.⁹⁷ As the spring came closer, rumours swirled that the Germans were preparing to launch a major offensive in their attempts to end the war. Owing to his already lengthy service, in which he had been awarded a Military Cross, St Leger was offered a well-earned six months' light duty in England. Torn between his duty to his mother and father to return home safely and his duty to his battalion, he rejected the opportunity, choosing instead to face his destiny.[98] On several occasions in the spring of 1918, he wondered if his dream would prove accurate.[99] It did. St Leger was killed on 27 April 1918.

Like Bird's comrades, St Leger's constant confrontation with death led to unconscious contemplations about his fate, experienced through premonitory dreams. But unlike Bird, St Leger was writing without the knowledge of hindsight, moving between moments of nihilism and optimism, accepting his destiny whatever it might be but not resigning himself to certain death. Rather, he was driven to stay in the line out of loyalty to his comrades, grasping at the spiritual to comfort himself and allay feelings of survivor's guilt. St Leger was not alone. Various soldiers reconciled industrial mass slaughter with religious and other numinous beliefs. For a number of soldiers, death and survival were not the result of wearing the right charm, conducting the right ritual or obeying certain rules, nor were they explained as the result of experience, morale or refined senses. Rather, intuition was psychic in nature, moods were premonitions, endurance was a test of faith and prayer could bring revelation or even divine intervention. It was the environment of war, in which some lived and some died indiscriminately, that provided glimpses of greater power and purpose. But this space was also potentially unstable, a no man's land of psychic abilities and spiritual awareness that could wreck the novice sensitive or fool the heathen. Often, it only made sense after the fact and could be used to come to grips with the crushing guilt of having witnessed your comrades die while you survived for no apparent reason. It was in these contexts that spiritualism manifested on the Great War's battlefields. Spiritualists emphasised experiment and observation and could accommodate various supernatural beliefs. The mass of supernatural stories emanating from the battlefields, which interwar spiritualists and psychical researchers promoted, offered Bill Bird a means with which he could understand his war experiences.

Spiritualism at the front

It has been established that magical, supernatural and psychic stories were hardly unusual on the battlefields, but were spiritualists correct in claiming this activity as their own? The historian Jay Winter has suggested they were. As he states 'wartime spiritualism was in vogue as much among serving men as among the families they had left behind'.[100] Michael Snape, on the contrary, finds 'little evidence to support' this statement. He argues that, although soldiers may have shown an interest in spiritualism, actual séances and automatic writing were rare, and spiritualists were unlikely to enlist given the prominence of pacifism within the movement.[101] Snape is partly correct. Spiritualists were not shy about voicing their support for the war, and spiritualist churches and societies boasted about their enlistment rates. As for the claim that spiritualism was rare at the front? Much depends on how one defines spiritualism. Winter uses the term broadly to refer to heterodox Christianity that includes angelic sightings, rituals and charms, alongside séances and spirit photography. Belief in ghosts and magic, however, did not necessitate an interest in séances or an affiliation with the spiritualist movement. It was spiritualism more narrowly defined that concerned the *Army and Religion* report when it concluded that there was 'some interest in spiritualism but not so much as there is outside the Army'.[102] But it is also misleading to associate spiritualism at the front solely with spiritualist practice since self-identified spiritualists in the BEF expressed their beliefs through much of the same phenomena already documented.

It is true that spiritualist practice was rare in the army even though some examples can be found, including in military intelligence. During the same time that the British Army was experimenting with sound-ranging and flash-spotting to improve the accuracy of their counter-battery operations, others were using the battlefield laboratory to conduct psychical research. One of the more peculiar examples is the story of Colonel Percy Fawcett of VI Corps. When he arrived at the front in late 1916 he terminated Captain H. H. Hemming's research into flash spotting. Fawcett would only target clearly visible batteries or those he had discovered through his Ouija board. According to Hemming, none of these shots hit anything but dirt.[103]

Other high-ranking individuals tried to solve the problems of trench warfare through supernormal means. While serving as Chief Experimental Officer on the Munitions Inventions Board, Major Clarence Christopher Colley claimed that various psychic and spiritual 'impressions' sent to him from 'scientists on the other side' were crucial to his war work. He described these moments of intuition as not '"heard" but felt', while also 'so strong and definite as almost to amount to a verbal order'. Some of the breakthroughs that he attributed to these impressions included the discovery of German espionage at the front, improved techniques for light signalling and the development of various inventions. For example, he received messages from his father's spirit stating 'coals of fire' and 'blood and fire'. When he met two inventors with the surnames Coles and Blood, he chose to fund their research based on his spirit messages. Sharing his experiences after the war with the elite Ghost Club, he believed that his testimony proved 'that our friends "on the other side" did their bit in the Great War just as much as those who were fortunate enough to service it'.[104] Fawcett and Colley had turned to the occult sciences in their own attempts to tame chance and master trench warfare.[105]

Spiritualism made its way to the front in various ways. One conduit was through the home front's burgeoning interest. British and Dominion soldiers received Oliver Lodge's *Raymond* as a gift and read the book at the front.[106] Some participated in spiritualist activities when on leave, while the mother of Corporal Henry G. Cleland mailed him séance messages.[107] George Smedley's wife sent her husband a worried letter in February 1917 after she was told by a medium that he had been killed. A very much alive Smedley advised her to stop seeing mediums.[108] Soldiers also poked fun at the home front's interest in spiritualism. The trench newspaper of the 14th Canadians, the *R.M.R. Growler*, included a séance between Mary and the spirit of her husband John who was killed in the war:

Are you happy, John?
Oh! Very happy, Mary.
Are you happier than when you were on earth with me, John?
Oh! yes, Mary; much happier.
Why, where are you?
I'm in hell, Mary.[109]

Chaplains took notice of spiritualism's wartime popularity. Reverend Railton received instruction about *Raymond* in March 1917 and some religious services erupted into discussions about the Occult revival.[110]

The spiritualist movement and SPR also made their presence known at the front. The SPR sent its journals to members serving abroad and the SNU sent 7,000 copies of spiritualist pamphlets to the Western Front in 1915.[111] They hoped that this would not only advance the cause but also provide comfort to the soldiers:

> by a perusal of the literature many a mind will be freed from perplexity regarding the future, many an hour of pain may be eased of its sting. While after the discord of the battlefield, it will come as balm to the spirit to realise that in the happy Summerland men shall live in unbroken amity, and be able to translate the doctrine of the Brotherhood of Man and the Fatherhood of God into the enduring terms of eternal progress, the pathway of which is strewn with the roses of eternal peace.[112]

Men like Driver J. R. Parker sent appreciations to 'all those kind friends who have so generously sent papers out to me, also pamphlets'.[113] Driver W. J. Plain with the 2nd Field Ambulance wrote with appreciation to *The Two Worlds* and commented that he read the paper at the front and passed it on 'to a chum who has recently become interested, and who, being level-headed, no doubt will be won over to our side'.[114]

As Plain's statements indicate, soldiers who were spiritualists before the war represented the movement at the front. One indication of spiritualists' contribution to the armed forces comes from the various rolls of honour erected by spiritualist churches.[115] Shortly after the outbreak of war, *The Two Worlds* created a weekly segment dedicated to recognising those spiritualists who had volunteered for service. The journal hoped to demonstrate that spiritualists played an equal part in the war effort and to remind future generations of this contribution.[116] The roll contains the names of 727 spiritualists and, in some cases, provides details about their rank, regiment and affiliated spiritualist society. The roll ended in the summer of 1916 after the Military Service Act came into force, not because spiritualists had soured on the righteousness of the war but because *The Two Worlds* believed that those who had to be compelled into service did not warrant recognition alongside those who volunteered.[117]

Efforts were made by spiritualist soldiers to spread the movement to others in training camps or at the front. A soldier training at Whitchurch Camp in Salop wrote that he was attempting to organise a Spiritualist Church Hut just as there were huts devoted to other churches. He claimed to have twenty-seven other men interested in using the facility.[118] Private E. Anderson wrote that he was leaving copies of *The Two Worlds* in the trenches and had managed to get 'a few interested in our Cause'.[119] The former president of Onward Spiritualist Church in Portsmouth, while stationed in India in 1916, boasted that he was 'able to create an interest in our Movement among the men, an interest which is spreading'.[120] It is debatable how successful these efforts were. Although 7,000 pamphlets sound impressive, as Owen Davies notes, when compared to the millions of Bibles that were sent overseas, the SNU's efforts represented a mere 'drop in the ocean'.[121]

Nevertheless, spiritualism was not just a homefront phenomenon, and it was expressed at the front in various ways. Some men found comfort in their spiritualist beliefs during those uncertain moments at the front. As Private Thomas Bell wrote to *The Two Worlds*, 'we know not when our time is come when we hear the shell and see them drop many yards away'.[122] J. T. Dillsen confided, 'the knowledge of Spiritualism makes a vast difference'. He attempted to spread his ideas to the other men within his unit for this reason.[123] Private Samuel Turner of the King's Shropshire Light Infantry was, much like St Leger, comforted by the fact of life after death and a reunion with loved ones. He explained that he was doing his bit in trying to spread spiritualism to the other men because 'a Spiritualist is far better off in this campaign than those of any other cause'.[124] Fatalism may have been expressed amongst spiritualists by accepting the 'facts' of life after death. One officer advocated for spiritualism on its scientific grounds, stating 'we have lost faith in the power of our clergy to clear up the mystery. We have ... more faith in the power of such men of science as Sir Oliver Lodge or Sir William Crookes'.[125] Other soldiers were the perfect image of the sacrificial spiritualist soldier who entered onto the battlefield because he had no fear of death. According to his mother, Arthur M. Lawrence of Reading enlisted because 'he thought it his duty to serve his country as any other young man. In fact, he considered himself more eligible, having a greater knowledge of the after-life'.[126]

Much like Bird, spiritualists also testified to being saved by the spirits. Colley was an artillery officer in the opening months of the war when he had his first experience. It occurred as he was desperately trying to save some British guns in a vulnerable position while under fire in the woods. On his own, and prepared to start dragging them out by hand, he suddenly heard his father's voice saying, 'Clarey my boy, wait'. Colley stopped in his tracks. 'Try as I would I could not move my right leg', he explained. Then 'as though by magic the firing ceased' and his gunners were able to make it to his position and remove the guns. 'And then, directly, my right leg was unshackled and I actually fell forward', he recalled. The pause in the fighting was just enough time to get the guns out safely. This proved a blessing, as he would have fallen victim to the shelling that was raining down in the woods.[127] Colley attributed his survival not to luck or an intuitive grasp of shellfire, but to a psychic intimation from spirits who anticipated the pause in the shelling before it happened. In fact, had Colley been allowed to follow his instincts he would have been killed. The spirits provided a needed corrective to his own intuition.

Private Alfred James Titmass also reported being guided by spirits in no man's land. On his second night on the frontlines, Titmass was detailed to go on listening patrol. As he neared the post, the Germans opened fire. He took cover but could not move from his position for almost three hours. When Titmass was finally able to make his way back, he became tangled in the barbed wire with 'the guns raining shot all around'. Fortunately, he returned safely owing to the telepathic guidance of his 'spirit friends'.[128]

Lance Corporal Alfred Perfect of the regular 1/Royal Warwickshire Regiment negotiated his morale through his spiritualist beliefs just as Christian soldiers turned to their faith. A Christian spiritualist, Perfect credited spiritualism with helping him endure the trying experiences of trench warfare. 'Under it all I have felt that God has been near giving me courage and nerve power', explaining, 'I feel a great angelic power which gives me not only spiritual but extra physical courage, thereby enabling me to endure hardships beyond my ordinary ability to do so'.[129] Titmass and Perfect were not unlike Bird, who had faith in his brother's ability to guide him to safety, thereby alleviating his nerves. Perfect expressed these mental states as both psychical-physical (nerve power) and the Divine (angels and God). Others approached their situation from a more scientific perspective. An anonymous soldier writing in *Light* was trying to experiment his way through solving morale at the front. He reasoned that depressed moods should correlate with the suffering and negative thought waves of destructive environments, but from his experience, they appeared to be random. He vowed to continue experimenting with various theories, since 'the science of psychic conditions and influences [is] in its infancy'.[130] As Tim Cook observes, the shellfire of the Western Front could literally charge the air, and spiritualists had long associated magnetic and electric waves with higher phenomena.[131] Soldiers could also become hyper-attuned to the various sensations of their unique environments. St Leger could recognise the 'wind of a passing shell' or 'the hot air of a shell-burst'. When he was moving along a road in the spring of 1918 he felt a peculiar sensation and wondered if it was a stray bullet. As he noted with curiosity, it was the first time he had felt 'the hot air of a passing bullet on my cheek'.[132] Such contexts might help us appreciate what spiritualists meant when they claimed to be able to *feel* a psychic presence.

Some spiritualist soldiers also claimed to see visions and received instructions from the spirits. Private Turner had been in France since September 1914. He had never heard anything at the time about angels in Mons but he did explain that 'I have seen spirit friends on the battlefield, and, what is more, I have some beautiful messages from them'. Much like Colley, the spirits provided directions that were essential to his survival. For example, he received the message 'keep to my left, as the right was very dangerous'. This he took as his rule to follow while under shellfire. On one occasion he kept to his left, even though most shells were landing to the left of him, and astonishingly, 'the shells were being transferred to the right, and the left was soon clear of all shells', allowing him free passage to safety. 'Now, the place I was making for on my right was soon a mass of ruins', he explained, 'so you see how my guides had helped me'. Turner believed that, had he not been a spiritualist, he would not have been cognisant of the guides' messages.[133] Spiritualism provided him with an occult knowledge at the same time that it commented on the absurdity of life and death in the trenches. A rational soldier would have moved to the right and would have been killed as a result. What else could account for his miraculous survival?

Turner's frontline mediumship earned him a reputation amongst the men as a prognosticator. His comrades began following his examples and frequently inquired if there was 'any fresh news' from the spirits. Some chose to keep close to Turner as if he were a lucky charm, and they would 'ask me if all was safe, and as far as possible I have set their minds at rest'. He believed his spiritualism was responsible for his platoon's performance, since between September 1914 and February 1915, only a fraction of the men had been wounded. 'Some people will say it is luck', he wrote, 'but we are the only section in the battalion which has been so fortunate'. He hoped his experiences would encourage others to 'use their gifts on the battlefield'.[134]

Turner's story raises questions about spiritualism as a practice, not just an identity or set of beliefs. Did soldiers engage in séances or automatic writing at the front? A few examples can be found. Tim Cook discovered the remarkable story of a group of Canadian soldiers who, after reading *Raymond*, conducted telepathic experiments on the Western Front using a blindfold.[135] Driver Parker of the Army Service Corps (ASC) informed *The Two Worlds* that he had a sympathetic parson in France who had given him a small room to conduct spiritualist meetings. Another officer reported a 'tendency towards dabbling' in spiritualism in his unit, but provided no details.[136] As was the case with conventional religious observance, time and opportunity would have been significant barriers.[137] As Titmass explained, 'war is not good for our work', since 'the conditions would be all against it'. The constant roar of the guns and the demands of army life would have made it hard to concentrate and initiate trance. Away from the frontlines, it may have been more practical, as in the case of a spiritualist circle that developed on board the HMS *Cordelia*. According to one participant, he and a group of other men conducted at least two séances that included messages from beyond and even materialisations. He believed their spirit friends had protected the ship through the Battle of Jutland.[138]

Time would not have been the only barrier. Since most mediums were women and male mediums were regarded as feminine, to engage in trance was to embrace a feminine sensitivity.[139] Mediumship in the BEF would have therefore been complicated by the presence of muscular Christianity in the British Army, where morality, athleticism and a healthy control over one's body were intertwined.[140] There was also the social stigma that might come with identifying as a spiritualist, just as there was with those who aligned themselves with a Christian piety.[141] When Smedley was discussing spiritualism with his wife, he made sure to use a green envelope so as to bypass the censor, who was often known to the soldier.[142] George Lee of the Salford Central Spiritualist Church claimed that when he identified as a spiritualist upon his enlistment, the recruiting officer was dismissive. It was only after Lee insisted that he write it down on his form that the officer complied.[143] Many soldiers who participated in the spiritualist movement identified themselves by their Christian denomination, but some soldiers, like Harold Earith with the 86th Canadian Battalion, did identify as 'Spiritualist' in their attestation papers.[144]

Overall, the infrequent mention of spiritualist practices in soldiers' writings, including from spiritualists themselves, suggests they were rare. Spiritualist phenomena were more likely to emerge spontaneously through psychic intuition, telepathic messages and guardian spirits. Titmass believed that although spiritualist practice was difficult, its philosophy was relevant and he had some success discussing it with the men.[145] Some spiritualists observed the popularity of an emergency religion just as the chaplains had, and saw this as an opportunity to spread the cause. William Gair of 1/7th Northumberland Fusiliers and formerly of the Hirst Lyceum and Society wrote to *The Two Worlds* in February 1916 offering to hand out any pamphlets, journals or books to the men because, as he explained,

> I find men who have never thought of the after-life, men who scorned the idea of our glorious truth, ready to listen and reason with me, instead of scoffing as in days of yore. To my mind, now is the time to give light to souls who will perhaps be ushered out into a life beyond. Now is the time to give knowledge to those who will come through the ordeal, so that when opportunity comes their way they may set about proving the thoughts we have placed before them.[146]

According to Gair, spiritualism could provide comfort to the soldiers but also prepare them for the spirit world, allowing them to become vehicles for the coming spiritual awakening. Just as significant was

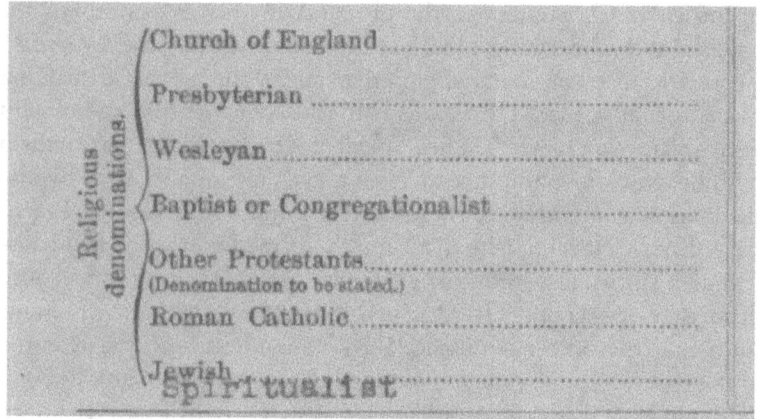

Figure 2.2 Segment of Harold Earith's attestation paper.

the ability of the environment of war to attune people to the reality of the spirit. If spiritualist ideas were planted, men would be able to ascribe their survival to the influence of the spirits. They could develop a type of mediumship more appropriate to the trenches, one that went beyond séances.

There is also some evidence of servicemen turning to spiritualism because of the suffering they witnessed at the front. The Reverend Alfred Allen Brockington served at the 15th CCS in June 1916, and then as the chaplain of the 43rd Brigade of the Royal Field Artillery (RFA). When he returned to England in 1917, he began engaging in automatic writing. The scripts remain in his diary and offer a unique look into how one padre dealt with the suffering of the war.[147] Brockington would have witnessed the worst that modern warfare could do to an individual's body and mind at a CCS. Although he includes few details, other examples offer an idea of some of the injuries that one witnessed within the RAMC. While with the 2/5th London Field Ambulance in 1916, Frank Steadman met a patient who had dislocated his thigh after being buried by a shell, a soldier who survived in no man's land but had his hands chewed to the bone by rats and another who had a piece of shrapnel lodged in his brain. 'I could not sleep for a while', he wrote home, 'the poor chap's ghastly face and wound was so vividly impressed upon my mind; every time I closed my eyes I could see him'. Just as bad were the sounds of the men screaming at night. As he explained,

'I had about twelve men in the ward now, suffering like this; all have had their friends killed by their sides'.[148] One RAMC worker sought the comfort of spiritualism under these conditions, noting that while he saw 'dozens pass away, and stood by to prepare them for their last resting place', he alleviated the torment by reminding himself of 'the facts and grand knowledge "there is no death"'.[149]

Whatever Brockington saw, his automatic writing scripts indicate that the war played a key role in his interest in spiritualism. These messages provide reassurances about God's love and mercies, and cite specific examples of his war experiences:

> <u>Jesus will hear all the cries of the wounded and those in pain wherever they are with His unfailing mercy and pity</u>. Tell the story of the wounded gunner to whom you advised the doc to give more morphia saying that you knew that he would die and that it was the will of God to spare men ...
>
> <u>Jesus will prove His love to men</u>. Tell the story of the man who came to you in the trench and said Do you think I shall have another chance ...
>
> <u>Jesus may reveal himself now to men through the direct mediation of the spirit</u>. Tell how you have had visions of him – at Whitecombe at the Battle of the Marne ... Say that you believe that all men are capable of such visions if only they will believe and look for them.[150]

Despite all the suffering that Brockington witnessed, these messages assured him that God was not silent on the battlefield. He was there when the men were suffering, working through the chaplain's mercy and faith in God. He was there when men experienced 'wind-up' before they went over the top, and the veil between this life and the other could periodically be lifted on the battlefield through visions.

Brockington's diary reveals a common response amongst chaplains who emphasised Christ's suffering on the cross to reconcile Christian values with the war and, in his case, spiritualism. Although chaplains found the men to be ignorant of doctrine, they saw within them an 'unconscious Christianity', indicating a set of values and virtues that they believed were important to living a Christian life, including unselfishness, generosity and humility.[151] Railton, for example, was touched by the selflessness that he witnessed during his time at the front and hoped that the war would create 'a new England'.[152] He was just as inspired by how soldiers endured in the face of suffering, which reminded him of Christ's passion. When Railton's faith was shaken by the war, he remembered that Christ suffered as well. 'If our Lord had not suffered on this earth', he wrote, 'I would blasphemy God all day ... I only believe in God in this war because I believe in Jesus Christ the crucified'.[153] Such ideas reinforced the view of the soldier as Christ-like. According to Railton, they were carrying 'out our Lord's ideals beyond anything we have ever seen in Churchmen and politicians'.[154] Chaplains projected this image back onto the men. The Reverend Harry Davies observed that chaplains were instructed to represent Christianity to the soldier 'as essentially a religion of sacrifice'.[155] Railton informed the troops that they were 'living the Christ life'.[156] Some took notice. After several close calls during Third Ypres, John Mellor Poucher remarked that 'they call us God's chosen people and I believe we are'.[157]

Brockington's spirit messages include detailed descriptions of Christ's crucifixion on the cross by the spirit of John the Apostle. Ministers of all denominations expressed concerns over spiritualism and some denounced it as diabolical. The Anglican Church feared a loss of authority over spiritual matters since the séance's emphasis on observation meant 'Every man is his own pope'.[158] For practical reasons, the Anglican Church often maintained a peaceful coexistence with spiritualists, allowing vicars such as Archdeacon Thomas Colley (Christopher Colley's father) to continue to minister to their congregations despite showing interest in spiritualism.[159] In the interwar period, some Anglican vicars such as George Vale Owen engaged with automatic writing to obtain new revelations.[160] After serving on the Western Front and perhaps struggling with God's silence, Brockington, like Railton, invoked a 'theology of the cross' to explain why humanity suffered. The concept was most famously articulated by Martin Luther to identify Christ's crucifixion as the source of all knowledge and revelation. As a solution to the problem of suffering, Christ's sacrifice reminds Christians that suffering sometimes has to be accepted with endurance and faith. Christ's acceptance also serves as an example to be emulated. Perhaps most significantly, Christ's crucifixion demonstrates his love for humanity by sharing in their suffering. To look towards the cross in the face of physical and emotional torment is to be reminded that one suffers *with* Christ.[161] Brockington and Railton were seeking answers to the war's destruction by bringing themselves closer to Christ's crucifixion. While Railton found it through the men's endurance and sacrificial character, Brockington found it through communications from beyond in the form of spiritualism. That he turned to spiritualism is telling, since God was clearly not silent but spoke back.

The evidence we have of spiritualism at the front suggests that although séances were rare, spiritualists found confirmation of their beliefs through premonitions, 'miraculous' survivals and the comforting notion of an afterlife based on 'facts'. A turn to some sort of numinous order was hardly an exceptional response, experienced by both religious and non-religious soldiers. The gravity with which the signs were acknowledged varied, but these signs were, nevertheless, a part of the soldiers' experiences. The congruence between superstition, religious beliefs and spiritualism also highlights the experimental and spontaneous nature of religious experiences at the front. Occult powers gradually revealed themselves as soldiers arbitrarily lived and died and came to terms with their environment.

Numinous experiences were not just part of a 'secret' culture 'known only to the soldiers'.[162] In addition to being shared in letters home, they were published in journals like *The Occult Review*, *Light*, *The Two Worlds* and *The Psychic Gazette*.[163] In August 1919, *Pearson Magazine* offered £100 in prizes for 'the weirdest stories of the war'.[164] Such experiences became part of a broader supernatural culture that reinforced various worldviews. Spiritualists and non-spiritualists, civilians and soldiers, championed the Angels of Mons as proof of the divine nature of Britain's cause and the existence of the afterlife, spirits and even telepathy. The rumour of a 'Comrade in White' ministering to the dying in no man's land was also reported at home. Sometimes this figure was Jesus Christ himself, and the story draws obvious parallels to some experiences documented above.[165] When the Reverend Bere met a soldier who had a mysterious companion, he thought it was proof of the White Comrade's existence.[166] Even charms could be used as examples of the existence of the supernatural.[167] For example, MacDonagh's report in *The Occult Review* included the story of Private Thomas Kelly of the 1st Royal Munster Fusiliers who believed he had experienced a miracle because of his Sacred Heart badge. This 'oval piece of red cloth' with a 'printed … picture of Jesus, standing before a cross, with His bleeding heart, encircled by thorns and flames, exposed on

His breast' added to the symbolism of the soldier as Christ-like.[168] Kelly's 'miraculous' story further established the connection. At Gallipoli, a bullet passed through his palm over his chest but was stopped by his sacred heart emblem. He was knocked to the ground and laid amongst the dead under fire for two hours but survived. Kelly suffered stigmata-like injuries and was metaphorically resurrected amongst the dead.[169]

Battlefield stories made their way into various books such as *Back of the Front*, *The War and the Weird*, *Dreams and Visions of the War* and *Psychical Phenomena and the War*.[170] These books reported cases of psychic premonitions, ghostly sightings, angelic interventions and miraculous survivals. Hereward Carrington, for example, shared the story of a soldier who saw a vision of his mother, and as he walked towards her, a shell landed in the very spot in which he had been standing, a story with a striking similarity to Bird's survival at Vimy. Another soldier accurately predicted he would be wounded three times and then killed once he returned from leave.[171] As previous examples demonstrate, one did not have to be a spiritualist to experience such incidents. They could be a momentary engagement with superstition born out of the urgency of the moment, an expression of the rituals and culture of the trenches or part of faith in divine providence. But the spiritualist movement's ability to incorporate these into their evidence-based, anti-orthodox philosophy was useful in a society in which traditional religious authority was deemed inadequate to the war's needs. Most importantly, the soldier's voice provided an authenticity of experience.[172] In *The War and the Weird*, Thurston Hopkins and the Reverend Forbes Phillips called the laboratory of the war 'the Great Revealer' and Tommy was its scientist, 'thinking over weird things [as] he comes to the conclusion, finding the lights by which he steers'.[173] After receiving a deluge of weird stories from the front, *Pearson Magazine* observed that the Great War had revealed that 'far more people are in possession of what is sometimes known as the "sixth sense" than is commonly supposed', providing 'further proof of the existence of those mysterious forces which modern civilisation seeks to find behind the veil'.[174] When combined with appeals to the authority of eminent scientists at home, these phenomena contributed to the wartime spiritualist movement no less significantly than home front séances.

Conclusion

The war stories of Will R. Bird are some of the more famous in Canadian history, though most historians have been inclined to overlook their supernatural elements.[175] Even Bird later minimised his strange experiences. Published in 1930, *And We Go On* contains over half a dozen psychic incidents that do not appear in his second memoir, *Ghosts Have Warm Hands*, published thirty-eight years later. Bird's decision to rewrite his memoirs reflected changing attitudes towards the war. Written after the war books boom of 1929, *And We Go On* was intended to counter how modernist writers depicted the soldiers' experience. As Bird stated, 'we are being deluged now, a decade after the war, by books that are putrid with so-called "realism". They portray the soldier as a coarse-minded, profane creature.' His latter memoir appears closer to our contemporary perspective of the war, portraying officers as donkeys and emphasising Bird's individual heroism over the bravery of his comrades or a psychic influence.[176]

Ghosts Have Warm Hands retains the seminal ghostly intervention at Vimy as the title suggests, but this was likely retained to honour the memory of his brother as the premonitions and other numinous experiences were removed. In doing so, Bird erased the wider context in which he initially framed his war experiences. Take for example the case of the atheist soldier named Christensen. Despite his lack of faith, Christensen experiences a death premonition. 'Something came to me', he explains. 'It was as if every sound in the world was stilled at once, as if there was nothing more for me to hear, and I knew what it meant. I'm not the least bit afraid.' Bird attempted to convince him this was nonsense but the atheist was certain. The premonition is essential to describing the courage and bravery with which Christensen sacrifices himself, but it also implies that the war was a revelation of a faith that could bridge science and religion. As Bird explained to Christensen, if he was correct then he was acknowledging that 'there was some power beyond the visible that imparted information'. The atheist conceded the point and Bird became just as convinced that he would never see him again. As with all premonitions in Bird's memoir, this one also came to pass.[177] In the modern myth of the war, Christensen's sacrifice is not brave and the spiritual science that united his and

Figure 2.3 Cover art for Rosa Stuart's *Dreams and Visions of the War* (1917).

Bird's philosophies appears equally naïve. *And We Go On* was not a memoir for the postwar age.

There is no evidence that Bird engaged in spiritualism after the war, but a supernormal culture is pervasive throughout his original memoir.[178] *And We Go On* promotes a more traditional image of war, portrays the battlefield as a psychic laboratory and references the British spiritualist movement. *Ghosts Have Warm Hands* leaves out Bird's brief relationship with a spiritualist medium in Britain, and we know that Canadian servicemen were exposed to the movement while on leave or in training on the home front.[179] Most revealing, however, is the similarities to Hereward Carrington's *Psychic Phenomena and the Great War*. Not only does it contain a case close to Bird's, but they share similar models of mind. Carrington's book includes instances of the supernormal and supernatural in the second half of the book, but in the first half, the contents are entirely devoted to the 'normal' psychology of the soldier. As we saw above, Bird's book does the same. When Bird claimed to be interested in the soldiers' 'psychic condition' he highlighted a culture in which both normal and abnormal psychology belonged under the definition of 'psychic'.[180] Even more interestingly, *Ghost Have Warm Hands* includes an uncharacteristic moment of intimacy between Bill and his brother's ghost. As the title suggests, in this memoir, Steve grasps Bill's hand to pull him out of the shelter at Vimy, before placing 'his warm hand over my mouth as I started to shout my happiness'.[181] Such a small detail may have been deliberate, since it would have had significant implications in 1930, implying a physical, not just a mental ghost, stretching the limits of credulity for all but the most ardent spiritualists at a time when physical phenomena were becoming increasingly associated with fraud. In *And We Go On*, on the other hand, Bill's ghost is more easily understood to be telepathic in nature, the only hint of intimacy being a 'tug' on Bill's arm when he was asleep. *And We Go On* was part of the broader supernormal trend to psychologise the ghost.

Any study of Bird must wrestle with an obvious question: did these stories really happen? Bird was a gifted and prolific creative writer who produced 600 short stories throughout his life. The Great War launched his writing career, providing him with ample material for stories through both his own war experiences and those of the thousands of veterans he encountered.[182] Perhaps Bird was more concerned with telling an interesting story by stretching the truth or repackaging the stories of others. Both are possible given his willingness to readapt his memoir in 1968 and his admission that his goal was to challenge 'realism' in 1930. But the entire point of *And We Go On* is that such realism was not always straightforward for the soldier. Bird makes the revealing but contradictory argument in his preface that men 'grasped' at fantasies but that his psychic experiences were 'actual fact'. Perhaps the author was just as unsure and looked towards the supernormal to frame a cluster of strange but nevertheless genuine experiences as 'real'. We cannot know for certain if the experiences in *And We Go On* were his own, but some details can be corroborated. We do know, for example, that he was a devout Christian and that Ira Black was indeed disciplined for refusing to go into the line on 12 July 1917.[183] Whether or not this was because of Freddy's prognostications is impossible to know, but we need not dwell on the question as enough examples of similar stories can be found to challenge the idea that these were less authentic representations of how some soldiers understood their service. In articulating the psychological effects of war, and in selling a less profane set of war experiences in 1930, Bird adopted an enchanted psyche that had been theorised by numerous thinkers since the late nineteenth century and which saw renewed public interest after the war in the form of spiritualism. Bird may not have been a spiritualist per se, but his book is perhaps its greatest literary rendition of the soldiers' experience.

Notes

1 Will R. Bird, *And We Go On: A Memoir of the Great War*, David Williams (ed.) (Montreal and Kingston, QC: McGill-Queen's University Press, 2014), pp. 3–4.
2 *Ibid.*, p. 48.
3 Paul Nash, *Outline: An Autobiography and Other Writings* (London: Faber & Faber, 1949), p. 211.
4 Bird, *And We Go On*, p. 4.
5 *Ibid.*
6 'Miscellaneous: Trench Mortar Mixtures', *The Shell Hole Advance*, 1:1 (1917), 7.
7 Trench newspapers represented an insider trench culture. In order to succeed and connect with their audience they had to convey something real about trench life while at the same time providing humour and escapism. See Graham Seal, *The Soldiers' Press: Trench Journals in the First World War* (London: Palgrave Macmillan, 2013), pp. 78–80 and J. G. Fuller, *Troop Morale and Popular Culture in the British and Dominion Armies, 1914–1918* (Oxford: Clarendon Press, 1990), pp. 7–20.
8 Dieter Storz, 'Artillery', *International Encyclopedia of the First World War*, last updated 16 December 2014, accessed February 2023, https://encyclopedia.1914-1918-online.net/article/artillery.

9 This number was based on a sample of 212,659 wounds at Casualty Clearing Stations (CCSs). 'Shells, trench mortars, etc.', accounted for 58.51 per cent. See T. J. Mitchell and G. M. Smith (eds), *History of the Great War Based on Official Documents. Medical Services. Casualties and Medical Statistics of the Great War* (London: His Majesty's Stationery Office, 1931), p. 40.
10 Richard Holmes, *Tommy: The British Soldier on the Western Front, 1914–1918* (London: Harper Collins, 2004), p. 275.
11 Alexander Watson, *Enduring the Great War: Combat, Morale and Collapse in the German and British Armies, 1914–1918* (Cambridge: Cambridge University Press, 2008), p. 87.
12 Imperial War Museum (hereafter IWM), Private Papers of G. W. Durham, Documents.348, Garnet W. Durham, 'My Experiences in the War, 1914–1918: Being Extracts from Letters Written by Me during the War and Returned to Me after the Armistice', n.d., pp. 94–5.
13 IWM, Private Papers of A. Jordens, Documents.18920, letter from Arthur Jordens to his mother, 29 August 1916.
14 IWM, Private Papers of T. G. Mohan, Documents.4804, Talbot G. Mohan, 'My War Diary', December 1919, p. 125.
15 Vanessa Chambers, 'Fighting Chance: War, Popular Belief and British Society, 1900–1951', unpublished PhD dissertation (Institute for Historical Research, University of London, 2007), p. 45; Owen Davies, *A Supernatural War: Magic, Divination, and Faith during the First World War* (Oxford: Oxford University Press, 2018), p. 137.
16 *Notes and Queries*, 12:1 (1916), 208.
17 IWM, Sound Archive, 22737, Bert Fearns, interview by Peter Barton, 1996–1997.
18 IWM, Sound Archive, 10648, George Peake, interview by Peter M. Hart, 1989.
19 Davies, *A Supernatural War*, pp. 135–59.
20 Michael MacDonagh, 'The Wearing of Religious Emblems at the Front', *The Occult Review*, 34:5 (1916), 266–74; Chambers, 'Fighting Chance', pp. 41–2.
21 Davies, *A Supernatural War*, pp. 160–8.
22 IWM, Sound Archive, 9202, George James Storey Wray, interviewed by Peter M. Hart, 1986.
23 Michael Snape, *God and the British Soldier: Religion and the British Army in the First and Second World Wars* (New York: Routledge, 2005), p. 37.
24 'Narrow Escapes in Battle', *The Balkan News*, 110 (1916), 3.
25 Jason Schweitzer, *The Cross and the Trenches: Religious Faith and Doubt among British and American Great War Soldiers* (London: Praeger, 2003), pp. 32–3.

26 Psalm 91:7 (KJV).
27 It has been argued that Catholicism was more popular on the battlefield than Anglicanism since the former had more to offer in the way of rituals and sacraments. See Edward Madigan, *Faith Under Fire: Anglican Army Chaplains and the Great War* (London: Palgrave Macmillan, 2011), pp. 167–8 and Snape, *God and the British Soldier*, p. 35.
28 This report was based upon a questionnaire, with sixty Catholic chaplains responding. By the end of the war there were 643 Catholic chaplains in the BEF, representing a sample size of approximately 9.3 per cent (however, this does not account for turnover throughout the war). See Charles Plater, *Catholic Soldiers* (London: Longmans, Green and Co., 1919), pp. 5–6, 24 and *Statistics of the Military Effort of the British Empire during the Great War: 1914–1920* (London: His Majesty's Stationery Office, 1922), p. 190.
29 IWM, Private Papers of G. Smedley, Documents.11745, George Smedley, 'The Diary of Gunner G. Smedley 66701', entry for 14 May 1916.
30 IWM, Private Papers of J. A. Johnston, Documents.12383, J. Anderson Johnston, 'The Diary of a Rifleman', ed. D. J. A Johnston and M. A. Johnston (1971, original written in 1924), p. 79.
31 Paul Fussell, *The Great War and Modern Memory* (Oxford: Oxford University Press, 1975, 2000), pp. 140–3.
32 I explore this connection and other themes from this chapter in Kyle Falcon, 'The Voiceless Dead: Francis Jenkins, Regina Trench, and Living and Dying on the Western Front', in Peter Farrugia and Evan Habkirk (eds), *Portraits of Battle: Courage, Grief, and Strength in Canada's Great War* (Vancouver, BC: University of British Columbia Press, 2021), pp. 63–83.
33 IWM, Private Papers of Reverend D. Railton, CF, Documents.4760, David Railton, 24 September 1916, p. 21.
34 IWM, Private Papers of W. C. Culliford, Documents.17089, 'War Diary of Walter Charles Culliford, 1915–1919', n.d., pp. 15, 32.
35 Snape, *God and the British Soldier*, pp. 33–4, 38.
36 For examples see Chambers, 'Fighting Chance', pp. 38–40 and Davies, *A Supernatural War*, pp. 146–7.
37 'Soldiers' Superstitions: Mascots and Luck-Bringers', *The Periscope*, 2:6 (1918), 294.
38 'Private Freeman Has His Fortune Told', *The Listening Post*, 12 (1916), pp. 3–4.
39 'Signs and Countersigns: An Article Especially Written for Superstitious M. T'ers', *The Pennington Press*, 2:40 (1917), 5.

A psychic laboratory

40 IWM, Private Papers of W. D. Darling, Documents.3472, letter from Walter Douglas Darling, 12 November 1916.
41 Watson, *Enduring the Great War*, pp. 100–7.
42 *Ibid.*, pp. 101–2.
43 Interview with Joseph Murray, recorded by Peter M. Hart, 1984.
44 IWM, Sound Archive, 8201, Joseph Pickard, interview by Peter M. Hart, 1986.
45 Davies, *A Supernatural War*, p. 138.
46 As Alexander Watson observes, soldiers focused on short term, in which one's chances of survival were higher rather than cumulative and long-term risk where the chances were lower. To think in the long term was to raise the possibility that one's luck might eventually run out (Watson, *Enduring the Great War*, pp. 100–3).
47 Fussell, *The Great War and Modern Memory*, pp. 135–40.
48 Watson, *Enduring the Great War*, pp. 85–92.
49 IWM, Mohan, 'My War Diary', p. 73.
50 D. Winter, *Death's Men: Soldiers of the Great War* (London: Penguin Books, 1979), p. 119.
51 IWM, Mohan, 'My War Diary', pp. 74–5; Holmes, *Tommy*, p. 411.
52 Seal, *The Soldiers' Press*, p. 156.
53 Private Papers of H. L. Adams, Documents.4300, Henry Lawrence Adams, 'My Life in the Army', n.d., p. 8.
54 Charles Edmonds (pseudonym), *A Subaltern's War: A Memoir of the Great War* (London: Peter Davies, 1929), pp. 161–2.
55 IWM, Private Papers of the Reverend J. M. Antsey, Documents.24295, diary entry under 12 June 1917.
56 Bird, *And We Go On*, p. 6.
57 *Ibid.*
58 Bird is vague on when this happened exactly but the unit's war diaries indicate that the action Bird describes took place on 24 March 1917. The date is also confirmed by Bird's mention of Lieutenant Stewart's death, which was also recorded in the unit diary (Library and Archives Canada [hereafter LAC], RG9-III-D-3, vol. 4938, f. 433, pt. 1, War Diary of 42nd Canadian Battalion, 3rd Canadian Division, Volume 18, 1 March to 31 March 1917, pp. 4–5).
59 Bird, *And We Go On*, pp. 33–4, 60.
60 *Ibid.*, pp. 81, 91. The full names of Arthur, Freddy, Herman, Ira, Mickey and Melville are identified in a glossary in Bird's second memoir, *Ghosts Have Warm Hands*. Arthur Silas Burke was killed on 24 March 1917. Herman Black and Frederick Gilbert Westcott were killed during the attack on Vimy Ridge on 9 April 1917. Ira Garnet Black was killed on 2 November 1917, the same day as Melville McKay Bailey.

Daniel 'Mickey' McGillivray was killed on 17 November 1917. The Sam referred to by Bird cannot be identified. See Will R. Bird, *Ghosts Have Warm Hands* (Ottawa, ON: CEF Books, 1968), pp. 178–82.
61 Bird, *And We Go On*, p. 67.
62 David Cairns (ed.), *The Army and Religion: An Enquiry and Its Bearing upon the Religious Life of the Nation* (London: Macmillan, 1919), p. 160.
63 *Ibid.*
64 IWM, Johnston, 'The Diary of a Rifleman', p. 31.
65 IWM, Private Papers of J. K. Best, Documents.102987, John Kenneth Best, France 1916, p. 6.
66 IWM, Bere, Letters from an Army Chaplain, p. 64; Jonathan H. Ebel, *Faith in the Fight: Religion and the American Soldier in the Great War* (Princeton, NJ: Princeton University Press, 2010), pp. 64–8.
67 Ebel, *Faith in the Fight*, pp. 54–75.
68 IWM, Private Papers of C. T. Newman, Documents.12494, Cyril Thomas Newman, note from his diary, p. 324.
69 IWM, letter from C. T. Newman to Winifred, 4 July 1916, p. 327.
70 Madigan, *Faith Under Fire*, pp. 180–2.
71 IWM, Johnston, 'The Diary of a Rifleman', p. 111.
72 Mohan, 'My War Diary', IWM, p. 116.
73 IWM, Adams, 'Life in the Army', p. 9.
74 Snape, *God and the British Soldier*, pp. 28–30.
75 A. M. Burrage (published as 'Ex-Private'), *War Is War* (Barnsley: Pen & Sword, 1930), chapter 9, paragraphs 54–5, Kindle.
76 LAC, Sir Archibald Cameron MacDonell Collection, R1894-0-6-E, A. E. Kennedy-Carefoot, unpublished biography of Sir Archibald Cameron MacDonell, n.d. (circa 1940), p. 164. Thank you to Mark Humphries for drawing my attention to this story.
77 IWM, Sound Archive, 4271, an anonymous Canadian Private, interview by the BBC, 1963.
78 Burrage, *War Is War*, chap. 9, paragraph 54, Kindle.
79 'Wit from the Trenches', *The Switchboard*, 2 (1916), 2.
80 IWM, Mohan, 'My War Diary', p. 2.
81 Schweitzer shows a variety of religious beliefs at the front from atheism to the devout, providing examples for various points along this spectrum. See Schweitzer, *The Cross and the Trenches*, pp. 17–62, 195–246.
82 *Ibid.*, pp. 187–92. See also Snape, *God and the British Soldier*, pp. 45–57; Madigan, *Faith Under Fire*, pp. 183–96. *The Army and Religion* report noted an 'almost universal resort to prayer in time of danger' (Cairns (ed.), *The Army and Religion*, pp. 74, 166–8).

83 IWM, Railton, 24 September 1916, pp. 13–14.
84 IWM, Private Papers of M. P. G. Leonard, Documents.16268, Letter 63, 18 August 1916.
85 IWM, Private Papers of W. H. Loosley, Documents.11783, Sydney Henry Loosley, diary.
86 Burrage, *War Is War*, chap. 1, paragraph 15, Kindle.
87 Madigan, *Faith Under Fire*, pp. 181–2.
88 IWM, Private Papers of C. R. T. Evans, Documents.1645, letter from C. R. T. Evans to his mother, 12 December 1916.
89 IWM, letter from C. R. T. Evans to his mother, 28 December 1916.
90 *Ibid.*
91 IWM, Adams, 'Life in the Army', p. 1.
92 *Ibid.*, p. 4.
93 Siegfried Sassoon, *Siegfried Sassoon Diaries: 1915–1918*, Rupert Hart-Davis (ed.) (London: Faber & Faber, 1983), pp. 161–2; Mark Dollar, 'Ghost Imagery in the War Poems of Siegfried Sassoon', *War, Literature & the Arts*, 16:1–2 (2004), 241.
94 IWM, Mohan, 'My War Diary', p. 97.
95 *Ibid.*, p. 137.
96 IWM, Private Papers of Lieutenant W. B. St Leger MC, Documents.20504, Diary, 9 September 1917 to 9 December 1917, pp. 109–12.
97 IWM, St Leger, Diary, September to December 1917, pp. 97–8.
98 *Ibid.*, Diary, 8 December 1917 to 28 March 1918, pp. 99–101.
99 *Ibid.*, pp. 202, 208–9, 217–20.
100 Jay Winter, *Sites of Memory, Sites of Mourning: The Great War in European Cultural History*, Canto Edition (Cambridge: Cambridge University Press, 1998), p. 64.
101 Snape, *God and the British Soldier*, p. 39.
102 Cairns (ed.), *The Army and Religion*, pp. 19–20. This is clear from the report's separation of spiritualism from other heterodox beliefs such as fatalism and superstition.
103 Paddy Griffith, *Battle Tactics of the Western Front: The British Army's Art of Attack, 1916–18* (New Haven, CT: Yale University Press, 1994), pp. 153, 251–2, fn. 56.
104 British Library (hereafter BL), Western Manuscripts, Add MS52272, The Ghost Club Minutes: Report File Corresponding with Minute Books, No. IX, pp. 17, 37.
105 Nor were they the only ones with high rank who had an interest in these matters. Major J. F. C. Fuller was an avid occultist who wrote several books on the topic and was a disciple of Aleister Crowley before the war. See for example J. F. C. Fuller, *The Star in The West: A*

Critical Essay Upon the Works of Aleister Crowley (London: Walter Scott Publishing Co., 1907).

106 Winter, *Sites of Memory, Sites of Mourning*, p. 65; Tim Cook, 'Grave Beliefs: Stories of the Supernatural and the Uncanny among Canada's Great War Trench Soldiers', *Journal of Military History*, 77 (2013), 4–5.

107 For example, Second Lieutenant Edward Saxelby Pearce of the Worcestershire Regiment was a friend of Oliver Lodge's secretary, Nea Walker. According to Walker, Pearce read *Raymond* and became interested in Nea's automatic writing while on leave, after his cousin died at the front. See CUL, MS SPR34, 24/9, Nea Walker, E. W. + N. W., Sitting with Mrs Leonard at Datchet, 19 April 1918, pp. 9, 16. A frequent reader of *Light* also sent the journal messages from his séances while on leave. See M. E., 'The Direct Voice: A Soldier's Notes of a Recent Séance', *Light*, 38:1945 (1918), 127. For the example of Cleland, see 'Roll of Honour', *The Two Worlds*, 28:1466 (1915), 640.

108 Chambers, 'Fighting Chance', pp. 116–17; IWM, Smedley, 4–5 February 1917.

109 'Wise and Otherwise', *RMR Growler*, 1:1 (1916), 3. Thank you to Brittany Dunn for sharing this example.

110 IWM, Private Papers of Reverend J. M. S. Walker, Documents.11462, Rev. John Michael Stanhope Walker, 'Letters Written from France by an Army Chaplain at a Casualty Clearing Station in 1915–16', M. L. Walker (ed.) (1971), p. 12.

111 'Report of the Council for the Year 1914', *JSPR*, 17:316 (1915), 19–28; 'The Spiritualists' National Union, LTD. A Report of the Proceedings of the Thirteenth Annual General Meeting Held in the Windsor Room, Metropole Hull, on Saturday July 3rd, 1915', *The Two Worlds*, 28:1444 (1915), 359.

112 'Spiritualist Literature at the Front: The S.N.U. Send 7,000 Pamphlets', *The Two Worlds* 28:1424 (1915), 102.

113 'The Roll of Honour', *The Two Worlds*, 29:1485 (1916), 203.

114 'A Commendation from the Front', *The Two Worlds*, 28:1461 (1915), 570.

115 A roll of honour plaque was unveiled at the Armley Theaker-lane Spiritualist Church in May 1916 listing thirty-three names of members who were serving in the war. This church no longer exists and it is unclear what happened to the roll. See 'Spiritualists in the War: A Roll of Honour for Twenty-Six Lyceums Unveiled at Armley', *The Two Worlds*, 29:1486 (1916), 209. Other similar plaques do still exist, for example that of the Hebden Bridge's Spiritualist Church. See IWM, War Memorials Register 2847, Hebden Bridge Association of Spiritualist (and Lyceum) Church, Imperial War Museum, accessed 24 October 2021, www.iwm.org.uk/memorials/item/memorial/2847. The

Roll of Honour at the Sowerby Bridge spiritualist church has also survived. See Gerald O'Hara, *Dead Men's Embers* (York: Saturday Night Press, 2006), p. 208.

116 The first list of names made its appearance in October 1914. See 'Roll of Honour', *The Two Worlds*, 27:1407 (1914), 538.
117 'The Roll of Honour', *The Two Worlds*, 29:1479 (1916), 140; 'The Roll of Honour', *The Two Worlds*, 29:1498 (1916), 342.
118 'Our Soldier Readers', *The Two Worlds*, 28:1458 (1915), 530–1.
119 'The Roll of Honour', *The Two Worlds*, 28:1435 (1915), 245.
120 'Roll of Honour', *The Two Worlds*, 29:1489 (1916), 249.
121 Davies, *A Supernatural War*, p. 82.
122 'The Roll of Honour', *The Two Worlds*, 28:1436 (1915), 256.
123 J. T. Dillsen, 'Experiences and Reflections by a Soldier', *The Two Worlds*, 28:1443 (1915), 344–5.
124 S. Turner, 'Spirit Guidance on the Battlefield', *The Two Worlds*, 28:1448 (1915), 403.
125 Cairns (ed.), *The Army and Religion*, p. 20.
126 'The Roll of Honour', *The Two Worlds*, 28:1443 (1915), 349.
127 Colley's story also appears in Leo Ruickbie, *Angels in the Trenches: Spiritualism, Superstition and the Supernatural during the First World War* (London: Robinson, 2019), pp. 105–6; BL, The Ghost Club Minutes, Volume VII, pp. 187–8.
128 A. Titmass, 'My First Experience of Trench Warfare', *The Two Worlds*, 28:1451 (1915), 438–9.
129 A. Perfect, 'Letters from the Front', *The Two Worlds*, 28:1418 (1915), 32.
130 C. V. T., 'Psychic Influences on the Battle-Field', *Light*, 36:1866 (1916), 333.
131 Cook, 'Grave Beliefs', 4–5.
132 IWM, St Leger, Diary, December 1917 to March 1918, p. 187.
133 S. Turner, 'Spirit Guidance on the Battlefield', *The Two Worlds*, 28:1448 (1915), 403.
134 *Ibid*.
135 Cook, 'Grave Beliefs', 5–6.
136 'The Roll of Honour', *The Two Worlds*, 29:1482 (1916), 164; Cairns (ed.), *Army and Religion Report*, p. 20.
137 Chaplains complained about low attendances at their voluntary services (Madigan, *Faith in the Fight*, pp. 90–2, 107–8). Part of this was contempt for clerical religion amongst the ranks but it was also true that religious soldiers complained about the lack of time for religious observance. As Mohan noted, free time on Sunday was like 'an oasis in the desert' (IWM, Mohan, 'My War Diary', p. 18).
138 William Kingshott of the HMS *Cordelia* described two séances on 18 and 19 June. During the former, he briefly saw a spirit and the next

night 'our spirit friends were with us in force. Messages were received and description of spirit friends given'. The medium was identified only as 'Rooke'. See 'The Roll of Honour', *The Two Worlds*, 29:1496 (1916), 323 and 'The Roll of Honour', *The Two Worlds*, 29:1498 (1916), 342.

139 Beth Robertson, *Science of the Séance: Transnational Network and Gendered Bodies in the Study of Psychic Phenomena, 1918–40* (Vancouver, BC: The University of British Columbia Press, 2016), pp. 10–17; Alex Owen, *The Darkened Room: Women, Power, and Spiritualism in Late Victorian England* (Chicago, IL: University of Chicago Press, 1989), pp. 14–15.

140 Aimée Fox, *Learning to Fight: Military Innovation and Change in the British Army, 1914–1918* (Cambridge: Cambridge University Press, 2017), pp. 22–3.

141 Schweitzer, *The Cross and the Trenches*, pp. 97–105.

142 IWM, Smedley, 19 February 1917.

143 'The Roll of Honour', *The Two Worlds*, 28:1464 (1915), 608.

144 LAC, RG 150, Accession 1992–93/166, Box 2801 – 39, Harold Earith, CEF Personnel File, Attestation Paper.

145 A. Titmass, 'From the Trenches', *The Two Worlds*, 28:1485 (1916), 208.

146 William Gair, 'From the Trenches', *The Two Worlds*, 29:1474 (1916), 69.

147 Brockington appears to have communicated with Oliver Lodge and attended séances with Gladys Osbourne Leonard sometime between the fall of 1916 and early 1917. Included in his diary are not only Lodge's contact information but also an address for a 'Mrs Leonard'. That this is the well-known medium is confirmed by the address listed, which was included in her advertisements in *Light*. Both state the address as '41 Clifton Gardens, Maida Vale'. See IWM, Private Papers of A. A. Brockington, Documents.4648, Alfred Allen Brockington, Diary, and 'The Personal Investigation of Spiritualism', *Light*, 36:1853 (1916), p. v.

148 IWM, Private Papers of Major F. St. J. Steadman DPH MRCS LRCP Lond. LDSRCS ENG, Documents.18927, Frank Steadman, 'My Darling Grace: Letters from an Army Doctor during the Great War' (unpublished transcription of his letters), Simon Miller (ed.), pp. 10, 21, 30, 41, 45.

149 'The Roll of Honour', *The Two Worlds*, 28:1425 (1915), 115.

150 IWM, Brockington, Diary.

151 Madigan, *Faith Under Fire*, pp. 7, 17, 91–2, 193.

152 IWM, Railton, 30 August 1916, p. 10.

153 IWM, Railton, 4 January 1917, p. 23; Madigan, *Faith in the Fight*, p. 179.
154 IWM, Railton, 12 March 1917, p. 33.
155 IWM, Private Papers of T. H. Davies, Documents.12740, Reverend Dr T. H. Davies, 'A War Diary' (unpublished transcription), Geoffrey and Kay (eds) (his grandchildren) (July 2002), pp. 10–11.
156 IWM, Railton, 14 January 1917 and 12 March 1917, pp. 23, 33; Madigan, *Faith Under Fire*, p. 179.
157 IWM, Private Papers of J. M. Poucher, Documents.6995, JMP2, John Mellor Poucher, diary entry under 5 June 1917.
158 Rene Kollar, *Searching for Raymond: Anglicanism, Spiritualism, and Bereavement between the Two World Wars* (Lanham, MD: Lexington Books, 2000), p. 166.
159 Janet Oppenheim, *The Other World: Spiritualism and Psychical Research in England, 1850–1914* (Cambridge: Cambridge University Press, 1988), pp. 68–71.
160 Georgina Byrne, October 2012, 'Owen, George Vale (1869–1931) Church of England Clergyman and Spiritualist Writer', *Oxford Dictionary of National Biography*, accessed October 2018, www.oxforddnb.com.libproxy.wlu.ca/view/10.1093/ref:odnb/9780198614128.001.0001/odnb-9780198614128-e-103376.
161 John R. W. Stott, *The Cross of Christ* (Downers Grove, IL: Inter Varsity Press, 1986), pp. 311–37.
162 Tim Cook, *The Secret History of Soldiers: How Canadians Survived the Great War* (Canada: Allen Lane, 2018), p. 10.
163 For more examples of supernatural and psychic phenomena reported from the battlefield see 'The Psychic Sense on the Battlefield: Visions and Premonitions at the Front', *Light*, 36:1832 (1916), 59; M. E., 'Conditions of Life in the Midst of Death: Wonderful Spiritual Protection in Times of Danger', *The International Psychic Gazette*, 41:4 (1917), 139–40; Edith K. Harper, 'Spirit Protection: A Verified Message', *The Occult Review*, 28:6 (1918), 334–6; Hereward Carrington, 'Psychic Phenomena Amidst the Warring Nations', *The Occult Review*, 21:4 (1915), 195–201.
164 'The Weirdest Stories of the War', *Pearson's Magazine*, 47:48 (1919), 190–4.
165 The Comrade in White first appeared in *Light* in June 1915. See 'The Friend of the Wounded', *Light*, 35:1795 (1915), 269. For a further examination of the Angel of Mons and the Comrade in White, including reactions from the spiritualist press see David Clarke, *The Angel of Mons: Phantom Soldiers and Ghostly Guardians* (Chichester: John Wiley & Sons, 2004).

166 IWM, Bere, p. 64.
167 *Light* also shared the example of a soldier being saved by a Bible in January 1915. See 'Strange Story from the Battle Field: The Adjutant and His Bible', *Light*, 35:1779 (1915), 80.
168 MacDonagh, 'Religious Emblems', 270; Ruickbie, *Angels in the Trenches*, p. 122. One Catholic padre observed, 'Sacred Heart badges were in constant demand among Catholics and frequently asked for by non-Catholics' (Plater, *Catholic Soldiers*, p. 27).
169 MacDonagh, 'Religious Emblems', 270–1.
170 See Forbes Phillips and R. Thurston Hopkins, *War and the Weird* (London: Simpkin Marshall, Hamilton, Kent & Co., 1916); Hereward Carrington, *Psychic Phenomena and the War*, New Edition (New York: American Universities Publishing Company, 1920); Rosa Stuart, *Dreams and Visions of the War* (London: C. Arthur Pearson Ltd., 1917); Phyllis Campbell, *Back of the Front* (London: George Newnes, 1915). See also Conan Doyle, *The History of Spiritualism*, Volume II (London and New York: Cassell & Company, 1926), pp. 235–6.
171 Carrington, *Psychic Phenomena*, pp. 154–5, 159.
172 Winter, *Sites of Memory, Sites of Mourning*, p. 67.
173 Phillips and Thurston Hopkins, *War and the Weird*, pp. 16–18.
174 'The Weirdest Stories of the War', 190.
175 Cook, 'Grave Beliefs', 3. Cook is one of the few historians to address Bird's ghostly encounter. His article was written before the reprint of Bird's original memoir, *And We Go On*, in 2014. Cook therefore examines Bird's experiences from *Ghosts Have Warm Hands*.
176 Bird, *And We Go On*, pp. 4–5. For an analysis of the differences between the two memoirs, see Monique Dumontet, '"Lest We Forget": Canadian Combatant Narratives of the Great War', unpublished PhD dissertation (University of Manitoba, 2010), pp. 338–48. See also the excellent preface and afterward by David Williams in *And We Go On*, pp. vii–xxi, 232–40.
177 Bird, *And We Go On*, pp. 30, 86–8, 143–4.
178 Williams in Bird, *And We Go On*, pp. xxviii–xxxi.
179 Bird, *And We Go On*, pp. 12, 97.
180 Carrington, *Psychic Phenomena*, pp. 31–100.
181 Bird, *Ghosts Have Warm Hands*, p. 27.
182 Ian McKay and Robert Bates, *The Province of History: The Making of the Public Past in Twentieth-Century Nova Scotia* (Montreal and Kingston, QC: McGill-Queen's University Press, 2010), pp. 132–5, 149–52.
183 LAC, RG 150, Accession 1992–93/166, Box 774 – 2, Ira Garnet Black, CEF Personnel File, Casualty Form – Active Service.

3

A war of sensation: telepathy, crisis apparitions and the moment of death on the home front

Marian M. Macklin was anxious after the Germans launched their major offensive in the spring of 1918. She knew her son David was somewhere near Arras and news of a German breakthrough in this region had reached the home front on 26 March.[1] The next day, Marian was in and out of sleep when she had a strange experience. While lying in bed she could hear footsteps along the veranda outside her bedroom window. Assuming it was David, she hurried outside to greet him, although she never physically left her bed. There she could see a figure dressed in khaki and wearing a tin helmet. 'Oh, David boy, you have never disgraced your officer's uniform and had to go back to Tommy's clothes', she thought to herself. The figure quickly vanished but Marian was certain it was her son. When she awoke the following morning, she was distracted by the waking dream. 'It was so vivid that it haunted me', she explained to the SPR, and she felt compelled to share the experience with her sister that day.[2]

On 3 April a telegram arrived announcing that David had been killed on 27 March. The news was no surprise to Marian, as she believed her vision was her son's way of fulfilling a pledge made earlier that year. The last time the two had seen each other was in January while David was on leave. Before he returned to France, his mother had told him, 'if what we can't help thinking about should happen, will you try to come to me?' As Marian stated in her correspondence with psychical researchers, 'I believe if it were in his power that he would have willed to come to me at the time of his death.' The SPR concluded that the incident was likely a telepathic message sent by David in his final moments to inform Marian of his death.[3] By 1918 hundreds of thousands of Britons had received a telegram notifying them of their loved one's passing, but Marian Macklin could claim to be the recipient of something far more immediate and intimate: a message sent from one mind to another.

During the Great War, people across the British Empire reported similar visions. While still in Saskatchewan working on the harvest, Will R. Bird saw the ghost of his brother Steve the day he went missing.[4] So did Harold Owen, the brother of the famous poet, Wilfred Owen. Harold was suffering from malaria onboard the HMS *Astraea* off the coast of Africa in November 1918 when he saw Wilfred. There he was in the ship's cabin, sitting in Harold's chair and distinctly out of place in his muddied khaki uniform, only to vanish as Harold's attention was diverted. Sick and exhausted, Harold went to sleep wondering if it was a dream or hallucination. When he awoke, he 'knew with absolute certainty that Wilfred was dead'.[5] The experiences of Bird and Owen were prototypical 'crisis apparitions' – in which an individual's ghost spontaneously appears to someone at a distance coinciding with a moment of crisis such as injury or death. The SPR's 1894 census on hallucinations estimated that approximately 10 per cent of the British population had gone through a similar experience at some point in their lives.[6]

Psychical researchers used crisis apparitions to construct their concept of telepathy. First coined in 1882, 'telepathy' arose out of a fascination with the unconscious alongside phenomena as diverse as mesmerism, hysteria, hypnotism, spiritualism, multiple personalities and psychoanalysis.[7] The recesses of the mind represented an undiscovered country ripe for imaginative speculation and experimentation. The SPR was founded to investigate a host of phenomena, but its greatest contribution to the new sciences of the mind was its telepathic project. British psychical researchers sought to validate their theories within psychology by relocating the ghost to the unconscious while simultaneously maintaining its mystical qualities as the product of a mysterious sympathy between minds.

Telepathy was not simply the invention of a handful of writers and theorists. It emerged to explain the curious explosion of crisis apparitions that were reported across the British Empire. As communities spread to the furthest reaches of the globe, Britons found new ways to express the intimacy and communal experiences of death. The Great War did not create the crisis apparition, but the conditions of a total and global conflict provided fertile ground from which they could emerge *en masse* within a short period of time. Crisis apparitions manifested within the emotional and communication networks that sustained affection and information between soldiers and their families. They mediated between certainty and uncertainty and intimacy and remoteness, providing a reassurance that in his last moments, the soldier was able to say goodbye.

What the SPR offered to those experiencing crisis apparitions was the veneer of scientific legitimacy and validation. Harold Owen recognised that it was possible he mistook a dream for a vision that had taken place before he fell asleep, but he could not shake 'the certainty of my conviction of Wilfred's death'. As he explained, it 'amounted ... to absolute knowledge ... I could no longer question it ... what I found impossible to explain was this self-existent awareness of mine'.[8] The telepathic hypothesis allowed for these subjective certainties and emotional experiences occurring in liminal states of consciousness to be framed as scientific facts. Although the SPR had intended to use telepathy to psychologise the ghost, many of those who experienced crisis apparitions during the war ultimately turned to spiritualism. The secular scientific concept of telepathy could not account for the haunting memories of the dead. The emotions of love and affection that informed visceral telepathic experiences continued to be felt long after the initial loss. Crisis apparitions were a symptom of affection both in life and after death.

Before telepathy

The SPR's concept of telepathy owes its roots to the development of animal magnetism and mesmerism, the belief that a magnetic fluid flows within bodies and minds and can be subject to manipulation by an external agent.[9] In nineteenth-century Britain, the most famous mesmerist was the physician John Elliotson who induced artificial somnambulism on his patients to demonstrate various abnormal behaviours known as the 'higher phenomena' of mesmerism. By controlling their wills through the magnetic fluid, Elliotson's subjects mimicked his movements outside his field of vision and shared his sense of taste, touch and smell.[10] More curiously, some demonstrated a 'sixth sense' by diagnosing ailments in other patients, predicting their evolution and prescribing the necessary treatments.[11] Mesmerism soon became a public spectacle. Stage performers placed ammonia under subjects' noses or struck their extremities as they remained completely still. Others subjects recited texts blindfolded or spoke a mesmerist's thoughts.[12] Public crowds were fascinated and puzzled by these altered states of consciousness as they raised the possibility of the fusion of minds, access to a higher state of sensation and 'an absence of being'.[13]

The popularity of mesmerism, and subsequently spiritualism, resulted in debates about the nature of the unconscious. Building upon the work of the physiologist Marshall Hall, William Benjamin Carpenter contended in the early 1850s that ideas could produce unintentional and automatic actions in what he called 'ideomotor action'.[14] Concerning table rapping, for example, Carpenter argued that laying hands on a table produced an expectation that it should move. The anticipation of movement formed an idea that created an automatic reflex in the muscles and caused the table to move without the sitter's conscious intent. According to Carpenter, ideomotor action was possible when the will was temporarily diminished by distraction or trance.[15]

The perceived value of trance to the study of the mind kept it alive in science even as mesmerism came under scrutiny and ridicule. In the 1840s, Scottish surgeon James Braid drew a scientific boundary around the unconscious by arguing that it was possible to physiologically produce deep trance via fixed attention, regulated breathing and relaxation of the muscles. In the 1850s he adopted a psychological approach, believing that since mental faculties could have physical counterparts, such as tears caused by grief, fixed ideas may also have a powerful influence. He used this new 'hypnotism' therapeutically to excite or depress unconscious 'dominant ideas' and evoke healthier physiological conditions.[16]

By the latter half of the nineteenth century, hypnotism was practised by two schools of French neurologists: the Salpêtrière school associated with Jean Martin-Charcot and the Nancy school of Hippolyte Bernheim. Charcot was concerned with diagnosis, arguing that the ability to become hypnotised was a symptom of hysteria. According to Charcot, traumatic events created a state similar to hypnotism in hysterics, thus allowing for unconscious suggestions to manifest physically, as in hysterical paralysis (a form of paralysis with no physical cause).[17] Bernheim, on the contrary, believed hypnotism was a latent universal ability and used it for therapeutic purposes. He eventually discovered that unconscious psychoneuroses could be removed through conversation without any need for hypnotism. Bernheim's new psychotherapy spread amongst neurologists looking to treat middle-class patients suffering from nervous disorders, including a young Sigmund Freud.[18]

The path from hypnotism to telepathy began in 1876 when William Barrett presented a paper on his hypnotic experiments at a meeting of the British Association for the Advancement of Science (BAAS). Barrett observed that 'sensations ... ideas or emotions occurring in the operator appeared to be reproduced in the subject without the intervention of any sign, or visible or audible communication'. Barrett distinguished his findings from the higher phenomena common to mesmerism by qualifying that his subjects could only read closed books if Barrett himself was familiar with the contents. Such cases were not simply examples of heightened senses but of a communication of thoughts.[19]

After the establishment of the SPR in 1882, two of its founding members, Edmund Gurney and Frederic Myers, expanded upon Barrett's research. In 1886, Myers visited France where he witnessed the work of French hypnotists such as Bernheim and Charcot and conducted hypnotic experiments with the neurologist Pierre Janet.[20] Janet's research involved the study of double personalities. His patients, including mediums, displayed a secondary personality that was accessible through hypnosis and of whom the normal waking consciousness was unaware.[21] In one experiment, Janet gave his patient Lucie five blank cards, two of which were marked. While under hypnosis, he suggested that she would be unable to see the marked cards. When she awoke, she had no memory of the conversation and could only see the three blank cards. The test presented a conundrum. Lucie had to identify specific cards before she could complete the action of not seeing them. Then she had to forget that she saw the marked cards in the first place. How to account for this paradox? After interrogating Lucie's double personality Adrienne, the latter explained that she saw the marked cards so that Lucie could not. Janet argued that it was incorrect to associate certain mental faculties with the 'unconscious' since Lucie's actions under hypnotic suggestion occurred thanks to the dissociated consciousness of her double. He concluded that the mind had a 'subconscious' of which the waking self remained unaware.[22]

British readers were first introduced to Janet within the pages of the SPR's *Proceedings* in 1886. Janet would not appear in *The Journal of Mental Science* until 1892. Myers was also the first to bring Sigmund Freud and Josef Breuer to British attention a year later.[23] Psychical researchers were therefore early proponents of a new dynamic psychiatry while British psychiatry remained focused on the psycho-physiology of the asylums. That these new sciences of the mind were still in their infancy is evident by the SPR's various influences. Myers, a classicist by training, pointed to the work of Wilhelm Wundt as an example that he wished to emulate in treating 'human thought and sensation as definite and measurable things'.[24] Charcot, Bernheim and Janet were used as illustrations of how to probe those faculties.[25] For their part, Myers and Gurney sought to establish a new science of the psyche that incorporated empirical methods but addressed metaphysical questions that were previously reserved for philosophers and theologians.[26] Although they claimed that they were probing natural law, the faculties they were examining were unlikely to be explicable through matter, hence the term 'supernormal'. It was time for a new science that would question a 'materialistic synthesis of human experience' by revealing the traces of a 'psychical element in man'.[27] The unconscious was the most promising object of study for Myers and Gurney's project, and it would lead them to the invention of telepathy.

Inventing telepathy

Myers and Gurney's telepathy was founded upon two lines of evidence. First were experiments in 'thought-transference'.[28] In April 1882, 382 trials were conducted with a clergyman, Andrew Macreight Creery, and his six children. Each trial ran as follows: one child was selected at random to be the 'percipient' of a telepathic message. The other children – the 'agents' of the message – were shown a playing card, a word or a number. The question was whether or not the percipient could accurately guess the content of the card in question. Barrett, Myers and Gurney concluded that the number of correct answers exceeded chance.[29]

The second line of evidence came from the public. The SPR requested documentation of extraordinary phenomena and received a massive collection of experiences in return, including 10,000 letters in 1883 alone.[30] They discovered what historians can observe as well, that 'by the beginning of the twentieth century there will scarcely be a family that does not have some legend of this sort: a terrible dream that comes at a certain time of night, when, it is later learned, a loved one died or almost died'.[31] Out of a sample of two thousand depositions, more than half were 'narratives of appearances or other impressions coincident either with the death of the person seen or with some critical moment in his life-history'.[32] Britons, it seemed, were prone to witnessing a particular type of ghost.

In 1886 Myers, Gurney and Frank Podmore provided their answer for the crisis apparition phenomena. In the two-volume *Phantasms of the Living*, they grouped thought-transference and crisis apparitions under the term telepathy, defined as 'the ability of one mind to impress or to be impressed by another mind otherwise than through the recognised channels of sense'.[33] Experiments in thought-transference demonstrated telepathy in a controlled scientific setting but most of the book was devoted to elaborating on the concept of 'phantasms of the living'. According to Myers and Gurney, this form of telepathy involves the transmission of an idea or 'impression' by an 'agent' that is received by the unconscious of the 'percipient'. The impression is cerebrally constructed into a sensory experience, such as a hallucination, using the percipient's memories. This transition mostly occurs in moments of liminal conscious states such as waking dreaming, and is triggered by the emotionally charged nature of the message.[34] It was reasoned that the message lingered in the subconscious of the individual until the right conditions emerged (if at all).[35]

A First World War case exemplifies the explanatory power of Gurney and Meyer's telepathy. Lieutenant G. E. W. Bridge of the Durham Light Infantry was wounded at the front on 24 July 1916 at 3.30 p.m. Sometime between 1 and 2 a.m. his mother-in-law, Mrs S. Jones, awoke in Enfield to see the figure of a small child with bandages across his neck and chin. The face resembled a photograph of her son-in-law that was taken when he was about three years old. Days later, the War Office informed her daughter that her husband was injured by shrapnel along his neck and chin. Jones and Lieutenant Bridge had discussed psychical research in the past, so it was reasoned that she was the percipient of his telepathic message because of their sympathetic psychic relationship. What Jones could not understand was why he appeared as a child. The SPR concluded the following: at 3.30 p.m., Bridge's subconscious telepathically conveyed to his mother-in-law that he was injured in the face. This message came to Jones's conscious awareness as she awoke from sleep. Two memories formed the nature of the image. When Jones's daughter was a child, she had an operation requiring bandages in a similar location. The nature of the message triggered this memory leading her to see Bridge as a child, whose likeness was formed according to his childhood photograph.[36]

Cases such as Enfield's were one indication to the SPR that phantasms of the living were possible. Since the crisis sometimes involved injury rather than death, one could not say that they were ghosts in the traditional sense. 'Phantasms of the dead' were treated far more sceptically. Gurney and the first president of the SPR, Henry Sidgwick, both objected to the idea but Myers was more sympathetic.[37] In the 1890s he began to develop his concept of the subliminal self.[38] In 1903, his posthumous two-volume magnum opus *Human Personality and Its Survival of Bodily Death* synthesised hysteria, dreams, hypnotism, thought transference, trance mediumship, automatic writing and phantasms of the living and dead. Drawing upon William James's concept of consciousness, Myers rejected the notion that mental faculties could ever be 'unconscious', though consciousness could be split into what James identified as separate 'streams of thought'.[39] Myers labelled the consciousness of everyday experience the 'supraliminal self', which had evolved in a terrestrial environment according to natural selection.[40] Below the threshold of consciousness existed the 'subliminal self', which although outside ordinary perceptions, occasionally rushed forth into the supraliminal, especially when the regular senses were dulled during trance or sleep.[41]

Myers noted that psychology had recognised that the self was fragmented and unstable, but he contended that this could be reconciled with a unifying Self (or soul), which originated and resided in a spiritual environment.[42] According to Myers, hysteria was caused by the loss of control of certain regular perceptions that had erroneously become submerged within the subliminal self. Examples included the hysterical paralyses of Charcot's patients, the double personalities of Janet and the otherwise stable patients of Breuer and Freud. Intensified emotions could disintegrate the personality, but they could also be reintegrated through hypnotism and psychotherapy. Since Janet believed hysteria was caused by traumatic memories, his method was to replace them with manufactured positive memories through suggestion.[43] Disintegration did not mean the unifying self was lost, and it could be reversed through hypnosis, which acted as a channel for the subliminal to communicate with the supraliminal.[44] For Myers, the implication was that if 'the Ego can and does survive ... the minor disintegration which affect it during earth-life', then so too might it survive 'the crowning disintegration of bodily death'.[45]

Myers contended that consciousness originated from a primordial spiritual germ – the source of all vitality – with the supraliminal and the subliminal representing different streams. Consciousness manifested along a spectrum from the simple to the more complex. On one end of the spectrum were automatic organic bodily functions such as the respiratory system, but on the other end were supernormal phenomena, which signified the evolutionary potential of humanity to access higher states of consciousness.[46] Since the supraliminal self was a sensory stream of consciousness as part of a greater unifying spiritual Self, whatever existed beyond bodily death was still a 'mind' with its own stream of consciousness.

For Myers, telepathy represented the universal mode of communication between these different states of consciousness, whether it was between two incarnate minds or an incarnate mind to a discarnate one:

> A communication ... from a departed person to a person on earth is a communication from a mind in one state of existence to a mind in a very different state of existence. And it is, moreover, a communication from one mind to another which passes through some channel other than the ordinary channels of sense, since on one side ... no material sense-organs exist.[47]

The subliminal self, not bound by the limits of earthly physical existence, acted as the channel, receiving telepathic impressions and sending them to the supraliminal. Because the latter was terrestrial, these impressions needed to be presented as hallucinations or dreams, or in the case of genuine mediumship, sensory and mental automatisms (as in Carpenter's ideomotor action).

Myers speculated on the mechanism for telepathy in his attempts to unify science and spirituality. If certain human faculties were not the product of natural selection, this might explain telepathy's underlying force. Myers raised the possibility that love was a transcendental faculty of the human spirit. 'Love is a kind of exalted, but unspecialised telepathy', he wrote, 'the simplest and most universal expression of that mutual gravitation or kinship of spirits which is the foundation of telepathic law'.[48] Not only could the mind survive the traumatic disintegration of the body, but the force of love could transcend distance and allow departed minds to invade one another's consciousness.

Myers's reconciliation of telepathy with the survival of personality was part of a growing acceptance of the spiritual within the SPR. The society's initially hostile relationship with spiritualists gradually diminished after the deaths of Gurney and Sidgwick in 1888 and 1900, respectively.[49] Still, Myers's synthesis did come with stipulations, including his caution that standard telepathy should be used as an explanation before resorting to the spiritual. His merging of spiritualism and telepathy made it difficult to discern, for example, if a medium's messages were the result of a discarnate personality or were from the mediums' or sitters' subliminal selves.[50] Endless ink was spilt by psychical researchers in the following decades debating these very questions. Only very rarely did they ever pause to consider the possibility that telepathy had not been adequately proven by the SPR's first generation. War-related crisis apparitions would therefore not be used as concrete proof of telepathy, but instead push psychical researchers more towards spiritualist interpretations.

An emotional history of telepathy

Any study that uses crisis apparitions as its source must address issues of interpretation and the reliability of the reported experiences. After the publication of *Phantasms of the Living*, the SPR was criticised for its reliance on witness testimony. It is clear that class prejudices clouded psychical researchers' judgement. Reports coming from within their social circles were considered to be genuine and trustworthy. The Reverend Creery was described as 'a clergyman of unblemished character, and whose integrity has, it so happens, been exceptionally tested'.[51] The Creery children were later caught by psychical researchers communicating with each other in code and admitted to cheating in past trials.[52]

Psychical researchers attempted to allay concerns over testimony by gathering as much corroborating evidence as possible. For a vision to be published by the SPR, it needed to have been recorded or communicated to another witness prior to the recipient receiving news of the death or injury of the agent. However, in his review of *Phantasms of the Living*, Scottish lawyer A. Taylor Innes observed that the authors could not provide a single letter unambiguously documenting an apparition within that proper timeframe.[53] Others, like the American philosopher and mathematician Charles S. Peirce argued that, even if these letters existed, crisis apparitions could arise purely from chance. As Peirce observed, we are often aware of a loved one's age, health and circumstances, and may harbour certain unconscious anxieties about their well-being. Crisis apparitions would correlate with those people in our lives most likely to die.[54] Gurney had incorporated cutting-edge probability statistics to help prove his case, but Peirce found his math wanting.[55] According to Peirce, it would take 30,000 hallucinations (not trillions as Gurney claimed) to produce by chance the thirty-one most remarkable cases presented by the SPR. Peirce contended that this was possible in a population of only two million.[56]

The value of crisis apparitions therefore lies not in their proof for or against telepathy, but instead as windows into the emotional lives of late nineteenth- and early twentieth-century Britons. Both proponents and critics of telepathy recognised that these were emotional experiences involving feelings of love, affection, anxiety, loss and grief. It was the precise expression and meaning of these emotions that were debated and which therefore grounds them within a specific time and place. Writing an emotional history of telepathy involves appreciating how crisis apparitions were constructed, narrated and comprehended (including as telepathic experiences) but also the contexts from which the experiences emerged – in an empire of dreaming, feeling and dying subjects communicating with one another across a zone of space that was simultaneously growing due to imperial expansion and shrinking thanks to efficient postal services and wireless communications. It is no wonder that the term chosen to describe a cluster of Britons' emotional experiences at the turn of the century, *telepathy*, literally meant 'distant feeling'. Myers's and Gurney's telepathy was not just a theory to be proven right or wrong but a historically specific description of how people felt.

An emotional history of crisis apparitions is particularly valuable to the historian of the Great War because it offers us a means of integrating the battlefields and home fronts, not as separate spheres requiring different methodologies to be studied in isolation but as part of a coherent whole with a shared emotional space.[57] That wartime crisis apparitions were so numerous and often led to an interest in spiritualism indicates a vibrant emotional network between firing line and home front that maintained personal relationships.[58] Postwar grief does not spring from a vacuum and needs to be contextualised within the moments leading to that grief. As the historian Martha Hanna explains, we need to consider 'how the bonds of affection that made loss so painful were sustained prior to death in the face of extended absence'.[59] Letters were particularly important in this regard. As one father communicated to his son, 'Write soon/write long/write often/+ then the distance + time will seem shorter.'[60] By April 1917, the British Army was sending nearly nine million letters home every week.[61] Many soldiers were like Alf Arnold of the RAMC, who considered letters to be 'worth many times their weight in gold'. He read them 'over and over again', as they served as comforting reminders that he was in his family's thoughts. As he expressed in August 1917, 'while I am writing this, I know you are thinking of me'.[62] That this was true for many families is evident in the number of parcels and letters sent from home. By 1917 the home front had shipped 114 million parcels and was sending 8.15 million letters every week to the Western Front alone.[63]

For those on the home front, letters helped alleviate anxiety, at least momentarily, and on the battlefields, they enriched a soldier's morale. Nevertheless, the link between the two fronts was always mediated, presenting contradictions. Letters sustained relationships and served as outlets of emotions but they also represented separation. If ingoing and outgoing mail were delayed, the absence of a letter could summon horrible thoughts. The British postal service only took three days to send letters to the front and six days to the British Isles, but during battles or movement, this process could be delayed significantly.[64] In Dominions such as South Africa, Canada and Australia, the process took weeks, slowing down the pace of letter writing from a daily activity in the British case to a weekly one for Canadians.[65] Those on the home front read about events in newspapers only to receive letters dated days or weeks before. A sense of time between home front and battlefield was therefore out of sync. To compensate, soldiers and their loved ones relied on more subjective feelings of affection. As one mother wrote to her son in the summer of 1916, 'I pray that what has now sustained you, may never fail you in your hour of need. I do not think it will, since you are a son of deep love + you must always feel that love stretching out to you, across the barriers of time + distance.'[66]

Dreams were another part of this culture of affection. SPR cases confirm others' observations that families and soldiers often dreamt about one another, recorded their dreams and shared them in correspondence.[67] Dreams offered families an opportunity to share intimate emotions and feelings of loneliness, homesickness, love and anxiety. Arnold's mother often dreamt about his safety. In September 1916, while Arnold was on the Somme, he wrote to her, 'I am sorry to read about your disturbing dream, mother. Of course, a lot is due to your anxious thoughts.'[68] Arnold, meanwhile, often dreamt that he was back home with his family, even watching his sister in school.[69] Dreams could transport families to their respective fronts. In 1916, a nun at St Katharine's School in Wantage had 'a remarkably vivid dream' in which she was flying with her brother over the Western Front. 'In my dream my brother and I were whirling through the air at a terrific speed', she recalled, explaining how 'we raced faster and faster until ... my brother veered sharp to the right and I was thrown out of the machine'.[70] Contemporary studies on sleep deprivation have discovered that exhaustion can increase the intensity of our dreams. It is no wonder that both anxious loved ones and fighting soldiers reported such vivid dreams.[71] Crisis apparitions offer us a rare glimpse into an otherwise hidden dreamscape.

The vivid feelings associated with dreams distinguished them from letters and suffused them with mystical and spiritual qualities. After losing her son, Wilfrid, Constance Wayte suddenly stopped dreaming of her boy. Disturbed by this development, she asked her son's spirit during a séance to visit her in her dreams.[72] In some cases, people reported having reciprocal dreams. In 1915, the SPR received testimony from Marion Camus who claimed that on the night of 7 November 1914, she had a dream she was with her friend Dorothy Kerin treating wounded soldiers on the battlefield. Later that day, Dorothy visited Marion and informed her, 'I saw you last night on the battlefield. I often pray I may go there ... in order to be used to heal the wounded.' A few days later Dorothy received a letter from a soldier who explained that he felt Dorothy's presence when he was recently wounded.[73]

At the heart of the crisis apparition phenomenon was separation. As British communities spread to other continents, numerous cases sent to the SPR came from the peripheries of the empire.[74] The war accelerated on a grand scale this process of separation. How much did the dispersal of communities affect conventional death rituals? We know, for instance, that a number of middle- and upper-class Victorians desired a 'Good Death', in which they were surrounded by family on their deathbed and provided with the opportunity to prepare for final judgement. An obsession with preparing for the moment of death corresponded with the evangelical revival in Britain and the United States, which peaked in the 1870s but declined thereafter.[75] The periodisation of the Good Death does not align with the crisis apparition phenomena. Nor does it seem to have been important to the Victorian generation during the Great War. If it was, we should expect to see in condolence letters and mourning rituals, assurances that soldiers were conscious and aware of what was happening to them as they died, as was the case during the American Civil War.[76] The exact opposite occurs during the Great War where the bereaved were comforted by an assurance of quick and sudden death.

Crisis apparitions do indicate the survival of other elements of prewar mourning rituals, including the importance of the deathbed and the presence of family. The remoteness of death in Imperial communities and battlefields was unfamiliar to a generation of Britons who had been raised to see death as a familial and communal affair. Telepathy brought the moment of death back into the domestic sphere and promised intimacy. It was at once an individual and collective experience – a union of thoughts and feelings in one's own unconscious. Crisis apparitions also implied agency on part of the dying. Marian Macklin believed David 'willed' his presence. Beryl Butterworth Hutchinson explained how her fiancé 'showed himself to his aunt' on the night of his death.[77] It is telling that the SPR chose the terms 'agent' and 'percipient' to describe the originator and passive receiver of telepathic messages, respectively. If crisis apparitions were a broad social phenomenon and not merely an intellectual one associated with psychical researchers, we should expect to see them reported across religious denominations. John Bailey Middlebrook's mother, a devout Christian, saw an apparition of him at the foot of her bed the same night he was injured. He attributed this act to God's will, which allowed him to communicate with his mother at this moment of crisis.[78] As Owen Davies observes, telepathy was also endorsed in Anglican communities. Camus, for example, was the wife of an Anglican vicar, and Dorothy Kerin was an Anglican worshipper.[79]

Soldiers and their loved ones thought intensely about each other, vividly dreamt of one another and maintained intimate relationships through correspondence. They felt a deep affection for one another despite absence, feelings that transcended distance and regular communication. No wonder so many believed that soldiers were willing agents of intimate notices of death. The SPRs concept of telepathy, approximately three decades old and suffused in the popular culture by the time of the war, likely anticipated and helped create unconsciously several of the experiences shared in this chapter. Most who experienced them were not psychical researchers, but the telepathic framework allowed dreams, thoughts and emotions to be framed into scientific knowledge exchanged across a culture of letters. Affection was a bias in the SPR's data according to Charles Peirce, but for Myers, it was the very force upon which telepathy operated. Intense emotions were not a sign of neuroses but proof of the transcendental powers of the human mind, capable of mediating the contradictions and practical limitations of affection in war.

'Most clearly borne in upon my mind'

Lieutenant Alec Leith Johnston of the 1st King's Shropshire Regiment was killed on 22 April 1916. Sometime the following morning, on

Easter Sunday, his father, Dr George Johnston of London, had a waking dream, which he communicated to the SPR:

> I saw two soldiers in khaki standing beside a pile of clothing and accoutrements which, in some way, I *knew* to be Alec's ... Then one of them took up a khaki shirt which was wrapped round something so as to form a kind of roll ... it unrolled itself and a pair of heavy, extremely muddy boots fell out and banged heavily on the floor, and something else fell which made a metallic jingle. I thought, 'That is his revolver', but immediately afterwards thought, 'No, it is too light to be his revolver, which would have made more of a clang.' ... And then the words 'Alec is dead and they are going through his kit', were most clearly borne in upon my mind. They were not spoken and I heard no voice, but they were just as clear as if I had done so. And then I became fully awake with these words repeating themselves in my mind and with the fullest conviction of their truth which I never lost. I suppose I still tried to persuade myself that it might not be true, but it was useless and when the official telegram arrived it only confirmed what I already knew.[80]

Alec had been near the frontlines since October 1914 but Dr Johnston had never experienced anything like this before.[81] Even more curious was that he had no reason to worry about his son's well-being at the time. 'I was not feeling at all anxious', he explained, since 'they were not due in the trenches until the Wednesday, but they were unexpectedly called upon in the evening of Good Friday'. It seemed to him unlikely that the dream was just a coincidence. He was also able to provide corroborating evidence. On 4 May, Alec's cousin had sent Dr Johnston a letter, stating, 'I hear that Alec has died at Ypres. Your dream has come true. Alec appears to have been trying to let you know.'[82]

Dr Johnston was so sure the dream was an intimation of Alec's death that he reiterated, 'when the official telegram came ... I felt that it was hardly necessary to open it'.[83] The military historian Sir John Keegan once wondered what could lead parents to 'give up the ghost' of their children in such a manner. He uses the example of his paternal grandmother, who, upon delivering her son to the train station in 1917, expressed her certainty that she would never see him again.[84] In contrast to the pessimism of Dr Johnston, many more maintained hope that a missing soldier was still alive, even as that possibility grew increasingly implausible. But Dr Johnston's confidence is also contradicted by his admission that 'I suppose I still tried to persuade myself that it might not be true'. If we dispense with hindsight and consider the psychological torment that accompanied having a loved one at the front, it is easier to sympathise with such statements as expressions of hopelessness and uncertainty rather than real conviction.

Studies on shell shock, war neuroses and the psychological state of the soldier are legion, but we know considerably less when it comes to their loved ones back home. The evidence we do have suggests that family members experienced an excruciating anxiety resulting in poor mental and physical health. Soldiers were well aware of this and expressed concern about these anxious states.[85] In May 1917, after he received a letter from his wife Rosie, John Mellor Poucher wondered, 'What it must be this waiting and waiting and hoping against hope each day that all will be well.'[86] We cannot know what she told him, as her letters were lost in the deluge of battle, but it was enough to make Poucher ponder her predicament. The anxiety of the home front, he believed, was quite different from what the soldier experienced. 'A man out here knows what is going on and does not have to worry', Poucher explained. A soldier, of course, had plenty of reason to worry, but generally, he grew to know when it was warranted. Those back home were not afforded this privilege. In Canada, where the Pouchers resided, mail was not only less frequent but soldiers had to spend their leaves in France or England, making any chance at a reunion unlikely until their war was over.[87] Rosie's war experience was just 'one long uncertainty', as Poucher explained.[88] A soldier's circumstances could not be known with any certainty. Underlying Dr Johnston's story is the realisation that what he took for granted to be Alec's safe condition was unreliable.

Death was usually first communicated to a relative through the War Office telegram, which the journalist E. S. Turner called 'the terror by day'. Once Kitchener's citizen soldiers started dying on the battlefield in 1915, the sight of a post office messenger in the streets or a knock on the door elicited panic. Some recalled women struggling to open envelopes with their trembling fingers and going pale at the sight of a telegram boy.[89] Vera Brittain described how 'ordinary households became a torment ... every ring at the door suggested a telegram, every telephone call a long-distance message giving bad news'. Writing in the 1930s she confessed, 'even now I cannot work comfortably in a room from which it is possible to hear the front-door bell'.[90] The possibility always lingered that the soldier was already dead, a realisation waiting to be confirmed with the arrival of a telegram.

Sometimes letters were sent from chaplains and fellow soldiers to describe a loved one's final moments. This privilege was especially granted to family members of officers. The regimental surgeon informed Dr Johnston about 'the gallant attack' and 'glorious achievement' of the battalion. He also explained that Alec had been 'shot through the heart gallantly superintending his company consolidating the captured position'.[91] Comforting assurances of bravery (and minimal suffering) offered a more personal account than the generic telegram. Second Lieutenant J. R. Leslie of the Black Watch sought to break the news to the mother of Corporal Ian Maclaren of Perthshire himself, hoping that 'a letter from me may break the terrible news a little easier than the bald War Office telegram'.[92] Battlefield deaths as experienced on the home front were depersonalised, reversing the affectionate relationships that were established through correspondence. Crisis apparitions filled this gap.

A soldier's personal items often followed the telegram.[93] These belongings brought the war close to home. Mary Lodge found that when she flipped through Raymond's diary, the edges were 'soaked, and some of the leaves stuck together with his blood'.[94] Amongst Alec's possessions was 'a French automatic pistol'. This material artefact provided evidence that Dr Johnston's vision was telepathic since the gun was light enough to account for the 'metallic jingle' that he heard in his dream. The correspondence was also revealing. The regimental surgeon explained that during the attack 'the mud was so deep that the men had to throw themselves down and crawl'. Could this account for the muddy boots in the dream?[95] The personal belongings, accounts of his son's last moments and Dr Johnston's vision all helped bridge the gap between Alec's death as it was experienced on the front and the blank canvass confronting those back home. Dr Johnston was 'there' and Alec was 'here'; the physical evidence made the subjective experience more real.

As in the case of Marian Macklin, news was another way that the war was mediated, and it could be a source of anxiety. After Vera Brittain was informed of the opening of the Somme offensive, she tried to keep herself occupied, knowing that her brother Edward was in the region. 'For the whole of my conscious mind resolved itself into one speculation', she recalled, 'was Edward still in the world – or not? ... For the next three days I lived and worked in hourly dread of a telegram.'[96] In L. M. Montgomery's 1920 novel *Rilla of Ingleside*, Rilla, the daughter of Anne of Green Gables, responds to the news of Canada's success during Second Ypres not with joy but concern: 'I can't feel pride or exultation or anything but a gnawing anxiety over Jem and Jerry and Mr. Grant.' In the days that follow, she finds herself avoiding any situation that might bring news of their deaths. She refuses to answer the telephone and avoids the newspapers as the casualty lists are published. 'I can't bear to read them for fear I'd find Jem's name', she states, 'for there *have* been cases where people have seen their boys' names in the casualty lists *before* the official telegram came'.[97] Rilla ignores channels of information as if doing so might prevent a potential death from happening. Those on the home front attempted to control and optimise the way in which the news of death was received.

Dr George Johnston disclosed in further correspondence with the SPR that his certainty of Alec's death was secured when he read the Sunday news. After his dream, he saw in the paper that Alec's 'battalion had accomplished this "fine feat", [and] ... I had no doubt whatever that my boy was dead'.[98] Note how time crucially impacts the nature of his experience. If Dr Johnston had his dream after reading the paper, it is likely that it would have been attributed to the anxiety of this unexpected news. Because the dream occurred when he had every reason to believe his son was safe, it was interpreted as a spontaneous and evidential telepathic impression. Regardless, the unexpected news, received through the papers, coincides with a much more intimate and personal experience.

As a piece of evidence for telepathy, Dr Johnston's case remains wanting. All of his evidence indicates that the dream contained no information that he could not have learned naturally. Nor was the dream communicated to anyone before Dr Johnston read the newspaper. As a window into the home front, however, the story confronts the ways in which Britons wrestled with the possibility and then reality of a loved one's death. It is difficult to know what Dr Johnston's spiritual beliefs were. It is easy to speculate on the significance of the dates involved as Alec's sacrifice began on

Good Friday and his 'resurrection' took place on Easter Sunday. In his correspondence, Dr Johnston explained that, although 'one does not want to read too much into such an experience', he was struck by the dream's symbolism. The muddy boots and pistol were all indications of a battle when Alec was supposed to be behind the lines. For him, the dream was simply 'Alec's way of letting me know what had happened'. To the SPR, the evidence suggested a standard case of telepathy: 'it seems ... probably, as he suggests, that the dream was a piece of symbolic imagery representing the fact telepathically conveyed to him, that his son had been killed in the attack on the previous day'.[99] Alec was an inspiring writer who contributed to *Punch* during the war, and so one might wonder if Dr Johnston saw the dream as another piece of Alec's writing from the front, its symbolism conveying a special message to an audience of one. Dr Johnston's experience was not any ordinary dream but an intimate last goodbye from a son to his father.[100]

What is particularly notable about the case of Dr Johnston is that it is the only male-centred crisis apparition published by the SPR during the war. Emotions are social codes, since where, when and how we express them are often dictated by cultural norms, attitudes and values. It was feminine to cry in the trenches but patriotic to show emotion at a funeral.[101] Although we cannot access Dr Johnston's subjective emotional states, we can appreciate how he chose to express them, that is, by sending his experiences to a fellow scientist, Oliver Lodge (who then passed it on to the SPR), as evidence of telepathy. If Dr Johnston was looking for validation, Lodge was an obvious choice as he was able to communicate and confirm his experiences through the SPR. The painful emotions associated with the process of confronting his son's death are hidden behind a telepathic case study; they are all presented as objects of scientific knowledge.

An empire of sensation

Dr Johnston was one of many on the British Isles who confronted the difficulties of uncertainty, anxiety and grief as their sons fought and died. The war also engulfed British subjects across the globe, expanding the geographical reach of loss. One did not have to be separated by continents to experience a crisis apparition, but the further the British diaspora reached the edges of the empire, the more telepathy offered a solution to bridge the physical and not just emotional distance of war.

On 11 March 1918, an anonymous associate of the SPR, identified only as 'Mrs C.', sent word of the following experience:

> In the early morning of Jan. 13th, 1918, my daughter V. had a vivid dream of Arthur S., an old school-friend of her brother 'G.'. Upon leaving school, this young fellow had gone out to Canada ... Arthur S. had thus virtually gone out of our lives, though he had written from time to time at rare intervals, the last occasion being some two years ago, on the death of his friend 'G.' to whom he was much attached. We knew that neither he nor his brother had been able to join the Army as they were running the homestead for their parents, and considered this to be their first duty. In her dream, V. saw Arthur S. very clearly, dressed in khaki ... – she also heard him say – (by impression), 'But I can never forget my old friend "G."' ... Two days later, on the 15th of Jan., V. received a letter from Arthur S ... In it he told her of his father's death a year ago, which had set him free to join up ... His letter ended with these words: 'I often think of my old friend "G." and keep his noble sacrifice before me ... I never forget "G."'[102]

Mrs C. stressed the value of the case by noting that, at the time of the dream, Arthur was not at all on V.'s mind. She had never dreamt about him before nor did she have any relationship with him outside of his friendship with her brother. As a psychical research enthusiast, Mrs C. made sure to record the experience in her journal and provided it to the SPR along with a copy of Arthur's letter. This case of telepathy could not pass Innes's test, however, since the envelope was torn, making it impossible to verify the date.[103]

If V.'s experience is notable, it is so for its mundaneness. Telepathic experiences do not contain those characteristics that made traditional ghost stories exciting and terrifying. There is no vengeful ghost, no haunted house and no tormented soul. It was this banality that made them ideal candidates for psychical researchers looking to avoid association with superstition. Such stories meshed 'firmly within the normality of everyday life'.[104] The everyday life that informed V.'s supernormal incident is that of a community of Britons on different continents. For some, telepathy offered the possibility of improving imperial communications. This was the opinion of journalist W. T. Stead, who believed that telepathy harboured the potential to transform mass media across the British Empire.[105] Some experimented with mesmerism on native populations in India in an attempt to use their subliminal consciousness as an instrument to communicate with other colonists.[106] Telepathy, in the context of imperialism, could serve as a form of control, subverting the passive colonial subject to the will of the colonisers.[107] The proximity of far-flung populations to magic and 'primitivism' was romanticised in the orientalism of British esoteric and occult movements, but these same people were actively excluded from the language of sympathy, closely tied as it was to British exceptionalism and progress.[108] In the case of V., telepathy was the symptom and channel of this imperial emotional network of white settlers united at war.

The British Empire was sustained not just through shared political institutions but also demographics. Dominion nations such as Canada were obligated to join Britain in war in August 1914, but the level of this commitment remained undetermined. By the end of the war, 1.3 million men had served from British Dominions, and 144,000 of them had died.[109] Ancestral ties were especially significant in the initial period of mobilisation. Of the 30,617 Canadians that formed the First Contingent, for example, 18,495 (60 per cent) of them were British-born.[110] This reflected Canada's status as a land of immigrants. It is estimated that between 1911 and 1914, approximately 1.5 million Britons lived in the Dominions.[111] Experiences like that of James Basil Green were common. Green immigrated to Canada in 1911 to work with his cousins, leaving his sweetheart behind in England. When war was declared, he returned home but chose to enlist with the Canadians, not out of loyalty to any Canadian nationalism but to serve alongside his friends from the Canadian militia. During the interwar period, he resettled in England, married his sweetheart and again served in the Second World War but this time for the British Home Guard.[112] Examples like Green's point to the personal relations that connected the empire. 'What made the empire, the Dominions, and the Commonwealth a reality', Jay Winter explains, 'were the family ties which bound core and periphery together'.[113]

Arthur S. enlisted much later than his fellow British immigrants. It would be absurd to speculate on the reasons why, given how little we know about this anonymous soldier, but a theme of V.'s dream is the communal bonds of empire. Arthur is portrayed as alone in a distant land with nobody left to serve but his homeland. The memory of his friend's sacrifice compels him to service. V. does not just receive this news through the ordinary channels of correspondence as the communion of empire is felt in the intimate space of telepathy. This telepathic experience is an expression and legitimisation of an empire united in war by bonds that are transcendent.

V.'s dream was not a crisis apparition, but these too occurred across the British Empire during the war. On 19 March 1917, Captain Eldred Wolferstan Bowyer-Bower of the Royal Flying Corps (RFC) was reported missing. In May, his father, Captain Thomas Bowyer-Bower, tragically discovered his remains. At a séance with the medium Annie Brittain, Eldred's fiancée, Æta Highett, was informed that Eldred's half-sister in India, Dorothy Spearman, 'has the power to communicate'. Curious, Æta wrote to Dorothy to see if she knew what this meant. She received the following experience in reply:

> Eldred was greatly on my mind when [my] baby was born, and I could only think of him. On march 19th [sic], in the late part of the morning, I was sewing and talking to baby ... I had a great feeling I must turn round and did to see Eldred; he looked so happy and ... I was so glad to see him, and told him I would just put baby in a safer place, then we could talk. 'Fancy coming out here', I said, turning round again, and was just putting my hands out to give him a hug and a kiss, but Eldred had gone ... At first I thought it was simply my brain. Then I did think for a second something must have happened to him and a terrible fear came over me. Then again I thought how stupid I was, and it must be my brain playing tricks. But now I know it was Eldred, and all the time in Church at baby's christening he was there, because I felt he was and know he was, only I could not see him. All the time I thought why do I feel like this when Eldred is safe.[114]

Dorothy's letter was written in January 1918, nearly a year after Eldred's death. She never told her husband because he did not believe in such phenomena, having dismissed reports of apparitions on the home front. Despite the lack of documentation, the SPR was willing to publish Dorothy's experience. The date of the event could be verified given that it was the same day as her baby's christening. 'It was very unlikely that Mrs. Spearman's memory would deceive her on such a point', the SPR reasoned. That the experience was so vivid was also considered a point in its favour: 'the apparition being so completely developed as to make her think ... that her brother was actually present in the flesh'.[115]

If Dorothy was hallucinating or lying, this was not considered. That was typical of how psychical researchers treated the testimony of members of their own class. But Dorothy certainly grappled with the reliability of her senses, wondering if 'it might be my own madness'. After all, Eldred had been on her mind that day and she was reluctant to share the experience with her husband lest he accuse her of credulity. It was the séance between Brittain and Eldred's fiancée that convinced her the experience was real.[116]

There was another reason that the SPR was confident in the story's authenticity. Two other people had intimations of Eldred's death. The first came from Eldred's other sister, Cecily Chater. According to her testimony, her three-year-old child declared one morning 'Uncle Alley Boy [Eldred's nickname] is downstairs'. This she recorded in a letter to Eldred's mother, Florence Margaret, which as it turned out was received before the War Office telegram (although no letter was provided to the SPR since it had been destroyed). Cecily did not attach much meaning to the experience even after Eldred's death, attributing it to ordinary childish behaviour.[117] For Eldred's mother, however, it was another thread in her growing interest in spiritualism.

The final piece of evidence involved correspondence from a family friend. On 19 March 1917, the same day Eldred was killed, Florence Margaret received a letter stating, 'Something tells *me* you are having a great anxiety about Eldred. Will you let me know?' According to her testimony to the SPR, Florence Margaret wrote back in bewilderment explaining, 'Eldred was fit and happy'. As she later wrote, 'a certain and awful feeling that he was killed' had prompted the family friend's anxiety.[118]

Three visions from opposite corners of the earth all claimed presentments of Eldred's death on the exact same day. As cases of telepathy, collective apparitions intrigued and perplexed Myers and Gurney, but they took on even greater significance during and after the Great War.[119] Multiple apparitions seemed to confirm that Eldred's external agency had penetrated and united a community through their collective unconscious.

As in the case of Dr Johnston, the experiences of Eldred's family were also underwritten by uncertainty and feelings of anxiety, made worse by Eldred's status as missing and Dorothy's isolation in India. Like the case of V., telepathy unified communal bonds across the empire. Dorothy was staying in a hotel in Calcutta, and according to Eldred's fiancée, 'did not of course know of Eldred's death or even that he was out in France again'. Eventually, she learned that he was missing but only through the newspapers. During this time she remained mostly alone, since she had few acquaintances in Calcutta and her husband was absent for months afterwards. Her knowledge of events came not through official channels but gradually through correspondence with Eldred's stepmother. This proved crucial in the exchange of telepathic experiences. Contrary to the cases of Marian Macklin and Dr Johnston, and perhaps reflecting her lack of previous knowledge, Dorothy never claimed any certainty over Eldred's well-being. Even after he had disappeared, she 'could not bring [her]self to believe he had passed away'.[120] Her vision was only constructed as a supernormal experience after corresponding with family members on the other side of the world.

Dorothy's vision was woven into a telepathic experience through the SPR's knowledge network and interests in spiritualism on the British home front. This framework, constructed through a community of grieving women, offered her social support to counter any fears of being labelled mad or hysterical by her husband. It also validated the feeling that Eldred was really with her, not only after he died but during a pivotal moment in their relationship, for Eldred was chosen as her baby's godfather and was to be present at the christening. Dorothy could now claim that this was the case. The physical and emotional distance of a world war was overcome thanks to spiritualism when a family separated by war and empire communally experienced Eldred's death.

Phantasms of the dead

Florence Margaret and Æta Highett continued to feel Eldred's influence for some time. They reported seeing vivid hallucinations of him at night, suggesting that the phenomena were spiritual, not just telepathic.[121] After accepting the secular-scientific concept of telepathy, people tended to gravitate towards the spiritual. Myers demonstrated this with his approval of survival after death in the 1890s. Arthur Conan Doyle cited his acceptance of telepathy as a gateway to spiritualism. 'If the mind ... could operate at a distance from the body', he stated, 'why then should it not exist on its own when the body was destroyed?'[122] Experiencing a crisis apparition appears to have awakened within many a spectre that could not be so easily explained away as a phantasm of the living.

'D.' was only three years old when her father was killed in October 1916. Her mother, 'Mrs X.', preferred to let her daughter believe that he was still in France, 'taking care of soldiers'.[123] One night, several days after her husband's death, Mrs X. was lying in bed with D. when she sensed two figures in the room. They were discussing whether Mrs X. was ready to join her husband, and she recalled a strong desire to follow him. While still sleeping, D. suddenly interjected, 'You won't go away from me, will you, Mummy?' Approximately two years later, Mrs X. finally decided to explain to her daughter that her father was dead. Afterwards, his spirit haunted D., as she frequently saw and engaged in conversations with him.[124]

The war had a profound influence on the family unit. Although males aged fifteen to twenty-four represented the largest demographic in the British Army, including in casualties, the number of fathers at the front was still significant.[125] Jay Winter estimates that over 350,000 children were left fatherless after the war.[126] Even when death did not intrude, separation could exercise a malign influence. In a father's absence, familial relationships and domestic roles had to be sustained through correspondence and fathers often attempted to re-insert themselves into family affairs. Given her age, D. must have spent most of her young life not knowing her father. He was not someone physically present and was only accessible through her mother's mediation, not unlike a medium.

War affected the lives of children in various ways. Schools taught students what they believed to be the most important lessons of the war and had them engage in activities designed to help boost the material comfort and morale of the soldiers.[127] War was also a game. Children played with board games and other toys inspired by the war, and sometimes they even played 'make-believe' war.[128] D., for example, liked to play 'at being Daddy', driving his horses around in France.[129] 'Daddy' was therefore known from a distance and was someone who could be embodied and imagined.

Within the literature on psychical research, children could be interpreted as more sensitive to the supernormal. Certain supernormal faculties were said to originate in childhood before they were forgotten.[130] Given that their physical senses were not fully developed and their personality was less mature, children more closely represented the simplistic consciousness on Myers's spectrum. They resembled primitive humanity's inability to recognise and appreciate the supernormal and to distinguish between subliminal and supraliminal influences.[131]

Mrs X. was an Associate of the SPR and theorised about the nature of her daughter's experiences. 'Probably most children are just as much aware of the unseen world at that age', she wrote, 'when their minds are so fresh'. Mrs X. previously suspected that her daughter was sensitive to telepathy. D. was able to describe what her father was doing and thinking at the front, statements which proved accurate according to subsequent correspondence between Mrs X and her husband.[132] Some couples did engage in telepathic experiments during the war. While Olive Field's husband was still alive in France, the two chose 9 p.m. as a time 'to think hard of each other', in order to establish a telepathic bond.[133] The Yoga Agency sold 'Yoga Crystals' advertised to help those on the home front receive telepathic messages from the battlefields should the worst happen. It warned that these thoughts could be left to expire in the subconscious. A 'thought wave ... intensified by the knowledge of the instant severing of the ties of love and relationship, can transcend time and space', it advertised, claiming, 'A "YOGA" CRYSTAL will help enable YOU to develop and read this message.'[134] In the case of D., her mediated relationship with her father at war was transcended through telepathy. The two of them were in loving sympathy with one another regardless of whether they could communicate personally. Furthermore, their subjective affection became objective knowledge in the form of a telepathic experiment in letters, and now Mrs X. had discovered evidence that her daughter's special relationship with her father continued beyond death. Mrs X. confessed to being sceptical of spiritualism, proclaiming, 'I may say that I knew nothing of spiritualism – rather hated its jargon – had never read a book about it, and rather laughed at it'. So what to make of her daughter's visions?

Some of D.'s experiences could be interpreted as telepathic. Mrs X. conjectured that perhaps what D. saw as her father was really her mother's thoughts telepathically conveyed to her. Telepathy might explain why D. seemed aware that her mother was speaking to spirits that night when they were lying in bed together. Both in liminal states of consciousness, Mrs X.'s visions were merely a dream that became impressed on her daughter's subconscious. But telepathy was not sufficient to explain all of the experiences, especially those of a physical nature. For example, D. seemed to be able to interact with her father's spirit. 'When I touch it there's no skin. I don't *know* if it's Daddy, but I think it is', she explained, and added, 'I hope he doesn't *mind* my finger going through him. It doesn't hurt him, does it?' Such incidents baffled Mrs X., leading her towards spiritual explanations. As she wrote to the SPR, 'There does seem to have been something more than [telepathy] at work.'[135]

D.'s sensitivity, which had united the family in war, promised to do so even in the case of his death. Wherever D. went, she seemed to bring her father's spirit with her. When her mother was tending to her younger son, 'P.' (born after her husband's death), D. became upset that she was not involved, stating, 'Daddy can't see P. unless we're there'. Over time, her experiences became more intimate and physical in nature. On one occasion, D. said 'D'you know, Mummy, Daddy's so close to me I can't help laughing ... I believe he's got right inside me; don't *you* feel him, Mummy? If you got right on top of me he might be able to hug us both.' What role Mrs X. had in fostering this belief can only be speculated, but it does appear that she engaged with her daughter's newfound interest in spirits. When D. asked her mother why he only visited at night, Mrs X. told her that he could come at any time and that while they were sleeping 'part of us would go to him'.[136] Still embodying her father, D. offered Mrs X. an opportunity to experience closeness, intimacy and touch with her deceased husband.

Perplexed by these experiences, Mrs X. sought the help of the SPR community, sending her story to the *Journal of the Society for Psychical Research* in the hopes that someone could offer satisfying explanations.[137] If the telepathic crisis apparitions had served the needs of Marian Macklin, Dr George Johnston and others, it offered little in the way of dealing with the haunting memories of the war dead. Instead, the disembodied mind opened the door for discarnate personalities. The affection established between Mrs X., her husband and their daughter was not severed after death. The innocent and creative imagination of the child embodying a father she had mostly known as a disembodied personality became a source of psychic and spiritual comfort. Where Myers had ventured once before, so too did Mrs X.

Conclusion

The story of Marian Macklin's crisis apparition has survived in the family history. In its present retelling, there are subtle but important changes in the details. Marian's apparition of David is said to have occurred while she was sitting on her veranda, not drifting in and out of sleep, and upon seeing him, she is said to have exclaimed, 'Oh, David how lovely, unexpected leave!' rather than commenting on his dishonourable uniform.[138] According to present-day standards, the idea that Marian's vision occurred in a semi-conscious state liable to hallucination challenges its authenticity. In 1916 this detail was what gave the story its legitimacy. The moment of shame that Marian feels when she sees her son in a Tommy's uniform reminds us of the lost generation and those privileged families who sent their children to fight and die under romantic illusions of combat. We have returned to that other world of naïve sciences and patriotic ideals which contrasts so sharply with our modern memory. Pull on either of these threads and the original meaning of Marian's experience becomes untangled.

The hallucinatory and unconscious nature was what gave these experiences their objective contribution to psychological sciences but also their subjective and emotional being. That some tried to structure these phenomena into scientific knowledge indicates the tension that these experiences elicited. As the case of Dorothy Spearman and Harold Owen demonstrates, those who experienced a crisis apparition could wrestle over their validity and meaning. As in the case of Mrs X, and Eldred Wolferstan Bowyer-Bower's family, apparitions could drive people towards experimentation with spiritualism. The SPR's framework of epistolary evidence allowed wartime Britons to represent the subjective nature of affection during and after death into something objective and tangible such as letters, just as they had done so while their loved ones were still alive. As telepathic experiences, they were structured into coherent narratives that affirmed through scientific authority what they believed to be true but struggled to validate.

For centuries, the Western intellectual tradition has relegated dreams to the realm of the irrational, only to be shared in private or on the fringes of respectability. Telepathy and the SPR, for all their faults, provided for a brief cultural moment an opportunity for Britons to communicate their dreams and to rationalise one-third of the human experience. It was perhaps this broader project that most typified the close relationship between psychical research and psychoanalysis.[139] We are well aware of the latter's role in uncovering psychological trauma and the nightmares of soldiers; we are far less familiar with the former's role in helping families comprehend death. First World War-related crisis apparitions offer us a valuable glimpse into an otherwise hidden emotional experience: an intimate space that can help us better understand how people felt.

We have also seen how these telepathic experiences were closely related to the experiences of empire and could be used to sustain the belief in a transcendental Imperial British character and community that was affirmed in its sacrifices. But behind sacrifice for community was the difficulty of accepting the extinction of the modern individual. That David Macklin appears as Tommy Atkins – that universal British rank-and-file soldier – instead of as a clearly defined individual (and an officer no less) is interesting. Was he just another British soldier mowed down in industrial warfare? How could Marian be sure that this one ghost amongst hundreds of thousands of others haunting Britain was really her son? How did the privileged classes reconcile the anonymous and indistinguishable slaughter of their children on a battlefield of thousands? Letters from comrades and chaplains often did their best to emphasise the heroic and gallant deeds of individual soldiers. The telepathic experience suggested an individual agency bound by familial relationships that transcended death in modern war. Their love, heroism and sacrifice could manifest as a spectre beyond death that reaffirmed their individuality and reinforced treasured narratives. That spectre, it turns out, would haunt them for years to come.

Notes

1 On 26 March, *The Times* reported that, 'The momentum of the German onslaught yesterday was felt mainly between Arras and Péronne ... against fresh forces flung in during the afternoon our troops were forced to retreat. At points near Maricourt the Germans reached the old trenches of 1916.' The next day the news was even grimmer, including a full-page map of German advances around the town of Albert where David was killed. See 'New Somme Battles', *The Times* (26 March 1918), p. 6; 'German Advance over the Old Somme Lines', *The Times* (27 March 1918), p. 4.
2 'Case L. 1220: Apparition at the Time of Death', *JSPR*, 19:351 (1919), 4–5.
3 'Case L. 1220: Apparition at the Time of Death', 5–7.
4 Will R. Bird, *And We Go On: A Memoir of the Great War*, David Williams (ed.) (Montreal and Kingston, QC: McGill-Queen's University Press, 2014), p. 8.
5 Harold Owen, *Journey from Obscurity, Wilfrid Owen 1893–1918: Memoirs of the Owen Family, Volume III: War* (London: Oxford University Press, 1965), p. 199.
6 This estimate was based on a sample of 17,000 respondents who were asked: 'Have you ever, when believing yourself to be completely awake, had a vivid impression of seeing or being touched by a living being or inanimate object, or of hearing a voice; which impression, so far as you could discover, was not due to any external physical cause?' Of the responses, 1,684 (9.9 per cent) were affirmative. See Henry Sidgwick et al., 'Report on the Census of Hallucinations', *PSPR*, 10:26 (1894), 33–9.
7 In their first report, the Literary Committee of the SPR stated, 'we venture to introduce the words *Telcesthesia* and *Telepathy* to cover all cases of impression received at a distance without the normal operation of the recognised sense organs'. See William F. Barrett et al., 'First Report of the Literary Committee', *PSPR*, 1 (1882), 147; The seminal work outlining the links between dynamic psychiatry and the history of mesmerism and hypnotism is Henri F. Ellenberger, *The Discovery of the Unconscious: The History and Evolution of Dynamic Psychiatry* (New York: Basic Books, 1970). See also Adam Crabtree, *From Mesmer to Freud: Magnetic Sleep and the Roots of Psychological Healing* (New Haven, CT and London: Yale University Press, 1993).
8 Owen, *Journey from Obscurity*, p. 199.
9 Crabtree, *From Mesmer to Freud*, pp. 3–11.
10 *Ibid.*, pp. 39–45; Alison Winter, *Mesmerized: Powers of Mind in Victorian Britain* (Chicago, IL: University of Chicago Press, 2000), p. 41.

11 Winter, *Mesmerized*, pp. 53–4, 75.
12 Peter Lamont, *Extraordinary Beliefs: A Historical Approach to A Psychological Problem* (Cambridge: Cambridge University Press, 2013), pp. 72–3, 80, 103–4.
13 Winter, *Mesmerized*, pp. 117–25.
14 Hall argued that some human behaviour was the result of a stimulation of the nervous system that was immune from sensation and independent of the mind (as in decapitated organisms that continued to respond to external stimuli). See Graham Richards, *Mental Machinery: The Origins and Consequences of Psychological Ideas, Part 1: 1600–1850* (Baltimore, MD: Johns Hopkins University Press, 1992), pp. 357–62; Winter, *Mesmerized*, p. 47; and William Benjamin Carpenter, 'On the Influence of Suggestion in Modifying and Directing Muscular Movement, Independently of Volition', *Proceedings of the Royal Institution of Great Britain*, 10 (1852), 128–9.
15 Kurt Danziger, 'Mid-Nineteenth-Century British Psycho-Physiology: A Neglected Chapter in the History of Psychology', in William R. Woodward and Mitchell G. Ash (eds), *The Problematic Science: Psychology in Nineteenth-Century Thought* (New York: Praeger Publishers, 1982), pp. 119–21, 131–6.
16 Crabtree, *From Mesmer to Freud*, pp. 155–62.
17 Ellenberger, *The Discovery of the Unconscious*, pp. 90–1.
18 Edward Shorter, *A History of Psychiatry: From the Era of the Asylum to the Age of Prozac* (New York: John Wiley & Sons, 1997), pp. 136–7, 140–8.
19 William F. Barrett, 'On Some Phenomena Associated with Abnormal Conditions of the Mind', *PSPR*, 1 (1883), 241–2.
20 It was Frederic Myers's brother, Alfred, who initially introduced the SPR to the work of the Nancy school in 1885, prompting Frederic to travel there in 1886. See Edmund Gurney and Frederic W. H. Myers, 'Some Higher Aspects of Mesmerism', *PSPR*, 3 (1885), 423; Frederic W. H. Myers, 'Human Personality in the Light of Hypnotic Suggestion', *PSPR*, 4 (1886–87), 6; and 'On Telepathic Hypnotism, and Its Relation to Other Forms of Hypnotic Suggestion', *PSPR*, 4 (1886–87), 127.
21 Sofie Lachapelle, *Investigating the Supernatural: To Spiritism and Occultism to Psychical Research and Metapsychics in France, 1853–1931* (Baltimore, MD: Johns Hopkins University Press, 2011), pp. 71–2.
22 Crabtree, *From Mesmer to Freud*, pp. 307–12.
23 Myers, 'On Telepathic Hypnotism, and Its Relation to Other Forms of Hypnotic Suggestion', 2. Janet's book *États mental de hystériques* (1892) was reviewed in the *Journal of Mental Science* in 1893 and

Janet reviewed Hack Tuke's *Dictionary of Psychological Medicine* (1892) in *Brain* in 1893. Cited in R. D. Hinshelwood, 'Psychodynamic Psychiatry before World War I', in German E. Berrior and Hugh Freeman (eds), *150 Years of British Psychiatry, 1841–1991* (London: The Royal College of Psychiatrists, 1991), pp. 199–201.

24 Edmund Gurney, Frederic W. H. Myers and Frank Podmore, *Phantasms of the Living*, vol. I (London: Rooms of the Society for Psychical Research, 1886), p. xli.

25 Myers, 'Human Personality in the Light of Hypnotic Suggestion', 2.

26 Gurney, Myers and Podmore, *Phantasms of the Living*, vol. I, p. 7.

27 *Ibid.*, pp. xli–xlx.

28 Roger Luckhurst, *The Invention of Telepathy, 1870–1901* (Oxford: Oxford University Press, 2002), pp. 60–9. The SPR ultimately chose 'thought-transference' over 'thought-reading' to avoid association with the tricks of stage magicians.

29 William F. Barrett, Edmund Gurney and Frederic W. H. Myers, 'Thought-Reading', *The Nineteenth Century*, 11 (1882), 890–900.

30 Shane McCorristine, *Spectres of the Self: Thinking about Ghosts and Ghost-Seeing in England, 1750–1920* (Cambridge: Cambridge University Press, 2010), p. 119.

31 Philippe Ariés, *The Hour of Our Death: The Classic History of Western Attitudes towards Death over the Last One Thousand Years*, trans. Helen Weaver (New York: Vintage Books, 1981), p. 456.

32 Gurney, Myers and Podmore, *Phantasms of the Living*, vol. I, p. lxiii.

33 *Ibid.*, p. xiii. Myers wrote the introduction and Frank Podmore collected the cases (701 of which formed the basis of the study in *Phantasms*). It was Gurney, however, who wrote the remaining body chapters and the bulk of the book.

34 For the relationship between telepathy and the intellectual history of hallucinations, see McCorristine, *Spectres of the Self*.

35 Gurney, Myers and Podmore, *Phantasms of the Living*, vol. I, p. 538.

36 'Case L. 1209: Apparition', *JSPR*, 18:334 (1917), 19–25.

37 For Myers's earliest writings on phantasms of the dead, see Frederic W. H. Myers, 'On Recognized Apparition Occurring More Than a Year after Death', *PSPR*, 6 (1889), 13–65; and 'A Defence of Phantasms of the Dead', *PSPR*, 6 (1890), 314–57.

38 Myers's subliminal self was first published in the *Proceedings* between 1891 and 1895. See Frederic W. H. Myers, 'The Subliminal Consciousness', *PSPR*, 7 (1891–92), 298–355; *PSPR*, 8 (1892), 333–404; *PSPR*, 9 (1893–94), 3–128; and *PSPR*, 11 (1896–97), 334–593. Janet's idea of a subconscious influenced William James theories on consciousness, which were published in 1890 in his *The Principles of*

Psychology. James is often considered 'the father of American psychology', but beginning in the late 1880s, he increasingly moved towards psychical research. He was the founder of the American Society for Psychical Research (ASPR), admired Gurney's work on hypnotism and developed a relationship with Frederic Myers in the 1890s. By 1896 he had declared that he was 'convinced of supernormal cognition'. In fact, the SPR's interest in Janet's work preceded that of James. See William James, *The Principles of Psychology*, Authorized Edition, vol. I (New York: Dover Publications, 1918), pp. 206–7; and Luckhurst, *The Invention of Telepathy*, pp. 237–9.

39 Alan Gauld, *The Founders of Psychical Research* (New York: Schocken Books, 1968), pp. 279–80; Luckhurst, *The Invention of Telepathy, 1870–1901*, p. 108.
40 Frederic W. H. Myers, *Human Personality and Its Survival after Bodily Death*, vol. I (London: Longmans, Green and Co., 1903), pp. xxi, 14.
41 *Ibid.*, p. 21.
42 *Ibid.*, pp. 10–12.
43 Myers, *Human Personality*, vol. I, pp. 34–69.
44 Gauld, *The Founders of Psychical Research*, pp. 277–93.
45 *Ibid.*, p. 11.
46 Luckhurst, *The Invention of Telepathy*, pp. 107–12; Myers, *Human Personality*, vol. II, pp. 76–80, 278–92.
47 Myers, *Human Personality*, vol. II, p. 6.
48 *Ibid.*, p. 282; Luckhurst, *The Invention of Telepathy*, p. 111.
49 See the relevant chapters in Gauld, *The Founders of Psychical Research*, pp. 186–274.
50 *Ibid.*, pp. 277–93.
51 Barrett et al., 'Thought-Reading', 893.
52 Trevor H. Hall, *The Strange Case of Edmund Gurney* (London: Gerald Duckworth, 1964), pp. 60–1. When dealing with playing cards, the children used the position of their head to indicate suit (up for hearts, down for diamonds, right for spades, left for clubs) and various hand movements for the cards' values.
53 A. Taylor Innes, 'Where Are the Letters? A Cross-Examination of Certain Phantasms', *The Nineteenth Century*, 22 (1887), 174–94; Edmund Gurney, 'Letters on Phantasms: A Reply', *The Nineteenth Century*, 22 (1887), 522–33.
54 McCorristine, *Spectres of the Self*, pp. 162–72.
55 Ian Hacking, 'Telepathy: Origins of Randomization in Experimental Design', *Isis*, 79:3 (1988), 427–51. Gurney was introduced to these methods through the French psychical researcher Charles Richet, whose research into thought-reading was one of the first examples of randomisation in experimentation.

56 C. S. Peirce, 'Mr. Peirce's Rejoinder', *Proceedings of the American Society for Psychical Research*, 1 (1885–89), 214; Gurney, Myers and Podmore, *Phantasms of the Living*, vol. II, pp. 16–17.

57 For good examples see Michael Roper, *The Secret Battle: Emotional Survival in the Great War* (Manchester: Manchester University Press, 2009) and Lucy Noakes, *Dying for the Nation: Death, Grief and Bereavement in Second World War Britain* (Manchester: Manchester University Press, 2020).

58 See Martha Hanna, 'A Republic of Letters: The Epistolary Tradition in France during World War I', *The American Historical Review*, 108:5 (2003), 1338–61; Carol Acton, *Grief in Wartime: Private Pain, Public Discourse* (New York: Palgrave Macmillan, 2007), pp. 1–16; Jessica Meyer, *Men of War: Masculinity and the First World War in Britain* (New York: Palgrave Macmillan, 2009), pp. 14–46; Roper, *The Secret Battle*, pp. 1–85; Anthony Fletcher, *Life, Death and Growing up on the Western Front* (New Haven, CT: Yale University Press, 2013), pp. 75–97; and Rosie Kennedy, *The Children's War: Britain, 1914–1918* (New York: Palgrave Macmillan, 2014), pp. 1–20.

59 Hanna, 'A Republic of Letters', 1341.

60 Quoted in Roper, *The Secret Battle*, p. 49.

61 Meyer, *Men of War*, p. 14.

62 IWM, Private Papers of A. J. Arnold, Documents.9691, letter from Alfred J. Arnold to his family, 29 August 1916, pp. 32–3.

63 Kennedy, *The Children's War*, p. 25.

64 Roper, *The Secret Battle*, p. 52.

65 Martha Hanna, *Anxious Days and Tearful Nights: Canadian War Wives during the Great War* (Montreal and Kingston, QC: McGill-Queen's University Press, 2020), pp. 61–5.

66 Quoted in Roper, *The Secret Battle*, p. 48.

67 For examples see Roper, *The Secret Battle*, pp. 85–6, 228, 230–2. Letters to family and the psychical research model of the mind offer very different portrait of soldiers' dreams than those from the psychoanalytical model. As one surgeon in a French hospital observed, the dream of the exhausted soldier 'is always the same, always of the enemy. It is never a pleasant pastoral dream, or a dream of home but a dream of the charge, of the bursting shell, of the bayonet thrust!' See Elliot Park Frost, 'Dreams', *Psychological Bulletin*, 13:1 (1916), 13; Alexander Watson, *Enduring the Great War: Combat, Morale and Collapse in the German and British Armies, 1914–1918* (Cambridge: Cambridge University Press, 2008), p. 89. See also F. W. Mott, 'War Psycho-Neurosis: The Psychologist of Soldiers' Dreams', *The Lancet*, 191:4927 (1918), 169–72.

68 IWM, letter from Arnold to his parents, 30 September 1916, p. 50.

69 IWM, letter from Arnold to his family, 2 November 1918, p. 144.
70 'Two Air Dreams', *S. Katharine's School Magazine*, Spring Term (1917), 16–18. Thank you to Sarah Wearne for sharing this example.
71 Christie Nicholson, 'Strange But True: Less Sleep Means More Dreams', 20 September 2007, *Scientific American*, accessed February 2023, www.scientificamerican.com/article/strange-but-true-less-sleep-means-more-dreams/. A study of First World War dreams has yet to be conducted but some of the interpretations and methods employed in this chapter were inspired by Jonathan W. White, *Midnight in America: Darkness, Sleep, and Dreams during the Civil War* (Chapel Hill, NC: University of North Carolina Press, 2017).
72 CUL, MS SPR34/24/5, Dorothy Wayte, 17 December 1917, pp. 3, 11, 37.
73 CUL, MS SPR, Research Files, Dreams: Telepathic, Folder 41, 'Camus, Mrs. Marion and Dorothy Kerin, Reciprocal Dream with Precognitive Element and Clairvoyant Content'.
74 McCorristine, *Spectres of the Self*, p. 147; Luckhurst, *The Invention of Telepathy*, pp. 148–80.
75 Pat Jalland, *Death in the Victorian Family* (Oxford: Oxford University Press, 1996), pp. 1–38.
76 Drew Gilpin Faust, *This Republic of Suffering: Death and the American Civil War* (New York: Alfred A. Knopf, 2008), p. 17. Faust notes that soldiers were so cognisant of the importance of the Good Death that they seemed to be following a checklist: 'the deceased had been conscious of his fate, had demonstrated willingness to accept it, had shown signs of belief in God and in his own salvation, and had left messages and instructive exhortations for those who should have been at his side'.
77 IWM, Sound Archive, 562, Beryl Butterworth Hutchinson, interview by Margaret A. Brooks, 1974.
78 Roper, *The Secret Battle*, p. 231.
79 Owen Davies, *A Supernatural War: Magic, Divination, and Faith during the First World War* (Oxford: Oxford University Press, 2018), pp. 92–3.
80 'Case L. 1212: Telepathic Dream', *JSPR*, 18:337 (1917), 52.
81 According to Sir Owen Seaman, the editor of *Punch*, Alec enlisted shortly after the declaration of war, and embarked for the front in October 1914. In February 1915 he received commission in the 1st King's Shropshire Light Infantry and was promoted to Lieutenant in September 1915. See Alec Johnston, *At the Front* (London: Constable, 1917), pp. v–vi.
82 'Case L. 1212', 51–4.
83 *Ibid.*, 53.

84 John Keegan, *War and Our World* (London: Hutchinson, 1998), p. 7.
85 Hanna, *Anxious Days and Tearful Nights*, p. 204.
86 IWM, Private Papers of J. M. Poucher, Documents.6995, JMP2, John Mellor Poucher, diary entry under 30 May 1917.
87 Hanna, *Anxious Days and Tearful Nights*, pp. 5–6, 126–8.
88 IWM, Poucher, diary entry under 30 May 1917.
89 E. S. Turner, *Dear Old Blighty* (London: Michael Joseph, 1980), pp. 130–1.
90 Vera Brittain, *Testament of Youth: An Autobiographical Study of the Years 1900–1925* (London: Victor Gollancz, 1933), p. 143.
91 'Case L. 1212', 55.
92 Quoted in Derek Young, *Scottish Voices from the Great War* (Stroud: The History Press, 2008), chapter 9, paragraph 12, Kindle.
93 Turner, *Dear Old Blighty*, p. 131.
94 Oliver Lodge, *Raymond: Or Life and Death* (New York: George H. Doran Company, 1916) p. 111.
95 'Case L. 1212', 53–5.
96 Brittain, *Testament of Youth*, p. 248.
97 L. M. Montgomery, *Rilla of Ingleside*, Canadian Favourites Edition (Toronto, ON: McClelland & Stewart, 1973), p. 105.
98 'Case L. 1212', 53.
99 'Case L. 1212', 53–4, 56.
100 His writings for *Punch* were published posthumously in the form of a memoir (Johnston, *At the Front*).
101 André Loez, 'Tears in the Trenches: A History of Emotions and the Experience of War', in Jenny Macleod and Pierre Purseigle (eds), *Uncovered Fields: Perspectives in First World War Studies* (Leiden: Brill, 2004), pp. 211–26.
102 'Case L. 1218: Telepathic Dream', *JSPR*, 18 (1918), 225.
103 *Ibid.*
104 McCorristine, *Spectres of the Self*, p. 158.
105 Luckhurst, *The Invention of Telepathy*, pp. 117–47.
106 *Ibid.*, pp. 152–3.
107 Winter, *Mesmerized*, pp. 187–212.
108 For orientalism see Chris Goto-Jones, *Conjuring Asia: Magic Orientalism and the Making of the Modern World* (Cambridge: Cambridge University Press, 2016) and for sympathy in an imperial context see Jane Lydon, *Imperial Emotions: The Politics of Empathy across the British Empire* (Cambridge: Cambridge University Press, 2019).
109 Jay Winter, *Remembering War: The Great War between Memory and History in the Twentieth Century* (New Haven, CT: Yale University Press, 2006), p. 170.

110 Tim Cook, *At the Sharp End: Canadians Fighting the Great War, 1914–1916* (Toronto, ON: Penguin Canada, 2007), pp. 28–9.
111 Winter, *Remembering War*, p. 161.
112 IWM, Private Papers of Lieutenant J. B. Green, Documents.15073, Basil James Green, 'The Autobiography of an Almost Nonagenarian: I Was That Choirboy', unpublished memoir, n.d.
113 Winter, *Remembering War*, p. 156.
114 'Case L. 1223: Apparition at the Time of Death', *JSPR*, 19 (1919), 40.
115 'Case L. 1223', 40.
116 *Ibid.*, 3.
117 *Ibid.*
118 *Ibid.*, 44.
119 For their analysis of collective apparitions see Gurney, Myers and Podmore, *Phantasms of the Living*, vol. II, pp. 168–270.
120 'Case L. 1223', 41–2.
121 *Ibid.*, 41–2.
122 Arthur Conan Doyle, *The New Revelation* (New York: George H. Doran, 1918), p. 41.
123 No name or alias is given to the mother in the SPR's article. Here she will simply be referred to as 'Mrs X.'.
124 'Hallucinatory and Other Experiences of a Young Child', *JSPR*, 18 (1918), 231–3.
125 Jay Winter notes that over two million men aged fifteen to twenty-four enlisted. The second highest demographic was twenty-five to twenty-nine with over 1.3 million. This leaves over 1.7 million aged thirty to forty-nine. Those between twenty and twenty-four had the highest death rate at 37.15 per cent (Jay Winter, *The Great War and the British People* (London: Macmillan, 1985), pp. 81–2).
126 Winter, *The Great War and the British People*, p. 273; Kennedy, *The Children's War*, p. 18.
127 The literature on this subject has grown considerably since Audoin-Rouzeau's seminal work on the topic. See Stéphane Audoin-Rouzeau, *La Guerre des enfants 1914–1918. Essai d'histoire culturelle* (Paris: A. Colin, 1993); Michael Paris, *Over the Top: The Great War and Juvenile Literature in Britain* (Westport, CT: Praeger, 2004); Dorothea Flothow, 'Popular Children's Literature and the Memory of the First World War, 1919–1939', *The Lion and the Unicorn*, 31:2 (2007), 147–61; Andrew Donson, *Youth in the Fatherless Land: War Pedagogy, Nationalism, and Authority in Germany, 1914–1918* (Cambridge, MA: Harvard University Press, 2010); Lissa Paul, Rosemary R. Johnston and Emma Short (eds), *Children's Literature and Culture of the First World War* (New York: Routledge, 2015); Susan Fisher, *Boys and Girls in No*

Man's Land: English Canadian Children and the First World War (Toronto, ON: University of Toronto Press, 2011).
128 Kennedy, *The Children's War*, p. 70.
129 'Hallucinatory and Other Experiences of a Young Child', 232.
130 Myers, *Human Personality*, vol. I, pp. xxix, 16–17, 346–7.
131 *Ibid.*, p. 41.
132 'Hallucinatory and Other Experiences of a Young Child', 232.
133 CUL, MS SPR34/19/02, letter from Olive Field to Helen Salter, 3 April 1918, pp. 5, 7.
134 'Telepathy from the Front', *The Two Worlds*, 27:1409 (1914), 556.
135 'Hallucinatory and Other Experiences of a Young Child', 233–5.
136 *Ibid.*, 234–5.
137 *Ibid.*, 235.
138 Christopher Dumergue, 'David Harold Macklin', *Duff's Blog*, last modified 23 December 2009, accessed February 2023, https://chrisandry.wordpress.com/2009/12/23/david-harold-macklin/. The author of this essay is his great-nephew.
139 Justin E. H. Smith, *Irrationality: A History of the Dark Side of Reason* (Princeton, NJ: Princeton University Press, 2019), pp. 75–7, 95–7.

4

Living with the ghosts of war: death and mourning in the séance room

Nea Walker was sensitive to noise in the spring of 1918. For several months now, Oliver Lodge's secretary and her sisters Damaris and Elsi had been attending séances with the medium Gladys Osborne Leonard to contact various soldiers killed in the Great War. Among the spirits was Elsi's sweetheart, Second Lieutenant Wilfrid Wayte, who served with the 103rd Brigade of the Royal Field Artillery (RFA) and died of wounds on 7 October 1917. When not in the séance room, Nea and Elsi experimented with trance at home and engaged in automatic writing on a regular basis to communicate with the war dead. With each passing session, their conviction was strengthened that those they had lost could break through the chasm between the spiritual and physical worlds. Elsi claimed she could feel Wilfrid's presence and heard peculiar noises that were described as 'like the noise in a shell, and sometimes like distant bells'.[1] At séances, Wilfrid's spirit reassured Elsi that he often visited her bedroom and made noises to attract her attention.

It is no wonder that on the night of Good Friday, 29 March 1918, Nea thought she heard a spirit when she was awoken by what sounded like 'three or four taps' coming from the bedroom fireplace. Curious, she reached out her right hand and it 'instantly … went perfectly cold. I did not feel any grip, but concluded that someone had taken it.' Nea quickly fell back to sleep but the incident left a vivid impression. The Walker sisters were sharing a bedroom while they visited their parents in Lampeter, and Nea wondered if Wilfrid had come for Elsi.[2] Further events during the weekend raised another troubling possibility.

While engaging in automatic writing with Elsi on Saturday evening, Nea's hand veered left off the page leaving only a few muddled strokes. Surprised, she tried again but placed her hand further to the right. This time the words 'Mother tell her' were written from right to left. When Nea asked who it was, her pencil wrote, 'Me, Ted, Yes'. With the events of the previous night on her mind, she enquired whether this was the same spirit who had touched her. The reply was affirmative: 'Yes, I came.' Nea and Elsi grew anxious. Their dear friend and Wilfrid's cousin, Ted Pearce, was currently on the Western Front as the German offensive raged. Could it be him? After all, Nea had recently sent Ted a letter informing him 'if he *did* go over during the great push' that 'he knew where to come to get messages through'.[3] Whether this was indeed Ted or just another lost soul looking for contact, Nea advised the spirit 'to try not to worry' and 'to work away with us' in order to help reunite him with his loved ones.[4]

Nea wrote to Ted's mother, an already anxious Mary Pearce, to enquire about Ted's well-being. Only a few days prior, Nea had received a letter from her with the prophetic sentence, 'perhaps you may hear or know something of [Ted] before I do'.[5] Nea kept her suspicions secret, as she did not want to upset Mary, but the latter's response was not reassuring.[6] The latest communication from Ted was a short note dated 21 March, the same day that the Germans launched their offensive on the Western Front. Ted informed his mother that he was on the move and would not be able to write for some time. This letter had not arrived until 1 April. Nea was left to wonder if Ted's correspondence was in limbo or if he had been killed.[7] Absent any normal communication, she turned to the supernormal. Perhaps Ted's spirit was waiting on the other side. If the War Office could not divulge his fate, maybe the séance could.

A missing soldier, a phantom visitor, an anxious mother and a group of women with access to a medium and planchette: it is a scenario that played out across Britain as the spectre of loss invaded British homes. In many respects, spiritualism was a continuation of Victorian spiritual practices.[8] Many spiritualists in the interwar period, such as Conan Doyle and Oliver Lodge, were already associated with the movement prior to the war. And then there were those like the Walker sisters, who were drawn to the séance because of the war. Conan Doyle claimed that out of the thirteen mothers that he personally knew who communicated with their sons, only one was acquainted with spiritualism before the war.[9] As bodies were eviscerated by industrial weaponry and swallowed into the abyss of the earth by successive artillery bombardments, conventional mourning rituals were difficult to sustain. Missing soldiers like Ted Pearce haunted the living as anonymous soldier-spirits appeared in séances across the country just as their loved ones were deprived of their bodies and left ignorant of their fate. In Kingston in 1919, the medium Elizabeth Cannock described how she saw endless lines of soldiers revealing themselves one by one as she described their appearances aloud waiting for someone in the audience to recognise them.[10] That spiritualism saw a resurgence on account of the war has long been acknowledged, but we know surprisingly little about what was said in these gatherings. Spirits provided information about the circumstances of death, the fate of the missing and guidance on how to mourn.

Britain's social and cultural elite were unprepared to deal with the nature and consequences of death in the Great War, but spiritualism made continuity possible. The individual personality of the soldier survived and performed his role as son, brother, sweetheart and husband. He had a future in the afterlife where he progressed and contributed to the construction of a spiritual science on earth. The rupture of identity has been a popular theme in Great War scholarship. Eric Leed interprets the war experience as a rite of passage. On the front, men entered a liminal zone between civilisation and the wild, living and dead, man and machine and man and beast. Their return to civilised life made it difficult to integrate these experiences into their civilised selves.[11] Shell shock represented the most devastating example, and historians have noted the emasculating influences of mental and physical disabilities. However, we also now know that civilian identities were sustained at the front, allowing for reintegration, and that conservative attitudes towards gender survived the war.[12] Prewar identities could also survive the death of a loved one. Studies of shell shock have naturally emphasised trauma, but the alternative psychiatry of psychical research offers another approach to understanding the war's psychological impact and the diverse coping methods that grieving family members employed. Just as psychoanalysts attempted to treat shell shock by reintegrating repressed memories into the self, some Britons reconciled who they were before the war by finding the soul of loved ones in the subconscious of themselves and mediums. The re-establishment of prewar relationships was only possible if social, as well as individual identities were continuous, and so soldier spirits and grieving sitters reverted to familiar domestic dynamics. In this way, Britons were able to maintain precarious relationships until they were prepared to let go of the ghosts of war.

The Walker circle

When Nea Walker was hired as Oliver Lodge's secretary in 1915, she 'knew nothing about' psychical research or spiritualism. The daughter of Hugh Walker, Professor of English and Philosophy at St David's College in Lampeter, Nea was introduced to Lodge through Britain's intellectual circles. Fresh into his spiritualist pursuits after the death of his son Raymond, Oliver Lodge was seeking a capable individual with knowledge of shorthand to transcribe his séances. Nea's new vocation brought her into contact with Gladys Osbourne Leonard, thus beginning a relationship that would last over twenty years and which would grow into a small network of grieving Britons.[13] As Britain's new citizen army was bloodied on the Somme, the Walkers, like many Britons, began to experience a series of devastating personal losses: Damaris's sweetheart, Sub-Lieutenant Jack Howell, died on 3 July 1916, the Walkers' close family friend, Lieutenant Samuel Bruce McLaren, was killed on the 13 August 1916 and Nea's friend (and possible romantic partner), Lance Corporal Hugh Russell Sommerville, was killed on 21 November 1916. Nea and Damaris began attending their own séances after the death of Jack Howell, and Elsi joined after the death of her sweetheart Wilfrid Wayte over a year later. Elsi had met Wilfrid, the son of a physician from Croydon, through his cousin Ted Pearce, whose mother, Mary Pearce, was one of the Walker family's oldest and closest friends.[14] Elsi and Nea in turn introduced the Wayte family as well as Ted and Mary Pearce to spiritualism after Wilfrid's death.[15]

Nea's association with the SPR has helped ensure the survival of her valuable séance notes. They are as close to an accurate record as was possible before audio recording. Most séances were transcribed in shorthand, allowing for precise documentation.[16] Once they were transliterated, they were sent to others present at the sitting to ensure accuracy. From there, they were shared with individuals who knew the alleged spirits in life for validation and further commentary, providing present-day readers with biographical details. The collections of séances surrounding the Walker investigations are especially valuable as they include various sitters and mediums allowing for a broader perspective. Wilfrid's mother Constance, his sister Dorothy and his brother Jack all attended sittings and the group conducted séances with the mediums Elizabeth Cannock, Annie Brittain, Violet Ortner (later Violet Warren-Elliot), Alfred Vout Peters and many others.

The Walker transcripts are also exceptional in the level of care and sophistication that went into their production. The Walkers approached séances in a manner that would have differed from the general public's interest in fortune tellers. For example, Elsi and Nea grew irritated at mediums when they 'fished' for information (a cold-reading tactic whereby mediums pose seemingly innocent questions designed to gather information from unsuspecting sitters).[17] A distinction between more careful and novice sitters is apparent during Constance Wayte's second sitting with Leonard, in which she murmured the name 'Ted' in reference to a description of someone close to Wilfrid at the front. Constance's blunder had to be recorded in the notes, as any subsequent mention of 'Ted' could not be used as evidence of supernormal communication.[18] Unlike Constance, when Nea suspected that Wilfrid's spirit was speaking about Ted on 19 April 1918, she refrained from mentioning his name for clarification, since she would prefer 'to come away with less knowledge than to risk giving away anything'.[19]

According to Nea, Constance also showed a lack of appreciation of finer details, once complaining that she could not get the Wayte family to comment on potentially evidential matters as they failed 'to realize the value of small points'.[20] Constance was likely far more representative of the wider public, who preferred more direct evidence over the careful weaving together of information that characterised SPR investigations. After analysing a poor sitting between the Walkers and Brittain, the psychical researcher J. Arthur Hill complained that public mediums tried too hard to sell themselves and avoided awkward silences. 'The ordinary sitter wants quantity for his money', he observed.[21] It is important to remember that the transcripts analysed here cannot serve as a universal

Figure 4.1 Nea Walker photographed by the spirit photographer Ada Deane in 1923.

standard that applied to everyone who attended séances during and after the war. For this reason, we also need to draw comparisons to other examples outside of the Walker group.

Despite some limitations, the Walker transcripts provide a unique perspective into the nature of the séance, giving us a sense of what people sought to achieve in séances, what was spoken to them and how they were consoled. Just as significantly, they reveal how strangers managed to convince sitters that they were communicating with the dead, individuals they had once known intimately.

How to discover a spirit

Séances developed according to who was sitting with whom and for what purpose. There were different styles of mediumship. Some mediums spoke through a trumpet, emitted ectoplasm, grew phantom limbs, manifested walking spirits, played musical instruments from a distance and levitated. The Walkers did not study any physical phenomena, although they did dabble in spirit photography at the height of its popularity in the early 1920s.[22] In the aftermath of the Great War, the Walkers' objective was to establish communion with specific spirits and provide evidence of the survival of personality.

The type of séance most conducive to the war's bereaved was therefore those conducted by 'trance mediums' and which followed a particular pattern. The two essential components were the 'sitter(s)' and the 'medium'. Sitters were present to establish communication with the dead while the medium acted as a gateway to the other world. Once in trance, the medium's consciousness gave way to discarnate personalities. The most common trance personality was the 'control', said to be a spirit guide that communicated with the living. Mediums usually had distinct controls with unique characteristics, patterns of speech and personal histories. William Stainton Moses had eighty-four controls including historical figures such as Plato, Benjamin Franklin and Beethoven.[23] The famous medium Leonora Piper, in turn, adopted Moses as one of her own after his death.[24] If the control was not the desired communicator, however, then séances included additional 'spirits' who did not communicate to the sitters directly but instead used the control as an intermediary.

Not every spiritualist communication met these conditions. Some made contact with spirits without an intermediary control.[25] Sometimes the spirit being sought by sitters was the control, and spoke directly through the medium in a trance state, which was called 'personal control'. Leonard and Ortner occasionally used personal controls with the Walkers, adopting a voice that sounded

Living with the ghosts of war 173

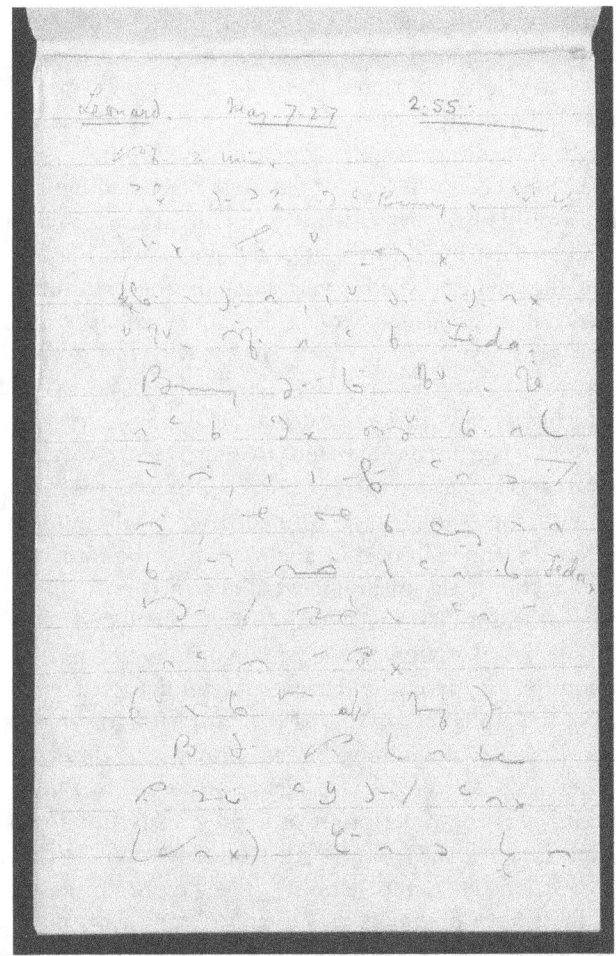

Figure 4.2 Nea Walker's original shorthand notes of a séance conducted on 7 May 1927.

masculine and which the sitters identified as similar to Wilfrid.[26] Communication could also be achieved through automatic writing, a crystal ball, an Ouija board or simply a table. Nea engaged in automatic writing frequently and she and Damaris experimented with a crystal ball in 1923.[27] The only compulsory conditions for successful communications were a participant for input and a material or human medium for output. Despite some exceptions, the majority of the Walkers' séances involved sitter(s), medium, control and spirit(s).

Leonard developed personal controls with a few sitters but she primarily used a single control known as Feda, who became as well known as the medium herself. Leonard's biographer, Suzy Smith, proclaimed that Feda was 'one of the most discussed figures in psychical research'.[28] Feda was allegedly the great-great-grandmother of Gladys. An East Indian by birth, she married an Englishman at the age of thirteen and died a year later during childbirth. Those familiar with Feda identified her as a distinct personality. Smith contrasted the 'gentle, sweet, and quiet' Gladys with the 'lively, shrewd, and sometimes noisey' Feda.[29] Una Troubridge, who by 1922 had claimed to have sat with Leonard over 180 times, described Feda as ignorant of basic norms. She once tossed Leonard's wedding ring into the fire and suggested a sitter burn her hair so that it could be replaced with something more attuned to Feda's liking.[30] A medium's success depended in part on their ability to be someone else. It is no wonder that many mediums were once actors.

Communications in a typical trance séance included descriptions of a spirit's physical attributes and personal characteristics as well as references to places, people and events. Mediums often listed names or letters of the alphabet associated with a spirit in order to demonstrate knowledge of something known only to the deceased or the sitter.[31] One of the key pieces of evidence presented by Oliver Lodge in *Raymond* was the description of a previously unknown group photograph taken at the front. Further investigations confirmed the photograph's existence and details.[32] The favoured method when investigating trance mediums was to share transcripts with a community of researchers attending unrelated séances with separate mediums. If similar messages could be found, it indicated the presence of an identity independent from the mediums and sitters. The messages about Raymond's group photograph, for example, came from both Leonard and Alfred Vout Peters, suggesting to Oliver Lodge and his wife Mary that Raymond's personality was external to any one medium.

To the present-day eye, the evidence presented at these séances may appear underwhelming and the sitters' enthusiasm credulous. Such an attitude is the natural consequence of the textual and epistolary nature of the sources, which by their design, failed to record or do proper justice to the emotions and subjective feelings that accompanied the process of talking to dead loved ones. We need to go beyond the transcripts themselves and consider the world that our subjects occupied. Consider, for example, a séance between Elsi, Nea and the medium Miss Bacon on 20 April 1918. The sitting itself was judged to be a failure as Bacon spent most of the time fishing, guessing names with little success and making inaccurate statements. Nea Walker must have judged Bacon a fraud, correct? On the contrary, despite Nea's criticism, she determined that some of the medium's powers were genuine based on a few observations. For starters, she described feeling a 'sort of electricity … in the room' and 'heard a very distinct buzzing' that she sometimes noticed when engaging in spiritualist communications.[33] Nea's comments took for granted the widely held association between psychical phenomena and modern technology. The Reverend Walter Wynn recalled that when he visited the trumpet medium Susannah Harris, the voice emanating from the trumpet 'was not exactly like [his son] Rupert's', but he 'made allowance for this, because I have noticed on a telephone that it is often difficult to detect the voices of your most intimate friends. How much more difficult, probably, through this trumpet.'[34] Twentieth-century communication technology legitimised what we would identify as defects in psychic and spiritual phenomena.

Nea placed most of the blame for the poor sitting on the control 'Sunbeam', who she described as 'very dictatorial', arrogant and 'a conceited … person'. She found it difficult to discern the difference between Sunbeam and the medium, as the former's 'voice and phrasing were remarkably like Miss Bacon's'. To the sceptical reader, Bacon has once again appeared to have slipped up and revealed herself to be an imposter. What did Nea make of this? According to her, Bacon's 'rather strong personality may have something to do with it … she may not be able to set herself aside sufficiently'. Nea's concern was that Bacon's conscious self was still active in the proceedings. She wondered if Bacon was 'shamming' the control or if Sunbeam was a secondary, rather than a discarnate, personality.[35] In other words, Nea was well versed in *fin-de-siècle* conceptions of the self and consciousness. British psychical research was founded in response to findings emanating from French neurologists studying hysteria and multiple personalities. The patients of Pierre Janet manifested radically different characters in altered states of consciousness, challenging the Enlightenment notion of the soul or self as a chain of memories and perceptions. These personalities were dissociated from one another's memories. It was as if the individuals studied had two selves or two souls. As the philosopher of science, Ian Hacking has observed, multiple personalities went hand-in-hand with the spiritualist craze. Janet's patients for example were often mediums and automatic writing was used as a prognostic device that allowed him to communicate with his patients' waking and trance personalities simultaneously.[36]

The study of multiple personalities, well known in the world of British psychical research, presented an open question as to the precise nature of controls. Most famously, in the 1930s, Whatley Carington conducted a series of word association tests on mediums, including Leonard, to determine if controls were secondary personalities. A list of stimulus words was read aloud to Leonard who was instructed to respond as quickly as possible. The test was first conducted while she was in a conscious state and repeated while under control. Influenced by Jung's work on word associations, Carington hypothesised that if controls were secondary personalities then the reactions in both states should be similar since, although the conscious memories of split personalities were dissociated from one another, each word would be associated with shared unconscious complexes.[37] Carrington concluded that Feda was a secondary personality of Leonard, 'probably formed round a nucleus of repressed material'.[38] His primary data were reaction times, under the assumption that delayed reaction indicated a word had special meaning. He observed that Feda's responses 'had a strong Oriental flavour', but he dismissed this as easily attributable to 'Leonard's own conscious or subconscious knowledge' given the simplicity of the terms.[39] By incorporating word association tests, Carington was hoping to move the problem of spirit controls out of the 'witness box' and into the 'laboratory'.[40]

When Carington first proposed his word association test in 1921, Nea and Elsi Walker were in their fourth year of séances with Leonard, and operating in the witness box.[41] Like Carrington, they were attempting to separate and compartmentalise identities emanating from the medium. Their efforts were influenced by Pierre Janet and William James rather than the works of Jung. During a sitting with Leonard on 29 December 1917, it was established through a personal control of Wilfrid that his mother would come to the next séance.[42] Two days later, the sitting began with Wilfrid as the control. When the voice asked 'Elsi' if his mother was there, this was identified as significant since only Wilfrid knew about the arrangements while Leonard or Feda were not informed, nor did they know Elsi's name.[43] The solution appears obvious. If Wilfrid knew Elsi's name and knew about the arrangements, so too did Leonard and any other of her personalities. But this applies only if we ignore the multiple layers that constituted a belief in spiritualism. Nea and Elsi were convinced of Wilfrid's presence, in part, because they presumed that Wilfrid, Feda and Leonard were dissociated personalities, with their own streams of consciousness, their own souls.

Not everyone who entered a séance room was as familiar with the works of Janet and William James as the Walker sisters were, but the ability to distinguish the identity of the communicator from personalities in the séance room was a requisite for any believer, even if the questions, methods and energy spent to get there varied. Books such as Lodge's *Raymond* and L. Kelway-Bamber's *Claude's Book*, for example, contain letters written by the soldiers while they were alive as well as biographical information in order to familiarise readers with their personalities prior to the presentation of séance evidence.[44] In *Raymond*, Oliver Lodge deciphers a cryptic literary allusion obtained in a séance that indicates the survival of his son's personality. In the correspondence section, we learn that Raymond liked to send his father acrostic puzzles while serving at the front, a habit apparently extended after his death in the form of séance communications.[45] In *Grenadier Rolf*, Ellen Little gradually discovers her son Rolf's personality through various mediums. After first attending séances with Peters, Little recalled that, at a sitting with Brittain, 'Rolf's own personality became clearer still'. She was particularly impressed that the spirit mentioned relatives using Rolf's personal nicknames.[46]

Trance mediumship had two benefits. From the perspective of the medium, it helped distance the sitter from the spirits. As Lodge admitted, the control enabled 'the investigator to be lenient to defects and to excuse modes of expression and misunderstandings and the like'.[47] For the sitters, it was important because it helped psychical researchers subvert the influence of the conscious subjective self. When Nea attempted to develop her own mediumistic powers in 1918, she refused to engage in sittings with Elsi over fears that she could not suppress her own personality.[48] Damaris's forays into professional mediumship in the 1920s appear to have been abandoned due to similar problems, and Elsi was initially unsure whether the noises she heard were from Wilfrid or her own imagination.[49] 'It's so difficult', she told Wilfrid's spirit on one occasion, adding that she did not want to be too credulous.[50] Spiritualists and psychical researchers underestimated their level of influence on the proceedings but they valued some sort of emotional distance. Far from suffering from a will to believe, sitters were only convinced if there were some objective grounds for dismissing the possibility of self-deception.[51] After Cynthia Asquith's brother, Yvo Allen Charteris, was killed in 1916, her mother went to a medium under 'the theory that the middle-man may still be necessary for communication – more on account of Yvo than Ego'.[52]

Mediums could be quite convincing if they were able to capture the personality of a spirit unknown to them. During their first sitting with Cannock, Nea observed,

> Wilfrid's presence [and] personality was very vivid indeed. It is very difficult to convey this in the notes, but we all there felt it ... Mrs. C. seemed to be in touch with the Wilfrid we all knew and did not appear to leave traces of her own personality.[53]

Despite the poor sitting, Nea still supposed Bacon was genuine in part because Wilfrid did seem to be present. Bacon not only identified him by name but also stated that he had career ambitions, that he was determined, that he rarely failed and that he was successful in life. He was also very clever and organised. All of this was true, Nea Walker observed, since 'he had got on very well, was very clever, and would never have been anywhere but at the top in whatever he did. He was also a "born organizer."'[54] Such a description would have resonated with most of Britain's 'lost generation' but the factual nature of the Walkers' séances underscores how moving the process of recognition could be to sitters. Like Nea, Walter Wynn considered the possibility that controls were just secondary personalities, but during a séance with Mrs Wesley Adams, he was struck by the medium's accurate description of his son.[55] When

Rupert's spirit proclaimed, 'that is my father, my guide, my teacher, my dear old Pa, I love him', Wynn was so shaken that he had to stop the proceedings. Even as he wrote about the experience later, he explained, 'the scene is so real to me as I write that I tremble with emotion'.[56]

Feelings of recognition and intimacy were triggered by memories of the dead, as relationships were re-established through remembrance in the séance room. After Dorothy and Constance Wayte sat with Leonard on 17 December 1918, Dorothy noted that the pace of the dialogue was very characteristic of her brother. It reminded her of a time a few years before he died when he visited her for a weekend. 'We talked for about three hours on end or more in just the same rapid way', she explained, as he disembarked 'himself of all his news, impressions [and] ideas'.[57] Nearly the exact opposite characterisation of Wilfrid as 'shy and reserved' was given by Cannock and affirmed by Nea, highlighting how much one's view depended upon individual memories of the dead. 'He's extremely sensitive', the medium kept repeating in frustration, complaining that she could not 'get to him as I want to'. Nea labelled this as 'appropriate', since when he was alive, Wilfrid was shy in expressing his affection towards Elsi whenever Nea was present. Jack Wayte was also impressed with how Cannock's dialogue matched Wilfrid's personality on earth, specifically that Wilfrid saw his older brother as a father figure.[58] Nea commented, and Jack agreed, that the sitting was 'a wonderfully good word picture of Wilfrid in look and in character ... We all came away feeling we certainly had been with Wilfrid.'[59]

It is easy to dismiss spiritualist pursuits as part of a credulous 'will to believe'. The experiences above indicate that some sitters struggled to separate a desire for contact with evidential proof. The survival of the other necessitated a subversion of the self, but paradoxically, communion was founded upon shared memories. The medium and trance state offered the best chance of clear evidence since information coming from a stranger or the unconscious suggested an independent identity. Modern technology and conceptions of the self provided both precedents as well as a certain level of imperfection in the communications. Once the survival of the personality was demonstrated, this opened the door to consoling messages for the bereaved and a continuity of relationships.

'The missing, but not the lost': information and consolation

During a sitting with Elizabeth Cannock on 29 March 1918, Dorothy and Jack Wayte were informed that Wilfrid could not attend the séance because he was 'with his cousin on the front' who was in danger. When Mary Pearce was informed of this development, she relayed the information to Nea and asked if she 'had anything relating to the sitting or to Ted by writing or other means?'[60] Mary was desperate for information. By 24 April she still had no official news. Inquiries made to the War Office provided no help.[61] All she could do was 'hope his letters are delayed in coming and I must just go on waiting till news does come'.[62]

Nea Walker was doing what she could to unravel the mystery, but she suspected the worst. In a séance with Leonard, she learned that Wilfrid was reunited with a newly passed spirit whom he was 'awfully pleased' to see again.[63] At a sitting with Miss Bacon on 20 April, she was informed that Wilfrid was with his cousin who was missing but who had recently passed away in the war. He was described as slender and tall with a thin nose and firm jaw. This was an accurate description of Ted.[64] Nea's fears were finally corroborated on 1 May. Mary received news from a chaplain informing her that Ted was killed at Cambrai on 21 March. 'The last that was seen of him was leading his men quite cheerfully into the battle', she explained to Nea, 'and he was bright and cheerful'.[65]

In some respects, Mary Pearce was lucky. She had received confirmatory evidence that her son was killed only weeks after he went missing. Many more would have to wait months, sometimes even years, if they received sufficient evidence at all. The war was 'a vanishing act'.[66] Consider the fate of Denis Buxton, comrade and friend of St Leger from a previous chapter. Buxton was hit in the neck by a shell fragment in no man's land during an attack on the German trenches. Under fire and with no stretcher-bearers present, a Corporal removed the shell fragment from his neck, bandaged the wound, placed his body in a shell hole under cover and told him he would return. After the battalion consolidated its objectives, the Corporal sent a man back to look for Buxton. Although he was able to uncover the shell hole, Denis had vanished.[67] He is now one of the 525,060 missing whose names are inscribed in stone in France and Belgium.[68] Was Denis taken prisoner? Did he attempt to crawl back to the trenches only to bleed out in no man's land? Was the shell hole hit with artillery, disintegrating or burying his body in the process? These were the kinds of questions that lingered in the minds of loved ones.

The scale of the missing created a shock within British culture. Traditional funerals involved a viewing of the dead body so that the bereaved could come to terms with the fact of death.[69] Britons were denied this practice, creating a need for alternative rituals. The body was essential to conventional mourning practices, but there were precedents in British history that suggested this absence could be met with ingenuity and adaptability. For example, while cremation was designed to disenchant the dead body by reducing it to base elements, modern societies continue to graft sacred meaning and identities onto ashes. Burial had long been viewed as necessary for resurrection, but some Christians accommodated cremation.[70] Combining the Anglican *Book of Common Prayer* with industrialisation, Sir Henry Thompson stated, 'never could the ... touching words "ashes to ashes, dust to dust", be more appropriately uttered than over a body about to be consigned to the furnace'.[71] In the context of the Great War, Britons turned to the names of the dead that were etched in bronze and stone. As the historian Thomas Lacqueur observes, 'We are still enchanted.' This is because biological death is distinguishable from social death. 'Death in culture takes time', explains Lacqueur, 'because it takes time for the rent in the social fabric to be rewoven'.[72] The séance can be located within the process of social death, a ritual in which death was both acknowledged but denied, and where the living dead helped the bereaved transition to a world without them.

In séances, soldiers' spirits appeared as they were before death, in both body and personality. Spiritualists attempted to downplay the importance of the physical body as it was dismembered and lost. Oliver Lodge's concept of a nonmaterial and indestructible body existing in the ether emerged out of the context of the Great War.[73] Arthur Conan Doyle explained that the etheric body was 'a perfect thing', which was comforting to know 'in these days when so many of our heroes have been mutilated in the wars. One cannot mutilate the etheric body'.[74] In Wesley Tudor-Pole's *Private Dowding*, the titular soldier spirit is at first perplexed and anxious about the fate of his body, but as he realises that he has passed into a greater existence, he begins to feel liberated. Dowding's spirit likens his journey to throwing away an old coat.[75] For many grieving Britons, the fate of the physical body was just as mysterious as the fate of the soul, but in the séance room, the departed were 'here'. The dead were 'the missing, but not the lost'.[76]

Spiritualism offered the possibility of uniting families with the missing. Caroline Rhys-Davids's son, Arthur (an Ace in the RFC), was reported missing in December 1917. Two of her neighbours began using planchette sometime in 1918 to contact their husbands, only to receive messages from anonymous soldiers. At one point they asked if Arthur Rhys-Davids was present in the spirit world and received the response, 'Let his mother call.' Carolyn started experimenting with automatic writing in June 1918 and continued to engage in dialogue with the spirit of her son for decades.[77] During a séance with J. J. Vango, W. T. Waters from Turnbridge recognised the description of an anonymous soldier as a local who had been reported missing. The spirit was desperate to establish communication with his mother and she was in deep agony over his fate. Waters initially refrained from contacting her, but after another resident received a similar message from the medium Miss McCreadie, the two joined forces to convince the family that spiritualism could help them.[78]

Mediums provided information about the fates of missing soldiers. Rudyard Kipling was sent unsolicited messages from mediums and fortune tellers after his only son John went missing in the Battle of Loos.[79] The psychical researcher Abraham Wallace reported a case where a medium successfully predicted that a missing soldier was still alive.[80] More likely, reassurances of survival were falsified as the work of the IWGC identified bodies or as the passage of time made survival less likely. These incidents were frequent enough to be the topic of a chapter in Kelway-Bamber's *Claude's Second Book*.[81] Carolyn Rhys-Davids used planchette in the late spring of 1918 to ask the spirit of her son about the fate of a family friend, Richard Maybery. Arthur's spirit confirmed that he was wounded but alive and in a POW camp.[82] She passed this information on to the family in India. Maybery was reported missing at the same time as Arthur, although his body was later found.[83] One woman received messages that her missing son Jack was alive in a POW camp. The information was revealed to be false in 1919. When she inquired into the reasons for this mistake, she was told that evil German spirits had deceived her son into believing he was a POW on earth.[84]

Some people experimented with supernormal modes of communication out of desperation, as was the case with Hazel Macnaghten.[85] Hazel's husband Angus was serving with the Black Watch during the opening months of the war. He was reported missing on 29 October 1914 and his wife was notified by telegram on 3 November. She received some hopeful information from fellow officers almost immediately. As far as they knew, Angus had received only a minor gunshot wound to the leg and had been taken prisoner by the Germans but was safe. Hazel, however, could not discover any reliable first-hand testimony about her husband. Officially, he was declared missing, and when no further information was provided she started her own investigation. She posted advertisements in the papers and contacted the War Office, the Red Cross and the embassies of neutral countries such as the United States in an attempt to reach German officials. She tracked down soldiers from the Black Watch in hospitals and those imprisoned in Germany. She sent letters addressed to Angus to various German POW camps only to have them returned. She even agreed to fund searches for missing soldiers in German camps, despite warnings that these expeditions may be the work of charlatans.[86] Hazel's efforts might appear delusional or fortuitous, but they were not irrational. There were stories of missing soldiers who, once presumed killed, suddenly reappeared or were reported alive in a CCS or POW camp. The comrades of James Case of the 24th Northumberland Fusiliers believed him to have been killed in July 1916: 'After I came out of the trenches two of my comrades nearly shook my hand off to see I was alive they were so pleased about it they said they saw me laying dead.' Word must have travelled back home quickly as he received two letters from family members who were told he was missing, presumed killed. 'I am very much alive', he was relieved to write back in response.[87]

By March 1915, Hazel was desperate enough to send one of Angus's letters to a fortune teller who conducted psychometric readings of personal objects to identify the owner's past, present and future. The fortune teller confirmed things that Hazel had already believed: Angus was shot in the leg and was taken prisoner by the Germans, but also added reasons for hope:

I follow him to Wittenberg, then Friedrichsfeld, and Munster, Osnabrück, and feel he is still in hospital and not able to walk fit. That does not mean that he will not walk again, for I get that he will recover quite nicely. He will be able to do things as usual; but not soldiering any more. He has written you and does not know that you have not heard or don't know of his whereabouts – he seems to be fairly well treated but looks thin and ill though I feel he had a wonderful recovery and will come back to you quite safely ... I feel so convinced that your husband is <u>alive</u> and that he will return.[88]

Hazel passed this information along to the German Red Cross in Berlin but after making inquiries at POW camps in Wittenberg, Friedrichsfeld, Munster and Osnabrück, they could not find Angus.[89] It was not until 1918, four years after he first went missing, that she finally received word from a soldier who witnessed her husband's death.[90]

Hazel's experience with psychics was negative, but it was indicative of the levels that family members of the missing would resort to when deprived of factual information. For those who received more convincing evidence from mediums, séances offered more than just details about the missing. Sitters were also reassured that their loved ones had passed away peacefully. Jack Wayte was informed that Wilfrid had 'passed over suddenly', although his personnel file indicates this was not the case.[91] During Dorothy and Constance's first sitting with Leonard, 'the painless passing over was emphasized'. Leonard explained that Wilfrid 'had an easy passing' and that his death was beyond anyone's control as 'there was nothing more anyone could do for him'.[92] Other mediums made similar statements. Cannock acknowledged that Wilfrid's death was 'violent' but also 'quick' with 'no time suffering'.[93] Bacon described a spirit who 'died in a hurry ... wasn't ill very long' and another who 'passed out quite suddenly'.[94] Sitters were eager to discover details about their loved ones' final moments. Walter Wynn asked Vango if Rupert experienced 'much pain in dying'. The medium responded, 'No ... too sudden.'[95] Rhys-Davids inquired with Arthur if he was wounded and if he passed over the same day he was reported missing.[96] Without more information, Carolyn was left to wonder if her son had survived the crash only to suffer a long agonising death alone.

Sitters also wanted to know if the deceased were happy in the spirit world. Carolyn Rhys-Davids observed that this was one of the 'usual questions' conducted during planchette.[97] According to mediums, spirits were elated to have passed over. Elsi was informed at a Leonard sitting on 21 October 1918 that Wilfrid was 'the happiest spirit in the spirit world!'[98] Wilfrid was said to be so happy in the afterlife that he had feelings of guilt: 'Sometimes I feel awfully selfish, how can I be so happy here.' But his spirit understood that those he left behind preferred him to be this way. 'He feels that you are asking him to be happy', it was explained, 'so I feel somehow that I ought to be'.[99] Brittain described a spirit killed in the war as 'strong and well and happy and bright'.[100] When Nea and Elsi engaged in automatic writing, they were given similar answers. During a session between Nea, Elsi and the Wayte family at their home in Croydon, Wilfrid's spirit 'emphasized his great happiness ... and kept repeating that he was all right and just the same'.[101]

Messages of painless death and happy spirits were part of a universal language of consolation, but séance dialogue also clearly depended upon the sitter's gender and precise relationship with the dead. With women, mediums adopted domestic masculine roles, embodying the providing husband, guardian soldier or dutiful son. Mediums were speaking the idiom of the time when they emphasised painless death and the well-being of the spirits.[102] The historian Jessica Meyer observes that in attempting to reinforce their roles as sons and husbands in letters home, soldiers often protected their loved ones from the horrific realities of the front.[103] Raymond Lodge frequently emphasised that he was enjoying his time in the trenches before he died, insisting that he was not simply trying to ease the anxiety of his parents.[104] The standard field postcard included the option 'I am quite well', with the only other choices being admission to hospital or 'sent down to base'.[105] When the spirit of Wilfrid stressed that he was both happy and safe to Dorothy and Constance, this was deemed appropriate because 'he knew how terribly anxious we used to be about him'.[106] Wilfrid's reassurances were hardly unique to the Wayte family and yet they reminded Dorothy and Constance of his protective nature. Caring messages represented a continuity of the domestic male as well as the survival of the individual personality.

With widows, there may have been an inclination on the part of mediums to grant them permission to find a new husband. The war impacted the way that widows mourned their deceased husbands.

Victorian mourning culture had placed significant burdens on widows.[107] As the historian Lucie Whitmore observes, early in the war, some women still felt expectations to uphold the memory of their heroic husbands and to function as 'living symbols of the glorious dead, regardless of their own needs or desires'. As the body count grew, however, it became unrealistic and indeed undesirable to expect so many young women to relinquish future emotional and sexual relationships.[108] There is evidence that some mediums encouraged young women to move on. Andrew Edward 'Teddy' Somerset Mulholland of the Irish Guards was killed in November 1914. Sometime thereafter, his wife Joan visited a medium. Teddy's spirit expressed his distress at seeing 'how miserable [she] was', and told her, 'if ever a really good and strong man comes into your life, I want you to know that ... I *want* you to marry again'. She responded that she 'could never do that for I can never love again like [I] have loved you ... and my heart is broken'. Teddy's spirit was insistent that she find 'companionship and someone to take care of you'.[109]

For mothers, there was an effort to reinforce wartime stoicism. During the war, mothers were expected to manage a 'maternal service' by relinquishing their 'sons to the nation'.[110] In order to maintain the spirit necessary to keep the home fires burning, women were encouraged to retain a stiff upper lip. In séances, mothers were instructed to overcome their grief.[111] On 17 December 1917, Wilfrid's spirit told his mother and sister that he would be with them on Christmas Day and that it was to be a positive occasion: 'Don't have the hump at Xmas. If only you knew how happy I am you would say it is worth the waiting ... Buck up and be good.'[112] If the living wanted to make the dead happy they could do so by being positive themselves. 'Be happy', Wilfrid told his mother on 31 December 1917, 'you help me far more by being happy than anything else'.[113] Stoicism was to be encouraged even in private. Carolyn Rhys-Davids asked the spirit of Arthur, 'Do you suffer when I sorrow?' Arthur's response was affirmative.[114] The frequency of these discussions indicates that British women struggled with an internal tension caused by their profound grief and demanding social expectations.[115] As mothers, their maternal role was emphasised in their sustained worry about the well-being of their sons, but as women in wartime, they were to refrain from expressing their grief. As a result, mediums tried to convince mothers that they could help their sons' spirits progress by overcoming their grief. It is possible that spiritualism may have assisted in this process as it allowed the bereaved to both give up their sons to the nation while also retaining their relationships in the séance room. But it is just as likely that British women suffered as they tried to follow impossible demands from spirits they believed to be their children. By insisting that they move on and be happy, mediums were invoking the memory of slain soldiers to ask mothers to accomplish something they simply could not do.[116] This disconnect between wartime expectations and the realities of losing a child must have caused mothers considerable pain.

One way that mediums tried to help sitters overcome their grief was through the promise of a reunion in the spirit world. For young women such as Elsi Walker, the war threatened the prospect of future marriage. In the séance room, however, the current separation between life and death was only temporary. 'I expect them to miss me', Wilfrid stated to Elsi, 'but … Don't you see, darling, we're going to be together for so many years, millions of years'.[117] This put wartime grief into perspective. As Claude's spirit explained to his mother, 'life is very happy here and full of interest even the grief and pain of those you love and have left behind does not affect one in the old way, for one can see beyond the trouble of the day and know it is I only for a little while'.[118]

Descriptions of the other side reinforced the notion that grief was unnecessary. Spiritualists articulated a 'thick description of heaven'. In 'Summerland' (as the afterlife was popularly known in spiritualist circles), familial and social relationships were maintained, as were art, culture and ethical and moral systems. Summerland was democratic, as the spirit was able to evolve and progress to higher stages of spiritual development. Those who sinned in life began at lower levels and had to work their way to greater spiritual progress, but there was no eternal damnation to hell.[119] The afterlife was also portrayed as a paradise. A home circle from Cornwall received a message from an RFA driver who explained that 'I am in a wonderful and glorious zone … my home now is far lovelier, far more beautiful, far more wonderful, than I had ever, or could ever, have conceived … this realm seems to be perfection itself'. The spirit described seeing singing angels, beautiful gardens, gigantic temples and buildings made of gold as well as hearing wonderful music.[120]

Summerland offered Britons the possibility of an escape from war's material destruction and a safe haven for loved ones brutally killed in the conflict. One could rest assured knowing that a family member was free from the dangers of war and was simultaneously allowed to enjoy certain earthly pleasures despite an early death. Raymond Lodge talked about the soldiers wanting to smoke cigars and drink whisky while Wilfrid Wayte had a house on the water as well as a garden.[121] 'The spirit world is the real world', Wilfrid explained, and putting the current troubles of the war into relief, he stated, 'everything here is indestructible [and] permanent'.[122]

Spiritualists' visions of the afterlife likely appealed to a broader number of people. Unlike the heaven of orthodox Christianity, an earthly afterlife was relatable and tangible, not abstract and unknowable.[123] A benevolent but earthly heaven also implied that it was possible to transform earth itself into heaven, to make the world free from class conflict and war. In Summerland, there were no coal mines, and individuals pursued the arts and psychic science to help humanity progress.[124] The soldiers' communications gave those on earth a vision to attain.

Perhaps most significantly, an earthly afterlife made it easier to imagine the survival of the personality, as spirits acted according to habits reflective of their character. On 31 December 1917, Wilfrid was described as conducting work on the other side involving 'lines' and 'special marks'. Nea and Elsi presumed this to be a reference to his interest in mathematics.[125] Death could not be the end if the dead still engaged in mathematics and talked to loved ones. Conan Doyle admitted as such, writing, 'If a human being has technical, literary, musical, or other tendencies, they are an essential part of his character, and to survive without them would be to lose his identity.'[126]

Spiritualists were steadfast in their belief that they could navigate grief more effectively. As we will see later, when this perceived moral authority was advocated publicly in the mid-1920s, it created a backlash in which mediums were cast as parasitic frauds. Events within the Walker circle indicate that the politics of spiritualism were seeping into private homes and damaging relationships at the familial level before the war was even over. Since the spiritualists' aim was to end conflict by proving the afterlife, any failure to pursue séances was akin to letting the soldiers die again. Men were described as abandoned on the other side as they waited for family members to contact them. Nea Walker, for example, was told that the spirit of her friend Hugh Russell Sommerville had been hurt by the refusal of friends and family members to attend séances. In a sitting with Ortner in May 1918, his spirit complained, 'we still have our human feelings when we are wronged' and compared this betrayal to that of a child throwing away an old toy.[127] In the fall of 1920, Arthur's spirit explained to Carolyn Rhys-Davids, 'It is not true that we want to "rest", or to be left alone. There is a great deal of unhappiness in our world, because people in your world think it is a very wrong thing to have communications with us.'[128] Carolyn Rhys-Davids was familiar with family squabbles over spiritualism as well. When the aunt of a friend discovered her niece was using planchette to communicate with her sweetheart, killed in the war, the aunt condemned the practice as the 'devil's craft'. 'What would Walter ... [a young evangelist] have said to it?' she asked.[129]

Divisions about spiritualism created a rift between Elsi and the Wayte family. The Waytes' foray into spiritualism was only temporary and their opinions were mixed. Jack was impressed with Cannock enough to arrange for two more sittings but was disappointed with Leonard. Dorothy was enthusiastic about the subject, once informing Nea that she wanted to develop trance on her own but that her mother was 'dead set against' the idea.[130] Constance did attend at least two sittings but cancelled a third on the one-year anniversary of her son's death. The reasons cited by Dorothy were fear of police raids and concerns regarding her father's reputation. 'It would do Dad such an awful lot of harm in a place like Croydon if it were known that his family went to sittings!' she explained to Nea.[131] These concerns were not unwarranted. Sine 1917, there had been persecutions against mediums for fortune telling, and embarrassing stories of hucksters and credulous sitters published in papers such as *The Times*.[132]

Elsi believed that the Waytes had a poor attitude. She complained in the fall of 1918 that they would not give 'the thing half a chance'.[133] The topic was raised at sittings, as Elsi expressed her concern about the impact it was having on Wilfrid's spirit and informed him that she would try to convince his brother and father to attend future sittings. In October 1919, Wilfrid's spirit complained that his mother 'worries and frets, and it is very irritable' and that she 'hasn't grown to miss me one little bit less'.[134] He stressed the differences that spiritualism fostered in the grieving process when he added, 'they don't realize how near we are, and why you can be so happy'.[135] Over a year earlier, when Elsi had asked how his mother's grief affected him, his spirit had replied: 'when I come to you, it makes me happy, when I come to her I feel so sorry'.[136] According to Leonard's mediumship, the Waytes were carrying an unnecessarily heavy burden by shutting out spiritual revelations and causing their son's spirit needless continued injury. If heaven on earth was to be realised, it necessitated an acceptance of the facts of survival and communication. In the interwar period, social divisions regarding spiritualism's religious and intellectual claims threatened these utopian visions.

These were some of the immediate benefits and consequences of spiritualism during the period of the Great War. Some Britons looked to the séance as a substitute for conventional mourning rituals and a solution to the problem of a missing body. Those who were convinced were given uplifting messages of painless death and superior existence in an afterlife that awaited all. Within official and unofficial networks, individual mourners were provided with a community of sympathetic men and women who were willing to share messages and experiences in order to prove the survival of personality beyond death. Social circles grew as phantom soldiers cried out to be recognised or as Britons heard about the comfort that a séance provided for a family member or friend. Clients of mediums bumped shoulders, and readers of books like *Raymond* and *Claude's Book* wrote to the authors for advice. Often, an experimental foray into talking with the dead was worth a shot; other times it led to fissures in communities and threatened to divide families. Most did not record their experiences, their temporary forays into spiritualism lost. But thanks to the devotion of psychical researchers and spiritualist leaders who sought to turn an interwar fad into a scientific and religious project, we have access to some of their stories. Still, in the long term, spiritualism allowed the living to retain communal relationships with the dead as they adjusted to life without their physical presence. Some gradually moved on, while others continued to be haunted by the Great War's dead.

Giving up the ghost

In October 1930, Nea Walker received a surprising letter from Constance Wayte asking to arrange a sitting with Leonard for the thirteenth anniversary of Wilfrid's death. As she explained to Nea, she had felt 'the wish for a long time now' to conduct another séance and lately her desire had 'grown stronger'.[137] This was Nea's first contact with the Waytes in approximately a decade, and by the 1930s, her initial community of spiritualists had narrowed considerably. In addition to the departure of the Wayte family, Mary Pearce's opinions towards spiritualism coarsened. In the 1920s, she suffered a decline in health and passed away in the early 1930s.[138] Ted's spirit gradually stopped appearing in séances as a result. Evolutionary concepts of the afterlife offered an explanation for such disappearances, as spirits were said to progress to greater states of existence once their work on a certain plane was completed. After Mary had come to terms with Ted's death, his spirit 'had other things to do'.[139] Wilfrid remained a significant figure in the lives of the Walker sisters. His 'presence is very real here, especially to Elsi', Nea explained to Constance in 1930. Elsi and Nea had known Wilfrid as a ghost longer than in life and continued to communicate with his spirit for at least another six years. How did spiritualists maintain personal relationships with the ghosts of war well after their deaths?

The historian Robert Cox describes spiritualism as 'an elaborate social physiology in which individuals', dead or alive, 'were integrated holistically within the structures of society, joined in thought, affect, and sensation into the fiber of a sympathetically united nation'.[140] Cox is writing about spiritualism in the nineteenth-century United States here, but his observations are equally relevant to interwar Britain. Spiritualists looked towards the unconscious and psychical as the site where a bounded community could be re-constructed in the modern world, across the British Empire, between the living and dead, and which was tightly bound with the ideals of progress and British exceptionalism. British spiritualists indicated that the dead surrounded the living and took part in earthly affairs while the living visited the spiritual world at night in their dreams. People's thoughts and feelings impinged on those in the other world and the world around them, and the thoughts of the spirit world affected those on earth leading to a more sympathetic and united empire at war. In the private realm, a sympathetic spiritualist philosophy could be used to maintain personal relationships with the war dead for extended periods while simultaneously suffusing their deaths with meaning.

From her very first séance, Elsi was informed that Wilfrid was watching over her, inside and outside the séance room, and that this connection would grow stronger over time. For example, in her first sitting with Leonard, Wilfrid was described as 'awful close' to her and that 'it's a wonder you can't feel the power'.[141] Eventually, Elsi would be able to develop a 'feeling' or 'sense' when his spirit was with her. The two could communicate in 'a mental way' and this would develop into something like an instinct. 'I will come so much more clearly in time', Wilfrid's spirit told her, 'that you will be able to get it without thinking'.[142] Similarly, Carolyn Rhys-Davids asked whether or not Arthur's spirit touched her and how she would know when he does. L. Kelway-Bamber had confessed to Rhys-Davids that she had learned to '*feel* her son (as a feather drawn across the skin), and had seen him once, seated by her'.[143] Elsi, Jack, Dorothy and Constance Wayte, as well as Damaris Walker, were all informed that the spirits of either Wilfrid or Jack Howell had attempted to make noises by tapping.[144] The implication was that the dead were always present but that it took certain states of awareness to coordinate that sympathy, as if adjusting a radio's frequency.

Mediums occasionally identified spirits as presiding over séance proceedings and physically interacting with the living. Their statements add an element of intimacy and touch that is otherwise difficult to discern in the textual record of investigative scripts. When Dorothy and Constance Wayte visited Leonard, it was mentioned that Wilfrid had taken Constance's hand.[145] During Joan Mulholland's séance, she claimed she could feel Teddy hugging her. The feeling was difficult to describe but she remembered him putting 'his arms around me and hugged me *exactly* as like he used to and I really felt it was him'.[146] For their part, mediums occasionally communicated the nature of a soldier's death as if they were experiencing the physical effects themselves. Some coughed to indicate gassing or influenza or complained about a pain in the shoulder.[147] The soldier's death was embodied by the medium, bringing the moment of death back into the domestic sphere and the afterlife into a lived, sensuous experience.

Sleep especially was presumed to be an ideal space for spiritual visitations. Sitters such as Constance Wayte were informed that their ethereal bodies travelled to the spirit world while sleeping and Arthur Rhys-Davids promised to visit Carolyn in her dreams.[148] These sentiments resonated with the Wayte and Davids families who had reported crisis apparitions on the night of Wilfrid and Arthur's deaths, respectively.[149] Mediums also promised the prospect of gaining the ability to see the dead in waking life. Leonard, for example, encouraged her sitters to anticipate visions. On 31 December 1917, Wilfrid's spirit told Elsi, Nea and Constance that Wilfrid would try to get through to them 'at an unexpected time' and challenged them to 'see if you can sense me'.[150]

The frequency with which Britons professed to sense the dead indicates one of the reasons why spiritualism found a ready audience in the era of the Great War. Spiritualism offered the possibility of a thinning of the veil between this life and the other just as Britain was haunted by the memories of 700,000 dead. It articulated feelings of closeness and intimacy with the departed in pseudo-mystical-scientific terms. Frederic Myers's view was that reminders of the dead could bring subliminal messages from the deceased to conscious awareness. Mediums advocated that memory was like a magnet. Bacon told Elsi that, when she looked at Wilfrid's photograph, her 'very strong thoughts' brought him closer.[151] Thinking of a certain spirit prior to a séance was believed to increase the chances of better communications.[152] Environments were also associated with the manifestation of appropriate spirits. When Elsi and Nea spent the weekend at the Waytes' home in Croydon, Nea described a moment when Wilfrid took control of one of her arms during an automatic writing session to shake Jack's hand and touch John's shoulder. She concluded, 'the link seemed to be very strong with Elsi in his own home'.[153] In October 1919, Wilfrid's spirit insinuated that if Elsi went to France to visit his grave, he would be able to explain more clearly what had happened to him.[154] It was no accident that Nea thought Ted might be contacting her in her parents' home in March 1918, since she had been thinking of him and Wilfrid that night. 'They had only in 1914 been members of a house party' in Lampeter, she explained, 'and being back in the old surroundings made one think of them more than usual'.[155] What others might find to be a bias – Nea dreamt of Ted because she had been thinking of him – was proof of a spiritualist sympathetic cosmos. To remember the dead was to summon their spirits. As certain soldiers faded from memory, so too did their ghosts.

One of the more revealing aspects of this intense sympathy was the ways in which spirits were said to be with those they left behind as they dealt with the struggles of daily life, including mourning over their deaths. The dead could sustain their previous domestic roles and soldierly duties as guardians and protectors. Spirits were often said to be influencing the living, guiding them, inspiring them and watching over them while the living also helped the dead progress. At a sitting with Ortner in October 1918, Wilfrid's spirit informed Elsi that '[w]hen you are in difficulties, remember your old Wilf will be with you'.[156] Leonard explained that Wilfrid was with her shortly after he died and that he telepathically helped his mother write the letter to Elsi informing her of his death.[157] Jack Wayte was also told that Wilfrid watched over him and helped him to do the right thing in difficult situations.[158] Jack confirmed that he had 'felt his presence' and wondered if Wilfrid's spirit was present at a meeting to discuss a war memorial at his old school.[159]

Wilfrid maintained his presence in the Walker sisters' lives as part of three larger narratives: the redemptive nature of the war's death toll, the personal life of Elsi and Nea's work as a psychical researcher. Wilfrid's spirit insinuated that his death carried meaning. When Elsi asked him when they would be reunited, Wilfrid explained: 'not yet I know that you've got something important to do for us you are staying here for me'.[160] Nea was told that 'there's something really important to be done, and we're helping'.[161] Their job was to help Wilfrid progress spiritually, as the sympathy they were building together allowed him to develop the knowledge necessary to master the bridge between the spiritual and physical worlds.[162] The spirits were also said to be doing important work. As Leonard told Dorothy Wayte, 'he was wanted on the other side' since 'there is a great work to do there'.[163] Carolyn Rhys-Davids was told that Arthur was doing important training regarding a mysterious ritual known as 'circle fire'. This work, it was explained, was like a 'purification' process that 'burns away false ideas' in the moments before the dead awake in the spirit world, a process that was deemed essential for the coming new millennium and the return of Christ.[164]

Living with the ghosts of war 195

The automatic writing of Rhys-Davids and the mediumships of Brittain, Bacon, Leonard and Ortner all indicated that the spirits were helping the deceased on the battlefield.[165] Brittain described hearing the 'clash of artillery' during a sitting on 18 July 1917 because the spirits were moving back and forth from the front.[166] The Walkers could also aid in the process. Wilfrid's spirit indicated that he was with Nea at the time of Ted's death because being in sympathy with her 'helped him to know what to say and what to do'.[167] Elsi was told she was able to assist Wilfrid in helping newly passed soldiers because, since she lived on the earthly plane, she was closer to their passing-over conditions than he was.[168] The concept of sympathy reinterpreted death on the battlefield as a communal affair, just like the war effort. The lines between the war front and home front, and individual and community, were as artificial as those that separated the two worlds.

For the Walkers, spiritualism was a consistent part of their lives for years after the war. Spirit communications could depend upon the sitter's gender, but the Walkers' story also reminds us of the importance of individual experiences. Despite losing her sweetheart at the age of twenty-six, Elsi was never instructed to move on – quite the contrary, as she continued to communicate with Wilfrid's spirit until at least the late 1930s. Neither Nea nor Elsi let go of Wilfrid for quite some time, but for different reasons. For Nea, her purpose was to be a psychic investigator who helped reunite the living with the dead. She eventually wrote two books that used the spirits of Jack Howell and Wilfrid as her communicators, and served as the editor of the SPR's *Journal* from 1934 to 1938.[169] The importance of investigation was especially stressed in séances with male participants. Messages encouraging stoicism are noticeably absent, reflecting prewar attitudes that women were expected to be more emotional than men. But through spiritualism and psychical research, men like Oliver Lodge and Conan Doyle were not simply mourning their children but participating in scientific research; bereavement was reframed as an intellectual pursuit, much in the same way that Rudyard Kipling channelled his grief into the work of IWGC. When speaking to Mary Lodge, Raymond's spirit insists that 'there must be no sadness', but when speaking with his father, Raymond emphasises the scientific value of their communications.

Elsi's attachment was related to her own personal struggles. She had to stop attending séances with Leonard after 1921 owing to her loss of hearing, an impairment that began a few years earlier (right around the time of Wilfrid's death, when she first described hearing noises that she believed might be from his spirit).[170] Nea continued to see Leonard and relayed messages from Wilfrid to Elsi. On 7 December 1929, she was informed, 'Wilfrid wants Elsi to know he's going to simply live with her at Christmas. Not going to be away from her at all.'[171] Elsi still believed her spirit travelled at night and that Wilfrid visited Elsi's bedroom. In 1929 while Damaris and Elsi were sharing a room, the former reported seeing a vision of a youthful Elsi and Wilfrid dancing while she lay in bed.[172] Their brief relationship on earth extended years after Wilfrid's death as Elsi struggled with deafness. Even as late as 1936, Feda was telling Nea, 'Wilfrid feels that Elsi needs him very much'.[173]

Elsi and Nea were able to find Wilfrid's influence as the years passed and his earthly life became more of a distant memory. Wilfrid's spirit was credited with helping treat Elsi's hearing. In a sitting on 15 March 1924, Wilfrid imparted advice from a spirit on the other side known as 'Dr Beale'. This brought the Walkers into touch with the medium Miss Harvey who claimed to be able to access Beale in trance and who in turn provided a diagnosis through a psychometric reading of Elsi's hair. Elsi's hearing was not cured, but Nea found that Harvey's diagnosis was similar to what had been described in a Leonard séance on 14 March by Wilfrid. The similarity confirmed for Nea that the whole affair was evidence that Wilfrid was trying 'to help [Elsi] and to watch over her and care for her'.[174]

Elsi's attachment to spiritualism may have been long given her age. Others moved on from spiritualism. Sara Nye of London had lost her two sons. On the night of her youngest son's death, she saw his vision at the foot of her bed. After losing her second son, she turned to the church. Nye struggled to understand why good Christians like her sons were taken at such a young age. Unsatisfied with the church's answers, she turned to spiritualism. Her sons explained that their death was not God's will but the result of sin, and humanity would now have to endure great suffering. Satisfied, her faith in God was restored. By 1921, her communications were less frequent. 'Having convinced me of their continuity of life', she explained, 'they are performing the work of their promotion'.[175] Their 'work' on earth was completed after helping Sara reclaim her faith.

Other parents, such as Rudyard Kipling, were unable to overcome their grief, and Carolyn Rhys-Davids and Oliver Lodge continued to engage with spiritualism until their deaths. Once this generation passed away, so too did many of spiritualism's wartime converts. After Lodge's death in 1940, the Walker sisters' work in psychical research appears to have ceased. Nea stopped producing content for the SPR, although she remained an honorary associate until her death in 1976, not long before Elsi passed away.[176] We do not know what happened to her and Elsi's relationship with spiritualism, but it is possible that Elsi never truly let go of Wilfrid and that the spirits continued to haunt the Walker home over a half-century after they first came knocking.

Conclusion

Enid Hudson was travelling through the Balkans in 1922 when she thought she saw a ghost. Her train stopped somewhere between Bulgaria and Trieste and when she looked outside she saw an old friend: Angus Macnaghten, who had gone missing in 1914 and whose body was never found despite the efforts of his widow, Hazel.[177] Upon reflection, Hudson figured it was probably just a 'likeness' as she was in 'a very dazed, ill condition' and 'frightfully over-tired'.[178] The incident went unrecorded until she casually mentioned it to Hazel Macnaghten in 1931.[179] Hazel never lost hope that her husband might be found, and this new piece of information ignited another round of fervent searching. She contacted German officials, including a photograph of Angus, to question whether or not POWs were ever held in Bulgaria.[180] She also returned to supernormal sources and sent Angus's personal items for psychometric readings. The only information the fortune teller could provide was a peculiar dream in which she sensed that Angus was in Belgium either alive or dead and something about a 'former life'.[181]

Hazel's son recalled that his mother's hopes were periodically lifted anytime she read about an amnesiac soldier being reunited with his family years after the war.[182] These men had no recollection of their lives before the war and had adopted new personalities.[183] What if Angus had been wandering around Europe all this time? Hazel's research brought her into contact with John Gouldney, who had served with the BEF before losing his memory in 1914. He was eventually discovered in California fifteen years later, living under a completely different identity. It was not until 1930 that he rediscovered his previous personality. In speculating on how he had arrived in California, he explained he had lived in the United States previously and probably 'acquired some personality that would have let the British authorities think I was an American'. At some point, he came into contact with a doctor familiar with fugue cases and multiple personalities. Gouldney was unable to help Hazel, but he was 'quite sure there are hundreds of such cases that would be as fortunate as me if they could only find the right man to handle there [sic] case'.[184] Angus's ghost refused to be buried.

Hazel was searching for her husband's personality in the subconscious of other men, just as Nea and Elsi Walker found Wilfrid in that of mediums. The uncertainty of life and death caused by the Great War's vanishing act and the rupture of identity in the shell shocked proved to be fertile ground for a new age of relativity and the irrational unconscious that signified modernism. But that world coexisted with the world of spirits. The loss of a body and practical information about Angus's death left open the possibility that the war had severed his identity, just as it had their relationship as husband and wife. Had Hazel discovered Angus as another personality, his identity might have been reintegrated through the gradual process of remembrance. For the Walkers, this process occurred in the séance room where proof of identity, shared memories and embodied domestic masculinity in the medium transformed the latter's trance personalities into the spirits of the dead. A study of psychoanalytical sources during the interwar period is a repository not just of traumatised soldiers, but also 'wandering unknown living soldiers' like John Gouldney, who bring us closer to the experiences of spiritualists and psychical researchers.

The industrial slaughter of the Great War led to the creation of a unique form of commemoration. The mangling of the corpse, the confusion of bones, the disappearance of the body and wandering amnesiacs all contributed to a 'potentially endless' mourning in which 'people could neither accept nor refuse the death of their loved ones'.[185] One solution was the creation of a Tomb of the Unknown Warrior. Through ritual and remembrance, this anonymous soldier's body became no one and everyone. His was a mystical body where biology was transcended and identity was both individual and universal. The spiritualist activities in the séance bear a striking resemblance to the more recognised memorial practices of the Great War era, sharing similar influences and attending to comparable needs.

It is not clear which of these approaches was more or less useful in the bereavement process. Elsi Walker, Constance Wayte, Hazel Macnaghten and Rudyard Kipling all experienced prolonged grief with no signs of overcoming their pain. But they were united by shared experiences, and their modes of grieving, although different, were not at odds with one another, causing their trajectories to overlap. If we end Hazel Macnaghten's story at her visit to Angus's name at the Menin Gate Memorial, not at her first or second correspondence with a fortune teller, it may be because Kipling's form of mourning has cast itself into solid stone that continues to dominate the French and Belgian countryside. If the ghosts that haunted the Walker sisters between 1917 and 1936 have proven more ephemeral, the answer may be as simple as the fact that the language of spiritualism served the immediate needs of a generation that had moved on or passed away by the Second World War. Sir Oliver Conan Doyle died in 1930, and Sir Oliver Lodge in 1940; the Walkers' devotion to spiritualism and psychical research followed suit. Nevertheless, spiritualists once attempted to graft their vision of the war dead onto stone at the very site where the ominous presence of the dead could be viscerally felt every year: the Cenotaph. The reasons for this endeavour and its consequences are the subject of the next chapter.

Notes

1 CUL MS SPR34/24/7, Nea Walker, E. W. and N. W. Sitting with Mrs Leonard, 29 December 1917, p. 10. These are Nea's words referring to Elsi's description.
2 CUL, MS SPR34/26/24, Nea Walker, Account of an Unverified Psychic Communication by N. W., 2 May 1918, pp. 1–2.

3 *Ibid.*, pp. 2–6.
4 *Ibid.*, p. 10.
5 CUL, MS SPR34/26/25, letter from Mary E. Pearce to Nea Walker, 28 March 1918, p. 1.
6 CUL, MS SPR34/24/9, Nea Walker, Sitting with Mrs Leonard at Datchet, 19 April 1918, p. 47.
7 CUL, MS SPR34/24/9, letter from Mary E. Pearce to Nea Walker, 13 April 1918, p. 1; CUL, MS SPR34/26/24, Nea Walker, 2 May 1918, pp. 3, 15.
8 Jay Winter, *Sites of Memory, Sites of Mourning: The Great War in European Cultural History*, Canto Edition (Cambridge: Cambridge University Press, 1998), pp. 54–5.
9 Arthur Conan Doyle, *The New Revelation* (New York: George H. Doran, 1918), p. 38.
10 Arthur Conan Doyle, *The History of Spiritualism*, vol. II (London and New York: Cassell & Company, 1926), pp. 235–6; 'From the Lighthouse Window', *Light*, 39:2008 (1919), 215.
11 Eric J. Leed, *No Man's Land: Combat and Identity in World War I* (Cambridge: Cambridge University Press, 1979), p. 1.
12 For masculinity, see Jessica Meyer, *Men of War: Masculinity and the First World War in Britain* (New York: Palgrave Macmillan, 2009); Joanna Bourke, *Dismembering the Male: Men's Bodies, Britain and the Great War* (Chicago, IL: University of Chicago Press, 1996); Deborah Cohen, *The War Come Home: Disabled Veterans in Britain and Germany, 1914–1939* (Chicago, IL: University of Chicago Press, 2001). For women, see Susan Grayzel, *Women and the First World War* (Abingdon: Taylor & Francis, 2013), pp. 101–16.
13 CUL, MS SPR34/24/4, Nea Walker, N. W. and D. W. Sitting at Mrs Leonard's, 17 July 1917, pp. 1, 28, 34–5; Nea Walker, 'Obituary: Sir Oliver Lodge, F. R. S. and Sir J. J. Thomson, O. M., F. R. S.', *PSPR*, 46:163 (1940–41), 218–23.
14 CUL, MS SPR34/25/15, Nea Walker, N. W. Group Portion of the Leonard Sitting, 13 June 1933, p. 4. Biographical details provided in the notes to this séance.
15 CUL, MS SPR34/24/9, Nea Walker, 19 April 1918, pp. 9, 16. Details regarding Ted's involvement with spiritualism are vague, but Nea noted that he had occasionally taken part in the Walkers' automatic writing communications with Wilfrid and had read *Raymond* but as far as she knew had never been to a medium.
16 In the transcript of 29 December 1917, Nea notes that they were done in shorthand (CUL, MS SPR34/24/7, Nea Walker, 29 December 1917, p. 1). Her original shorthand notes for 7 May 1927 also survive (CUL,

MS SPR34/25/6. Nea Walker, N. W. Leonard, 7 May 1927). There were a few instances when someone other than Nea recorded the séances, including Dorothy Wayte and Elsi Walker, and it is unlikely they were done using shorthand. These transcripts are identified by their authors in subsequent notes.

17 Nea was especially critical of the medium Miss Bacon on this point, indicating that she would not recommend her to novice sitters because of her constant 'fishing' (CUL, MS SPR34/26/1, Nea Walker, E. W. and N. W. Sitting with Miss Bacon at 131 Castellian Mansions, 20 April 1918, pp. 1–2, 4, 7). The same criticism was communicated by Nea to Lodge regarding the medium Hester Dowden (formally Hester Travers Smith) (CUL, MS SPR34/400, letter from Nea Walker to Sir Oliver Lodge, 30 March 1932, p. 2).

18 CUL, MS SPR34/24/8, Nea Walker, Sitting at Mrs Leonard's, 31 December 1917, pp. 30–1, 36. In another example, on 19 April 1918, Nea mistakenly referred to Elsi by name in front of Leonard. She felt obligated to make a note so as not to confuse the subsequent use of Elsi's name as evidence of supernormal abilities (CUL, MS SPR34/24/9, Nea Walker, 19 April 1918, p. 1).

19 CUL, MS SPR34/24/9, Nea Walker, 19 April 1918, p. 42.

20 CUL, MS SPR34/24/8, Nea Walker, 31 December 1918, p. 4.

21 CUL, MS SPR34/26/2, letter from J. Arthur Hill to Nea Walker, August 1917, pp. 1–2.

22 Sessions were conducted with the spirit photographer Ada Deane in 1923. See CUL, MS SPR34/24/21, Nea Walker, Sitting with Mrs Deane for Photography, 5 May 1923; and CUL, MS SPR34/24/22, Nea Walker, Sitting with Mrs Deane, 8 September 1923.

23 A list of his controls can be found in A. W. Trethewy, *The 'Controls' of Stainton Moses ('M. A. Oxon')* (London: Hurst & Blackett Ltd., 1923), pp. 21–3.

24 W. H. Salter, *Trance Mediumship: An Introductory Study on Mrs. Piper and Mrs. Leonard* (Glasgow: Society for Psychical Research, 1950), pp. 8, 16.

25 The Walkers encountered this method with Cannock and the medium Miss Pearson. Cannock did have a control but not during this sitting. Nea referred to Cannock's methods here as 'normal clairvoyance' (CUL SPRMS34/26/4, Nea Walker, Sitting at Mrs Cannock's, 31 December 1917, p. 2). Miss Pearson's state was labelled 'semi-trance' (CUL, MS SPR34/26/13, Nea Walker, N. W. at Miss Pearson's, 20 July 1918, p. 15).

26 Leonard first conducted a personal control of Wilfrid on 29 December 1917 (CUL, MS SPR34/24/7, 2, Nea Walker, 29 December 1917, pp.

7–8). Between May and October 1918 Ortner began doing personal controls of Wilfrid, and Leonard seems to have abandoned the practice around this time. It was identified in the notes of 20 October that Ortner's control was far superior and that the Walkers had intended to stop trying with Leonard (CUL, MS SPR34/24/10, Elsi Walker and Nea Walker, Elsi Sitting at Mrs Leonard's, at Datchet, 20 October 1918, p. 15).

27 CUL, MS SPR34/26/21, Damaris and Nea Walker, Mrs P. Using Crystal, March–May 1923.
28 Susy Smith, *The Mediumship of Mrs. Leonard* (New York: University Books, 1964), p. 43.
29 Ibid., pp. 19–20, 51.
30 Una Troubridge, 'The Modus Operandi in So-Called Mediumistic Trance', *PSPR*, 32:84 (1922), 353–4.
31 Ibid., 367–8.
32 Oliver Lodge, *Raymond: Or Life and Death* (New York: George H. Doran Company, 1916), pp. 105–16.
33 CUL, MS SPR34/26/1, Nea Walker, 20 April 1918, p. 2.
34 Walter Wynn, *Rupert Lives!* (London: Kingsley Press, 1919), p. 165.
35 CUL, MS SPR34/26/1, Nea Walker, 20 April 1918, pp. 1–2, 4.
36 Adam Crabtree, *From Mesmer to Freud: Magnetic Sleep and the Roots of Psychological Healing* (New Haven, CT: Yale University Press, 1993), p. 311.
37 Whatley Carington, 'The Quantitative Study of Trance Personalities I', *PSPR*, 42:136 (1934), 173–83.
38 Whatley Carington, 'The Quantitative Study of Trance Personalities II', *PSPR*, 43:141 (1935), 410.
39 Carington, 'Trance Personalities II', 410.
40 Carington, 'Trance Personalities I', 173.
41 Carington first made the proposal in 1921, although his name was then Whatley Smith. See Whatley Smith, 'A Suggested New Method of Research', *PSPR*, 31:81 (1921), 401–12.
42 CUL, MS SPR34/24/7, Nea Walker, 29 December 1917, pp. 3–4, 13, 18–20.
43 CUL, MS SPR34/24/8, Nea Walker, 31 December 1917, p. 2.
44 Lodge, *Raymond*, pp. 3–82; L. Kelway-Bamber, *Claude's Book* (London: Psychic Book Club, 1919), pp. 115–49.
45 Lodge, *Raymond*, pp. 19–21, 25, 51, 90–104.
46 Ellen Little (published anonymously), *Grenadier Rolf* (London: Kingsley Press, 1920), p. 38.
47 CUL MS SPR35/1141, Oliver Lodge, Reply to a Question from an Old Lady, Who on Reading *Raymond* Is Puzzled by the Perpetual Youth of Feda, n.d.

48 CUL MS SPR34/24/6, Nea Walker, Sitting with Mrs Leonard, 28 December 1917, pp. 38–40.
49 Damaris conducted several experimental trance séances as a medium between February and April 1923 in the Walker sisters' home. In one of her last recorded sittings, it was noted that Hugh Walker (their father) had to stop doing sittings with Damaris because her mediumship was too fragile, and it was also observed that Damaris 'could hear herself speaking in patches' (CUL, MS SPR34/26/19, Nea Walker, E. W. and D. W., 7 April 1923, pp. 2, 4). Damaris's struggles with trance were the topic of a séance with Leonard in May 1923 and there was talk about whether or not she should continue (CUL, MS SPR34/24/21, Nea Walker, N. W. at Mrs Leonard's, 5 May 1923, pp. 10–14, 19–25).
50 CUL, MS SPR34/24/7, Nea Walker, 29 December 1917, pp. 5–7.
51 Peter Lamont, *Extraordinary Beliefs: A Historical Approach to a Psychological Problem* (Cambridge: Cambridge University Press, 2013), p. 45. Using conjuring theories, Lamont observes that people do not willingly suspend their disbelief at a magic show, but instead look for explanations. The strength of the effect is dependent upon the conjuror's ability to eliminate ordinary explanations. The same is true with extraordinary beliefs. In order to be convinced of them, ordinary explanations have to be explored by the observer and deemed inadequate.
52 Lady Cynthia Asquith, *Diaries: 1915–1918* (London: Hutchinson, 1968), p. 236.
53 CUL, MS SPR34/26/4, Nea Walker, 31 December 1917, p. 2.
54 CUL, MS SPR34/26/1, Nea Walker, 20 April 1918, pp. 16, 36.
55 Wynn, *Rupert Lives!*, p. 120.
56 Ibid., pp. 148–9.
57 CUL, MS SPR34/24/5, Dorothy Wayte, Notes by Dorothy Wayte, 17 December 1917, p. 4.
58 CUL, MS SPR34/26/4, Nea Walker, 31 December 1917, pp. 10, 18–20.
59 Ibid., p. 30.
60 CUL, MS SPR34/24/9, letter from Mary E. Pearce to Nea Walker, 3 April 1918, p. 1.
61 CUL, MS SPR34/24/9, Nea Walker, 19 April 1918. Jack Wayte, who served in the RAMC, contacted the War Office on her behalf. For details of his war record and life, see his obituary, 'Dr J. W. Wayte', *The British Medical Journal*, 2:4903 (1954), 1553.
62 CUL, MS SPR34/26/25, letter from Mary E. Pearce to Nea Walker, 25 April 1918.
63 CUL, MS SPR34/24/9, Nea Walker, 19 April 1918, p. 6.
64 CUL, MS SPR34/26/1, Nea Walker, 20 April 1918, p. 23.
65 CUL, MS SPR34/26/25, letter from Mary E. Pearce to Nea Walker, 1 May 1918.

66 Jay Winter, *War beyond Words: Languages of Remembrance from the Great War to the Present* (Cambridge: Cambridge University Press, 2017), p. 49.
67 IWM, Private Papers of Lieutenant W. B. St Leger MC, Documents.20504, Diary 9 September 1917 to 9 December 1917, pp. 99–101.
68 Commonwealth War Graves Commission, *Annual Report, 2014–2015*, accessed November 2018, https://issuu.com/wargravescommission/docs/ar_2014-2015?e=4065448/31764375, 39.
69 Pat Jalland, *Death in the Victorian Family* (Oxford: Oxford University Press, 1996), pp. 210–13.
70 Thomas Lacqueur, *The Work of the Dead: A Cultural History of Mortal Remains* (Princeton, NJ: Princeton University Press, 2015), pp. 495–548.
71 Quoted in Jennifer Leaney, 'Ashes to Ashes: Cremation and the Celebration of Death in Nineteenth-Century Britain', in Ralph Houlbrooke (ed.), *Death, Ritual, and Bereavement* (London and New York: Routledge, 1989), pp. 131–2.
72 Lacqueur, *The Work of the Dead*, pp. 10, 18.
73 Richard Noakes, *Physics and Psychics: The Occult and the Sciences in Modern Britain* (Cambridge: Cambridge University Press, 2019), pp. 304–11.
74 Arthur Conan Doyle, *The Vital Message* (London: George H. Doran Company, 1919), pp. 93–4.
75 Wesley Tudor Pole, *Private Dowding* (London: John M. Watkins, 1918), pp. 6–13.
76 J. Cuming Walters, 'Spiritualism and War', *The Two Worlds*, 43:2243 (1930), 712.
77 Senate House Library (hereafter SHL), University of London, Caroline Augusta Foley Rhys-Davids Papers, MS1082/1/1, Caroline Rhys-Davids, 'Chronicle of First Steps', pp. 1–3.
78 W. T. Waters, 'The Same Message through Two Mediums', *Light*, 39:2032 (1919), 407.
79 Winter, *Sites of Memory, Sites of Mourning*, pp. 72–3; Tonie and Valmai Holt, *My Boy Jack? The Search for Kipling's Only Son* (Barnsley: Pen & Sword, 2011), chapter 7, Kindle.
80 Abraham Wallace, 'Missing Soldiers: Remarkable Evidence', *Light*, 39:1985 (1919), 29.
81 L. Kelway-Bamber, *Claude's Second Book* (London: Methuen & Co., 1919), pp. 43–6. Claude's spirit explanation was that sometimes it was difficult to tell if an astral body was merely visiting the spirit world or had been severed permanently from the physical body.

82 SHL, MS1082/1/1, Rhys-Davids, 'Chronicle of First Steps', p. 10.
83 Commonwealth War Graves Commission, 'Captain Richard Aveline Maybery', accessed 26 April 2018, www.cwgc.org/find-war-dead/casualty/336959/maybery,-richard-aveline/. His date of death is listed as 19 December 1917.
84 Mary Hamilton, 'Message from a "Missing" Soldier', *The International Psychic Gazette*, 6:69 (1919), 134.
85 The Macnaghtens' story also appears in Richard van Emden, *The Quick and the Dead: Fallen Soldiers and Their Families in the Great War* (London and New York: Bloomsbury, 2011), pp. 174–88.
86 Angus Macnaghten, *'Missing': An Account of the Efforts Made to Find an Officer of the Black Watch, Reported 'Missing' on 29th October, 1914, during the First Battle of Ypres* (Bala, North Wales: Dragon Books, 1970), pp. 11, 16, 21–5, 34–5, 42–3.
87 IWM, Private Papers of Reverend E. E. Hayward, Documents.7073, letter from James Case to Rev. Hayward, 19 July 1916.
88 IWM, Private Papers of Captain A. C. R. S. Macnaghten, Documents.3696, Captain A. C. R. S. Macnaghten: Correspondence with his widow after ACRSM was reported missing-February-March 1915, letter from Otto von Bourg to Hazel Macnaghten, 18 March 1915.
89 Macnaghten, *Missing*, pp. 43–5.
90 *Ibid.*, pp. 51–5.
91 CUL, MS SPR34/19/12, Helen Salter, Sitting with Mrs Leonard, 28 January 1918, p. 2. Wilfrid Wayte was shot in the right thigh on 6 October 1917 at the latest (it is unclear from his file if he was shot on this day or took a turn for the worse). He died on 7 October 1917 (National Archives, WO 339/82885 1215570, Samuel Wilfrid Wayte, Personnel File).
92 CUL, MS SPR34/24/5, Dorothy Wayte, 17 December 1917, pp. i, 2–3.
93 CUL SPRMS34/26/4, Nea Walker, 31 December 1917, p. 5.
94 CUL, MS SPR34/26/1, Nea Walker, 20 April 1918, p. 21.
95 Wynn, *Rupert Lives!*, p. 49.
96 SHL, MS1082/1/1, Rhys-Davids, 'Chronicle of First Steps', p. 5.
97 *Ibid.*
98 CUL, MS SPR34/26/12, Elsi Walker, E. W. at V. O'.s, 21 October 1918, p. 6.
99 CUL, MS SPR34/24/5, Dorothy Wayte, 17 December 1917, pp. 12–13.
100 CUL, MS SPR34/26/2, N. W. and D. W. Sitting at Mrs. Brittain's, 18 July 1917, p. 13.
101 CUL, MS SPR34/24/8, Nea Walker, 31 December 1917, p. 18.
102 For examples see Meyer, *Men of War*, pp. 84–6.

103 *Ibid.*, pp. 15–17, 29–31.
104 In his letter of 29 May 1915, he wrote, 'No, I am not making things out better than they really are. I like to write mostly about the pleasant parts, of course' (Lodge, *Raymond*, pp. 18–19, 29, 30, 42).
105 Anthony Fletcher, *Life, Death and Growing up on the Western Front* (New Haven, CT and London: Yale University Press, 2013), p. 87.
106 CUL, MS SPR34/24/5, Dorothy Wayte, 17 December 1917, pp. 1, 30.
107 Jalland, *Death in the Victorian Family*, p. 301.
108 Lucie Whitmore, '"A Matter of Individual Opinion and Feeling": The Changing Culture of Mourning Dress in the First World War', *Women's History Review*, 27:4 (2018), 579.
109 IWM, Private Papers of Captain A. E. S. Mulholland, Documents.16816, Joan Mulholland, note on séance, n.d.
110 Michael Roper, *The Secret Battle: Emotional Survival in the Great War* (Manchester and New York: Manchester University Press, 2009), p. 224; Nicoletta Gullace, *The Blood of Our Sons: Men, Women and the Renegotiation of British Citizenship During the First World War* (New York: Palgrave Macmillan, 2004).
111 Pat Jalland, *Death in War and Peace: A History of Loss and Grief in England, 1914–1970* (Oxford: Oxford University Press, 2010), p. 59.
112 CUL, MS SPR34/24/5, Dorothy Wayte, 17 December 1917, pp. 24–5, 30.
113 CUL, MS SPR34/24/8, Nea Walker, 31 December 1917, p. 50.
114 SHL, MS1082/1/1, Rhys-Davids, Chronicle of First Steps, p. 8.
115 For the interaction between public expectation and private grief, see Carol Acton, *Grief in Wartime: Private Pain, Public Discourse* (New York: Palgrave Macmillan, 2007).
116 I am grateful to Janet Watson for making this observation.
117 CUL, MS SPR34/24/8, Nea Walker, 31 December 1917, p. 21.
118 Kelway-Bamber, *Claude's Book*, p. 55.
119 Colleen McDannell and Bernhard Lang, *Heaven: A History* (New Haven, CT and London: Yale University Press, 1988), pp. 292–6.
120 '"My Life After Death": A Series of Automatic Messages Given to the Cornish Circle by a Driver of the R.F.A.', *The Two Worlds*, 33:1697 (1920), 317.
121 Lodge, *Raymond*, pp. 197–8. The comments about cigars elicited ridicule and criticism from the public and clergy. See Ruth Brandon, *The Spiritualists: The Passion for the Occult in the Nineteenth and Twentieth Centuries* (New York: Alfred A. Knopf, 1983), pp. 216–18; Georgina Byrne, *Modern Spiritualism and the Church of England, 1850–1939* (Woodbridge: The Boydell Press, 2010), p. 77.
122 CUL, MS SPR34/24/5, Dorothy Wayte, 17 December 1917, pp. 16, 21.

123 Rene Kollar, *Searching for Raymond: Anglicanism, Spiritualism, and Bereavement between the Two World Wars* (Lanham, MD: Lexington Books, 2000), pp. 1–32.
124 McDannell and Lang, *Heaven*, pp. 297–8, 303.
125 CUL, MS SPR34/24/8, Nea Walker, 31 December 1917, pp. 49–50.
126 Conan Doyle, *The Vital Message*, p. 107.
127 CUL, MS SPR34/26/12, Nea Walker, N. W. Sitting with V. O., 30 May 1918, pp. 40–3.
128 SHL, MS1082/5/4, Rhys-Davids, Introductory written by Arthur, 23 September 1920, p. 1. It is not clear from the writing if the Walter in question is the woman's sweetheart or another family member.
129 SHL, MS1082/1/4, Carolyn Rhys-Davids, Report, 25 June–9 August 1918, p. 61.
130 CUL, MS SPR34/24/9, letter from Dorothy Wayte to Nea Walker, 4 May 1918, p. 1.
131 CUL, MS SPR34/24/11, letter from Dorothy Wayte to Nea Walker, 8 January 1919, p. 1.
132 Vanessa Chambers, 'Fighting Chance: War, Popular Belief and British Society, 1900–1951', unpublished PhD dissertation (Institute for Historical Research, University of London, 2007), p. 233.
133 CUL, MS SPR34/24/10, Elsi and Nea Walker, 20 October 1918, p. 4.
134 CUL, MS SPR34/24/14, Nea Walker, N. W. with Mrs. Leonard at Datchet, 6 October 1919, pp. 36d–f.
135 CUL, MS SPR34/26/12, Elsi Walker, 21 October 1918, p. 6.
136 CUL, MS SPR34/24/9, Nea Walker, 19 April 1918, p. 36.
137 CUL, MS SPR34/25/15, letter from Constance Wayte to Nea Walker, 3 October 1930.
138 In a 1933 letter to Mary Pearce's daughter, Nea noted that, 'Mrs. Pearce didn't latterly quite approve of this subject' (CUL, MS SPR34/25/15, Nea Walker to Doris, 11 August 1933).
139 Nea Walker, June 13, 1933, Leonard Papers, CUL, MS SPR34/25/15, 4.
140 Robert S. Cox, *Body and Soul: A Sympathetic History of American Spiritualism* (Charlottesville, VA: University of Virginia Press, 2003), introduction, third paragraph, Kindle.
141 CUL, MS SPR34/24/6, Nea Walker, 28 December 1917, pp. 36–7.
142 CUL, MS SPR34/24/9, Nea Walker, 19 April 1918, p. 42.
143 SHL, MS1082/1/4, Rhys-Davids, p. 18.
144 CUL, MS SPR34/19/12, Helen Salter, 28 January 1918, p. 10; CUL, MS SPR34/24/5, Dorothy Wayte, 17 December 1917, p. 17; CUL, MS SPR34/24/6, Nea Walker, 28 December 1917, p. 17.
145 CUL, MS SPR34/24/5, Dorothy Wayte, 7 December 1917, pp. 3, 11, 37.

146 IWM, Joan Mulholland, Note on séance.
147 CUL, MS SPR34/24/5, Dorothy Wayte, 17 December 1917, p. 10; CUL, MS SPR34/26/2, Nea Walker, Sitting with Mrs Brittain, 27 December 1917, p. 28.
148 SHL, MS1082/1/4, Carolyn Rhys-Davids, p. 33.
149 CUL, MS SPR34/24/5, Dorothy Wayte, 17 December 1917, pp. 3, 11, 37.
150 CUL, MS SPR34/24/8, Nea Walker, 31 December 1917, p. 7.
151 CUL, MS SPR34/26/1, Nea Walker, 20 April 1918, p. 30.
152 CUL, MS SPR34/24/14, Nea Walker, 6 October 1919, pp. 46–7.
153 CUL, MS SPR34/24/7, Nea Walker, 29 December 1917.
154 CUL, MS SPR34/24/14, Nea Walker, 6 October 1919, p. 36a.
155 CUL, MS SPR34/26/24, Nea Walker, 2 May 1918, p. 2.
156 CUL, MS SPR34/26/12, Elsi Walker, 21 October 1918, p. 11.
157 CUL, MS SPR34/24/8, Nea Walker, 31 December 1917, p. 4.
158 CUL, MS SPR34/19/12, Helen Salter, 28 January 1918, p. 10.
159 CUL, MS SPR34/19/12, letter from Jack Wayte to Helen Salter, 11 February 1918, p. 3; CUL, MS SPR34/24/9, Nea Walker, 19 April 1918, p. 25.
160 CUL, MS SPR34/25/20, Elsi Walker, Leonard Sitting, 26 August 1918, p. 9b.
161 CUL, MS SPR34/24/19, Nea Walker, E. W. Sitting with Mrs Leonard, 28 December 1921, p. 33.
162 CUL, MS SPR34/24/9, Nea Walker, 19 April 1918, pp. 32, 91.
163 CUL, MS SPR34/24/5, Dorothy Wayte, 17 December 1917, p. 30.
164 SHL, MS1082/1/4, Carolyn Rhys-Davids, p. 74.
165 CUL, MS SPR34/26/2, Nea Walker, 18 July 1917, p. 28; CUL, MS SPR34/26/11, Nea Walker (Second Sitting) Sitting with Miss Ortner at York Road. E. W. and N. W., 17 May 1918, p. 14.
166 CUL, MS SPR34/26/2, Nea Walker, 18 July 1917, p. 28.
167 CUL, MS SPR34/24/9, Nea Walker, 19 April 1918, p. 7.
168 CUL, MS SPR34/25/20, Elsi Walker, 26 August 1918, p. 10b.
169 'Annual Report of the Council', *JSPR*, 30:542 (1938), 161–5.
170 CUL, MS SPR34/26/29, Nea Walker and Elsi Walker, Diagnoses by 'Dr Beale', for E. W. and N. W., n.d., p. 6.
171 CUL, MS SPR34/25/13, Nea Walker, Family Part of the N. W. Leonard Sitting, 7 December 1929, p. 1.
172 CUL, MS SPR34/26/32, letter from Nea Walker to Eleanor Sidgwick, 24 October 1927, p. 7; CUL, MS SPR34/25/11, Damaris Walker, Report Made by D. W., and Shown to N. W. on Her Return from London after the Leonard Sitting, 7 January 1929, p. 1.

173 CUL, MS SPR34/25/18, Nea Walker, N. W. Part, Leonard, 28 January 1936, p. 24b.
174 CUL, MS SPR34/26/29, 6, Nea Walker and Elsi Walker, Diagnoses by 'Dr Beale', n.d., p. 1.
175 Sara Nye, 'A Mother's Story of Her Sons' Return', *Light*, 41:2118 (1921), 519.
176 'Public Notices', *The London Gazette* (27 September 1976), 13118 and (12 October 1976), 13863. In the 1974 list of members, Nea is still listed as an honorary member. See 'List of Officers and Members', *PSPR*, 56:209 (1974), 149.
177 Macnaghten, *Missing*, p. 59.
178 IWM, 'Correspondence, April 1915–June 1932', letter from Enid Hudson to Hazel Macnaghten, 30 June 1931.
179 IWM, Correspondence, April 1915–June 1932, letter from Enid Hudson to Hazel Macnaghten, 7 December 1931.
180 Macnaghten, *Missing*, pp. 59–61.
181 IWM, Miscellaneous Papers and Press Cuttings, Some relating to the Black Watch, First World War, letter from Rachel A. Grant to Hazel Macnaghten, n.d. (c. 1930–31).
182 Macnaghten, *Missing*, p. 58.
183 Laura Wittman, *The Tomb of the Unknown Soldier, Modern Mourning and the Reinvention of the Mystical Body* (Toronto, ON: University of Toronto Press, 2011), p. 21.
184 IWM, Miscellaneous Papers, letter from John Gouldney to Hazel Macnaghten, 28 October 1931.
185 Wittman, *The Tomb of the Unknown Soldier*, p. 24. See also Neil Hanson, *The Unknown Soldier: The Story of the Missing of the Great War* (London: Doubleday, 2005) and Adrian Gregory, *The Silence of Memory: Armistice Day, 1919–1946* (London: Bloomsbury, 1994), pp. 27–30.

5

The army of the living dead: spirit photography and the public denial of death

On 11 November 1922, spectators flocked to the London Cenotaph to remember the Great War's dead. A parade of fathers and mothers, brothers and sisters, comrades, friends and widows marched down Whitehall four years after the guns fell silent. As Big Ben signalled the eleventh hour, 'the rustle of the crowd ceased'. The only sound to be heard thereafter was 'some dim, brief wailing noise of unexplained origin' so contrasted by the great silence that it 'seemed to come from another world'.[1] At that moment, the spirit photographer Ada Deane was on a nearby rooftop overlooking the procession. With her camera pointed towards the Cenotaph, she exposed her plate for the two minutes of silence. Accompanying her was Estelle Stead, the daughter of the late journalist W. T. Stead. 'We were asked from the other side to arrange it so', Stead later explained.[2] Once the plates were developed it seemed that this request had not been in vain. Surrounding the Cenotaph were the spirit faces of young men. Arthur Conan Doyle later referred to it as the 'greatest spirit photograph ever taken'. In the spring of 1923, he displayed the picture before a stunned crowd at Carnegie Hall in New York City. Convulsive sobbing interrupted the initial shock of silence and one woman in the crowd shouted 'Don't you see them? Don't you see them?'[3]

Stead and Deane returned to the Cenotaph in November 1923 with further success. That year's photograph showed approximately fifty youthful faces 'smiling through' a white haze.[4] After publishing the images in *The Illustrated Sunday Herald*, Stead received countless letters from people who recognised their loved ones.[5] Conan Doyle professed to see his son amongst the faces, and possibly his nephew.[6] The promising results of the previous two years compelled the women to return to the Cenotaph once again in 1924. Stead was informed at séances in the weeks before Armistice Day that preparations were well underway.[7] According to one spirit, there was great excitement in the spirit world as 'the boys were all posing themselves in position'.[8] At Whitehall, Stead could 'sense the presence there of thousands of spirits – more, I should think, than there were living people present'.[9] Deane's camera rendered this sensation visible. The results were even more impressive than on previous occasions, with the developed photograph showing dozens of clearly defined faces.

Stead's enthusiasm turned out to be misplaced. This time it was not just the grieving who recognised the spirits. Two days after the *Daily Sketch* published the photos, the paper alleged that the faces were not those of deceased soldiers but well-known living athletes.[10] Conan Doyle rushed to Deane's defence. In front of a crowd at Surbiton on 25 November, he made clear what was at stake:

> we have that newspaper branding Mrs. Deane as an imposter! Their report is a tissue of lies. Mediums are our most precious people, and we must stand by them and protect them. There is not a clergyman in the country up to the Archbishop of Canterbury, who can, as they do prove immortality to you.[11]

Spiritualism's future was in jeopardy if the press was allowed to attack its revered mediums.

Spiritualists were on the defensive yet again thanks to their embrace of the photographic medium. Only two years earlier, the SPR had published evidence that the British spirit photographer, William Hope of the famous 'Crewe Circle', was a fraud.[12] Now the public accused spiritualists of preying on the emotionally vulnerable and insulting the war dead, the very people that spiritualists claimed they were trying to help. One reader of the *Daily Sketch* stated 'that the Cenotaph on Armistice Day was chosen as the spirit photographs cannot be too strongly deplored'.[13] How did the spiritualist movement find itself embroiled in such a bitter feud? Why was Ada Deane taking spirit photographs at the Cenotaph on Armistice Day and why did Estelle Stead publish these photographs in the press, where they were likely to arouse scepticism?

The Deane photographs were the culmination of two trends. Spirit photography originated in the 1860s but gained a new following after the Great War and the influenza pandemic. Thousands of people from Britain and around the world travelled to Crewe and London in the 1920s to obtain photographic evidence of an afterlife. Those who recognised their loved ones shared their stories in the spiritualist press. Unrecognised faces were also published with hopes of reuniting the living and the dead and therefore attracting new converts to the movement. Spirit photography became a crucial front in the project to redeem the Great War's sacrifices.

By 1924, Armistice Day had also become a sacred annual event within the spiritualist movement. Spiritualists gathered in the thousands at public halls each year to remember that the 'dead' were not dead and that they were enjoying a fuller, more enlightened existence.[14] The two minutes of silence were interpreted as an opportunity to telepathically link the two worlds together on a massive scale through remembrance and bring spiritualists one step closer to creating a heaven on earth. Three days before Deane took the fateful photograph in 1924, *Light* informed readers that 'it will yet become common knowledge that in the great Rite of Remembrance an atmosphere of "awareness" is created, in which spirit with spirit may meet and prove that Death is but the gateway to a brighter, freer, fuller life'.[15] The work of Stead and Deane brought these developments together. Deane's spirit photographs documented the presence of the dead during the two minutes of silence while Stead utilised the popular press to reunite the living with those they had lost and demonstrate the 'facts' of spiritualism to a larger audience.

British spiritualism in the 1920s has been interpreted as an alternative expression of the 'cult of memory' that informed civic rituals. Some scholars have argued, for example, that spiritualist beliefs were 'directly at odds with official forms of commemoration' since the denial of death 'makes a proper commitment to memory impossible'.[16] Similarly, the British historian David Cannadine states, 'If Armistice Day was the *public recognition of bereavement*, the Spiritualist movement, by contrast, was the *private denial of death*.'[17] These characterisations do not hold when we consider the relationships between private spiritualist practices and the public denial of death. Spiritualists' commemorations of the war shared many similarities with the national discourse and they utilised the public platform to spread the movement. But it is also the case that their accompanying religious, scientific and political contentions were not homogeneous. In the 1920s, spirit photography was part of a broader crisis of authenticity that followed the Great War, and which threatened social and cultural sensibilities. As spiritualists moved from the private to the public, they faced increased scrutiny. Deane's 1924 photograph exposed the paradox. Attempts to spread the movement and redeem the Great War's sacrifices led to accusations that they had desecrated the memory of their own prophets. After Deane's fall, spirit photography and spiritualism's public profile waned as surely as the faithful's hopes for achieving heaven on earth.

Spirit photography and private grief

Armed conflict shaped spirit photography from its conception. In the spring of 1861, shortly after the outbreak of the American Civil War, the engraver William Mumler was taking self-portraits in Boston through the wet-collodion process when a figure appeared on one of his plates.[18] This he recognised as his deceased cousin.[19] Mumler's discovery was announced in the spiritualist press in the fall of 1862. The *Banner of Light* declared that his photographs marked the dawn of a 'new phase' that would 'tangibly connect the two worlds, the material and the spiritual, to the palpable recognition of sensuous perception'.[20] The spirit photograph was recognised as a means of uniting the material and spiritual worlds by rendering the invisible spirit as a material object that could be both seen and touched.

The year 1839 marked the emergence of a practical photographic process, but spirit photography profited from later technologies that made photographs cheaper and easier to produce, as well as creating a more receptive market. The invention of glass plate negatives in the early 1850s allowed for a single negative to produce countless prints.[21] Mumler sold his spirit photographs in the form of *cartes-de-visite* (visiting cards). These small and inexpensive portraits were produced from a single plate that could hold eight images with varying poses. *Cartes-de-visite* were popular in the 1850s and 1860s, and were produced in the millions as the public collected portraits of famous individuals.[22] Mumler benefited from this trend, and he quickly established a following in Boston and later New York. His clientele included William Lloyd Garrison and Mary Todd Lincoln, giving him the dubious honour of 'the man who captured Lincoln's ghost'.[23] Mumler also utilised the post to sell his prints and advertised them through *Spiritual Magazine*. One of his customers was the amateur English medium, Georgina Houghton. Ten years after Mumler's discovery, Houghton partnered with the photographer Frederick Hudson and announced that the first successful spirit photograph had been taken in London.[24]

The first generation of spirit photographers was more commercially motivated than their twentieth-century, research-oriented successors.[25] For example, Mumler sold his *cartes-de-visite* for $10 apiece when a single photograph typically sold for 25¢.[26] Britain became the epicentre of spirit photography only in the early twentieth century as psychical researchers became more interested in the spirit hypothesis. William Hope, a carpenter from Crewe, and his partner, the medium Mrs Buxton, began taking spirit photographs in 1905. Hope apparently stumbled upon spirit photography accidentally, just like Mumler. While photographing a friend, a mysterious figure appeared, which the friend recognised as his deceased sister. The Crewe Circle gained wider attention in 1908 after Archdeacon Thomas Colley sat with Hope and identified an extra as his mother. Colley was so impressed that he provided Hope with a Lancaster quarter plate camera, which he continued to use well into the 1920s.[27] Hope's popularity grew in the interwar period, and he was eventually endorsed by the Society for the Study of Supernormal Pictures (SSSP) and the British College of Psychic Science (BCPS), founded in 1918 and 1920, respectively. The former included well-known spiritualists such as Arthur Conan Doyle.[28]

It is tempting to attribute the rise of spirit photography to unquestioning faith in photographic technology. The camera offered the possibility of 'mechanical objectivity' since nature could automatically imprint itself onto the photographic plate without the tainted influence of the subjective artist.[29] In 1844, Henry Fox Talbot famously introduced his photographs with the explanation that they were drawn 'without any aid of the artist's pencil' and were instead 'impressed by nature's hand'.[30] The writer Maurice Hewlett criticised Conan Doyle's endorsement of the Cottingley Fairies on these grounds, stating,

If he believes in the photographs ... he must believe ... that a mechanical operation, where human agency has done nothing but prepare a plate, focus an object, press a button, and print a picture, has rendered visible something which is not otherwise visible to the common naked eye. That is really all that Sir Arthur has to tell us.[31]

Mechanical objectivity was certainly one argument made in favour of spirit photography.[32] One spiritualist remarked, 'we will believe even the modern ghost if it can be fixed on paper ... liable to no delusions, has no brains to be diseased, and is exact in its testimony'.[33] The spirit photograph appeared to refute spiritualism's critics, since it could not be accused of madness or error.

Mechanical objectivity is an appealing although insufficient explanation for spirit photography's popularity. Photography's claims of objectivity have always been contested. Even before spirit photography, Britons and Americans were well aware that the photographic medium was not always objective.[34] When Mumler shared his first spirit photograph with a friend, it was not accepted uncritically but dismissed as a double exposure.[35] Early photographers manipulated and combined images to produce illusions and famous photographers such as Henry Peach Robinson took it for granted that his audience would recognise his mediating influence.[36] Scientists were also aware that photographs were liable to distortion.[37] Far from being purely mechanical, photography was a labour-intensive affair, which meant that gender and class could impact who could be trusted to use photography for scientific purposes.[38] There were debates about when photography counted as science and when it was art. Scientists tended to emphasise the need to reduce the influence of the self as much as possible, while artistic movements such as pictorialism embraced interference.[39]

Spiritualists were also conscious of trickery. Mumler's French counterpart, Edouard Buguet, was convicted of fraud in 1875. Police discovered dummies, shrouds, fake beards and hundreds of facial portraits in his Paris studio. Buguet confessed that his assistants conversed with clients to gather information while he prepared for sittings. Details about the deceased were passed onto Buguet, who proceeded to photograph a disguised dummy or a portrait that resembled the description.[40] Even Conan Doyle accepted Buguet's deception, cautioning that, when it came to spirit photography, 'fraud must be carefully guarded against, having been admitted in the case of ... Buguet'.[41] Nevertheless, spirit photography and mechanical objectivity were encouraged by photographs of objects 'on the threshold of vision' beginning in the latter half of the nineteenth century, including aerial views of cities, bullets in movement, birds in flight, galloping horses, celestial bodies and microbes.[42] In his book on spirit photography, Arthur Coates used the examples of X-rays, observing that, if the camera could capture the 'material invisible', then why not the 'immaterial invisible'?[43]

Spirit photography's claims of mechanical objectivity were also undermined by a series of inconsistencies. In the nineteenth century, it was common to argue that extras were objective spirits captured by light-sensitive plates, but by the 1920s, proponents of spirit photography were more likely to argue that the extra was a representation of the spirit. It was observed that identical extras appeared at different sittings and with unrelated sitters. Experiments with spectroscopic cameras also found that extras remained two-dimensional, even if plates were exposed from different angles simultaneously. Finally, some spirit photographers produced extras on plates that never left their packaging. To the sceptical observer, such peculiarities indicate obvious fraud, but to the editor of the *British Journal of Photography*, John Traill Taylor, these inconsistencies indicated that spirit photographs were actually *psychic* photographs: images of thoughts impressed onto the plates.[44] In other words, they were the visualisation of telepathy, not physical spirits. It was an interpretation that would find a ready audience in the more psychically minded spiritualist movement of the twentieth century. By the outbreak of the Great War, the most common explanation was the 'memory-mould theory'. First articulated through a séance with W. T. Stead in 1895, the theory argued that the extra is a re-printable 'mould' formed out of etheric substances according to a spirit's thoughts. The mould was then impressed onto the plate through natural chemical laws using the medium's psychic power as a channel.[45]

The memory-mould theory was taken for granted when Stead explained the production of the Deane Armistice Day photographs. According to Stead, the moulds were prepared ahead of time in groups, and 'were either impressed upon the plates before, during or after the two-minute exposure'. All that was required on the earthly

The army of the living dead 217

Figure 5.1 The first of two spirit photographs showing identical extras at different sittings. The same extra appears in two separate spirit photographs taken by Ada Deane in the early 1920s.

side was the medium and a sensitive plate or film.[46] The implication was that the extra was a specific artist willing himself onto the plate. As one spiritualist stated, 'they speak to us all of will, purposeful and courageous beyond the barriers of death, constant and untiring-love, which finds a way to its object ... as only intelligent, persistent effort could discover'.[47] So much for mechanical objectivity.

Spirit photographs did not just exist within a culture of science but also one of mourning where proof of continued existence was

Figure 5.2 The second of two spirit photographs showing identical extras at different sittings.

desired. The most common explanation for belief in spirit photography was recognition.[48] The psychical researcher Fred Barlow argued that 'there is no doubt that the whole fabric of the evidence for the reality of psychic photography is based on the claim that ... sitters who were quite unknown to the medium have obtained "extras" of dead friend or relatives'.[49] Despite Buguet's admission of guilt, numerous former clients came forth to speak in his defence. They testified to the unmistakable likeness between the extras and their loved ones as proof.[50] This was part of a larger pattern throughout the history of spiritualism. Once someone had become convinced of spiritualism's veracity, it was extremely difficult to admit that they had been the victims of fraud or gullibility. When it came to spirit photography, it was the visceral feeling of recognising a loved one's face that moved people to accept the extraordinary.

The shock – or the 'incontrovertible thud of recognition' as the historian Martyn Jolly describes it – appears in many testimonies related to the Great War.⁵¹ After R. Hipwood's son was killed in France in August 1918, he sought the comfort of the church, but the minister was unable to offer anything 'beyond a joyful resurrection in ages to come, perhaps'.⁵² He and his wife turned to spiritualism instead, and in June of 1921, they attended a sitting with Hope. The extra that appeared in the Hipwoods' photograph was 'such a well-recognized photo' of their son that even their 'nine-year-old grandchild could tell who the "extra" was'. The Hipwoods thanked the Crewe Circle for 'their work in trying to prove in such a tangible way to broken-hearted ones that there is no death'.⁵³ Their desire for definite evidence of an afterlife led them to experiment with spiritualism and the recognition of their son through a stranger's camera provided the proof.⁵⁴

Psychical researchers and spiritualists also referenced procedures that they believed eliminated the possibility of fraud. Hope gave his sitters a considerable amount of control in the proceedings and his supporters struggled to explain the phenomenon they observed. A London businessman, identified only by the initials J. L. H., visited Hope in January 1919. His report in *Light* is written as if he were conducting an experiment, and in fact, the BCPS referred to personal sittings with Hope as 'experiments' and distinguished these from 'tests'.⁵⁵ J. L. H. reasoned that he could not have been a victim of trickery because he brought his own plates and never left them out of his sight. He opened the package, signed the plates and placed them into the slides. He then followed Hope into the dark room where he moved the plates from the slides and into the developing dish. These experiments were a success. On the first plate, he saw his recently deceased wife, and on the second was a 'vivid likeness' of his son killed in the war.⁵⁶

Critics of spirit photography were not convinced by cases of recognition. Whatley Smith (later Carington) argued that the extra might be based upon an existing photograph of the deceased or was a case of mistaken identity. He observed that the number of extras 'clear enough to be *capable of definite recognition at all is extremely small*'. The faces were usually 'blurred, out-of-focus', covered in cloth or surrounded by a white haze 'as to leave no more than two eyes, a nose and a mouth visible'.⁵⁷ In anticipation of this criticism, one woman who recognised her son killed in France in 1916, explained that the extra was 'not vague or shadowy, but clear for all to see'. Nor did she believe it possible that the photograph was a doctored image of her son since 'neither Mr. Hope nor Mrs. Buxton knew that I was going, what my name was ... or that I had lost a son'. Despite the extra's resemblance to a real photograph taken a year before her son passed away, it was not identical, as the extra's 'face looks somewhat thinner and younger, and the pose is different'. She also noticed 'two distinct marks' on the temple, and she had been informed that her son 'was twice hit in the head by bursting shells'. His death wounds made it clear that this was not just an ordinary photograph of her son.[58]

Additional witnesses testified to instances of personal recognition. *Light* compared both of J. L. H.'s spirit photographs with those taken of the man's wife and son while they were alive. The journal corroborated the 'unmistakable likeness' and declared them to be 'amongst the best psychic photographs we have seen'.[59] In 1925, the *Two Worlds* announced that its staff had conducted experiments through the BCPS with a new spirit photographer, George Moss. During the proceedings, an extra appeared which was recognised by one of the experimenters as his friend, Rifleman George Carnt of the London Rifle Brigade, who was also a member of a spiritualist church in Portsmouth. Carnt was declared missing, presumed killed, and his body was never recovered. The photograph was sent to his widow who recognised George and asked for personal copies. After they carefully examined more photos of Carnt, *The Two Worlds* concluded, 'We have no hesitation ... that the extra is a likeness of Rifleman G. Carnt', and added, 'many members of the Portsmouth Temple were able to instantly recognise the likeness'.[60]

As material objects, spirit photographs could unite grieving communities with dead and vanished soldiers. James Hewat and Barbara McKenzie's son, Second Lieutenant William McKenzie of the 2nd London Scottish Regiment, was killed on 12 June 1918 in Jerusalem. They took a sitting with Hope the following November. The results were inconclusive and perhaps the matter would have ended there if it were not for a séance between Barbara and Gladys Osborne Leonard on 7 December 1918. Feda informed her that William had 'done well' on the plate of another grieving mother, and that William's spirit had become friendly with this woman's son in the spirit world. The description of the mother resembled the writer Pamela Glenconner, with whom McKenzie was familiar, although they had no personal relationship. The McKenzies obtained Glenconner's photo and the spirit presented 'an unmistakable likeness of William'. The McKenzies also identified what looked like a bullet wound in the extra's temple, which happened to be the cause of William's death.[61]

There remained the issue of why William appeared at Glenconner's sitting. J. Arthur Hill suggested that unidentified extras might be the result of spirits from previous sittings leaving behind their 'influence'.[62] The McKenzies learned that the spirit of Glenconner's son had helped William transition to the other side and taught him how to manifest his presence on earth. 'There was thus a link established', *Light* explained, 'the value of which was shown in the successful results of the photographic experiment'.[63] The two women were united in a community of mourning through their shared interests in spiritualism.[64] The relationship was initiated by a spirit photograph that presented an unrecognised figure to one grieving mother, but a recognisable image to another, helping one woman mourn and demonstrating to both the reality of spiritualism. Afterwards, the McKenzies became staunch supporters of Hope and Deane.[65] In 1920, they established the BCPS and offered sittings with the Crewe Circle for £1 and 1s (or £2 and 2s for non-members). In their opening week, an exhibit of psychic photographs attracted 500 visitors.[66] By 1922, the BCPS had an annual income of over £4,000.[67]

For every grieving person who recognised a loved one, there were far more extras that went unidentified. Hope appears to have had a success rate of only 5 per cent, although he liked to claim that it was 25 per cent.[68] Barbara McKenzie admitted that 'it is a well known fact that only a small proportion of … the "extras" … are recognised by those with whom they appear'.[69] This meant that there were countless spirits looking for their loved ones, and many of the extras appeared to be former soldiers.[70] Albums of photographs by Deane and Hope housed at the SPR's archives show hundreds of people posing with the heads of young men, some in uniform, hovering above.[71] It is impossible to tell who these unidentified sitters were there to find, but the haunting presence of the nation's war dead is pronounced. Unidentified extras provided a visual form and potential identity to the war's missing. McKenzie explained that these extras were 'of the utmost value, if only the right link is obtained' since they could reunite the dead with the living and provide proof of spiritualism.[72] Spirit photography had a significant moral and scientific role to play in the spiritualist movement during the interwar period. It is no wonder that Conan Doyle, having devoted his later life to the cause, was so wounded by accusations of fraud.

Attempts were made to connect unidentified extras with the living. In the fall of 1920, McKenzie held a viewing at the BCPS, and *Light* agreed to publish them in a weekly feature.[73] The paper appealed to readers for help under the assumption 'that many of the public will realise how deep is the desire on the part of those on the other side to obtain recognition from their dear ones'. Publishing them would fulfil 'a sacred duty to our friends beyond the veil'.[74] After three weeks, they received a substantial number of letters and photographs from readers asking *Light* to compare the unidentified extras with their loved ones. The response prompted the editor to state, 'we wish to point out very clearly to all our readers that we cannot undertake or decide for them whether the photographs submitted to us are identical'. From their experience, recognition was a personal and subjective certainty. 'When anyone *does* recognise psychic "extras" there is never any doubt about it', *Light* explained, 'and it is not necessary to call in the assistance of others who did not know the original in the flesh to convince one'.[75]

In the early 1920s, spiritualists viewed spirit photography as one means of uniting the missing war dead with the living, which could be achieved through the camera of a tested and endorsed medium on the one hand, and the recognition of an extra on the other. Some grieving families were able to arrange sittings with Hope and Deane and to conduct the 'experiments' themselves, while others had to rely on the spiritualist press to potentially connect them with these unidentified extras. If a link could be established between the two worlds, this could not only help the living, but also prove spiritualism and redeem the sacrifices of the Great War. It was this message that was delivered at spiritualist Armistice Day ceremonies, which were conceived as giant public séances. What would happen if those séances were photographed? Could the results help spiritualists validate their aims on a grander scale?

The army of the living dead 223

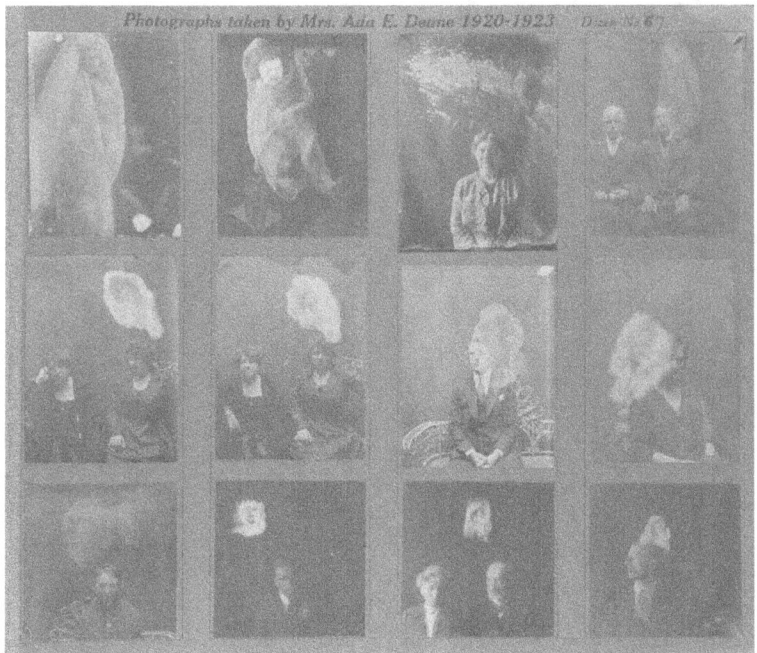

Figures 5.3 The first of two spirit photographs by Ada Deane with unidentified sitters.

The 'Great Séance': spiritualism and Armistice Day ceremonies

Stories about ghosts at Whitehall were reported in the spiritualist press from the moment the permanent Cenotaph was unveiled in November 1920. One spiritualist, Jessie Freeman, for example, told the story of her visit to the Cenotaph late one night in the fall of 1920. The endless crowds of the previous days had finally ceased and there was nobody else present at the monument. 'Suddenly I became aware I was not alone', she explained, 'for around the empty tomb, standing silently, were an army of soldiers'. There was something peculiar about these soldiers, however; 'their faces were not sad, like others I had seen previously at the Cenotaph, but shining with a great joy and peace'. It then dawned upon her that these were not the faces of living men but of the dead:

224 Haunted Britain

Figure 5.4 The second of two spirit photographs by Ada Deane with unidentified sitters.

> as my eyes scanned the happy faces, bronzed and strong, I recognised with surprise for one, and then another, of my friends who had died. I was greatly startled at first, then a great joy overwhelmed me; I knew that this must be the Army of the Living Dead.[76]

Freeman also noticed a woman, standing out of place amidst the ghosts, her 'face was ... saddened by a great grief'. As the grief-stricken woman prepared to lay down a wreath of white blossoms, one of the soldiers emerged from the crowd, placed his hand on her shoulder and whispered 'Mother'. The woman's solemn face was suddenly 'shining with a new hope, a perfect joy and the sublime knowledge that HE LIVED'.[77] Freeman's story captures the central message that spiritualists conveyed every November: the dead were not dead, the living could find them, and with this knowledge established, Armistice Day could become the occasion of a joyous reunion. Spirit photography gave these beliefs tangibility. Like the woman in Freeman's story, the public could identify a loved one's face amongst the spirits that surrounded the Cenotaph. In doing so, they would find comfort in the fact of survival after death and achieve heaven on earth.

Armistice Day rituals emerged in the specific context of 1919. Occurring at the peak of the 'first memory boom', and in an uncertain political and social climate, there was a great urge to remember the sacrifice of the Great War's dead one year after the conflict. As Jay Winter notes, from the 1890s to the 1920s, memory was used to formulate national, cultural and social identities.[78] A nationwide moment of silence seemed very appropriate as it reinforced a national community during the unstable period of demobilisation and the transition from a wartime to postwar economy. To one observer, the silence meant that 'all classes must combine as they did to win the war, unselfishly and harmoniously. There must be a truce in domestic quarrels, and end to industrial strife. We must all pull together lest the rewards of victory be thrown away.'[79] The silence momentarily realised the cause for which the men had died, reminded people of the blood that had been spilt to achieve this, and so sought to ensure that their lives had not been given in vain.[80]

The silence had other benefits. It provided a civic alternative to prayer while alluding to the moment when the guns went silent. It was both collective and private, since the entire nation was united in remembrance for two minutes but left alone with their own thoughts.[81] Silence could also express aspects of the war that were beyond words. One writer in the *Evening Standard* struggled to communicate his feelings during the silence and instead wished that he could paint 'the passing of the Great White Army which lived for two minutes to-day in the mind of every man and woman'. He wondered if it was true that 'the veil between Life and Death is very thin'.[82] During the silence, this seemed possible. At the original Cenotaph in 1919, Australian ex-serviceman Bill Grant similarly imagined 'a Great Phantom army ... Swiftly, Silently & singing as they went'.[83] These commentators resorted to ghostly metaphors to try and articulate their thoughts during the silence. A similar sentiment led Will Longstaff to paint phantom soldiers in *Menin Gate at Midnight* in 1928 and *The Ghosts of Vimy Ridge* in 1929. His motivations were metaphorical, not spiritual. The figures were not literally ghosts, he explained, but 'the only way in which I can symbolize the dead'.[84]

The relationship between thoughts and ghosts was not just metaphorical according to psychic theories. Telepathy popularised the idea that thoughts were analogous to the invisible fields and light waves that made wireless telegraphy, X-rays and photography possible. In 1896, William Crookes pointed to Röntgen's discovery to suggest that thoughts might also be a form of radiation.[85] Psychic photographers such as Hippolyte Baraduc, Louis Darget and Tomokichi Fukurai attempted to photograph these thought waves.[86] Myers argued that thoughts transcended not just the gulf between the normal and supernormal but also the living and the dead. Mediums told sitters that thoughts of the dead brought them closer together, and twentieth-century British spirit photographers argued that it was memories that made the materialisation of faces possible. An entire Empire joined in thought focused on the Great War's dead would surely have psychic and spiritual implications. Conan Doyle referred to Armistice Day as 'the great psychic feast' and *Light* called the great silence 'a great séance – the greatest and noblest ever held … A gigantic thought wave to the other side.'[87]

It was repeatedly mentioned at remembrance ceremonies that to think about the dead during the silence was to bring their spirits into sympathy with the living. These public spaces became 'thin places'. *The Two Worlds* described in 1923 how 'the silence could be felt. To the physically alive the two worlds were blended, for memory opened the gates, and the risen comrades of the strenuous years joined with us.'[88] In 1919, mediums attested to the dead's presence. Alfred Vout Peters felt 'a tremendous psychic power flooding the hall, a power too strong to be almost borne at one time', and Mary Gordon described how she 'saw a great concourse of our heroic soldiers … the whole vast interior of the Albert Hall seemed to be thronged with them'.[89] Conan Doyle rejoiced that, thanks to spiritualism, 'we can extend our arms and with smiling faces look up, knowing that we are looking straight into those unchanged faces which once we knew upon earth'.[90] Years later he showed photographs of faces around the Cenotaph to audiences around the world.

Spiritualists embraced the two minutes of silence and had even anticipated the ritual (at least in England) by several months.[91] At the memorial event in April 1919, Ernest Oaten, the president of the SNU, asked the audience for a minute of silence 'to concentrate …

thought upon the dear ones who have crossed over, and by thought and desire to bridge that gulf'.[92] The silence's ability to express what was beyond words found natural accommodation with telepathy, which suggested subconscious links between minds (both living and dead), which were empowered by feelings of love and community. In 1920, the spirit of W. T. Stead acknowledged that people might grieve over what they did or did not say to their loved ones while they were still alive. 'But words have passed beyond our need', he assured readers, since 'your thoughts reveal to all our spirit "boys" the greatness of your love ... There is more expressed in your thoughts than in all the eloquence of words used by great men.'[93] An individual's private thoughts could be telepathically communicated to the dead during the 'great séance' and thus lift the burden of guilt, loss and grief.

The silence was also used to remember the purpose of the sacrifice, lest the soldiers' deaths be in vain. Spiritualist commemorations of the war therefore stressed the 'fact' of survival. As Stead's spirit proclaimed,

> I would speak to mankind and tell them not of the horrors and the suffering of the dear men who have 'died' ... but rather of the everlasting love that is between you ... I would speak of the joy they have in knowing themselves remembered and remembered as being in the family circle still. I would tell all the vast masses to rejoice, to meet together in gladness, not in sorrow at the foot of your memorial. Meet to celebrate the victory of life over suffering and horror. *Death enters not here! There is no death!*[94]

Spiritualist services were to be celebrations, not solemn funerals. It was 'not a Memorial Service, though we call it so', Conan Doyle asserted, but 'rather a joyous reunion'.[95] In remembering what the soldiers had died for, spiritualists looked towards a future in which survival was proven. In 1919, Ernest Keeling from Liverpool offered prayers that the dead 'will again co-operate with us even as you did on earth and help spread this truth of ours throughout the whole of this earth-world – this truth that there is no death'.[96] Keeling appealed to spirits on the other side to show themselves and work with the living. The number of spirits that appeared at séances and as photographic extras in the ensuing years indicated that they were answering the call. All that was left was to establish more connections. As Stead's spirit explained, by doing so, the grieving could come 'face to face with material and spiritual facts', and by re-establishing familial connections with the dead, 'you can have a Heaven among yourselves'.[97]

Another message conveyed at spiritualist ceremonies was that the triumph of spiritualism would unite the world's philosophies and humanity. Heaven on earth was not just a personal project but a communal one as well. At the Armistice Day service in Queen's Hall in 1924, Conan Doyle explained that his 'ambition is to see the day when Mohammedans, Buddhists, Parsees, Jews and Christians will all stand together to testify to this same truth'. According to Conan Doyle, religious simplicity was needed before a true human brotherhood could be realised since 'nothing will be settled until religion is settled, because that is the basis upon which all rests'.[98] At a ceremony in 1923, the medium W. E. Long stated that, when he heard Conan Doyle's call for spiritualists to support the League of Nations, he saw 'a mighty army (in spirit) of every country and colour – a *real* League of Nations – united in the fellowship of the spirit to bear witness of man's immortality, irrespective of creed or racial distinctions'.[99] Long's thoughts of a universal brotherhood were represented as ghosts, just as others had used ghostly visuals to explain the silence. But his vision was far more political, as it represented the internationalism and pacificism being advocated by the LNU. Nor were his visions meant to be just allegoric. The ghosts were really there, and represented not only the fact of spiritualism, but also its social implications.

Conan Doyle hoped that society would progress to a point where the veil was entirely lifted and the deaths of the Great War were redeemed. He recalled the story of Admiral Togo during the Russo-Japanese War, who, after battle, summoned the dead to tell them why they had died and thank them for their sacrifice. 'When we have got to the level of Japan in psychical civilization', Conan Doyle explained, 'it will be they who will stand here in a great meeting of this sort and we will welcome them and thank them for their services'.[100] The analogy implied that this moment would allow the Great War's dead to see that their sacrifice had atoned for humanity's sins and thus redeemed the bloodshed. At Armistice Day, individuals momentarily achieved this in their own private thoughts by reopening the connection between the two worlds in the public sphere.

Armistice Day spirit photographs were therefore a natural extension of interwar spiritualist rhetoric. First, they visualised and objectified the notion that the dead were present during the two-minute silence. It was one thing to make this claim, but spiritualists also wanted a demonstration, which spirit photography provided.[101] Second, Armistice Day spirit photographs were similar to Togo's summoning of the dead. Although they were mediated rather than direct forms of communion, the dead were still showing themselves as the living thanked them for their sacrifice. Finally, spirit photography could help ensure that this sacrifice was not in vain. If faces could be shown to hover above the Cenotaph, the public might recognise the extras as their loved ones. This would establish more connections between the living and dead, proving spiritualism in the process and creating a heaven on earth. Spiritualists were therefore not unlike other Britons commemorating the war. The silence was easily appropriated and linked with spiritualist concepts of telepathy and sympathy, and it was used to both remember the individual dead and the ideals for which they had fought. The silence was a personal and political act.[102]

The spiritualists' mistake was overestimating the popularity of their worldview and the integrity of their mediums. There was evident hubris amongst members of Estelle Stead's Borderland Library. In January 1924, for example, Felicia Scatchered, one of the collaborators in the Cenotaph photographs, proclaimed that Armistice Day was bringing people closer to the movement. As Scatchered explained, Armistice Day rituals were only conducted once a year by the general public, but were a daily philosophy for spiritualists. 'For the essence of Armistice Day in the minds of the people is *remembrance*', she wrote, 'and so, with unerring intuition this day developed to the memory of those who died in the Great War is called *Remembrance Day*'.[103] Months earlier, *The Two Worlds* attributed the decision to swap the Last Post for Reveille as a 'call to life and action instead of the solemn good-bye which we used to hear', and which represented 'a striking testimony to the work which Spiritualism has done'.[104] The Borderland Library and *The Two Worlds* were suggesting that Armistice Day was spiritualist by its very nature. 'Is it any wonder that the future is with us and for us?' Scatchered asked.[105] By the end of the year, she would be involved in one of the movement's greatest controversies in the interwar period.

'A strange and disappointing world': fraud and the press

Estelle Stead understood the power of print media. Her father, W. T. Stead, was at the forefront of the 'new journalism' of the late nineteenth century, characterised by larger headlines, shorter paragraphs and more interviews, gossip columns and sensational stories that would appeal to a burgeoning mass market.[106] W. T. Stead also believed that a democratisation of the press was part of a historical trend towards 'downward' government.[107] His infamous 1885 series on child prostitution in London's East End represented the potential influence of this new style of journalism. The story caused moral panic, political reform and even Stead's imprisonment. Critics feared the potential dangers of rule by popular opinion. Matthew Arnold blamed the new journalism for recent public support for Irish Home Rule and dismissed it as 'feather-brained' just like 'the new voters, the democracy'.[108]

Beginning in the 1890s, as editor of *Review of Reviews*, Stead's interests turned to spiritualism and psychical research. In 1893, he established a separate paper, *Borderland*, entirely devoted to the subject. *Borderland*'s role was to help democratise scientific knowledge by providing a public forum where facts and knowledge could be exchanged.[109] The combination of spiritualism with the new journalism further tarnished the latter's reputation and prompted concerns from those in positions of scientific authority.[110] Stead proclaimed that in order to reach a mass audience, editors should 'never employ an expert to write a popular article' but instead use 'someone who knows nothing about it to tap the expert's brains'.[111] Stead's positions led to conflict with not only scientific naturalists such as Thomas Huxley, but also members of the SPR, who feared losing control of concepts such as telepathy.[112]

After W. T. Stead was killed in the *Titanic* disaster, Estelle Stead attempted to follow in her father's footsteps. In November 1920, she published an Armistice Day message from her father's spirit as a pamphlet for public consumption. She printed 5,000 copies, of which 3,000 were given to the crowds at the Cenotaph. After placing an advertisement in *Light*, she had to print a further 5,000 pamphlets to meet the demand.[113] In 1921 and 1922, she published Deane's first Armistice Day photographs in *Light*, which had only begun to print photographs after the war.[114] Spirit photography's revival coincided with the rapid expansion of illustrated journalism in the 1920s.[115] Stead and Deane's work was also bolstered by Conan Doyle's lectures abroad. He recognised the value of spirit photography in the battle to spread spiritualism, as it was the only phenomenon appropriate for large audiences. As he explained, 'it is difficult and unseemly to produce actual mediumistic results upon a public platform'.[116]

By 1924, Stead and Deane's work was successful, but the spirits were demanding greater publicity. 'We want to bring them to the notice of non-Spiritualists', W. T. Stead's spirit explained to Estelle; 'those are the people we want to force to take notice'.[117] Similar statements were made at the Queen's Hall Armistice Day ceremony. Ernest Oaten stated, 'our duty and responsibility to those lads is to put our backs into the work and see that every unit in this country does its bit as they did'.[118]

Calls to action partly reflected a growing optimism within the spiritualist movement. *Light* noted in May 1923 that 'daily inspection of Press cuttings covering the whole range of newspapers and periodicals ... [caused] little occasion for complaint'.[119] Horace Leaf believed that press attention had revealed 'that the great interest aroused in psychic subjects during the war was of a durable nature, and not rooting in hysteria'.[120] A noteworthy example was James Douglas's exposé on spiritualism in *The Sunday Express* between 1921 and 1922. His conclusions were mixed, but he left open the possibility of spirit phenomena.[121] Douglas had a successful sitting with Hope and admitted that 'the mystery seems to me unfathomable and I do not pretend to have fathomed it'.[122] To ensure caution, he asked readers if anyone could replicate Hope's results under natural methods. The conjurer William Marriott answered his call and successfully reproduced a spirit extra at the BCPS in front of Conan Doyle without detection. Douglas concluded that the possibility of fraud could not be eliminated but that more stringent tests were needed to determine if Hope was genuine.[123]

Douglas did not offer a ringing endorsement but he was not disparaging either, and spiritualists welcomed the publicity.[124] In 1922, the popular magazine *Scientific American* also agreed to award $2,500 each to anyone who could demonstrate genuine spirit photography and physical mediumship. Conan Doyle helped arrange the tests and early results seemed promising.[125] After his

1922 tour of the United States, Conan Doyle believed that overall, the press was more sympathetic to spiritualism, spiritualists were more aggressive and proof was accumulating. In 1923, the editors of *The Two Worlds* and *Light* both boasted about record circulation numbers.[126] Horace Leaf declared, 'during my long association with Spiritualism, no more successful a year than 1923'.[127] There was a sense that this may be spiritualism's moment.

Despite the optimism, there were forebodings of the coming crisis. Not all press exposure had been neutral or positive. One of the more suspicious aspects of Deane's mediumship was that she requested sitters to send her their plates ahead of time so that they could be 'magnetized'. Even Conan Doyle admitted that Deane's policy was 'embarrassing' and 'unnecessary'.[128] When the staff of *John Bull* refused to comply and brought their own plates, they received no results (although Deane attempted to claim a 'smudge' as genuine spirit phenomenon).[129] The assistant editor, W. Charles Pilley, condemned Deane: 'this is a sample of the childish maneuvers which ... have served to deceive brilliant journalists, learned scientists and erudite philosophers! It is a strange and disappointing world'.[130] Meanwhile, a society of conjurers known as the Occult Committee of the Magic Circle complied with Deane's request, but unbeknownst to the spirit photographer, they had secretly marked the plates with numbers and carefully arranged them so that film was against film with the first plate film side down. When they opened the plates during the session, they noticed the first plate was film side up, a sign that they had been tampered with and repackaged. After receiving their final results, they found that the only plate missing the secret markings was the plate that showed extras.[131]

Conjurers represented a significant challenge to spiritualists in the twentieth century since they could replicate many of the phenomena through natural means while also evading detection.[132] Stage performers took advantage of the public's interest in spiritualism by reproducing similar feats, but they tended to differentiate themselves as entertainers and honest illusionists.[133] Many conjurers were antagonistic towards those who used the art of deception for other purposes.[134] For example, Conan Doyle and Houdini initially had a cordial relationship but in the 1920s, they increasingly argued with one another over the legitimacy of spiritualism.[135]

The Crewe circle was also targeted by conjurers. In 1922, Harry Price, a member of the Magic Circle, exposed Hope in one of spiritualism's most infamous controversies.[136] Price had arranged to have a sitting with Hope at the BCPS in February 1922. Working with the SPR, he was given a set of specialised plates from the Imperial Dry Plate Company. The plates were all cut from the same sheet of glass and secretly marked with the company's logo using X-rays. The invisible markings would only appear once the plates were developed. During his sitting with Hope, Price also secretly pinpricked the plate holders and noticed that Hope suspiciously placed them in his breast pocket very briefly. The marks were gone when they were returned to Price before the exposure. An extra of a woman did appear beside Price after the plates were developed, but there was no sign of the X-rayed logos. Price also noticed that the developed plates were of a different thickness than the rest of the Imperial plates in his possession. He concluded that Hope likely swapped the marked plates with those from his own collection, which were hiding in his breast pocket.[137] Price published his findings in the SPR's journal weeks later and in a pamphlet titled, *Cold Light on Spiritualistic 'Phenomena'*.[138]

Arguments over spiritualism were not just dispassionate debates about objectivity and truth, but also about claims to authority. Price, for example, had established his own society to rival that of the SPR, and he endorsed plenty of spiritualist and psychic phenomena, even as he debunked Hope. Ironically, Eric J. Dingwall, the SPR's research officer, once criticised the standards of Price's society as comparable to that of the BCPS.[139] Debates over spirit photography also occurred against a backdrop of social and political change. The extension of the voting franchise to women and non-property-owning men in 1918 tripled the number of eligible voters in Britain from 7.6 million to 21.7 million.[140] This was followed by the collapse of the Liberal party and the election of the first Labour prime minister in January 1924, the same year that the *Daily Sketch* exposed Ada Deane.

Gender figured prominently in developments surrounding conjuring and spiritualism. It was perhaps no coincidence that the conjurer's most popular illusion in the 1920s was the 'sawing a *woman* in half' trick.[141] Stage magic was a male profession. As the historian Sofie Lachapelle has noted, a key distinction between conjurers and mediums was that the latter tended to be women, acting in passive roles, who made no claims to understand the phenomena in question. In contrast, conjurers were usually men who could demonstrate their control of scientific knowledge as well as their bodies. Houdini's famous escape act put the power of the masculine form on full display.[142] If women wanted to use the tricks of the conjurer, they had to do so as mediums, making them a target of professional conjurers like Houdini. And it was usually men, such as Harry Price, who discovered women with certain talents before grooming them into spiritualist mediums, or who poked and prodded their naked bodies to rule out trickery in physical séances.[143]

Issues regarding gender and class impacted debates about spirit photography. Conan Doyle's rejoinder to Price contained the usual lines of defence used by spiritualists: he appealed to the scientific authority of William Crookes who endorsed Hope and placed a premium on positive evidence obtained in (apparently) controlled settings. But Conan Doyle also naively believed that fraudulent mediums were 'so easily found out that one could hardly make a living at so precarious a trade'.[144] His failure to see through Hope reflected prewar social power dynamics. The rise of Labour had demonstrated just how much the Liberal party relied on a small electorate of elite middle-class male voters. This could not be sustained given an enlarged voting franchise and increasing class consciousness.[145] Hope and Deane also represented a growing access to photography which had spread beyond middle-class males.[146] Spiritualists could not see beyond their own images of Deane and Hope as passive simpletons through which the spirits operated. How could a carpenter like Hope trick scientific men like William Crookes? As Conan Doyle wrote, 'his hands with their worn nails and square-ended fingers are those of the worker, and the least adapted to sleight-of-hand tricks of any that I have seen'.[147]

The same biases manifested in controversies surrounding Ada Deane. The spirit photographer insisted on carrying a handbag during experiments, which raised further suspicions. Dingwall once witnessed Deane place her right hand, which was holding his plates, into her bag as she retrieved her hymnbook. According to Dingwall, she 'fumbled about and then withdrew ... what were apparently the same four slides and two hymn books'. His accomplice, meanwhile, never noticed this potential sleight of hand.[148] As in the case of Hope, Deane's supporters found it hard to accept that she was using the tricks of a conjurer. She came from humble origins, was a single mother of three and was in her fifties when she started producing spirit photographs. Commenting on the handbag, Oliver Lodge stated, 'if she knew more about conjuring she would be more careful, but I doubt if she knows anything worth talking about'.[149] After the *Sketch* exposed Deane, *The Two Worlds* thought it ludicrous that 'a quiet and mature woman who has no interest whatever in sport, has carefully selected a number of prominent athletes and patched up a photograph … which would take a skilled photographer eight or ten hours to produce'.[150] Estelle Stead similarly protested to the *Sketch*, 'you have seen Mrs. Deane; do you think she appears to have the technical knowledge or skill to fake such a truly wonderful result?'[151]

Gender norms prohibited Deane from a career as a conjurer, meaning that her public persona was either that of a genuine medium or a dangerous fraud. As the historian Jenny Hazelgrove notes, it was not uncommon for mediums to be portrayed as swindlers preying on the bereaved.[152] Elliot O'Donnell proclaimed in 1920 that for every well-intentioned medium, 'there are ninety-nine who … rely on their powers of deception, in order to rake in the shekels'.[153] After Deane's exposure, one reader of the *Sketch* found it 'dastardly cruel that individuals, especially women, should resort to these spirit photographs, thereby ridiculing the heroes of the war and … causing sorrow and distress in many homes'.[154] Reports of sobbing women at Carnegie Hall left one *Evening Standard* reporter 'appalled' by Deane's 'seeming lack of reverence' and exploitation of 'hysterical women'.[155]

Anxieties about charlatans and hysteria had a long history, but were given new urgency in the aftermath of the Great War. Public disdain over war profiteers led to a postwar antagonism against 'profiteering'.[156] The image of the evil and greedy opportunist made for an ideal villain in popular novels in the 1920s, such as E. Phillips Oppenheim's *The Profiteers*.[157] Spirit photography had elicited controversy and criticism from conjurers but the location of the Cenotaph had raised the stakes. Spiritualists had projected private thoughts onto the public monument and grafted their political, religious and scientific claims onto something that was meant to be sacred. The exposure of spiritualists' views to a broader public – and during a period when their claims were filled with tension – invited a level of scrutiny that spiritualists were unprepared to address.

The social and political environment of 1920s Britain provided a motive for exposing spirit photographers such as Deane, but other factors made it feasible. The rapid expansion of news photography in the interwar period created a demand (especially in the daily tabloids) for expert photographers.[158] It was the *Sketch*'s photographer, W. Lord, who led the campaign against Deane in 1924. Utilising the lessons provided in the preceding years by Marriot, Price and other conjurers, Lord published his own spirit photographs that he obtained through natural methods.[159] He challenged Deane to demonstrate the veracity of her mediumship under strict conditions and agreed to donate £1,000 to a hospital if she was successful.[160] Deane protested that she could not produce phenomena 'under any *conditions*' since 'they come from some power which works through me, and over which I have no control'.[161] Stead also countered that Deane had produced phenomena under more restrictive circumstances than those of Lord. She issued her own challenge: if Lord could obtain results in the same setting as Deane, she would donate £100 to charity.[162] But the *Sketch*'s challenge had publicly backed Deane into a corner that she could not escape with her reputation intact. As the paper sarcastically remarked: 'Mrs. Deane's familiar spirit will not help her to obtain £1,000 for ... the Middlesex Hospital.'[163]

Stead blamed the controversy on the pressure that the press placed upon her in the days before and after the famous Armistice Day photograph was taken. The *Daily Graphic* and the *Sunday Express* had indeed expressed interest in the results. After the photos were first published in the *Sketch*, Stead sent prints to the Topical Press Agency so they could be circulated within the press. The following morning she was informed that they could not be reproduced because they had violated copyright. The *Daily Sketch*, meanwhile, had been informed of the development. The ensuing publicity arose not just because the press was interested, but because Stead was willing to oblige. She seemed to be following the advice of her father's spirit to spread the urgent truth of spiritualism.[164] Before Armistice Day, W. T. Stead's spirit issued a call to action. 'Many of you are frightened to come out and testify to that knowledge', Stead's spirit explained, 'fearing ridicule, fearing your social position, fearing your business position'. Stead's spirit used the memory of the soldier's sacrifice to remind spiritualists to act on these principles:

> Think of them – these vast hosts ... will you fail them? Will you not be brave as they were when they went forth to fight for King and Country? They thought not of social position. They listened not to ridicule. They went forth, steadfast in the faith that it was their duty.[165]

Whatever setbacks had occurred over the previous years were outweighed by a sense of urgency and duty. Stead recalled that in the weeks leading to the 1924 photographs, 'there seemed to be a great deal of excitement about them on both sides of the Veil. We were continually getting messages about the preparations going on the Other Side, where there seemed to be a great deal of training and grouping.' Demands were also made of Stead and Deane. The former was informed to stop smoking until 11 November so that the spirits could draw from her 'clear and pure' psychic power. Since Estelle was 'a rather keen smoker this was a test of endurance'. The sacredness of the ritual emphasised just how important Stead viewed their work on Armistice Day.[166]

Ironically, it was the democratisation of knowledge advocated by W. T. Stead that compromised Estelle's efforts. As the *Daily Sketch* wrote, their exposure 'would not have been possible if the *Daily Sketch* had not, at the risk of obloquy to itself, submitted the pictures to the rigorous searchlight of publicity'.[167] It was also amateur conjurers and photographers, not scientific experts, that exposed Deane and Hope. Perhaps the greatest irony was that spiritualists found themselves mobilising the same arguments that had historically been used to discredit spirit photography. Since one of the extras was of African descent, Deane accused observers of mistaking the likeness, since 'all negroes were much alike to an outsider'.[168] Stead claimed, 'it only needs a careful examination of the faces to realise that those on the Armistice photographs may be somewhat similar in type to the footballer' and that 'surely there were many of a similar type of face who "passed on" in the war'. One spiritualist was irritated that sceptics denied previous cases of clear recognition but suddenly found the recognition of footballers enough to discredit the entire enterprise.[169] Likewise, *The Two Worlds* wrote, 'judging by the reproduction in the *Sketch*, somebody has a vivid imagination ...We are sometimes told that Spiritualists will recognise *anything*, but our critics are putting us in the shade.'[170] The *Daily Sketch* exposure was just a case of mistaken identity, which was easy to do given the general likeness of the extras' faces. If spiritualists appreciated the irony, they may not have appreciated that they were compromising their most important line of evidence regarding spiritualism.

Stead still drew upon the testimonies of those who had lost loved ones in the Great War. Accumulation of evidence was more important than negative evidence, and the relatives of deceased soldiers were given sacred status. G. Pratt wrote to inform Stead that he and his wife 'recognise our son Harry, who was killed in action March 2nd, 1918'. They had shown the photograph to several of their friends who verified the likeness. 'This knocks the *Daily Sketch* argument that they are faked on the head', he wrote, 'for if only one is claimed, the case for genuine spirit photography is made out'.[171] Stead's defence rested on the visceral feelings and subjective certainty of personal recognition and the moral good that spirit photography offered.

The potential damage inflicted by the *Daily Sketch* article was evident in the spiritualist response. In a raucous open letter, the spiritualist, journalist and former employee of the *Daily Sketch*, Hannen Swaffer, called on spiritualists to pester editors of papers if they spoke negatively of spiritualism.[172] He complained that spiritualists were held to a double standard. If a medium was caught in fraud, they were always identified as a spiritualist, but no paper ever referenced a 'Rape by Presbyterian' or 'Conservative found Guilty'.[173] *The Two Worlds* pledged to copy Swaffer's letter and send it to the offices of all of the nation's leading newspapers. This was a 'call to action to every Spiritualist in the United Kingdom'.[174]

There were attempts to see the developments that followed the controversy over the Armistice Day photographs more optimistically. Stead claimed victory although feeling no less persecuted. She maintained that the *Daily Sketch* exposure brought 'many people ... wanting to know about Spiritualism'.[175] *The Two Worlds* also thanked the press for 'drawing attention to this matter ... there will be many dozens who will ... investigate the matter for themselves in a calm, collected and deliberative state of mind, and it is pretty certain that ninety per cent of these will come our way'.[176] Any press was good press. In reality, the exposure was a devastating blow to spiritualists' hopes that the press was growing more interested and that public outlets could be used to advance the cause. In November 1924, W. T. Stead's spirit called on spiritualists to be more proactive, but in the years that followed, Deane receded from the public eye. If 1924 had begun favourably for spiritualists, the year ended on a bitter and pessimistic note.

Conclusion

Deane still produced spirit photographs after 1924, including ones taken during Armistice Day ceremonies, but only in the safe confines of spiritualist lodgings.[177] After 1924, there was noticeably more scepticism and caution in reports of spirit photography. In 1925, for example, *The Two Worlds* acknowledged that some people were too swift to 'cheerfully identify any face with a chance resemblance to some departed friend, and we agree that there is tendency … to attach too much importance to recognition'. Instead of claiming that recognition was a subjective certainty and the most important piece of evidence for spirit photography, it was now recognised as unreliable. As the paper cautioned, 'it must not be forgotten that such phenomena is [sic] very easily simulated'.[178] In comparison, four years earlier this same journal exclaimed that 'psychic photography [was] one of the most evidential forms of Spiritualistic phenomena in vogue today. The evidence of the sensitive plate is invaluable'.[179] The numerous cases of fraud had undermined such naïve hopes.

Time was not kind to spirit photography. Spiritualists exposed more frauds in the years ahead instead of uncovering new talent and more evidence. In 1925, the once promising new spirit photographer, George Moss, admitted to deception, and in 1933, Oaten was part of a committee that uncovered another fraudulent spirit photographer, E. R. Mandeville.[180] It was also in 1933 that further secrets came to light about once-revered mediums. Fred Barlow defended Deane and Hope against fraud in the early 1920s but now denounced them both. As he wrote, 'I was at one time a very strenuous advocate for … supernormal photography', but now he believed that Hope 'tricked every time', which 'involved a considerable amount of thought and preparation beforehand'.[181] The tipping point was Barlow's discovery in the 1920s that Hope may have been using a flashlight apparatus with a positive extra taped to the lens. Hope could 'stamp' extras onto plates by quickly turning on the device's bulb and pressing it against the plate. A newly suspicious Barlow began secretly conducting his own experiments during subsequent sittings. He conjectured that Hope had transitioned from substituting pre-made plates to using this 'ghost stamp' method after his feud with Price. Barlow observed that whenever he gave Hope the opportunity to substitute plates, extras appeared veiled in cotton or wool. When substitution was not possible, the extras were unveiled as if impressed by a flashlight during the sitting. If tests were too stringent to allow for the use of substitutions or a device, no extras appeared.[182] After Hope's death in 1933, Barbara McKenzie confirmed that her husband had discovered evidence that Hope began using a flashlight apparatus after 1922. Nevertheless, McKenzie defended Hope as genuine; the spectre of William's face on Glenconner's photograph continued to cloud her judgement.[183]

There were other scandals in the late 1920s as well. The tests with *Scientific American* ended poorly. Conan Doyle recommended the Boston medium Margery Crandon for the $2,500 prize for successful demonstration of genuine mediumship and scientists on the committee were sincerely impressed by the phenomena she produced, including direct voice, the moving of lights, the materialisation of objects and the ringing of bells from a distance. In a July 1924 issue of *Scientific American*, the committee hinted that she might win the $2,500 prize. Houdini, who was a member of the committee, was not impressed. He uncovered that Margery used her head to ring bells and to manifest objects, while her feet and hands remained in contact with the sitters. Houdini called one of her exploits 'the "slickest" ruse I have ever seen'.[184] Women, apparently, were capable of conjuring. Conan Doyle defended Crandon against Houdini, but two additional members of the committee publicly denounced her in 1925, noting that stricter conditions failed to produce any interesting phenomena.[185]

Conan Doyle did not live to see Barlow's denunciation of Hope and Deane, but he showed no signs of abandoning spirit photography. In 1928, he endorsed a spirit photograph taken during Douglas Haig's funeral that appeared to show the former Field Marshall's face above his coffin. Conan Doyle believed this photograph vindicated Deane. As he wrote in the *Sunday Express*, 'this authentic case of Lord Haig must cause some heart-searching among those who condemned the Cenotaph pictures of Mrs. Deane'.[186]

The revelation of a spirit photograph taken during Haig's funeral highlights the connection between spiritualist worldviews and changing war perspectives. Spiritualists claimed Haig as one of their own just as in the case of Armistice Day. Conan Doyle stated that although Haig was not a spiritualist per se, 'he was extremely sympathetic to our cause, and sent us more than once a message of encouragement at our big Queen's Hall meetings'.[187] Haig's burial and the spirit photograph in question symbolised a dying mythology. In 1929, veterans released books condemning the war's futility and the elites who prosecuted the war effort. Today Haig has come to symbolise futility and incompetence, and the question of whether or not Deane and Hope were charlatans is tragically evident.[188] After Deane's fall, Conan Doyle's support for spirit photography is evidence of 'a more credulous past'.[189] In his reminiscences in 1928, Conan Doyle spoke of a bygone age that the world had failed to embrace. The Cenotaph photographs were 'a great miracle wrought in three separate years in the heart of London', he explained, but 'the people heeded it not ... it was one of the wonders of the world, and passed almost unnoticed'.[190] Spirit photography had of course earned the public's attention, but mostly in the form of controversy and exposure. Spiritualists failed to appreciate that, in the modern world, enchantment also brought disenchantment.[191] By 1928, the ghosts that had haunted Britain in the aftermath of the Great War were fading from memory and being replaced by a new sensibility.

Notes

1 'Four Years Ago', *The Times*, 12 November 1922, p. 7.
2 'Spiritualists at the Cenotaph: Miss Stead and Medium's Photographs', *West Australian*, 6 June 1923.
3 'Spirit Picture Stirs Spectators to Sobs', *New York Times*, 7 April 1923, pp. 1, 8.
4 'The Cenotaph Psychic Photograph: Wonderful Results on Armistice Day', *Light*, 43:2236 (1923), 727.
5 'The Observatory: Light on Things in General', *Light*, 32:3237 (1923), 745.

6 CUL, MS SPR35/453, letter from Arthur Conan Doyle to Oliver Lodge, n.d. (likely December 1923).
7 'Unseen Men at Cenotaph: Spirit Photograph Claims of Miss Estelle Stead', *Daily Sketch*, 13 November 1924, pp. 2, 10–11.
8 F. W. Warrick, *Experiments in Psychics: Practical Studies in Direct Writing, Supernormal Photography, and Other Phenomena, Mainly with Mrs. Ada Emma Deane* (New York: E. P. Dutton, 1939), p. 234.
9 'Unseen Men at Cenotaph', pp. 2, 10–11.
10 'How the Daily Sketch Exposed "Spirit Photography"', *Daily Sketch*, 15 November 1924, p. 1.
11 *Ibid.*
12 'A Case of Fraud with the Crewe Circle', *JSPR*, 20 (1922), 271–83.
13 'Readers' Views on Faced Spirits: "Ridiculing Heroes of the War"', *Daily Sketch*, 18 November 1924, p. 15.
14 Between 1919 to 1924, spiritualists gathered in large crowds to commemorate the war, first at the Royal Albert Hall and later Queen's Hall. According to the spiritualist press, there was an estimated 'six or seven thousand in attendance', despite the unseasonably snowy weather in 1919 ('The National Memorial Service for the Fallen in the War: Royal Albert Hall', *Light*, Special Supplement (1919), 1). In 1923, *The Two Worlds* estimated that the crowd was 5,000. Apparently, there were so many in attendance that an estimated 1,000 people had to stay outside and were greeted to a secondary service ('The Great Commemoration: A Memorable Meeting at the Queen's Hall', *Light*, 43:2236 (1923), 724). This happened again in 1924 ('Armistice Day in London: Great Meeting at the Queen's Hall', *The Two Worlds*, 36:1879 (1923), 382).
15 F. R. S., 'The Great Remembrance: Some Thoughts for Armistice Day', *Light*, 44:2287 (1924), 688.
16 Neil Matheson, 'The Ghost Stamp, the Detective and the Hospital for Boots: *Light* and the Post-War Battle over Spirit-Photography', *Early Popular Visual Culture*, 4:1 (2006), 40.
17 David Cannadine, 'War and Death, Grief and Mourning in Modern Britain', in Joachim Whaley (ed.), *Mirrors of Mortality: Studies in the Social History of Death* (London: Europa Publications, 1981), p. 227.
18 For spiritualism and the Civil War see Bridget Bennett, '"There Is No Death": Spiritualism and the Civil War', in *Transatlantic Spiritualism and Nineteenth-Century American Literature* (New York: Palgrave Macmillan, 2007), pp. 147–76; Drew Gilpin Faust, *This Republic of Suffering: Death and the American Civil War* (New York: Alfred A. Knopf, 2008), pp. 180–5; and Mark A. Lause, *Free Spirits: Spiritualism, Republicanism, and Radicalism in the Civil War Era* (Urbana, IL: University of Illinois Press, 2016).

19 Martyn Jolly, *Faces of the Living Dead: The Belief in Spirit Photography* (New York: Mark Batty Publisher, 2006), p. 16; Crista Cloutier, 'Mumler's Ghosts', in Clément Chéroux et al. (eds), *The Perfect Medium: Photography and the Occult* (New Haven, CT: Yale University Press, 2004), pp. 20–3.
20 A. B. Child, 'Spirit Photographs', *Banner of Light* (8 November 1862), p. 4, in Louis Kaplan (ed.), *The Strange Case of William Mumler, Spirit Photographer* (Minneapolis, MN: University of Minnesota Press, 2008), pp. 39–44.
21 Naomi Rosenblum, *A World History of Photography*, Fourth Edition (New York and London: Abbeville Press, 2007), p. 56.
22 Mary Warner Marien, *Photography: A Cultural History*, Third Edition (London: Prentice Hall, 2011), p. 83; Robert Hirsch, *Seizing the Light: A History of Photography* (Boston, MA: McGraw Hill, 2000), pp. 78–80.
23 Peter Manseau, *The Apparitionists: A Tale of Phantoms, Fraud, Photography and the Man Who Captured Lincoln's Ghost* (Boston, MA and New York: Houghton Mifflin Harcourt, 2017).
24 Jolly, *Faces of the Living Dead*, p. 24.
25 Pierre Apraxine and Sophie Schmit, 'Photography and the Occult', in Chéroux et al. (eds), *The Perfect Medium*.
26 Cloutier, 'Mumler's Ghosts', p. 21.
27 By the time Doyle wrote his *History of Spiritualism* in 1926, Hope was still using this camera. Arthur Conan Doyle, *The History of Spiritualism*, vol. II (London and New York: Cassell & Company, 1926), p. 146.
28 Jolly, *Faces of the Living Dead*, p. 90.
29 Daston and Galison define mechanical objectivity as 'the insistent drive to repress the willful intervention of the artist-author, and to put in its stead a set of procedures that would, as it were, move nature to the page through a strict protocol, if not automatically' (Lorraine Daston and Peter Galison, *Objectivity* (New York: Zone Books, 2007), p. 121).
30 Henry Fox Talbot, *The Pencil of Nature* (London: Longman, Brown, Green and Longman, 1844), p. 1.
31 Quoted in Alex Owen, '"Borderland Forms": Arthur Conan Doyle, Albion's Daughters and the Politics of the Cottingley Fairies', *History Workshop Journal*, 38:1 (1994), 65.
32 For the link between science and spirit photography see John Harvey, *Photography and Spirit* (London: Reaktion Books, 2007), pp. 70–106.
33 Quoted in Jennifer Tucker, *Nature Exposed: Photography as Eyewitness in Victorian Science* (Baltimore, MD: Johns Hopkins University Press, 2005), p. 70.

34 See Jordan Bear, *Disillusioned: Victorian Photography and the Discerning Subject* (University Park, PA: The Pennsylvania State University Press, 2015), p. 5. For early examples of photographic tricks before spirit photography, see Tucker, *Nature Exposed*, pp. 71–3.
35 William H. Mumler, *The Personal Experiences of William H. Mumler in Spirit-Photography* (Boston, MA: Colby and Rich, 1875), in Kaplan (ed.), *Strange Case of William Mumler*, p. 70.
36 Bear, *Disillusioned*, pp. 32–79.
37 Daston and Galison, *Objectivity*, pp. 126–30.
38 Tucker, *Nature Exposed*, pp. 3–4, 17–64.
39 Daston and Galison, *Objectivity*, pp. 131–7; Marien, *Photography*, pp. 172–4.
40 Jolly, *Faces of the Living Dead*, p. 22.
41 Arthur Conan Doyle, *The Vital Message* (London: George H. Doran Company, 1919), p. 156.
42 Tucker, *Nature Exposed*, pp. 67–8; Daston and Galison, *Objectivity*, p. 126; Rosenblum, *A World History of Photography*, pp. 245–57.
43 James Coates, *Photographing the Invisible: Practical Studies in Spirit Photography, Spirit Portraiture, and Other Rare But Allied Phenomena* (London: L. N. Fowler, 1911), p. 1.
44 J. Traill Taylor, 'Spirit Photograph: Are Spirit Photographs of Spirits?', *Borderland*, 2:9 (1895), 239–41.
45 Jolly, *Faces of the Living Dead*, pp. 47–8.
46 Estelle Stead, *Faces of the Living Dead: Remembrance Day Messages and Photographs* (Manchester: 'The Two Worlds' Publishing, 1925), p. 22.
47 Barbara McKenzie, 'The Unknown Face', *Light*, 40:2082 (1920), 440.
48 Jolly, *Faces of the Living Dead*, p. 111.
49 Fred Barlow and Major W. Rampling-Rose, 'Report of an Investigation into Spirit Photography', *PSPR*, 41 (1932–33), 124.
50 Jolly, *Faces of the Living Dead*, p. 22.
51 *Ibid.*, p. 111.
52 R. Hipwood, 'Spirit-Photograph of a Soldier Son', *The International Psychic Gazette*, 96:8 (1921), 178.
53 *Ibid.*
54 Mrs M. S. Hipwood attended at least one other Hope sitting in 1924. 'Another Spirit Photograph', *The Two Worlds*, 37:1936 (1924), 722.
55 For example, the Assistant Secretary of BCPS, E. Ford, informed Harry Price that he could 'experiment' with Hope but that he 'will not undertake tests' ('A Case of Fraud with the Crewe Circle', 271–83).
56 J. L. H., 'Psychic Photography: Successful Experiments', *Light*, 39:1987 (1919), 46.
57 Whatley Smith, 'Psychic Photography', *The Psychic Research Quarterly*, 1:1–4 (1920–21), 348–9.

58 'Spirit Photograph: Another Success of the Crewe Circle', *Light*, 39:2015 (1919), 267.
59 J. L. H., 'Psychic Photography', 46.
60 'A Good Case for Spirit Photography', *The Two Worlds*, 38:1946 (1925), 129.
61 'The Return of a Soldier Boy', *Light*, 40: 2078 (1920), 364.
62 J. Arthur Hill, 'Unidentified Psychic Photographs', *Light*, 40:11 (1920), 420.
63 'The Return of a Soldier Boy', 364.
64 Jay Winter, *Sites of Memory, Sites of Mourning: The Great War in European Cultural History*, Canto Edition (Cambridge: Cambridge University Press, 1998), pp. 29–31.
65 James Hewat McKenzie was interested in spiritualism, including spirit photography, before his son's death. But the incident was the catalyst that led them to invest so much time and money into Hope. For his writings on spirit photography before 1918, see J. Hewat McKenzie, *Spirit Intercourses: Its Theory and Practice* (New York: M. Kennerley, 1917), pp. 102–7.
66 Senate House Library, Eric J. Dingwall Papers (hereafter Dingwall Papers), MS912/1/2, 'Notes for Members', *British College of Psychic Science*, May 1920, pp. 76–9.
67 'Balance Sheet', *British College of Psychic Science*, July 19, 1922, in *ibid.*, p. 82.
68 Arthur Conan Doyle claimed to Dingwall that Hope's success rate was 25 per cent but this contradicted earlier reports of 5 per cent (Dingwall Papers, Scrapbook (Q), SHL, MS912/1/383, letter from Arthur Conan Doyle to Eric J. Dingwall, 4 December 1923, p. 9).
69 McKenzie, 'The Unknown Face', 440.
70 Allerton Cusham sat with Mrs. Deane and recognised an extra as his fifteen-year-old daughter. That the extra was not a soldier was a point in Deane's favour 'since the great majority of Mrs. Deane's sitters ... are mourning soldier sons it would hardly seem reasonable to believe that her repertory happened to contain a picture of young girl a perfect simulacrum of our daughter'. See Allerton S. Cushman, 'An Evidential Case of Spirit Photography', *Light*, 42:2157 (1922), 298.
71 For photographs taken by Deane see CUL, MS SPR, Spirit Photographs (hereafter 54), Warrick Collection, four volumes (hereafter 1–4), 1920–23. For those taken with the Crewe Circle see CUL, MS SPR 54, Crewe Circle (hereafter 6). See also, British Library, General Reference Collection, Cup. 407.a.1, Eric J. Dingwall, The Barlow Collection of Psychic Photography.
72 McKenzie, 'The Unknown Face', 440.
73 *Ibid.*

74 'Unknown Psychic "Extras": Can Our Readers Recognize Them?', *Light*, 40:2080 (1918), 404.
75 'Unseen Psychic "Extras": Can Our Readers Recognize Them?', *Light*, 40:2082 (1920), 440.
76 Jessie Freeman, 'At the Cenotaph', *The International Psychic Gazette*, 87:8 (1920), 34.
77 *Ibid.*
78 Jay Winter, *Remembering War: The Great War Between Memory and History in the Twentieth Century* (New Haven, CT: Yale University Press, 2006), 18.
79 Quoted in Adrian Gregory, *The Silence of Memory: Armistice Day, 1919–1946* (London: Bloomsbury, 1994), p. 16.
80 As Adrian Gregory argues, Armistice Day originated as more of 'an aspiration towards a genuine international peace rather than a celebration of its reality' (*ibid.*, p. 17).
81 *Ibid.*, p. 22.
82 Quoted in 'Armistice Day', *The International Psychic Gazette*, 6:75 (1919), 33.
83 Quoted in Gregory, *The Silence of Memory*, p. 19.
84 Winter, *Sites of Memory, Sites of Mourning*, p. 61.
85 Seymour H. Mauskopf and Michael R. McVaugh, *The Elusive Science: Origins of Experimental Psychical Research* (Baltimore, MD: Johns Hopkins University Press, 1980), p. 115.
86 Tucker, *Nature Exposed*, pp. 139–41; Andreas Fischer, '"La Lune au Front": Remarks on the History of the Photography of Thought', in Chéroux et al. (eds), *The Perfect Medium*, pp. 139–54.
87 Arthur Conan Doyle, 'For Armistice Day: A Symposium of Reflections and Messages by Some Distinguished Readers of, and Contributors to, "Light"', *Light*, 43:2235 (1923), 710; 'Armistice Day: The Arisen Dead', *Light*, 40:2078 (1920), 868.
88 'Armistice Day in London: Great Meeting at Queen's Hall', *The Two Worlds*, 36:1879 (1923), 382.
89 'A Mighty Host! Clairvoyant Impression by Two Noted Mediums', *Light*, Special Supplement (1919), 5.
90 'Sir Arthur Conan Doyle', *Light*, Special Supplement (1919), 3.
91 As Gregory observes, the silence originated in South Africa during the war (Gregory, *Silence of Memory*, p. 9).
92 'Mr. Ernest Oaten, President, S.N.U.', *Light*, Special Supplement (1919), 2.
93 Stead, *Faces of the Living Dead*, pp. 10–11.
94 W. T. S., 'An Armistice Day Message from Mr. W. T. Stead', *Light*, 40:2079 (1920), 378.

95 'The National Memorial Service for the Fallen in the War', *Light*, Special Supplement (1919), 1.
96 'The White Insignia', *Light*, Special Supplement (1919), 2.
97 Stead, *Faces of the Living Dead*, p. 13.
98 'Armistice Sunday: Great Service at Queen's Hall', *Light*, 44:2258 (1924), 698.
99 W. E. Long, 'Remembrance Day in London', *Light*, 43: 3237 (1923), 749.
100 'Sir Arthur Conan Doyle', 3.
101 Some ceremonies included clairvoyant descriptions. In 1924, one medium engaged in this activity and the crowd recognised a dozen personalities. See 'Armistice Rally in London: Service of Remembrance in Queen's Hall', *The Two Worlds*, 37:1931 (1924), 646.
102 See Jay Winter, *War beyond Words: Languages of Remembrance from the Great War to the Present* (Cambridge: Cambridge University Press, 2017), 173.
103 'Special New Year Messages', 1.
104 'Armistice Day in London: Great Meeting at the Queen's Hall', *The Two Worlds*, 36:1879 (1923), 382.
105 'Special New Year Messages', 4.
106 See Peter Broks, *Media Science before the Great War* (London: Macmillan Press, 1996), pp. 5–8, 14–16; W. Hamish Fraser, *The Coming of the Mass Market, 1850–1914* (London: Macmillan Press, 1981), pp. 225–9. For the history of the new journalism see Alan J. Lee, *The Origins of the Popular Press in England: 1855–1914* (London: Croom Helm, 1976), pp. 117–30.
107 W. T. Stead, 'Government by Journalism', *Contemporary Review*, 49 (1886), 653.
108 Quoted in Broks, *Media Science before the Great War*, p. 15.
109 Roger Luckhurst, *The Invention of Telepathy, 1870–1901* (Oxford: Oxford University Press, 2002), pp. 131–2.
110 Ibid., pp. 125–6, 146.
111 Quoted in Broks, *Media Science before the Great War*, 34. See also Bernard Lightman, *Victorian Popularizers of Science: Designing Nature for New Audiences* (Chicago, IL: University of Chicago Press, 2007), pp. 28–9. For the popularisation of science in the twentieth century, see Peter J. Bowler, *Science for All: The Popularization of Science in Early Twentieth-Century Britain* (Chicago, IL: University of Chicago Press, 2009).
112 Lightman, *Victorian Popularizers of Science*, pp. 331–2; Luckhurst, *The Invention of Telepathy*, pp. 125–6, 146. For more on Stead and spiritualism, including spirit photography, see Ruth Brandon,

The Spiritualists: The Passion for the Occult in the Nineteenth and Twentieth Centuries (New York: Alfred A. Knopf, 1983), pp. 190–205; Tucker, *Nature Exposed*, pp. 114–24.

113 Stead, *Faces of the Living Dead*, p. 31.
114 *Ibid.*, p. 27. The first Armistice Day spirit photograph was taken during the two minutes of silence at the W. T. Stead Bureau and Library (later renamed the W. T. Stead Borderland Library).
115 Marien, *Photography*, pp. 235–8.
116 '"Criticism" of Psychic Photographs', *International Psychic Gazette*, 98:9 (1921), 20.
117 Stead, *Faces of the Living Dead*, p. 31.
118 'The Great Commemoration: A Memorable Meeting at Queen's Hall', *Light*, 43:2236 (1923), 725.
119 As *Light* explained, 'We have more than once referred to the remarkable change of attitude on the part of both Press and public, as contrasted with that which prevailed some twenty years ago, or even less.' See 'Notes by the Way', *Light*, 43:2211 (1923), 321.
120 'Special New Year Messages to Our Readers', *The Two Worlds*, 37:1886 (1924), 1.
121 James Douglas, 'Grappling with the Unknown: The Dark Cabinet', *The Sunday Express*, 27 November 1921, p. 6.
122 James Douglas, 'Are the Dead Alive? Is Spirit Photography Genuine?', *The Sunday Express*, 6 November 1921, p. 8.
123 James Douglas, 'Is Spirit Photography Genuine? The Results of My Second Experiment', *The Sunday Express*, 11 December 1921, p. 6.
124 *Light* commented that the introductory 'article deserves to be read by all for it is the fine, manly statement of a seeker after truth. We are informed that there will be further instalments, and these will be awaited with eagerness by many.' See 'Form the Lighthouse Window', *Light*, 41:2128 (1921), 685.
125 The *Daily Express* reported favourably on the competition in the fall of 1923. See 'Spiritualism in Daylight: Feats of an American Woman Medium', *Daily Express*, 18 October 1923, p. 1.
126 'Exit, 1924', *The Two Worlds*, 37:1937 (1924), 734; '1923: Our Outlook', *Light*, 43:2191 (1923), 8.
127 'Special New Year Messages to Our Readers', *Two Worlds*, 37:1886 (1924), 1.
128 Arthur Conan Doyle, *The Case for Spirit Photography* (New York: George H. Doran Company, 1923), p. 61.
129 W. Charles Pilley, 'Amazing Spirit Camera Frauds: Psychic Experimenters Caught Red-Handed in Transparent Deception and Trickery', *John Bull*, 17 December 1921, p. 4.

130 *Ibid.*, p. 4.
131 Jolly, *Faces of the Living Dead*, pp. 115–17; CUL, MS SPR, Medium Files, Mrs Ada Deane, File 23, 'Magic Circle Deane Test', 17 February 1923.
132 As Sofie Lachapelle notes, psychical researchers had a poor familiarity with the art of deception. See Sofie Lachapelle, *Conjuring Science: A History of Scientific Entertainment and Stage Magic in Modern France* (New York: Palgrave Macmillan, 2015), p. 67.
133 Houdini pretended to have spiritual and psychic powers very early in his career, but he abandoned the act for reportedly moral reasons. See Michael Mangan, *Performing Dark Arts: A Cultural History of Conjuring* (Chicago, IL: Intellect Books, 2007), pp. 162–3.
134 As Peter Lamont notes, the difference between the magician and the fraud is that the former demonstrates fabrications while the latter fabricates demonstrations (Peter Lamont, *Extraordinary Beliefs: A Historical Approach to A Psychological Problem* (Cambridge: Cambridge University Press, 2013), pp. 36–54). For more on the relationship between spiritualists and conjurers see Lachapelle, *Conjuring Science*, pp. 59–88.
135 See Mangen, *Performing Dark Arts*, pp. 162–71.
136 For an overview of Marriot's experiments see Everard Fielding, 'An Experiment in "Faking" Spirit Photographs', *JSPR*, 20 (1920–21), 219–23; Douglas, 'Is Spirit Photography Genuine?', p. 6.
137 Jolly, *Faces of the Living Dead*, p. 101.
138 'A Case of Fraud with the Crewe Circle', 271–83; Harry Price, *Cold Light on Spiritualistic 'Phenomena:' An Experiment with the Crewe Circle* (London: Kegan Paul, Trench, Trubner, 1922).
139 Mauskopf and McVaugh, *The Elusive Science*, p. 26.
140 Pat Thane, 'The Impact of Mass Democracy on British Political Culture, 1918–1939', in Julie V. Gottlieb and Richard Toye (eds), *The Aftermath of Suffrage: Women, Gender and Politics in Britain* (London: Palgrave Macmillan, 2013), p. 54.
141 Mangen, *Performing Dark Arts*, p. xiii.
142 Lachapelle, *Conjuring Science*, p. 87.
143 Jenny Hazelgrove, *Spiritualism and British Society between the Wars* (Manchester: Manchester University Press, 2000), p. 250.
144 Conan Doyle, *Case for Spirit Photography*, pp. 13, 17.
145 As Waites argues, the war introduced greater segments of the working class to issues regarding fairness, 'equality of sacrifice' and 'profiteering'. See Bernard Waites, *A Class Society at War: England 1914–1918* (New York: Berg, 1987), pp. 16–17, 235.
146 Rosenblum, *A World History of Photography*, p. 267.

147 Conan Doyle, *Case for Spirit Photography*, pp. 15–17.
148 CUL, MS SPR, Medium Files, Deane, report by E. J. Dingwall, 9 March 1922,
149 CUL, MS SPR., letter from Oliver Lodge to E. J. Dingwall, 8 April 1922,
150 'Much Ado About a Psychic Photograph', *The Two Worlds*, 37:1932 (1924), 660.
151 Stead, *Faces of the Living Dead*, p. 44.
152 Hazelgrove, *Spiritualism and British Society between the Wars*, p. 151.
153 Elliott O'Donnell, *The Menace of Spiritualism* (London: Werner & Laurie, 1920), p. 137.
154 'Readers' Views on Faced Spirits: "Ridiculing Heroes of the War"', *Daily Sketch*, 18 November 1924, p. 15.
155 Quoted in 'The Observatory: Light on Things in General', *Light*, 43:2206 (1923), 249.
156 Waites, *A Class Society at War*, pp. 221–2.
157 See Christine Grandy, '"Avarice" and "Evil Doers": Profiteers, Politicians, and Popular Fiction in the 1920s', *Journal of British Studies*, 50:3 (2011), 667–89.
158 Peter Twaites, 'Circles of Confusion and Sharp Vision: British News Photography 1919–39', in Peter Catterall et al. (eds), *Northcliffe's Legacy: Aspects of the British Popular Press, 1896–1996* (London: Macmillan, 2000), pp. 106–7.
159 '"Spirits" – While You Wait', 18 November 1924, p. 2.
160 '£1,000 Challenge Declined: Mrs. Deane a Charlatan and a Fraud', *Daily Sketch*, 21 November 1924, p. 2.
161 Ada Deane, 'Mrs. Deane's Reply: Doubts if Money Would Tempt Her Wonderful Power', *Daily Sketch*, 21 November 1924, p. 2.
162 'Mrs. Deane and the "Daily Sketch"', *Light*, 44:2290 (1924), 729.
163 '£1,000 Challenge Declined', *Daily Sketch*, p. 2.
164 Stead, *Faces of the Living Dead*, pp. 39–42.
165 *Ibid.*, pp. 34–6.
166 *Ibid.*, p. 37.
167 'How the Daily Sketch Exposed "Spirit Photography"', *Daily Sketch*, p. 1.
168 Warrick, *Experiments in Psychics*, p. 259.
169 Rose Ch. De. Crespigny, 'Letters to the Editor: The Cenotaph Photograph', *Light*, 44:2289 (1924), 721.
170 'Much Ado About a Psychic Photograph', 660.
171 Stead, *Faces of the Living Dead*, pp. 60–2.
172 Dennis Griffiths (ed.), *The Encyclopedia of the British Press, 1422–1922* (New York: St. Martin's Press, 1992), p. 550. Swaffer also worked

for Lord Northcliffe for many years and later wrote a book purporting to contain messages from the press magnate after his death in 1922. See Hannen Swaffer, *Northcliffe's Return* (London: Hutchinson & Company, 1925).
173 Hannen Swaffer, 'Spiritualist Services and Insulting Press References', *Light*, 44:2258 (1924), 703.
174 'A Protest and a Personal Experience', *The Two Worlds*, 37:1933 (1924), 676.
175 Stead, *Faces of the Living Dead*, p. 58.
176 Quoted in *ibid.*, p. 58.
177 Deane photographed the spiritualist Remembrance ceremony at the Borderland Library in 1929 and at Albert Hall in 1927 and 1931. In the latter, Conan Doyle's face appeared, a year after his death (Warrick, *Experiments in Psychics*, pp. 21, 24, 276).
178 'Psychic Pictures and Identification', *The Two Worlds*, 38:1941 (1925), 56.
179 'Spirit Photography', *The Two Worlds*, 33:1684 (1920), 20.
180 'Fraudulent Psychic Photographer Exposed: Further Evidence of Imposture', *The Two Worlds*, 46:2402 (1933), 943.
181 Barlow and Rose, 'Report of an Investigation into Spirit Photography', 121; Fred Barlow, 'Mr. Barlow Replies to His Critics', *Light*, 53:2736 (1933), 374.
182 *Ibid.*, 121–38.
183 Barbara McKenzie, 'Afterthoughts on "Hope" Debate: Facts of the Flash-Lamp "Discovery" at the British College', *Light*, 53:2734 (1933), 342.
184 Quoted in Brandon, *The Spiritualists*, p. 181.
185 *Ibid.*, pp. 174–89.
186 CUL MSPR, Research Files, Psychic Photography, File 20, Earl Haig's Funeral, Arthur Conan Doyle, '"Spirit" Photographs: The Face at the Haig Funeral', *The Sunday Express*, n.d. (circa February 1928).
187 *Ibid.*
188 For a more nuanced and favourable assessment of Haig, see Gary Sheffield, *The Chief: Douglas Haig and the British Army* (London: Autumn Press, 2011).
189 Matheson, 'The Ghost Stamp', 40.
190 Conan Doyle, '"Spirit" Photographs'.
191 Owen, 'Borderland Forms', 80.

Conclusion

After the outbreak of war in September 1939, David Anderson took a walk to contemplate the news. A veteran of the Great War, he was filled with terror as he remembered the battlefield. His horror was contrasted by the peaceful moonlit night, which made him think 'that it was impossible there could be a war on'. The following morning, he was reminded that the coming cataclysm was very real; the news reported that the SS *Athenia* had been sunk with 1,400 passengers on board. 'This is only the beginning', he thought to himself; 'it seems a ghastly nightmare'. After surviving the Western Front, Anderson once 'wished that I could die in peace time', but as he wrote to his former comrade, Alister Hardy, 'the hounds of war are loose and we have the heartbreaking sight of our babies being disfigured with gas masks'. Frightful of the future, Anderson informed Hardy: 'If I happen to go west – one never knows – I will try and let you know where you may be. That is if I am not a way down in the infernal regions.'[1]

David Anderson was a coal fireman from Spital Tongues writing to the biologist Alister Hardy. The unlikely friends had met during the Great War when Hardy served as Anderson's Captain in the C Company of the Northern Cyclist Battalion (NCB). When the war began, Hardy was nineteen and studying forestry at Oxford. Like most men of his class and age, he enlisted in the war shortly thereafter and received a commission as a Second Lieutenant. By all accounts, he was well respected by the men, and he established lifelong friendships with many of them.[2] In the 1920s, while corresponding with David Anderson, the conversation had turned to the recent passing of one of their former comrades. Anderson could not help but reveal his interest in spiritualism:

This might sound strange to you, but my wife Ann and myself do not grieve about Archie, tho [sic] we pray for his progression at the other side of the veil. We are spiritualists (Christian) and quite convinced about the future. Where uncertainty – fear and unhappiness preyed on me – I have instead Happiness, Contentment and Love and all foreboding [sic] have vanished like a mist.[3]

This level of certainty and optimism is a far cry from the agony and despair that Anderson felt in the immediate days after the Second World War. In the interwar period, spiritualists had anticipated a heaven on earth, but instead, between 1914 and 1945, Europe went 'to hell and back'.[4]

Hardy, it turns out, was very interested in Anderson's spiritualist pursuits. Behind the confident young man that commanded C Company was a soul in travail. Hardy was raised in a different world, where the Bible and Christianity were taken for granted. His exposure to the works of Darwin and Huxley at Oxford had deeply troubled his worldview.[5] When war erupted he made a vow that shaped the course of his life: '[I] vowed to what I called God that if I should survive the war I would devote my life to attempting to bring about such a reconciliation that would satisfy the intellectual world.'[6] Most of the subjects examined in this book passed away or moved on from spiritualism by the 1950s. Hardy's efforts, on the contrary, spanned over seven decades. His story offers an informative case study on the rise and fall of the supernormal explanation of the Great War.

Hardy's biographer observes that it is hard not to smirk at a naïve young man's cocksure attitude that he could 'satisfy the intellectual' world by uniting science and religion.[7] But Hardy never wavered in his commitment. As he wrote in his memoirs, which he titled *A Life with a Vow*, 'the working of this vow has been very real to me'.[8] Looking back on his life in the 1980s, he could not help but think that he had been guided by providence to see his promise through. His first stroke of luck came shortly after his vow. Hardy was fortunate to never set foot on the battlefield. He was transferred from the NCB to the Camouflage School in 1915 in a case of mistaken identity. He applied to the Royal Engineers in the hope of potentially becoming a pilot, but the colonel at the Camouflage School mistook Hardy for someone else. The appointment was a perfect fit for someone interested in science and skilled at art (he was an amateur artist) and Hardy attributed this twist of fate to providence.[9] After the war, he transferred from forestry to biology where he became famous (and knighted) for his work on plankton. As he explained to Anderson, this was a deliberate choice meant to obtain the knowledge and scientific authority that would allow him to fulfil his vow. '[I] am trying to get a good established position in the scientific world from which to speak', he explained, 'it will take a long time yet but I have hopes. In the meantime I am ... preparing for the future work.'[10] Hardy kept his hopes secret from most of his family, friends and colleagues until the 1960s when he retired from his position as Linacre Chair of Zoology and Comparative Anatomy at Oxford.

In Hardy's biography and correspondence, one can see the influence of both the Victorian crisis of faith and the Great War on his spiritual thinking. He was an admirer of George Frederic Watts's 1886 painting, *Hope*, which depicts a blindfolded woman sitting atop a globe, attempting to play a harp with only one string. Contemporaries interpreted the painting as emphasising the importance of faith in a material world. This was Hardy's interpretation, as he believed that the female figure was 'blinded by science' and unable to engage in the art of music.[11] The spiritualist Ellen Little was fond of the painting as well, and thought that it represented 'the hope of another and endless life after this physical life is over'. The imagery was spiritualist in nature, she reasoned, as the figure '*is not* playing but *listening, listening intently* for any sound which may come to her, *along that one string*, from Beyond'.[12] The sound waves and vibrations from the string were analogous to the forces that made supernormal communications possible.

The Great War also shaped Hardy's vow and directed him towards psychical research. As he explained to Anderson, the war convinced him that man needed spirituality more than ever. 'I have been feeling ever since the war', he wrote, 'that men cannot live without some sort of religion', although not of a clerical variety. Spirituality made men happy and contented, and its void in the modern world resulted in commercialism and class conflict. He believed socialism was appealing because 'men are wanting some great ideal to follow', which industrial life had failed to provide. The war had at least achieved this on some level, and Hardy hoped that it would result in 'much more love and sympathy between men and the classes'.

As the General Strike of 1926 demonstrated, this potential had not been fully realised by 1927, but Hardy could still hope 'that a time will come soon when there will be a great spiritual awakening'.[13] Like Conan Doyle, Hardy believed that a spiritual synthesis with modern science would provide a holistic remedy for the modern world, one that traditional religion had failed to achieve.

Hardy's hope for a classless society was less superficial and more firmly grounded in his experiences than that of Conan Doyle. Bernard Waites observes that the class levelling that did occur on account of the war had a mythic power in the cultural memory. One shoemaker recalled, 'It is a paradox of war that whatever the position of a man or woman, whatever may be the attitude of "others" toward him in times of peace, he suddenly seems to be elevated and mysteriously becomes a better person in times of war.'[14] The war had revealed to Hardy the artificiality of class division. As he later wrote, he was raised 'to look upon the working classes as if they were quite a different race almost. They were never treated at all like social equals – one should never mix with them.' His commission into the NCB introduced him to the working class for the first time. This represented a culture shock, but over time he developed a deep affection for his men. After the war, he maintained correspondence with dozens of them for the rest of his life.[15] Hardy also organised an annual reunion that was held until the 1970s. In both his scientific pursuits and private life, he was committed to the vow he made in 1914. It was not until 1984, at the age of eighty-eight, that he published his last book outlining his synthesis of Darwinism and spirituality.[16] He died the following year, his vow complete.

Hardy's work can be interpreted as the last effort to realise the hopes of the Britons examined in this book. He believed that a spiritual science was the answer to the intellectual, cultural and social issues that afflicted modern Europe in the decades immediately before and after the Great War. The conflict between 1914 and 1918 also offered an opportunity to rejuvenate humanity's spiritual nature through sacrifice, suffering and redemption. Hardy was not a spiritualist, but like many men of science who were interested in spiritual matters, he did attend some séances. He did not deny the possibility of the survival of human personality or communion with the dead. As he explained to Anderson, he was 'sure that the spirit of man ... will survive bodily death', and that it was 'much more improbable that the part of our friends we love should end at the bodily death than otherwise'. Hardy also admired the work of Oliver Lodge, William Crookes, William Barrett and the SPR, but he did not like the 'cult' of spiritualism, distrusted mediums because of fraud and believed that much of the phenomena could be explained as subconscious imagination.[17] These positions meant that Hardy sympathised with what was identified as the right wing and High-and-Dry School of psychical researchers, when spiritualism dominated discussions about psychic phenomena, regardless of one's own views on the matter. The so-called 'right wing' of psychical research tended to be sceptical of spiritualism, and were solely interested in telepathy, while the 'left wing' advocated for exploring a broader range of phenomena. J. G. Piddington drew another distinction between what he labelled the 'High-and-Dry School' and the 'Not-So-High-and-Dry School'. The former were those who insisted on the strictest levels of evidential standards possible and were generally more conservative in their approaches. The Not-So-High-and Dry, which included Conan Doyle, tended to be liberal in their investigations, believing that 'so much has been established beyond cavil that we can now safely relax to some extent the stringent cautions and ... very high standard of evidence'.[18] Thus, when Hardy first engaged in psychical research in the 1960s after his retirement, the intellectual foundations, practices, assumptions, questions and methods that had shaped the field between the 1880s and 1930s had changed.

There is one other striking distinction between Hardy's earlier and later careers. In his memoirs, written towards the end of his life, Hardy's vow is much more personal and presented as the fulfilment of his destiny rather than as a part of a communal enterprise that will usher in a new spiritual age or redeem the sacrifices of the Great War. Just as Will R. Bird was honouring his brother in *Ghosts Have War Hands*, Hardy appeared to be honouring his vow. What accounts for this contrast? What changed after the Second World War?

From the supernormal to the paranormal

Between the 1880s and the 1930s, psychical research had five general defining characteristics. The first was its chosen method of investigation. With a few exceptions, most psychical researchers followed a 'natural-historical approach' characterised by 'meticulous observation', 'fact gathering' and an 'unwavering commitment to the facts thus established'.[19] Examples include the letters used for *Phantasms of the Living* and the cross-correspondence studies of the SPR. The second major characteristic was the significance of the spiritualist hypothesis. Telepathy was originally intended to be separate from this question, but, as was observed in Chapter 3, Myers's synthesis brought the two directly into contact with one another. In the aftermath of the war, the question was probed with greater energy, and even those within the High-and-Dry School of psychical research such as Eric J. Dingwall devoted their resources to mediums and spirit photography.[20] A third feature of psychical research was that telepathy's existence was taken for granted. Researchers rarely asked if mind-to-mind communication was possible and instead tried to discern if a trance medium's communications came from discarnate spirits or originated in the subconscious of the medium or sitter. During the war, more Britons within the SPR's social circles began gravitating from the established facts of telepathy to the open question of spiritualism. Fourth, two intellectual traditions influenced the field. The first was nineteenth-century physics as typified by the work of Crookes, Barrett and Lodge, and the second was *fin-de-siècle* dynamic psychiatry. Finally, the field was dominated mostly by amateurs with diverse backgrounds who operated through various societies in Europe and the United States.

The established paradigm after the Second World War bore increasingly fewer of these characteristics. The transition from psychical research to parapsychology is perhaps best exemplified through the career of J. B. Rhine. In some respects, Rhine's story is quite familiar. He was raised in a Protestant family from Pennsylvania and underwent a crisis of faith just as the United States entered the Great War. He was introduced to spiritualism and psychical research during Conan Doyle's 1922 tour of the United States. Intrigued by spiritualism's potential to unite science and the supernatural, Rhine joined the American Society for Psychical Research (ASPR) while pursuing his PhD in botany. From 1927 onwards, his sympathies shifted more towards psychology and the right wing of psychical research. The Margery Crandon controversy convinced him that spiritualism was fraudulent, and while most other researchers were consumed with séances, Rhine became more interested in mental phenomena.[21] He was particularly intrigued by the work of Ina Jephson, who hypothesised in the early 1920s that previous experimental tests into telepathy were flawed. Jephson observed that in card-guessing experiments, the agent looked at the card's contents in full view of the percipient. What if the latter was not receiving telepathic impressions but was actually clairvoyant?[22] This led Rhine to group telepathy and clairvoyance under the umbrella term 'extrasensory perception' (ESP), which was also the name of his famous 1934 book.[23]

Although Rhine drew upon a lengthy history of psychical research, *Extrasensory Perception* is generally regarded as ushering in a new era of parapsychology.[24] For starters, Rhine emphasised the experimental method over the natural historical approach. The SPR's *Phantasms of the Living* had included an experimental component, but it had placed far more significance on cases of spontaneous crisis apparitions. This precedent made subsequent researchers biased against controlled experiments.[25] Not only did Rhine reject spiritualism, but he was not convinced that telepathy had been proven. Previous experiments lacked rigour and failed to distinguish between telepathy and clairvoyance. Rhine also incorporated contemporary psychology into his studies. He considered what effect mental states such as stress or boredom might have on the results, and this required the integration of the latest research into 'perception, cognition, motivation, personality, and learning'.[26] Finally, Rhine was a specialist operating within the psychology department at Duke University, and he used graduate students as research assistants and subjects.[27]

So far, this book has been solely interested in phenomena belonging to the era of the supernormal. The distinction is not just one of semantics. Parapsychological experiences were qualitatively different from supernormal experiences, as they were validated through controlled scientific experiments and expert statistical analyses. Individuals were clairvoyant or telepathic according to a series of specially designed card-guessing exercises that controlled for different factors under different assumptions.[28] Eric J. Dingwall recalled how Rhine's book inspired a wave of private circles to try their hand at these experiments.[29] The supernormal experience was heavily structured around the idea that moments of crises and intense emotional feelings stimulated telepathic phenomena. A telepathic experience usually occurred between dreaming and waking, and involved a hallucination. These were not just abstract theories invented by a small group of isolated elites. Gurney and Myers came to their conclusions because people were having these experiences. Geographical distance and communal bonds such as empire, nation or family informed these spontaneous phenomena. During the war, a number of British subjects felt these connections, experienced crisis apparitions and looked for scientific validation through telepathic theory.

Another key difference in post-1945 investigations is the lack of trance, which had allowed for the supernormal to encompass spiritualism and multiple personalities. This connection meant that spirit phenomena, ghosts or anything related to post-mortem survival were consumed by the supernormal, in dialogue with questions that parapsychology neatly closed off into its own space. Instead, the general term *paranormal* has become commonplace and encompasses a host of phenomena that do not necessarily indicate any association with parapsychology (see Figures 6.1 to 6.3). The term telepathy has likewise survived in popular culture but is no longer associated with dreams or hallucinations.

Hardy was operating within a new register when he conducted his own tests into telepathy in 1967. His interest in the subject originated from supernormal experiences during the First World War. While serving in England with the NCB, the medium Mrs Wedgewood had grown acquainted with some of the battalion's officers. In her conversations with Hardy, she was able to vividly explain what Hardy's mother looked like and correctly described his brother as sitting in a German POW camp.[30] Wedgewood's visions appeared to imply telepathic ability. If Hardy could prove telepathy scientifically, then it was a potentially revolutionary finding towards fulfilling his vow. As he stated,

> it would at once lend plausibility to the possibility that the influence which religious people feel when they say they are in touch with what seems to them to be some transcendental element ... may be something within the same field as extrasensory telepathic communication. Could it perhaps be ... that the element that is at the back of all religion might be some extrasensory shared spiritual experience?[31]

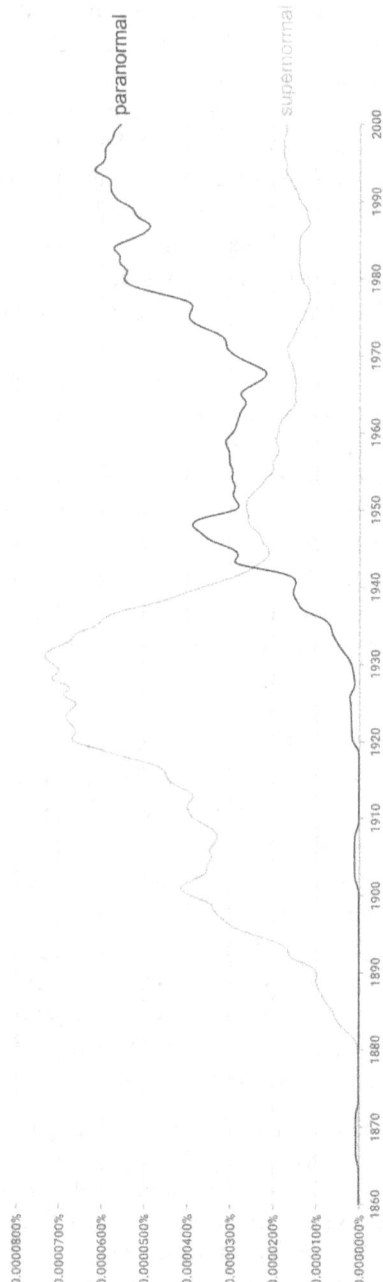

Figure 6.1 Google Ngram search for 'supernormal' and 'paranormal' in British English books, 1880–2000. Note the peak for 'supernormal' during the interwar period followed by a surge of 'paranormal' in the latter half of the twentieth century.

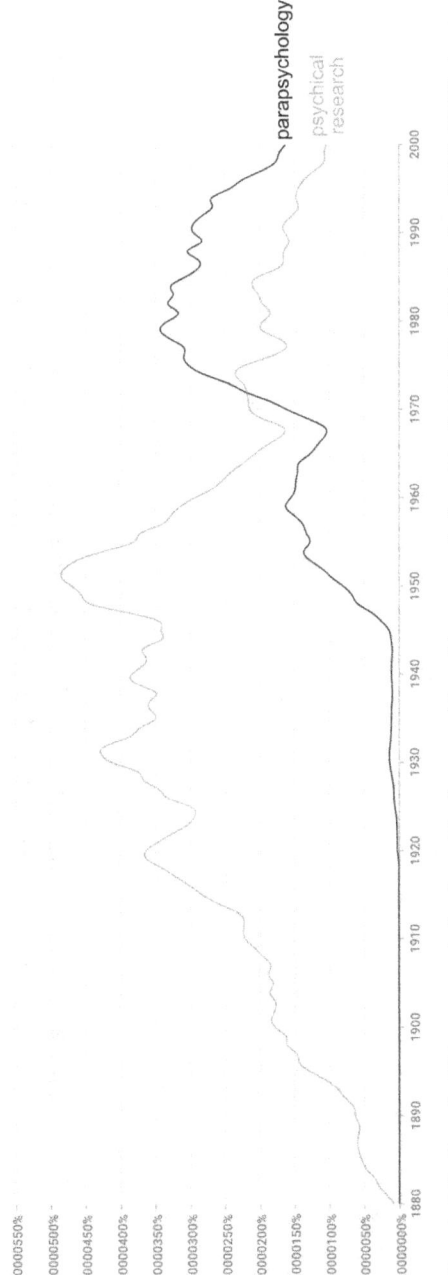

Figure 6.2 Google Ngram search for 'psychical research' and 'parapsychology' in British English books, 1880–2000. Again we see an interwar peak followed by a steady decline. Note that as compared to the American context (see Figure 6.3), 'psychical research' remained a frequently used term. This is likely because of the SPR, which still operates.

Figure 6.3 Google Ngram search for 'psychical research' and 'parapsychology' in American English books, 1880–2000. 'Parapsychology' was more common in the American lexicon probably because of Rhine's influence.

Five decades removed from his experiences, Hardy now believed that science was ready for the task. He followed Rhine's work but argued that it was insufficient. He observed that Rhine's card-guessing tests showed evidence of both telepathy and clairvoyance. Even when the agent did not see the card, the percipient was still able to correctly guess the contents. This was Rhine's point, but Hardy found clairvoyance to be too improbable. He thought it far more likely that Rhine's statistical results were flawed and that different methods were necessary.[32]

Hardy conducted a mass experiment involving 200 subjects with the SPR. Each agent viewed a series of drawings, rather than cards, to avoid the possibility of lucky guesses. The percipients were separated from the agents in adjacent booths and were instructed to draw what they perceived in their minds. Hardy hoped that by using hundreds of subjects he could increase the chances of discovering genuine telepathic phenomena. Although the statistical results were inconclusive, Hardy noticed a series of curious coincidences. In some cases, a percipient's drawings appeared to combine the thoughts from two other agents, or from someone sitting non-adjacently to them, thus indicating possible telepathy as opposed to clairvoyance.[33]

Hardy recognised that if he wanted to prove telepathy, then controlled and rigorous experiments were necessary. The age of the natural-historical approach was over, and an era of laboratory science had taken hold of a new generation of researchers. The work conducted by the early SPR was interesting for historical purposes, but it did not constitute definitive proof. Spiritualism was now rejected as an embarrassing detour prompted by a will to believe in the aftermath of the Great War. Writing in 1973, and now disillusioned with the field, the former SPR research secretary, Eric J. Dingwall, denounced psychical research and pleaded with parapsychologists to learn from the mistakes of the past and avoid the allure of superstition. According to Dingwall, the Great War had clouded the minds of otherwise 'extremely intelligent' individuals. Those like Fred Barlow had fallen victim to 'crazy beliefs' such as spirit photography and devoted their lives to studying and defending fraudulent phenomena. Trying to argue with them was 'as useless as to argue with a Capuchin about the devils on the lettuce', he explained. But eventually the 'rational prevailed over the magical, and [Barlow] realized that all this work had been in vain'. The Great War was a lesson about the 'deadly effect occultism could have' on the mind. Dingwall reframed wartime spiritualism as 'occultism', 'magic' and 'superstition'.[34] He was engaging in a long tradition, in which terms such as 'religion' and 'science' are constructed in opposition to 'superstition' or 'magic'.[35] Decades removed from the events, and with hindsight as his guide, Dingwall could now distinguish between the profound and the absurd.

New physics, old psychics

Laboratory science was not the only intellectual harbinger of doom for spiritualists. Quantum physics and Einstein's theories of special and general relativity were also damaging. When Oliver Lodge began his scientific career, he was engaging in problems that were at the forefront of physics. The introduction of field theory and discoveries such as X-rays and electromagnetic radiation (which Lodge had almost discovered himself) necessitated a conceptual shift in explaining the propagation of forces. The favoured solution was the existence of a 'continuous and all-pervading' ether, 'through which forces propagated with a finite speed'.[36] British scientists in the 1890s, such as J. J. Thomson, William Hicks and Karl Pearson, sought to construct a 'theory of everything' by explaining all physical phenomena as merely different manifestations of the ether. This presented an awkward dualism between matter and energy and so the former was reconceived as an epiphenomenon of the transcendental and immaterial ether. For example, the French psychologist and amateur physicist Gustave LeBon argued that matter was an evolved state of a pure ethereal state. According to LeBon, radioactivity was the degradation of matter into 'the final nirvana to which all things return after a more or less ephemeral existence'. His ideas appealed to anti-materialist and anti-positivist physicists at the turn of the century.[37]

For Oliver Lodge, psychical research was a means for constructing his own ethereal theory of everything. At the same time that he was designing physical experiments to detect the ether, he was attending séances. For Lodge, the ether served as a universal continuum between physical matter and the spiritual world. He speculated that the soul was actually the ethereal component of the physical body. Others adopted the language of *fin-de-siècle* physics to understand spiritualist phenomena. The ether was used to explain how extras appeared in a photograph and how a divine intelligence could guide evolution. As William Barrett wrote in 1917, 'If the grosser matter we are familiar with is able to be the vehicle of life, and respond to the Divine spirit, the finer and more plastic matter of the ether might more perfectly manifest and more easily respond to the instructable Power that lies behind these phenomena.'[38] Relativity and quantum mechanics accelerated the death of ether physics in the interwar period and threatened to pull the intellectual rug out from underneath spiritualists. 'There could hardly be a material universe at all' without the ether, wrote Lodge, and the same was true of the spiritual world that he had spent the latter part of his life trying to discover.[39]

The end of ether physics did not necessarily mean the end of a unification of science with the supernatural, or even the end of spiritualism. The new physics was peculiar. Light was both waves and particles depending upon how it was observed, and quantum particles could influence one another despite being at opposite ends of the universe. Einstein's description of this quantum entanglement as 'spooky action at a distance' is about as close to a telepathic analogy as wireless communication. Heisenberg's uncertainty principle overturned the stable laws sought by Lodge and other spiritualists, but it was also a blow to the materialism that they were rallying against. Even some leading scientists of the new physics, such as A. S. Eddington, constructed new mystical worldviews. Eddington was on the expedition that validated relativity in 1919. In the 1920s, he advocated for a new kind of idealism based upon mind-dependent reality. Eddington wondered if it was possible that 'the mystical illusions of man ... [are] a reflection of an underlying reality'. Or perhaps the universe itself might necessitate a sort of 'universal mind' for reality to exist.[40] Plenty of mystically inclined thinkers were inspired by the new physics. In a new twist on the old cosmological argument, J. W. Dunne argued that if the observer is necessary for localised descriptions of the universe, then this required an observer to describe the observer's position, and so forth into infinity.[41] The spiritual was just as elastic as it was in previous eras.

Relativity also initially faced opposition from within Britain, not least because a German scientist was claiming to have proved Newton wrong. Those supporting relativity did not necessarily understand the theory, and if they did, it was difficult to explain to lay audiences. There was plenty of room for exaggeration, misconceptions and stretching of the facts.[42] Some even skirted the boundaries between the old and the new. Dunne's popular book, *An Experiment With Time*, fused Myers's subliminal self with the new physics.[43] According to Dunne, the mind was composed of two conscious observers, one occupying the waking normal state and another occupying the unconscious. This second observer existed in a higher dimension where past, present and future coexisted. Perhaps dreams were glimpses into the future? Dunne designed a simple experiment. He instructed readers to record their dreams as soon as they awoke so they could be compared to subsequent events.[44] Some spiritualists' ideas, like Geraldine Cummins's 'Great Memory' from Chapter 1, were clearly influenced by Dunne's ideas. However, Cummins was far more in line with the Myers tradition since her 'Great Memory' existed in the ether. As a new generation of scientists was making exciting new discoveries in quantum mechanics and relativity, Lodge was still attending séances and asking Frederic Myers's spirit whether he should abandon the ether. 'You feel I am right in sticking to the ether hypothesis', Lodge asked Myers's spirit, adding, 'Everything would be in chaos if it did not exist.'[45] In June 1940, Nazi Germany entered Paris, thus succeeding where the Germans had failed between 1914 and 1918. Two months later, Lodge passed away. The spiritual universe he had envisioned had indeed collapsed into chaos.

The 'decline' of spiritualism

Spiritualism did not vanish after the Second World War.[46] A group of psychical researchers in Kitchener, Ontario, continued to experiment with séances into the 1960s. Doris Stokes practised a traditional and popular mediumship in Britain into the 1970s.[47] But something had changed. One study in the 1960s found that physical mediumship had almost vanished and high-quality trance mediums remained rare.[48] As we saw in Chapter 1, the Second World War did not produce another Conan Doyle or Oliver Lodge, and in the late 1950s, the number of spiritualists dropped dramatically and never recovered.

There were many reasons why spiritualism's influence waned in British culture. As Chapter 4 argues, the scale and nature of death in the First World War led people to experiment with spiritualism. The Second World War resulted in fewer British casualties and unidentified remains. For the First World War, the CWGC cites 187,744 unidentified burials and 525,060 missing (47 per cent of all the dead). For the Second World War, these numbers are 24,341 and 232,662 (40 per cent), respectively.[49] Still high, but the shock of a mass vanishing act is clearly absent. The historian Pat Jalland further argues that before the Great War, it was generally accepted that women were bound to be emotional during the bereavement process. During the war, women were then expected to retain a stiff upper lip.[50] The shock of the Great War led people to the séance, where death was acknowledged but also denied, and where grief was reframed as scientific study. In the case of the Second World War, there was perhaps less incentive to seek non-conventional forms of mourning.[51] The way people die and experience the death of others also changed in the second half of the twentieth century. Average life expectancy has risen significantly, making cancer and death in old age far more common. Death is professionalised, and frequently occurs in hospitals and hospices over prolonged periods in the presence of specialists.[52] The precedents of the Great War and the influenza pandemic suggest that, if another shock to established customs, patterns and rituals were to occur, we might anticipate more experimentation with less conventional responses to death. It is no wonder that as the COVID-19 pandemic ravaged the United States and hospital lockdowns left people to die in isolation apart from their families, reports of mystical experiences and demand for virtual psychic readings increased.[53]

The study of psychology has also undergone significant alteration since the days of Charcot and Janet. As Chapters 3 and 4 demonstrated, psychical research and spiritualism were closely related to the psychological sciences. The postwar popularity of psychoanalysis offered the bereaved an alternative to spiritualism as a form of therapy. As multiple personalities returned in the 1980s and 1990s, leading experts in the fields of medicine or psychiatry were unlikely to probe these patients as gateways to the spirit world.[54] Biological psychiatry surpassed psychoanalysis in the era after the Second World War. The historian Edward Shorter has boldly stated, 'If there is one central intellectual reality at the end of the twentieth century, it is that the biological approach to psychiatry ... has been a smashing success.'[55] Shorter notes the decline of the asylum system, and views dynamic psychiatry as a 'hiatus' from the more successful biological approach.[56] Contemporary popular images of the First World War have emphasised the stories of shell shocked soldiers and the work of psychiatrists such as W. H. R. Rivers, who treated Siegfried Sassoon and Wilfred Owen.[57] The emphasis is now on trauma and the war's futility. The progress of the psychological sciences discourages any interest in stories of séances. The modern ghost represents a more traumatic haunting than the happy and glorified ghosts of Gladys Osborne Leonard and other mediums.

Britain's relationship with Christianity has also changed, especially since the 1960s. The spiritual revival of the late nineteenth century was influenced by Eastern mysticism in addition to Christianity, but, as this book has shown, spiritualism in the interwar period was a form of diffusive Christianity. Soldiers were granted resurrection for their service, the sins of modernity were atoned for and the war would bring redemption. Spiritualism advocated for a democratic heaven, but a heaven nonetheless, and this influenced the church's attitudes towards the afterlife. Conan Doyle and Lodge were both Christian, and they sought to improve the teachings of Christianity. Although the church's authority had declined in the nineteenth century, Christian culture was still a pervasive element in Britain in the early twentieth century. Callum Brown has argued that Christianity's influence on British culture declined drastically in the 1960s, owing to the erosion of traditional values concerning the home and family. The 1960s saw the end of censorship of theatre, the legalisation of abortion and homosexuality and the rise of liberation and student movements that rebelled against conservatism. The change was so sudden, argues Brown, as to happen virtually overnight.[58] The sudden drop in spiritualist churches and members in 1959 is evidence in favour of his thesis.

Jenny Hazelgrove argues convincingly that changing attitudes towards women in the second half of the twentieth century were a significant factor in spiritualism's decline. The Great War offered women opportunities for new employment but these gains were mostly temporary and they dwindled as men returned from the front. The continued presence of women in traditionally male occupations was potentially emasculating for ex-servicemen facing unemployment, making a reversion to prewar norms easier. Female employment remained provisional, and motherhood and domestic service were still considered to be a woman's primary social function.[59]

The war created opportunities for women in spiritualism and psychical research as it had in other industries. As noted in Chapter 1, the demand for mediums increased and the conflict launched the careers of towering figures such as Gladys Osborne Leonard. Nea Walker was able to conduct her research because of Oliver Lodge's burgeoning public profile. Unlike male-dominated industries, spiritualism and psychical research continued to offer women an outlet for their creativity and intelligence in the interwar period. Spiritualism may be interpreted as a form of creative writing. Geraldine Cummins was a playwright before she became a medium. In 1918, the writer and a member of the SPR, May Sinclair, used William James's concept of 'streams of consciousness' to describe a new literary device most famously adopted by Virginia Woolf.[60] In séance transcripts, Nea Walker sorted streams of consciousness to delineate spirit identities. For example, during a sitting with Leonard on 28 December 1917, three spirits seemed to be present, but the details and descriptions overlapped or were inconsistent. Psychical researchers solved these problems through a combination of supernormal theories and creative writing. The artist Una Troubridge used the term 'compound descriptions' to describe situations in which one spirit shared characteristics belonging to two or more personalities. She reasoned that since controls received communications from spirits through telepathic impressions, this required significant concentration on the part of the communicator. If the communicator's thoughts wavered for only a moment, such as thinking of another spirit known to the sitter, the impression could become combined with the latter's characteristics and project a composite of two personalities.[61] Nea Walker concluded that Feda was too excited and therefore muddled the communications. She explained that 'at the time' the sitting was 'hopelessly confusing', but after 'writing it out, I see that it is not so bad'.[62] Troubridge and

Walker were able to use psychical research to freely engage in creative writing as well as scientific study.

Spiritualism empowered women, but only to a certain extent. Consider the case of L. A. Meurig-Morris. During the interwar period, she was a prolific trance lecturer, having spoken for 105 consecutive Sundays (with the exception of Christmas Day) in the 1930s. Sometimes her lectures lasted for over an hour. In October 1933, she signed a one-year contract with Aeolian Hall (which could seat between 500 and 1,000) to give weekly lectures on Sundays. Each lecture was transcribed verbatim exclusively in *The Two Worlds*.[63] Despite Meurig-Morris's labour and celebrity status, it was her male spirit control, named 'Power', who received credit and authorship for the spiritual revelations. Her career was also managed and financed by the playwright Lawrence Cowen. When the spiritualist press covered her mediumship, it was either Cowen or Power who spoke on Meurig-Morris's behalf.[64] Although Ada Deane was able to deceive Arthur Conan Doyle and earn a significant following, she was unable to take any credit for her work. Instead, she portrayed herself as a passive vehicle and had to deny authorship over her spirit photographs lest she be accused of fraud.

In the interwar period, women were the ideal mediums because of their apparent sensitivity, simplicity and domesticity.[65] In Chapter 4, we saw how spiritualism could reinforce domestic masculinity and femininity. It was no accident that psychical researchers conducted mediumistic experiments in the domestic sphere: the mediums' or researchers' homes.[66] In the second half of the twentieth century, women received more opportunities. As Hazelgrove argues, late twentieth-century feminism rejected the idea that 'men should occupy the public sphere, women the private; that men are active, women are passive; and that maternity is the sole function and destiny of women'.[67] Mediums such as Eileen Garrett were able to continue their careers in the postwar era by embracing cultural change. Garrett moved to the United States, established a publishing house and in 1951 co-founded the Parapsychology Foundation. Such self-assertiveness and independence were more reflective of the postwar age than the gendered norms that shaped her mediumship in the interwar period.[68]

The elements of Victorian and Edwardian culture that had made spiritualism a socio-cultural force had been significantly challenged by the 1960s. Victorian sexual restraints led women to transgress conservative values through mediumship. By the 1920s, after the outbreak of the war, women mediums became sacred objects and were groomed according to conservative images and domestic values. In the post-1945 era, these attitudes were challenged. The idea of any universal codes of morality was further eroded by the new physics. Although Einstein was quick to emphasise that relativity was an abstract scientific principle, numerous Britons associated it with moral relativism. Morality depended on one's relative position, not an inherent code of ethics from a divine source.[69] The type of spiritualism analysed in this book could hardly find the same popular support after these broad changes to British culture and society.

(Re)enchantment, myth and memory

If spiritualism declined in the 1950s, it was not because Western society was finally disenchanted. The postwar period saw the rise of UFOs, Scientology, Wiccans, New Age mysticism and parapsychology. In the 1970s, psychics such as Uri Geller claimed to be able to bend spoons with their minds.[70] Many of these movements share histories with the previous occult practices. Theosophy has been identified as a precursor to the UFO religions of the 1980s and 1990s. Blavatsky's occult knowledge was said to come from a group of Eastern 'masters' who imparted an 'ancient wisdom' and new scientific ideas to save humanity from potential catastrophe. The Blavatsky tradition is mirrored in the belief that extraterrestrial 'masters' are privy to a new science so advanced that it appears as magic or occult to earthly subjects.[71] There has also been a continuity between spiritualism and the history of parapsychology. The magician James Randi used conjuring to discredit various paranormal claims, much like Houdini. In a tactic that is reminiscent of those used against spirit photographers, Randi offered $1 million to anyone who could demonstrate paranormal abilities under controlled settings. He also utilised television to great effect when he exposed Uri Geller on Johnny Carson's *The Tonight Show* in 1973.[72] If the exposure of mediums by the likes of Houdini represented the end of enchantment, it is difficult to explain why history continues to repeat itself.

Statistics attest to a sustained belief in the paranormal. A survey of British paranormal beliefs in 2007 found that 62 per cent believe in souls, 58 per cent in premonitions, 47 per cent in life after death, 42 per cent in ghosts, 41 per cent in telepathy, 32 per cent in necromancy and 31 per cent in UFOs. A significant number believe that 'dreams can predict the future' (35 per cent) and 'that it is possible to receive communication from the dead' (32 per cent), while 36 per cent have reported seeing a ghost.[73] The occult has also thrived in contemporary Western culture in television shows such as *Twin Peaks*, *The X-Files* and *Stranger Things*, not to mention countless movies, novels and comic books.[74] Some have therefore argued that postmodern disillusionment with the grand narratives of the Enlightenment and modernity has led to a re-enchantment in the West.[75]

Enchantment is also necessary for conventional forms of remembrance. On 1 July 2016, 1,400 volunteers dressed in First World War uniforms across the United Kingdom to commemorate the first day of the Somme Offensive. The actors were unable to speak, and were instead instructed to share cards that identified them as a soldier who died on 1 July 1916. The concept was 'partly inspired by tales of sightings during and after the First World War by people who believed they had seen a dead loved one'.[76] Dark tourism has also transformed former battlefields into sacred places. For example, Australians conduct annual pilgrimages to Gallipoli. Before the practice was banned in 2000, it was common for travellers to sleep on the graves on Anzac eve. Other acts, such as swimming in Anzac Cove, are considered taboo. Many walk the former battlefields, or climb Shrapnel Gully to retrace the steps of the legendary John Simpson Kirkpatrick and his donkey.[77] As Bruce Scates observes, these pilgrimages indicate 'a "hunger for meaning", a craving for ritual, a search for transcendence' in a secular age.[78] It takes enchantment to believe that names chiselled into stone, or actors, are the remains of the dead. Just as Britons in 1920 used ritual and remembrance to transform the individual biological remains of one soldier into everyone and no one, so too do we continue to conduct rituals in order to transcend the distance between the past and the present. The war has passed from memory to history, but those killed in the Great War remain simultaneously absent and present.[79]

Given the persistence of enchantment, it would be wrong to argue that spiritualism's rise and fall can simply be attributed to the Great War and its aftermath. Rather, we see the gradual rise and fall of a particular narrative and specific experiences associated with this movement and which was profoundly shaped by the war. Supernormal enchantment made claims about destiny, the evolution of life, universal brotherhood and the meaning of suffering that are too romantic for the post-1945 order. Spiritualists' views regarding the Great War were shaped during the height of the British Empire and a period of class conflict. Where was the social utopia during the General Strike of 1926 and the Great Depression? The traumatic experiences of shell shocked soldiers placed them 'out of time' and space. In an age of relativity, perhaps time was not linear and humanity could regress instead of progress.[80] These developments spoke to modernist writers and artists who rejected the high ideals of the war generation and whose views have come to dominate our understanding of the war. If spiritualist conceptions of the war were in crisis during the 1920s and 1930s, they spoke to even fewer Britons after the Second World War. How could a devotion to evolutionary progress and an unshakable faith in England's destiny be sustained as Europe lay in rubble in 1945 and national liberation movements threatened empires?

It is no coincidence that beginning in the 1960s, the historiography of the Great War underwent significant transformations. Enchantment did not cease, but the meaning of the war and its lessons changed. Part of the reason was Britain's ambivalent place in the war. France had been invaded by Germany, and victory had restored French control of Alsace and Lorraine. In Germany and Italy, millions had 'died for nothing', leading the German occult into far more revolutionary and virulently racist apocalyptic directions.[81] But in Britain, it was a 'pyrrhic victory' that domestic and international events of the interwar period helped cast in a far more pessimistic light. Terms like 'glory', 'duty' and 'honour' became hollow over time. Books such as Alan Clark's *The Donkeys* portrayed Douglas Haig as incompetent and stupid, and the losses under his command as unnecessary and wasteful.[82] The BBC's successful *Great War* documentary series that marked the fiftieth anniversary of the conflict cemented the myths of futility, waste, disillusionment and incompetence.[83] Dan Todman attributes the dominance of the more sceptical attitudes, at least partly, to the death of veterans, which made it difficult for those who experienced the war to counter this emerging narrative.[84] However, there was a significant effort to interview remaining veterans of the Great War starting in the 1980s, and these subjects included those who once believed in the causes for which the war was fought.[85] It was not just that alternative narratives had died away, but also that veterans misremembered or rewrote their experiences in the face of new sensibilities.[86]

Spiritualism and psychical research can tell us much about the war's changing cultural legacy. The prophecies that were popular amongst spiritualists reflected an unerring faith in progress; spiritualists tolerated the war under the assumption that it would lead to a new millennium or spiritual utopia. Will R. Bird could write about his abnormal experiences on the Western Front in 1930 but had to remove most of them in 1968 to sell his memoir. During the war, a national and imperial community was viscerally felt across geography and class. At the same time, the novelty of wireless telegraphy and telephones left people to wonder if it was possible for the living and Great War's dead to communicate through the mysterious and uncharted world of the subconscious. Or maybe they would appear on the photographic plate to prove that the war had been fought for a higher purpose. It was not just that these people were suffering from a will to believe. They were learning how to respond to and cope with mass death during a war that they had reason to believe was righteous and just. They were intrigued by scientific experts and notable public figures who told them that the veil between life and death was very thin. They recognised the familiar Christian notions of sacrifice, suffering, resurrection and redemption that had been so essential in their upbringing. They had strange experiences and experimented with séances and spirit photography in order to understand them. Sometimes they simply could not explain what they witnessed. The broader effect was to believe in a universe filled with purpose and the promise of a better world. After Auschwitz and Hiroshima, it was difficult to believe in these ideals or remain confident that a great new spiritual age could be achieved through bloodshed.

Perhaps the most significant reason spiritualism and psychical research did not have the same potency after the Second World War was because of that conflict's less ambiguous nature. The Great War was fought to maintain the status quo, leading to a host of contradictions and exaggerated hopes that enchanted syncretic philosophies such as spiritualism were equipped to reconcile. The consent and sacrifices of the masses had to be rewarded with tangible economic benefits, but these could only come at the expense of the elites. The war was justified as a struggle between democracy and autocracy, but Britain suffered from its own inequality. Britons were promised a greater society, but the financial, material and human resources necessary for such a reconstruction were brought to the brink by 1918. The idealism of national self-determination stimulated spiritualists' hopes of a new brotherhood as well as national liberation movements that threatened British Imperialism.[87] For the privileged classes, spiritualism represented continuity of power and culture, and a validation of their patriotism and spirituality through demonstrable scientific 'facts'. In the séance, the war was revealed to be the beginning of a heaven on earth forged in their image by their own children. The Second World War was less ambiguous and the victory less pyrrhic. Was the necessity of the war in doubt as the Nazi invasion spread across Europe and threatened the British Isles or when British soldiers entered Bergen-Belsen?[88] Public knowledge of the Holocaust only solidified the myth of the 'good war' versus the futile farce of 'the war to end all war'. British soldiers consented to fight on the promise not of a spiritual awakening but of real social change. Salvation would not come from the séance but through the construction of the welfare state.[89] This time, memorials erected across the former British Empire were to be useful 'living' memorials such as hospitals, not mystical bodies or tombs.[90]

In Sassoon's *Memoirs of a Fox-Hunting Man*, George Sherston is in the hospital when he meets an older gentleman who trains labradors. The 'Theosophist', as Sherston identifies him, wears a monocle and has 'iron grey hair'. Perhaps he is a member of the old 'pre-war virilists' that so disgusted Charles Montague. As Sherston grumbles about the war, the Theosophist assures him of eternal progress in 'higher planes of existence'. The war, he explains, is the work of the 'Celestial Surgeon' improving humanity. Sherston responds by asking him if his dogs won prizes by biting 'one another to death'.[91] The views of the Theosophist here are little different than those of the spiritualist, and yet, while clever, Sassoon's prose would not be enough to disenchant the British populace. As Britain's war dead appeared on the battlefields and in dreams, séances and photographs, their loved ones turned to the comforting notion that the war was part of a grand design and their deaths a vehicle towards spiritual renewal and intellectual and social unity. Sassoon's portrait has become typical of mainstream thought, but between 1914 and 1939, very different ghosts haunted Britain.

Notes

1 University of Oxford, Bodleian Library, A. C. Hardy Papers (hereafter A. C. Hardy Papers), Ms.Eng.Misc.c. 1091, letter from David Anderson to Alister Hardy, 4 September 1939.
2 David Hay, *God's Biologist: A Life of Alister Hardy* (London: Darton, Longman and Todd, 2011), pp. 58–70.
3 A. C. Hardy Papers, Anderson to Hardy, 4 September 1939.
4 Ian Kershaw, *To Hell and Back: Europe: 1914–1949* (London: Allen Lane, 2015).
5 Hay, *God's Biologist*, pp. 55–6.
6 A. C. Hardy Papers, Ms.Eng.Misc.c. 1091, A.55, Alister C. Hardy, *A Life with a Vow* (unpublished autobiography), n.d. (circa 1977–85), p. 52.
7 Hay, *God's Biologist*, p. 57.
8 Hardy, *A Life with a Vow*, p. 1.
9 Hay, *God's Biologist*, pp. 67–70.
10 A. C. Hardy Papers, Ms.Eng.Misc.c. 1091, letter from Alister Hardy to Dave Anderson, 9 November 1927.
11 Hardy, *A Life with a Vow*, pp. 50–2.
12 Ellen Little (published anonymously), *Grenadier Rolf* (London: Kingsley Press, 1920), pp. 6–8.
13 A. C. Hardy Papers, Hardy to Anderson, 9 November 1927.
14 Quoted in Bernard Waites, *A Class Society at War: England 1914–1918* (New York: Berg, 1987), p. 238. On the contrary, Leed argues that the war exposed this vision of class levelling to be an illusion. Once officers learned that the working-class ranks did not share their high ideals about the war, the resulting tension 'collapsed the entire "meaning" of the war in its ideological aspect'. Leed's analysis is a European-wide study, and like that of Fussell, relies on a limited range of sources (Eric J. Leed, *No Man's Land: Combat & Identity in World War I* (Cambridge: Cambridge University Press, 1979), pp. 81–2).
15 Hardy, *A Life with a Vow*, p. 59.

16 For his synthesis see Alister Hardy, *The Living Stream* (London: Collins, 1965); *The Divine Flame* (London: Collins, 1966); *The Spiritual Nature of Man* (Oxford: Clarendon Press, 1979); and *Darwin and the Spirit of Man* (London: Collins, 1984).
17 A. C. Hardy Papers, Hardy to Anderson, 9 November 1927. As Chapter 5 demonstrated, by 1927, mediums' scientific claims were in a far more precarious position than they had been immediately after the Great War.
18 Seymour H. Mauskopf and Michael R. McVaugh, *The Elusive Science: Origins of Experimental Psychical Research* (Baltimore, MD: Johns Hopkins University Press, 1980), pp. 25–6.
19 Ibid., pp. 6–7.
20 Ibid., p. 26.
21 Ibid., pp. 71–7.
22 Ibid., pp. 32–6.
23 J. B. Rhine, *Extrasensory Perception* (Boston, MA: Boston Society for Psychic Research, 1934), p. xiv. ESP was defined simply as 'perception without the function of the recognized senses'. Telepathy was renamed 'Pure telepathy' and defined as 'extra-sensory perception of the mental processes of another person. "Pure" refers to the absence of objective representation of the mental act or image, which might permit of clairvoyance by the percipient.' And 'pure clairvoyance' was defined as 'extra-sensory perception of objective facts. "Pure" refers to the elimination of telepathy from the experimental situation.'
24 Mauskopf and McVaugh, *The Elusive Science*, p. 102.
25 Ibid., pp. 12–13.
26 Ibid., p. 117.
27 Ibid., p. 102.
28 For example, Rhine used a 'before touching' and 'down through' method to find evidence of pure clairvoyance. In the first instance, the percipient would guess the contents of the first card in a deck, then touch the card and place it aside. The task was repeated for the twenty-five cards in the deck. In a 'down through' test, the percipient guessed the contents of all twenty-five cards in sequential order without touching any of the cards (Mauskopf and McVaugh, *Elusive Science*, p. 311).
29 Eric J. Dingwall, 'The Need for Responsibility in Parapsychology: My Sixty Years in Psychical Research', in Paul Kurtz (ed.), *A Skeptic's Handbook for Parapsychology* (New York: Prometheus Books, 1985), p. 168.
30 Alister Hardy, *The Challenge of Chance: A Mass Experiment in Telepathy and an Unexpected Outcome* (New York: Vintage Books, 1975), pp. 4–6.

31 *Ibid.*, p. 8.
32 *Ibid.*, pp. 15–16.
33 *Ibid.*, pp. 18–19, 28–71.
34 Dingwall, 'The Need for Responsibility in Parapsychology', p. 168.
35 Owen Davies, *Magic: A Very Short Introduction* (Oxford: Oxford University Press, 2012), pp. 1–8. See also Jason A. Josephson-Storm, *The Myth of Disenchantment: Magic, Modernity, and the Birth of the Human Sciences* (Chicago, IL: University of Chicago Press, 2017), pp. 14–16.
36 Helge Kragh, *Quantum Generations: A History of Physics in the Twentieth-Century* (Princeton, NJ: Princeton University Press, 1999), p. 4.
37 *Ibid.*, pp. 5–11.
38 Quoted in Peter J. Bowler, *Reconciling Science and Religion: The Debate in Early-Twentieth-Century Britain* (Chicago, IL: University of Chicago Press, 2001), pp. 94, 101–2.
39 Quoted in Janet Oppenheim, *The Other World: Spiritualism and Psychical Research in England, 1850–1914* (Cambridge: Cambridge University Press, 1988), pp. 382–5.
40 Bowler, *Reconciling Religion*, pp. 88, 103–8.
41 *Ibid.*, p. 103.
42 For examples see Katy Price, *Loving Faster Than Light: Romance and Readers in Einstein's Universe* (Chicago, IL: University of Chicago Press, 2012); Peter J. Bowler, *Science for All: The Popularization of Science in Early Twentieth-Century Britain* (Chicago, IL: University of Chicago Press, 2009), pp. 40–2; and Gerald Holton, *Einstein, History, and Other Passions: The Rebellion against Science at the End of the Twentieth Century* (Cambridge, MA: Harvard University, 2000).
43 J. W. Dunne, *An Experiment in Time* (New York: Macmillan, 1927). Dunne never mentions Myers, nor does he use the terms 'subliminal' or 'supraliminal', but the idea that the mind had a dreaming self that accessed other planes of existence is distinctly Myers.
44 Dunne, *An Experiment with Time*, p. 59.
45 Geraldine Cummins, *Beyond Human Personality: Being Detailed Description of the Future Life Purporting to Be Communicated by the Late F. W. H. Myers* (London: Ivor Nicholson & Watson, 1935), p. xiii. The séance occurred on 10 December 1933.
46 The SNU still exists today with 327 churches. 'Our Churches', Spiritualist National Union, accessed 29 June 2018, www.snu.org.uk /Pages/Events/Category/churches.
47 Stan McMullin, *Anatomy of a Séance: A History of Spirit Communication in Central Canada* (Montreal and Kingston, QC: McGill-Queen's

University Press, 2004), p. 161; Jenny Hazelgrove, *Spiritualism and British Society between the Wars* (Manchester: Manchester University Press, 2000), pp. 286–7, fn. 36.
48 Hazelgrove, *Spiritualism and British Society between the Wars*, p. 275.
49 *Annual Report, 2014–2015*, Commonwealth War Graves Commission, accessed November 2018, https://issuu.com/wargravescommission/docs/ar_2014-2015?e=4065448/31764375, p. 39.
50 Pat Jalland, *Death in War and Peace: A History of Loss and Grief in England, 1914–1970* (Oxford: Oxford University Press, 2010), p. 226.
51 Jalland uses Geoffrey Gorer's data from the 1960s to reach this conclusion (Jalland, *Death in War and Peace*, pp. 218–26). See also Geoffrey Gorer, *Death, Grief, and Mourning in Contemporary Britain* (London: Cresset Press, 1965).
52 Jalland, *Death in War and Peace*, pp. 5–7.
53 John Blake, 'They Lost Their Loved Ones to Covid. Then They Heard from Them Again', CNN, accessed 5 August 2020, www.cnn.com/2021/06/20/health/supernatural-encounters-pandemic-loved-ones-blake/index.html.
54 See Ian Hacking, *Rewriting the Soul: Multiple Personality and the Sciences of Memory* (Princeton, NJ: Princeton University Press, 1995).
55 Edward Shorter, *A History of Psychiatry: From the Era of the Asylum to the Age of Prozac* (New York: John Wiley & Sons, 1997), p. vii.
56 Ibid., p. 145.
57 See, for example, Pat Barker's successful *Regeneration* trilogy. Pat Barker, *The Regeneration Trilogy* (London: Penguin, 2013). The first novel, *Regeneration*, was published in 1991, followed by *The Eye in the Door* (1993) and *The Ghost Road* (1995).
58 Callum Brown, *The Death of Christian Britain: Understanding Secularisation 1800–2000* (New York: Routledge, 2001), pp. 175–80.
59 Susan Grayzel, *Women and the First World War* (Abingdon: Taylor & Francis, 2013), p. 101; Trevor Wilson, *The Myriad Faces of War: Britain and the Great War, 1914–1918* (Cambridge: Polity Press, 1986), pp. 720–2.
60 George M. Johnson, *Mourning and Mysticism in First World War Literature and Beyond: Grappling with Ghosts* (New York: Palgrave Macmillan, 2015), pp. 153–86; Diane F. Gillespie, 'May Sinclair and the Stream of Consciousness: Metaphors and Metaphysics', *English Literature in Transition, 1880–1920*, 21:2 (1978), 134–42.
61 Una Troubridge, 'The Modus Operandi in So-Called Mediumistic Trance', *PSPR*, 32:84 (1922), 374–7.
62 CUL, MS SPR34/24/6, Nea Walker, 28 December 1917, p. 32.

63 See '"Power's" Second Anniversary', *The Two Worlds*, 46:2356 (1933), 45; 'Mrs. Meurig Morris to Establish New Centre', *The Two Worlds*, 46:2391 (1933), 732; and 'Power's Work: Important Announcement', *The Two Worlds*, 46:2392 (1933), 754.
64 James Leigh, 'The Story of "Power" and His Mediumship', *The Two Worlds*, 46: 2391 (1933), p. 733.
65 Hazelgrove, *Spiritualism and British Society between the Wars*, p. 276.
66 Beth Robertson, *Science of the Séance: Transnational Network and Gendered Bodies in the Study of Psychic Phenomena, 1918–40* (Vancouver, BC: The University of British Columbia Press, 2016), pp. 43–5.
67 Hazelgrove, *Spiritualism and British Society between the Wars*, p. 276.
68 Ibid., p. 280.
69 Price, *Loving Faster Than Light*, pp. 26, 35–6.
70 For Geller and spoon-bending see H. M. Collins and T. J. Pinch, *Frames of Meaning: The Social Construction of Extraordinary Science* (London: Routledge & Kegan Paul, 1982), pp. 25–46.
71 Christopher Partridge, 'Understanding UFO Religions and Abduction Spiritualties', in Christopher Partridge (ed.), *UFO Religions* (London and New York: Routledge, 2003), pp. 8–12.
72 For more on Randi, see Collins and Pinch, *Frames of Meaning*, pp. 154–76.
73 Ben Schott, 'Survey of Beliefs', IpsosMORI, accessed 29 June 2018, www.ipsos.com/ipsos-mori/en-uk/survey-beliefs.
74 See Jeffrey Kripal, *Mutants and Mystics: Science Fiction, Super Hero Comics and the Paranormal* (Chicago, IL: University of Chicago Press, 2011).
75 Josephson-Storm, *Myth of Disenchantment*, pp. 35–7.
76 'About', 14–18 NOW, accessed November 2018, https://becausewearehere.co.uk/we-are-here-about/.
77 John Hannaford and Janice Newton, 'Sacrifice, Grief and the Sacred at the Contemporary "Secular" Pilgrimage to Gallipoli', *Borderlands*, 7:1 (2008), 25–33.
78 Bruce Scates, *Return to Gallipoli: Walking the Battlefields of the Great War* (Cambridge: Cambridge University Press, 2006), p. xx.
79 Thank you to Jay Winter for making this observation.
80 Christopher White, *Other Worlds: Spirituality and the Search for Invisible Dimensions* (Cambridge, MA: Harvard University Press, 2018), pp. 175–8; and Price, *Loving Faster Than Light*, pp. 26, 76–8.
81 Nicholas Goodrick-Clarke, *The Occult Roots of Nazism: Secret Aryan Cults and Their Influence on Nazi Ideology* (New York: New York University Press, 1985), pp. 78–89.

82 Alan Clark, *The Donkeys* (London: Pimlico, 1961); Dan Todman, *The Great War: Myth and Memory* (London: Hambledon & London, 2005), pp. 99–101.
83 *Ibid.*, pp. 39–49, 132–6, 183–4.
84 *Ibid.*, pp. 205–38.
85 See for example Peter Hart, *Voices from the Front: An Oral History of the Great War* (Oxford: Oxford University Press, 2016).
86 Todman, *The Great War*, pp. 187–90.
87 Wilson, *The Myriad Faces of War*, p. 801.
88 For the British liberation of Bergen-Belsen see Mark Celinscak, *Distance from the Belsen Heap: Allied Forces and the Liberation of a Nazi Concentration Camp* (Toronto, ON: University of Toronto Press, 2015).
89 See Jonathan Fennell, *Fighting the People's War: The British and Commonwealth Armies and the Second World War* (Cambridge: Cambridge University Press, 2019).
90 Tim Cook, *The Fight for History: 75 Years of Forgetting, Remembering, and Remaking Canada's Second World War* (Canada: Allen Lane, 2020), pp. 89–97; Lucy Noakes, *Dying for the Nation: Death, Grief and Bereavement in Second World War Britain* (Manchester: Manchester University Press, 2020), pp. 249–57.
91 Siegfried Sassoon, *The Complete Memoirs of George Sherston* (London: Faber & Faber, 1937), pp. 526–7.

Bibliography

Primary sources: archival material

Bodleian Library, University of Oxford
Sir Alister Clavering Hardy Papers.

British Library
The Barlow Collection of Psychic Photography, General Reference Collection, Cup. 407.a.1.
Conan Doyle, Sir Arthur, Add MS 88924.
The Ghost Club Archives, Add MS 52258–Add MS 52273.

Imperial War Museum

Private papers

Private Papers of H. L. Adams, Documents.4300.
Private Papers of the Reverend J. M. Antsey, Documents.24295.
Private Papers of A. J. Arnold, Documents.9691.
Private Paper of M. A. Bere, Documents.12105.
Private Papers of J. K. Best, Documents.102987.
Private Papers of A. A. Brockington, Documents.4648.
Private Papers of H. R. Butt, Documents.6771.
Private Papers of W. C. Culliford, Documents.17089.
Private Papers of W. D. Darling, Documents.3472.
Private Papers of T. H. Davies, Documents.12740.
Private Papers of G. W. Durham, Documents.348.
Private Papers of C. R. T. Evans, Documents.1645.
Private Papers of B. J. Green, Documents.15073.

Private Paper of J. A. Johnston, Documents.12383.
Private Papers of A. Jordens, Documents.18920.
Private Papers of M. P. G. Leonard, Documents.1626.
Private Papers of W. H. Loosley, Documents.11783.
Private Papers A. C. R. S. Macnaghten, Documents.3696.
Private Papers of T. G. Mohan, Documents.4804.
Private Papers of A. E. S. Mulholland, Documents.16816.
Private Papers of C. T. Newman, Documents.12494.
Private Papers of J. M. Poucher, Documents.6995.
Private Papers of D. Railton, Documents.4760.
Private Papers of G. Smedley, Documents.11745.
Private Papers of F. St J. Steadman, Documents.18927.
Private Papers of Lieutenant W. B. St Leger MC, Documents.20504.
Private Papers of Reverend J. M. S. Walker, Documents.11462.

Sound archive

Anon., 4271.
Fearns, Bert, 22737.
Hutchinson, Beryl Butterworth, 562.
Murray, Joseph, 8201.
Peake, George, 10648.
Pickard, Joseph, 8946.
Storey Wray, James, 9202.

Library and Archives Canada

Sir Archibald Cameron MacDonell Collection, R1894-0-6-E, Kennedy-Carefoot, A. E. Unpublished biography of Sir Archibald Cameron MacDonell, circa. 1940.
Record Group 9, War Diary of 42nd Canadian Battalion, 3rd Canadian Division. Volume 18, March 1 to March 31, 1917.
Record Group 150, CEF Personnel Files, 774–2, 2801–39.

National Archives, Kew

Wayte, Samuel Wilfrid, Personnel File.

Senate House Library, University of London

Dingwall, Eric J., MS 912.
Rhys-Davids, Caroline Augusta Foley, MS 1082.

Society for Psychical Research Archives, Cambridge University Library

Medium files

Cummins, Miss Geraldine.
Deane, Mrs Ada.

Papers

Carington, Whatley, MS SPR 11.
Leonard, Mrs Gladys Osborne, MS SPR 34.
Lodge, Sir Oliver, MS SPR 35.
Spirit Photographs, MS SPR 54.

Research files

Dreams – Telepathic.
Predictions.
Psychic Photography.

Primary sources: manuscripts and articles

Asquith, Lady Cynthia. *Diaries: 1915–1918*. London: Hutchinson, 1968.
Barlow, Fred. 'Mr. Barlow Replies to His Critics'. *Light*, 53:2736 (1933), 374–5.
Barlow, Fred and Major W. Rampling-Rose. 'Report of an Investigation into Spirit Photography'. *PSPR*, 41 (1932–33), 121–38.
Barrett, William F. 'On Some Phenomena Associated with Abnormal Conditions of the Mind'. *PSPR*, 1 (1883), 238–44.
———. 'War in Its Psychical and Religious Aspects'. *Light*, 34:1763 (1914), 507.
Barrett, William F., Edmund Gurney and Frederic W. H. Myers. 'Thought-Reading'. *The Nineteenth Century*, 11 (1882), 890–900.
Barrett, William F. et al. 'First Report of the Literary Committee'. *PSPR*, 1 (1882), 116–55.
Begbie, Harold. *On the Side of Angels: A Reply to Arthur Machen*. London: Hodder and Stoughton, 1915.
Berry, George F. '"Beyond These Voices": Peaceful Thoughts for Troublous Times'. *Light*, 34:1758 (1914), 453.
Bird, Will R. *And We Go On: A Memoir of the Great War*, edited by David Williams. Montreal and Kingston, QC: McGill-Queen's University Press, 2014.

———. *Ghosts Have Warm Hands: A Memoir of the Great War, 1916–1919*. Ottawa, ON: CEF Books, 1968.

Blatchford, Robert. *My Eighty Years*. London: Cassell, 1931.

Blake, Frank T. 'Prophecies'. *The Two Worlds*, 52:1708 (1939), 641, 646.

———. 'Spiritualists and the War: Manifesto by the Council of the Spiritualists' National Union'. *The Two Worlds*, 52:2710 (1939), 665.

Brittain, Vera. *Testament of Youth: An Autobiographical Study of the Years 1900–1925*. London: Victor Gollancz, 1933.

Burrage, A. M. (published as 'Ex-Private'). *War Is War*. Barnsley: Pen & Sword, 1930. Kindle.

Cairns, David (ed.). *The Army and Religion: An Enquiry and Its Bearing upon the Religious Life of the Nation*. London: Macmillan, 1919.

Cammell, C. R. 'Peril Which Threatens Humanity: Spiritual Revival the Only Way to Salvation'. *Light*, 46:2877 (1936), 129–31.

Campbell, Phyllis. *Back of the Front*. London: George Newnes, 1916.

Carington, Whatley. 'The Quantitative Study of Trance Personalities'. Part I, *PSPR*, 42 (1934), 173–240; Part II, *PSPR*, 43 (1936), 319–61; Part III, *PSPR*, 44 (1937), 189–222.

——— (as Smith). 'A Suggested New Method of Research', *PSPR*, 31:81 (1921), 401–12.

——— (as Smith). 'Psychic Photography'. *The Psychic Research Quarterly*, 1:1–4 (1920–21), 348–9.

Carpenter, William Benjamin. 'On the Influence of Suggestion in Modifying and Directing Muscular Movement, Independently of Volition'. *Proceedings of the Royal Institution of Great Britain*, 10 (1852), 147–54.

Carrington, Hereward. 'Psychic Phenomena Amidst the Warring Nations'. *The Occult Review*, 21:4 (1915), 195–201.

———. *Psychical Phenomena and the War*, New Edition. New York: American Universities Publishing Company, 1920.

Child, A. B. 'Spirit Photographs'. *Banner of Light*, 8 November 1862, p. 4. In Louis Kaplan (ed.), *The Strange Case of William Mumler, Spirit Photographer*, pp. 39–44. Minneapolis, MN and London: University of Minnesota Press, 2008.

Coates, James. *Photographing the Invisible: Practical Studies in Spirit Photography, Spirit Portraiture, and Other Rare But Allied Phenomena*. London: L. N. Fowler, 1911.

Conan Doyle, Arthur. 'A New Revelation: Spiritualism and Religion'. *Light*, 36:1869 (1916), 357–8.

———. *The Case for Spirit Photography*. New York: George H. Doran Company, 1923.

———. *The History of Spiritualism*, Volumes I and II. London: Cassell, 1926.

———. 'How the World Will End: A Strange Prophecy and A Description of the "Last Day"'. *Sunday Express*, 20 July 1930.

———. *The New Revelation*. London: George H. Doran Company, 1918.

———. *Pheneas Speaks: Direct Spirit Communications in the Family Circle*. London: The Psychic Press and Bookshop, 1927.

———. '"Spirit" Photographs: The Face at the Haig Funeral'. *The Sunday Express*, circa February 1928.

———. *The Vital Message*. London: George H. Doran Company, 1919.

Cummins, Geraldine Dorothy. *Beyond Human Personality: Being Detailed Description of the Future Life Purporting to Be Communicated by the Late F. W. H. Myers*. London: Ivor Nicholson & Watson, 1935.

———. *The Road to Immortality: Being a Description of the Afterlife Purporting to Be Communicated by the Late F. W. H. Myers*. London: Ivor Nicholson & Watson, 1933.

———. *Unseen Adventures: An Autobiography Covering Thirty-Four Years of Work in Psychical Research*. London: Rider, 1951.

Cummins, Geraldine Dorothy and E. Beatrice Gibbes. *No War: The Coming European Crisis*. London: Goodmount Press, 1939.

Deane, Ada. 'Mrs. Deane's Reply: Doubts if Money Would Tempt Her Wonderful Power'. *Daily Sketch*, 21 November 1924.

Delaisi, Francis. *A Prophecy Fulfilled: The Present War Predicted in 1911*. Omaha, NB: Swartz Printing Co., 1916.

Desmond, Shaw. 'The Guides Have Not Failed Us'. *Light*, 59:3062 (1939), 591.

Dingwall, Eric J. 'The Need for Responsibility in Parapsychology: My Sixty Years in Psychical Research'. In Paul Kurtz (ed.), *A Skeptic's Handbook for Parapsychology*, pp. 161–74. New York: Prometheus Books, 1985.

Douglas, James. 'Are the Dead Alive? Is Spirit Photography Genuine?' *The Sunday Express*, 6 November 1921.

———. 'Grappling with the Unknown: The Dark Cabinet'. *The Sunday Express*, 27 November 1921.

———. 'Is Spirit Photography Genuine? The Results of My Second Experiment'. *The Sunday Express*, 11 December 1921.

Duffie-Boylan, Grace (originally published anonymously). *Thy Son Liveth: Messages from a Soldier to His Mother*. Boston, MA: Little, Brown and Company, 1918.

Dumergue, Christopher. 'David Harold Macklin'. *Duff's Blog*. Last modified 23 December 2009, accessed February 2023. https://chrisandry.wordpress.com/2009/12/23/david-harold-macklin/.

Dunne, J. W. *An Experiment in Time*. New York: Macmillan, 1927.

Edmonds, Charles (pseudonym). *A Subaltern's War: A Memoir of the Great War*. London: Peter Davies, 1929.

Einstein, Lewis. *A Prophecy of the War (1913–1914)*. New York: Columbia University Press, 1918.
Evans, W. H. 'An Open Letter to Spiritualists'. *The Two Worlds*, 27:1399 (1914), 438.
———. 'Peace Prophecies That Failed'. *Light*, 59:3060 (1939), 568.
———. 'Spiritualism and the Peace Ideal'. *The Two Worlds*, 27:1411 (1914), 581–2.
———. 'Spiritualism and War'. *The Two Worlds*, 52:2707 (1939), 636; *The Two Worlds*, 52:2709 (1939), 660.
Fielding, Everard. 'An Experiment in "Faking" Spirit Photographs'. *JSPR*, 20 (1920–21), 219–23.
Forster, E. M. *Goldsworthy Lowes Dickinson and Related Writings*. London and Southampton: Edward Arnold, 1934.
Frost, Elliot P. 'Dreams'. *Psychological Bulletin*, 13:1 (1916), 12–14.
Fuller, J. F. C. *The Star in the West: A Critical Essay upon the Works of Aleister Crowley*. London: Walter Scott Publishing Co., 1907.
Gibbes, E. B. 'After-Thoughts on Peace Prediction Failure'. *Light*, 59:3063 (1939), 601–2.
Gow, David. '"Power" on the Final World-Peace: Armistice Celebrations at the Aeolian Hall'. *The Two Worlds*, 46:2399 (1933), 390.
———. 'Spiritualism: Its Position and Its Prospects'. *The Quest*, 11:2 (1920), 254–7.
Gurney, Edmund. 'Letters on Phantasms: A Reply'. *The Nineteenth Century*, 22 (1887), 522–33.
Gurney, Edmund and Frederic W. H. Myers. 'Some Higher Aspects of Mesmerism'. *PSPR*, 3 (1885), 401–23.
Gurney, Edmund, Frederic W. H. Myers and Frank Podmore. *Phantasms of the Living*, Volumes I and II. London: Rooms of the Society for Psychical Research, 1886.
Hambling, Horace S. 'Does Spiritualism Really Grow?' *The Two Worlds*, 30:1970 (1925), 499.
Hardy, Alister. *The Challenge of Chance: A Mass Experiment in Telepathy and an Unexpected Outcome*. New York: Vintage Books, 1975.
———. *Darwin and the Spirit of Man*. London: Collins, 1984.
———. *The Divine Flame*. London: Collins, 1966.
———. *The Living Stream*. London: Collins, 1965.
———. *The Spiritual Nature of Man*. Oxford: Clarendon Press, 1979.
Harper, Edith K. 'Spirit Protection: A Verified Message'. *The Occult Review*, 28:6 (1918), 334–6.
Hunt, Ernest H. '"A Scrap of Paper": Material Might Versus Spiritual Law'. *Light*, 34:1757 (1914), 436.

Innes, A. Taylor. 'Where Are the Letters? A Cross-Examination of Certain Phantasms'. *The Nineteenth Century*, 22 (1887), 174–94.
James, William. *The Principles of Psychology*, Authorized Edition, Volume I. New York: Dover Publications, 1918.
Johnston, Alec. *At the Front*. London: Constable & Company, 1917.
Kelway-Bamber, L. *Claude's Book*. London: Psychic Book Club, 1919.
———. *Claude's Second Book*, London: Methuen and Company, 1919.
Kenyon, Lieut.-Colonel Sir Frederic. *War Graves: How the Cemeteries Abroad Will Be Designed*. London: His Majesty's Stationery Office, 1918.
Leadbeater, C. W. *An Occult View of the War*. Los Angeles, CA: Theosophical Publishing House, 1917.
Leaf, Horace. 'Prophecies, the War, and a Call'. *Light*, 3061:59 (1939), 579.
———. 'Spiritualism and World Federation'. *The Two Worlds*, 47:2411 (1934), 91.
———. 'Spirits, the War and a Call'. *The Two Worlds*, 52:2703 (1939), 580.
Leonard, Gladys Osbourne. *Brief Darkness*. London: Cassell, 1942.
Little, Ellen (published anonymously). *Grenadier Rolf*. London: Kingsley Press, 1920.
Lodge, Oliver. *Christopher: A Study in Human Personality*. London: Cassell, 1918.
———. 'Public Service versus Private Expenditure'. In *Socialism and Individualism*, pp. 92–102. New York: John Lane Company, 1905.
———. *Raymond: Or Life and Death*. New York: George H. Doran Company, 1916.
———. *The War and After: Short Chapters on Subjects of Serious Practical Import for the Average Citizen from A. D. 1915 Onwards*. New York: George H. Doran Company, 1915.
MacDonagh, Michael. 'The Wearing of Religious Emblems at the Front'. *The Occult Review*, 34:5 (1916), 266–74.
Machen, Arthur. *The Bowmen and Other Legends of the War*. London: G. P. Putnam's Sons, 1915.
Maeterlinck, Maurice. *The Wrack of the Storm*, translated by Alexander Teixeira de Mattos. New York: Dodd, Mead and Company, 1916.
McKenzie, Barbara. 'Afterthoughts on "Hope" Debate: Facts of the Flash-Lamp "Discovery" at the British College'. *Light*, 53:2734 (1933), 342.
———. 'The Unknown Face'. *Light*, 40:2082 (1920), 440.
McKenzie, J. Hewat. *Spirit Intercourse: Its Theory and Practice*. New York: M. Kennerley, 1917.

Mitchell, T. G. and G. M. Smith (eds). *History of the Great War Based on Official Documents. Medical Services. Casualties and Medical Statistics of the Great War*. London: His Majesty's Stationery Office, 1931.

Montague, Charles Edward. *Disenchantment*. New York: Brentano's Publishers, 1922.

Montgomery, L. A. *Rilla of Ingleside*, Canadian Favourites Edition. Toronto, ON: McClelland & Stewart, 1973.

Morse, James J. *Leaves from My Life: A Narrative of Personal Experiences*. London: James Burn, 1877.

Mott, F. W. 'War Psycho-Neurosis: The Psychologist of Soldiers' Dreams'. *The Lancet*, 191:4927 (1918), 169–72.

Moynihan, Michael (ed.). *God on Our Side: The British Padres in World War I*. London: Leo Cooper, 1983.

Mumler, William H. *The Personal Experiences of William H. Mumler in Spirit-Photography*. Boston, MA: Colby and Rich, 1875. In Louis Kaplan (ed.), *The Strange Case of William Mumler*, pp. 69–139. Minneapolis, MN and London: University of Minnesota Press, 2008.

Myers, Frederic W. H. 'A Defence of Phantasms of the Dead'. *PSPR*, 6 (1890), 314–15.

———. *Human Personality and its Survival of Bodily Death*, Volumes I and II. London: Longmans, Green and Co., 1903.

———. 'Human Personality in the Light of Hypnotic Suggestion'. *PSPR*, 4 (1886–87), 1–24.

———. 'On Recognized Apparition Occurring More Than a Year after Death'. *PSPR*, 6 (1889), 13–65; *PSPR*, 6 (1890), 314–57.

———. 'On Telepathic Hypnotism, and Its Relation to Other Forms of Hypnotic Suggestion'. *PSPR*, 4 (1886–87), 127–57.

———. 'The Subliminal Consciousness'. *PSPR*, 7 (1891–92), 298–355; *PSPR*, 8 (1892), 333–404; *PSPR*, 9 (1893–94), 3–128; *PSPR*, 11 (1896–97), 334–593.

Nash, Paul. *Outline: An Autobiography and Other Writings*. London: Faber & Faber, 1949.

O'Donnell, Elliott. *The Menace of Spiritualism*. London: Werner & Laurie, 1920.

Owen, Harold. *Journey from Obscurity, Wilfrid Owen 1893–1918: Memoirs of the Owen Family*, Volume III: War. London: Oxford University Press, 1965.

Perice, C. S. 'Mr. Peirce's Rejoinder'. *Proceedings of the American Society for Psychical Research*, 1 (1885–89), 180–214.

Phillips, Forbes and Robert Thurston Hopkins. *War and the Weird*. London: Simpkin Marshall, Hamilton, Kent & Co., 1916.

Piddington, J. G. 'Forecasts in Scripts Concerning the War'. *PSPR*, 33:87 (1923), 439–605.

Pilley, W. Charles. 'Amazing Spirit Camera Frauds: Psychic Experimenters Caught Red-Handed in Transparent Deception and Trickery'. *John Bull*, 17 December 1921.

Pixley, Olive Charlotte Blyth. *Listening in: A Record of a Singular Experience*. London: Psychic Bookshop and Library, 1928.

Plater, Charles. *Catholic Soldiers*. London: Longmans, Green and Co., 1919.

Price, Harry. *Cold Light on Spiritualistic 'Phenomena:' An Experiment with the Crewe Circle*. London: Kegan Paul, Trench, Trubner, 1922.

Radclyffe-Hall, Marguerite and Una Troubridge. 'On a Series of Sittings with Mrs. Osborne Leonard'. *PSPR*, 30:78 (1919), 339–453.

Rhine, J. B. *Extrasensory Perception*. Boston, MA: Boston Society for Psychic Research, 1934.

Salter, Helen. 'An Enquiry Concerning "the Angels at Mons"'. *JSPR*, 17:324 (1915), 106–18.

Salter, William Henry. *Trance Mediumship: An Introductory Study on Mrs. Piper and Mrs. Leonard*. Glasgow: Society for Psychical Research, 1950.

Sassoon, Siegfried. *The Complete Memoirs of George Sherston*. London: Faber & Faber, 1937.

———. *Siegfried Sassoon Diaries, 1915–1918*, edited by Rupert Hart-Davis. London: Faber & Faber, 1983.

Schiller, F. C. S. 'War Prophecies'. *JSPR*, 17:330 (1916), 185–92.

Sheridan, Claire. 'Soldiers of St. Martin's: Visions and Voices Seen and Heard in the Crypt and in the Church'. *Light*, 59:3031 (1939), 92–3.

Shirley, Ralph. *Prophecies and Omens of the Great War*. London: William Rider & Son, 1914.

Sidgwick, Henry et al. 'Report on the Census of Hallucinations'. *PSPR*, 10:26 (1894), 25–423.

Spiritualist National Union. 'Churches'. Accessed June 2018. www.snu.org.uk/Pages/Events/Category/churches.

Stainton Moses, William. *More Spirit Teachings through the Mediumship of William Stainton Moses*. London: L. N. Fowler, n.d., likely 1892.

Statistics of the Military Effort of the British Empire during the Great War: 1914–1920. London: His Majesty's Stationery Office, 1922.

Stead, Estelle. *Faces of the Living Dead: Remembrance Day Messages and Photographs*. Manchester: 'The Two Worlds' Publishing, 1925.

Stead, W. T. 'Government by Journalism'. *Contemporary Review*, 49 (1886), 653–74.

———. 'The Great Pacifist: An Autobiographical Sketch'. *The Review of Reviews for Australia* (August 1912), 609–20.

Stuart, Rosa. *Dreams and Visions of the War*. London: C. Arthur Pearson, Ltd., 1917.
Swaffer, Hanne. *Northcliffe's Return*. London: Hutchinson & Company, 1925.
———. 'Spiritualist Services and Insulting Press References'. *Light*, 44:2258 (1924), 703.
Talbot, Henry Fox. *The Pencil of Nature*. London: Longman, Brown, Green and Longman, 1844.
Taylor, J. Traill. 'Spirit Photograph: Are Spirit Photographs of Spirits?' *Borderland*, 2:9 (1895), 239–41.
Thurston, Herbert. *The Church and Spiritualism*. Milwaukee, WI: The Bruce Publishing Company, 1933.
———. 'Spiritualists and Their "No War" Predictions'. *The Tablet* (16 September 1939), 357.
———. *The War and the Prophets: Notes on Certain Popular Predictions Current in this Later Age*. London: Burns & Oats, 1915.
Tiplady, Thomas. *The Soul of the Soldier: Sketches of Life at the Front*. London: Methuen, 1918.
Trethewy, A. W. *The 'Controls' of Stainton Moses ('M. A. Oxon')*. London: Hurst & Blackett, 1923.
Troubridge, Una. 'The Modus Operandi in So-Called Mediumistic Trance'. *PSRP*, 32:84 (1922), 344–78.
Tudor Pole, Wesley. *Private Dowding: The Personal Story of a Soldier Killed in Battle*. Norwich: Pilgrims Book, 1917.
Walker, Nea. *The Bridge: A Case for Survival*. London: Cassell, 1927.
———. 'Obituary: Sir Oliver Lodge, F.R.S. and Sir J. J. Thomson, O.M., F.R.S'. *PSPR*, 46:163 (1940–41), 218–23.
———. *Through a Stranger's Hand*. London: Hutchinson, 1935.
Wallace, Abraham. 'Missing Soldiers: Remarkable Evidence'. *Light*, 39:1985 (1919), 29.
Wallace, Alfred Russel. *Contributions to the Theory of Natural Selection: A Series of Essays*. London: Macmillan, 1870.
Wann, Chas E. 'The War from a Spiritualist Point of View'. *The Two Worlds*, 27:1402 (1914), 473–5.
Ward, J. S. M. *Gone West: Three Narrative of After-Death Experiences*. London: William Rider & Son, 1920.
———. *A Subaltern in Spirit Land. A Sequel to 'Gone West'*. London: William Rider & Son, 1920.
Warrick, F. W. *Experiments in Psychics: Practical Studies in Direct Writing, Supernormal Photography, and Other Phenomena, Mainly with Mrs. Ada Emma Deane*. New York: E.P. Dutton, 1939.

Weber, Max. 'Science as Vocation'. In *The Vocation Lectures*, edited by David Owen and Tracy B. Strong, translated by Rodney Livingstone. Indianapolis, IN: Hackett Publishing Company, 2004.
Wynn, Walter. *Rupert Lives!* London: Kingsley Press, 1919.
Zalinski, Countess. *Noted Prophecies, Prediction, Omens and Legends Concerning the Great War and the Changes to Follow*. Chicago, IL: Yogi Publishing, 1917.

Primary sources: journals and newspapers

British Medical Journal, 1954.
Daily Express, 1923.
Daily Sketch, 1924.
International Psychic Gazette, 1917–22.
Journal of the Society for Psychical Research (JSPR), 1914–39.
Light, 1914–39.
London Gazette, 1976.
The New York Times, 1923.
Occult Review, 1915–18.
Pearson's Magazine, 1919.
Prediction, 1939.
Proceedings for the Journal of the Society for Psychical Research (PSPR), 1882–1974.
Psychic News, 1933–39.
Sunday Express, 1921–30.
St Katharine's School Magazine, 1917.
The Times, 1918–22.
The Two Worlds, 1914–39.
Western Australia, 1923.

Primary sources: journals, trench newspapers

The Balkan News, 1916.
The Listening Post, 1916.
The Pennington Press, 1917.
The Periscope, 1918.
R.M.R. Growler, 1916.
Shell Hole Advance, 1917.
The Switchboard, 1916.

Secondary sources

14–18 NOW. 'About'. Accessed November 2018. https://becausewearehere.co.uk/we-are-here-about/.

Acton, Carol. *Grief in Wartime: Private Pain, Public Discourse*. New York: Palgrave Macmillan, 2007.

Allport, Allan. *Britain at Bay: The Epic Story of the Second World War, 1938–1941*. New York: Alfred A. Knopf, 2020.

Apraxine, Pierre and Sophie Schmit. 'Photography and the Occult'. In Clément Chéroux et al. (eds), *The Perfect Medium*, pp. 12–20. New Haven, CT and London: Yale University Press, 2004.

Ariés, Philippe. *The Hour of Our Death: The Classic History of Western Attitudes towards Death over the Last One Thousand Years*, translated by Helen Weaver. New York: Alfred A. Knopf, 1981.

Ashcraft, W. Michael. 'Progressive Millennialism'. In Catherine Wessinger (ed.), *The Oxford Handbook of Millennialism*, pp. 44–65. New Haven, CT: Yale University Press, 2006.

Ashworth, Tony. *Trench Warfare: The Live and Let Live System*. London: Macmillan, 1980.

Audoin-Rouzeau, Stéphane. *La Guerre des enfants 1914–1918. Essai d'histoire culturelle*. Paris: A. Colin, 1993.

Barker, Pat. *The Regeneration Trilogy*. London: Penguin, 2013.

Barrow, Logie. *Independent Spirits: English Plebeians, 1850–1910*. London and New York: Routledge, 1986.

Bassett, Jean. *100 Years of National Spiritualism*. London: Spiritualist National Union, 1990.

Bear, Jordan. *Disillusioned: Victorian Photography and the Discerning Subject*. University Park, PA: Pennsylvania State University Press, 2015.

Becker, Annette. *War and Faith: The Religious Imagination in France, 1914–1930*, translated by Helen McPhail. Oxford and New York: Berg Publishers, 1998.

Bennett, Bridget. *Transatlantic Spiritualism and Nineteenth-Century American Literature*. New York: Palgrave Macmillan, 2007.

Béres, Laura. 'A Thin Place: Narratives of Space and Place, Celtic Spirituality and Meaning'. *Journal of Religion and Spirituality in Social Work*, 31 (2012), 394–413.

Black, Monica. *A Demon Haunted Land: Witches, Wonder Doctors, and the Ghosts of the Past in Post-WWII Germany*. New York: Metropolitan Books, 2020.

Blake, John. 'They Lost Their Loved Ones to Covid. Then They Heard from Them Again'. CNN. Accessed 5 August 2020. www.cnn.com/2021/06/20/health/supernatural-encounters-pandemic-loved-ones-blake/index.html.

Boddice, Rob. *A History of Feelings*. Chicago, IL: University of Chicago Press, 2018.
———. *The History of Emotions*. Manchester: Manchester University Press, 2018.
———. 'The History of Emotions'. In Sasha Handley, Rohan McWilliam and Lucy Noakes (eds), *New Directions in Cultural and Social History*, pp. 45–63. London and New York: Bloomsbury, 2018.
Bourke, Joanne. *Dismembering the Male: Men's Bodies, Britain and the Great War*. Chicago, IL: University of Chicago Press, 1996.
Bowler, Peter J. *The Invention of Progress: The Victorians and the Past*. Oxford: Basil Blackwell, 1989.
———. *The Non-Darwinian Revolution: Revisiting a Historical Myth*. Baltimore, MD: Johns Hopkins University Press, 1988.
———. *Reconciling Science and Religion: The Debate in Early Twentieth-Century Britain*. Chicago, IL: University of Chicago Press, 1988.
———. *Science for All: The Popularization of Science in Early Twentieth-Century Britain*. Chicago, IL: University of Chicago Press, 2009.
Brandon, Ruth. *The Spiritualists: The Passion for the Occult in the Nineteenth and Twentieth Centuries*. New York: Alfred A. Knopf, 1983.
Broks, Peter. *Media Science before the Great War*. London: Macmillan Press, 1996.
Brown, Callum G. *The Death of Christian Britain: Understanding Secularisation, 1800–2000*. London: Taylor & Francis, 2009.
Byrne, Georgina. *Modern Spiritualism and the Church of England, 1850–1939*. Woodbridge: Boydell Press, 2010.
———. 'Owen, George Vale (1869–1931) Church of England Clergyman and Spiritualist Writer'. October 2012. *Oxford Dictionary of National Biography*. Accessed October 2018. www.oxforddnb.com.libproxy.wlu.ca/view/10.1093/ref:odnb/9780198614128.001.0001/odnb-9780198614128-e-103376.
Campbell, Bruce F. *Ancient Wisdom Revived: A History of the Theosophical Movement*. Berkeley, CA: University of California Press, 1980.
Cannadine, David. 'War and Death, Grief and Mourning in Modern Britain'. In Joachim Whaley (ed.), *Mirrors of Mortality: Studies in the Social History of Death*, pp. 187–242. London: Europa Publications, 1981.
Ceadel, Martin. 'Gilbert Murray and International Politics'. In Christopher Stray (ed.), *Gilbert Murray Reassessed: Hellenism, Theatre, and International Politics*, pp. 217–38. Oxford: Oxford University Press, 2007.
———. *Pacifism in Britain, 1914–1945: The Defining of a Faith*. Oxford: Clarendon Press, 1980.

Celinscak, Mark. *Distance from the Belsen Heap: Allied Forces and the Liberation of a Nazi Concentration Camp*. Toronto, ON: University of Toronto Press, 2015.

Cerullo, John. *The Secularization of the Soul: Psychical Research in Modern Britain*. Philadelphia, PA: Institute for the Study of Human Issues, 1982.

Chambers, Vanessa Ann. 'A Shell with My Name on It: The Reliance on the Supernatural during the First World War'. *Journal for the Academic Study of Magic*, 2 (2004), 86–7.

———. 'Fighting Chance: War, Popular Belief and British Society 1900–1951'. PhD diss., Institute of Historical Research, University of London, 2007.

Chéroux, Clément, Sophie Schmit, Andreas Fischer, Denis Canguilhem and Pierre Apraxine (eds). *The Perfect Medium: Photography and the Occult*. New Haven, CT and London: Yale University Press, 2004.

Clark, Alan. *The Donkeys*. London: Pimlico, 1961.

Clarke, David. *The Angel of Mons: Phantom Soldiers and Ghostly Guardians*. Chichester: John Wiley & Sons, 2004.

Clarke, I. F. *Voices Prophesying War: Future Wars, 1763–3749*. Oxford: Oxford University Press, 1992.

Cloutier, Crista. 'Mumler's Ghosts'. In Clément Chéroux et al. (eds), *The Perfect Medium: Photography and the Occult*, pp. 20–8. New Haven, CT and London: Yale University Press, 2004.

Cohen, Deborah. *The War Come Home: Disabled Veterans in Britain and Germany, 1914–1939*. Chicago, IL: University of Chicago Press, 2001.

Collins, H. M. and T. J. Pinch. *Frames of Meaning: The Social Construction of Extraordinary Science*. London: Routledge & Kegan Paul, 1982.

Commonwealth War Graves Commission. 'Annual Report: 2014–2015'. Accessed November 2018. https://issuu.com/wargravescommission/docs/ar_2014-2015?e=4065448/31764375.

Connelly, Mark. *The Great War, Memory and Ritual: Commemoration in the City and East London, 1916–1939*. Suffolk: The Boydell Press, 2002.

Cook, Tim. *At the Sharp End: Canadians Fighting the Great War, 1914–1916*. Toronto, ON: Penguin Canada, 2007.

———. 'Grave Beliefs: Stories of the Supernatural and the Uncanny among Canada's Great War Trench Soldiers'. *Journal of Military History*, 77:2 (2013), 521–42.

———. *Secret History of Soldiers: How Canadians Survived the Great War*. Canada: Allen Lane, 2018.

Cork, Richard. *A Bitter Truth: Avant-Garde Art and the Great War*. New Haven, CT: Yale University Press, 1994.

Cox, Jeffrey. *The English Churches in a Secular Society: Lambeth, 1870–1930*. New York and Oxford: Oxford University Press, 1982.

Cox, Robert S. *Body and Soul: A Sympathetic History of American Spiritualism*. Charlottesville, VA and London: University of Virginia Press, 2003. Kindle.

Crabtree, Adam. *From Mesmer to Freud: Magnetic Sleep and the Roots of Psychological Healing*. New Haven, CT and London: Yale University Press, 1993.

Currie, Robert, Alan Gilbert and Lee Horsley. *Churches and Churchgoers: Patterns of Church Growth in the British Isles Since 1700*. Oxford: Clarendon Press, 1977.

Danziger, Kurt. 'Mid-Nineteenth-Century British Psycho-Physiology: A Neglected Chapter in the History of Psychology'. In William R. Woodward and Mitchell G. Ash (eds), *The Problematic Science: Psychology in Nineteenth-Century Thought*, pp. 119–46. New York: Praeger Publishers, 1982.

Daston, Lorraine and Peter Galison, *Objectivity*. New York: Zone Books, 2007.

Davies, Owen. *America Bewitched: The Story of Witchcraft After Salem*. Oxford: Oxford University Press, 2013.

———. *Magic: A Very Short Introduction*. Oxford: Oxford University Press, 2012.

———. *A Supernatural War Magic, Divination and Faith During the First World War*. Oxford: Oxford University Press, 2018.

———. *Witchcraft, Magic and Culture, 1736–1951*. Manchester: Manchester University Press, 1999.

Dollar, Mark. 'Ghost Imagery in the War Poems of Siegfried Sassoon'. *War, Literature & the Arts*, 16:1–2 (2004), 235–45.

Donson, Andrew. *Youth in the Fatherless Land. War Pedagogy, Nationalism, and Authority in Germany, 1914–1918*. Cambridge, MA: Harvard University Press, 2010.

Dumontet, Monique. '"Lest We Forget": Canadian Combatant Narratives of the Great War'. PhD diss., University of Manitoba, 2010.

Ebel, Jonathan H. *Faith in the Fight: Religion and the American Soldier in the Great War*. Princeton, NJ: Princeton University Press, 2010.

Eksteins, Modris. *Rites of Spring: The Great War and the Birth of the Modern Age*. Boston, MA: Houghton Mifflin, 1989.

Ellenberger, Henri F. *The Discovery of the Unconscious: The History and Evolution of Dynamic Psychiatry*. New York: Basic Books, 1970.

Falcon, Kyle. 'The Voiceless Dead: Francis Jenkins, Regina Trench, and Living and Dying on the Western Front'. In Peter Farrugia and Evan Habkirk (eds), *Portraits of Battle: Courage, Grief, and Strength in Canada's Great War*, pp. 63–83. Vancouver, BC: University of British Columbia Press, 2021.

Festinger, Leon, Henry Riecken and Stanley Schachter. *When Prophecy Fails: A Social and Psychological Study of a Modern Group That Predicted the Destruction of the World*. Minneapolis, MN: University of Minnesota Press, 1956.
Fischer, Andreas. '"La Lune au Front": Remarks on the History of the Photography of Thought'. In Clément Chéroux et al. (eds), *The Perfect Medium: Photography and the Occult*, pp. 139–54. New Haven, CT and London: Yale University Press, 2004.
Fisher, Susan. *Boys and Girls in No Man's Land: English Canadian Children and the First World War*. Toronto, ON: University of Toronto Press, 2011.
Fleming, John V. *The Dark Side of the Enlightenment: Wizards, Alchemists and Spiritual Seekers in the Age of Reason*. New York: W. W. Norton and Company, 2013.
Fletcher, Anthony. *Life, Death and Growing up on the Western Front*. New Haven, CT and London: Yale University Press, 2013.
Flothow, Dorothea. 'Popular Children's Literature and the Memory of the First World War, 1919–1939'. *The Lion and the Unicorn*, 31:2 (2007), 147–61.
Forster, E. M. *Goldsworthy Lowes Dickinson and Related Writings*. London and Southampton: Edward Arnold, 1934.
Fox, Aimée. *Learning to Fight: Military Innovation and the Changes in the British Army, 1914–1918*. Cambridge: Cambridge University Press, 2017.
Freedman, Lawrence. *The Future of War: A History*. New York: Public Affairs, 2017.
French, Sophia. 'British Spiritualism and the Experience of War'. In Christopher M. Moreman (ed.), *The Spiritualist Movement: Speaking with the Dead in America and around the World, Volume 3: Social and Cultural Responses*, pp. 189–206. Santa Barbara, CA: Praeger, 2013.
Fuller, J. G. *Troop Morale and Popular Culture in the British and Dominion Armies, 1914–1918*. Oxford: Clarendon Press, 1990.
Fussell, Paul. *The Great War and Modern Memory*. Oxford: Oxford University Press, 2000.
Gauld, Alan. *The Founders of Psychical Research*. New York: Schocken Books, 1968.
Gillespie, Diane F. 'May Sinclair and the Stream of Consciousness: Metaphors and Metaphysics'. *English Literature in Transition, 1880–1920*, 21:2 (1978), 134–42.
Gilpin Faust, Drew. *This Republic of Suffering: Death and the American Civil War*. New York: Alfred A. Knopf, 2008.
Glenney, Brian Edmund. '"Light, More Light": The "Light" Newspaper, Spiritualism, and British Society, 1881–1920'. Master's thesis. Clemson University, 2009.

Goldsworthy, Simon. 'English Nonconformity and the Pioneering of the Modern Newspaper Campaign'. *Journalism Studies*, 7:3 (2006), 387–402.
Gonzales, Alexander G. *Irish Women Writers: An A-to-Z Guide*. Westport, CT: Greenwood Publishing Group, 2006.
Gorer, Geoffrey. *Death, Grief, and Mourning in Contemporary Britain*. London: Cresset Press, 1965.
Goto-Jones, Chris. *Conjuring Asia: Magic, Orientalism, and the Making of the Modern World*. Cambridge: Cambridge University Press, 2016.
Grandy, Christine. '"Avarice" and "Evil Doers": Profiteers, Politicians, and Popular Fiction in the 1920s'. *Journal of British Studies*, 50:3 (2011), 667–89.
Grayzel, Susan. *At Home and Under Fire: Air Raids and Culture in Britain from the Great War to the Blitz*. Cambridge: Cambridge University Press, 2012.
———. *Women and the First World War*. Abingdon: Taylor & Francis, 2013.
Gregory, Adrian. 'Beliefs and Religion'. In Jay Winter (ed.), *The Cambridge History of the First World War Volume 3: Civil Society*, pp. 418–43. Cambridge: Cambridge University Press, 2014.
———. *The Last Great War: British Society and the First World War*. Cambridge: Cambridge University Press, 2008.
———. *The Silence of Memory: Armistice Day, 1919–1946*. London: Bloomsbury, 1994.
Griffith, Paddy. *Battle Tactics of the Western Front: The British Army's Art of Attack, 1916–18*. New Haven, CT and London: Yale University Press, 1994.
Griffiths, Dennis (ed.). *The Encyclopedia of the British Press, 1422–1922*. New York: St. Martin's Press, 1992.
Hacking, Ian. *Historical Ontology*. Cambridge, MA: Harvard University Press, 2002.
———. *Mad Travelers: Reflections on the Reality of Transient Mental Illness*. Charlottesville, VA and London: University Press of Virginia, 1998.
———. *Rewriting the Soul: Multiple Personality and the Sciences of Memory*. Princeton, NJ: Princeton University Press, 1995.
———. 'Telepathy: Origins of Randomization in Experimental Design'. *Isis*, 79:3 (1988), 427–51.
Hall, Trevor H. *The Strange Case of Edmund Gurney*. London: Gerald Duckworth & Co., 1964.
Hannaford, John and Janice Newton. 'Sacrifice, Grief and the Sacred at the Contemporary "Secular" Pilgrimage to Gallipoli'. *Borderlands*, 7:1 (2008), 1–45.

Hanna, Martha. *Anxious Days and Tearful Nights: Canadian War Wives during the Great War.* Montreal and Kingston, QC: McGill-Queen's University Press, 2020.

———. 'A Republic of Letters: The Epistolary Tradition in France during World War I'. *The American Historical Review*, 108:5 (2003), 1338–61.

Hanson, Neil. *The Unknown Soldier: The Story of the Missing of the Great War.* London: Doubleday, 2005.

Harrison, J. F. C. *The Second Coming: Popular Millenarianism, 1780–1850.* New Brunswick, NJ: Rutgers University Press, 1979.

Hart, Peter. *Voices from the Front: An Oral History of the Great War.* Oxford: Oxford University Press, 2016.

Harvey, John. *Photography and Spirit.* London: Reaktion Books, 2007.

Hay, David. *God's Biologist: A Life of Alister Hardy.* London: Darton, Longman and Todd, 2011.

Hayward, Rhodri R. 'From Millennial Future to the Unconscious Past: The Transformation of Prophecy in Early Twentieth-Century Britain'. In Bertrand Taithe and Tim Thornton (eds), *Prophecy: The Power of Inspired Language in History, 1300–2000*, pp. 161–80. Phoenix Mill: Sutton Publishing, 1997.

Hazelgrove, Jenny. *Spiritualism and British Society between the Wars.* Manchester: Manchester University Press, 2000.

Heukelom, Floris (ed.). *Behavioral Economics: A History.* Cambridge: Cambridge University Press, 2014.

Hinshelwood, R. D. 'Psychodynamic Psychiatry before World War I'. In German E. Berrior and Hugh Freeman (eds), *150 Years of British Psychiatry, 1841–1991*, pp. 197–205. London: The Royal College of Psychiatrists, 1991.

Hirsch, Robert. *Seizing the Light: A History of Photography.* Boston, MA: McGraw Hill, 2000.

Holmes, Richard. *Tommy: The British Soldier on the Western Front, 1914–1918.* London: Harper Collins, 2004.

Holt, Tonie and Valmai Holt. *My Boy Jack? The Search for Kipling's Only Son.* Barnsley: Pen & Sword, 2011. Kindle.

Horne, John N. *Labour at War: France and Britain, 1914–1918.* Oxford: Oxford University Press, 1991.

Houlbrook, Matt. *The Prince of Tricksters: The Incredible True Story of Netley Lucas, Gentleman Crook.* Chicago, IL: University of Chicago Press, 2016.

Humphrey, Robert. *Stream of Consciousness in the Modern Novel.* Berkeley, CA: University of California Press, 1954.

Humphries, Mark. *A Weary Road: Shell Shock in the Canadian Expeditionary Force, 1914–1918.* Toronto, ON: University of Toronto Press, 2018.

Hunter, Michael. *The Decline of Magic: Britain in the Age of Enlightenment*. New Haven, CT and London: Yale University Press, 2020.
Hynes, Samuel. *A War Imagined: The First World War and English Culture*. London: Bodley Head, 1990.
Imperial War Museum. 'War Memorials Register'. Accessed 9 April 2018. www.iwm.org.uk/memorials.
IpsosMORI and Ben Schott. 'Survey of Beliefs'. Accessed 29 June 2018. www.ipsos.com/ipsos-mori/en-uk/survey-beliefs.
Jalland, Pat. *Death in the Victorian Family*. Oxford: Oxford University Press, 1996.
———. *Death in War and Peace*. Oxford: Oxford University Press, 2010.
Jenkins, Philip. *The Great and Holy War: How World War I Became a Religious Crusade*. New York: Harper One, 2014.
Jenkinson, Jacqueline. *Black 1919: Riots, Racism and Resistance in Imperial Britain*. Liverpool: Liverpool University Press, 2009.
Johnson, George M. *Mourning and Mysticism in First World War Literature and Beyond: Grappling with Ghosts*. New York: Palgrave Macmillan, 2015.
Johnson, K. Paul. *The Masters Revealed: Madame Blavatsky and the Myth of the Great White Lodge*. New York: State University of New York Press, 1994.
Jolly, Martyn. *Faces of the Living Dead: The Belief in Spirit Photography*. New York: Mark Batty Publisher, 2006.
Jones, Edgar and Simon Wessely. *Shell Shock to PTSD: Military Psychiatry from 1900 to the Gulf War*. Hove and New York: Psychology Press, 2005.
Jones, Kevin I. *Conan Doyle and the Spirits: The Spiritualist Career of Sir Arthur Conan Doyle*. Detroit, MI: Aquarian Press, 1989.
Josephson-Storm, Jason A. *The Myth of Disenchantment: Magic and Modernity, and the Birth of the Human Sciences*. Chicago, IL: University of Chicago Press, 2017.
——— (as Jason Ānanda Josephson). 'An Empowered World: Buddhist Medicine and the Potency of Prayer in Japan'. In Jeremy Stolow (ed.), *Deus in Machina: Religion, Technology, and the Things in Between*, pp. 117–41. New York: Fordham University Press, 2012.
Jundt, Tony. *Postwar: A History of Europe since 1945*. London and New York: Penguin, 2005.
Kaplan, Louis. *The Strange Case of William Mumler, Spirit Photographer*. Minneapolis, MN and London: University of Minnesota Press, 2008.
Kean, Hilda. *The Great Cat and Dog Massacre: The Real Story of World War II's Unknown Tragedy*. Chicago, IL: University of Chicago Press, 2017.
Keegan, John. *War and Our World*. London: Hutchinson, 1998.

Kennedy, Rosie. *The Children's War: Britain 1914–1918*. London: Palgrave Macmillan, 2014.

Kerghan, Helge. *Quantum Generations: A History of Physics in the Twentieth-Century*. Princeton, NJ: Princeton University Press, 1999.

Kershaw, Ian. *To Hell and Back: Europe: 1914–1949*. London: Allen Lane, 2015.

Khun, Thomas S. *The Structures of Scientific Revolutions*. Chicago, IL: University of Chicago Press, 1970.

Kollar, Rene. *Searching for Raymond: Anglicanism, Spiritualism, and Bereavement between the Two World Wars*. Lanham, MD: Lexington Books, 2000.

Kripal, Jeffrey J. *Authors of the Impossible: The Paranormal and the Sacred*. Chicago, IL: University of Chicago Press, 2011.

———. *Mutants and Mystics: Science Fiction, Super Hero Comics and the Paranormal*. Chicago, IL: University of Chicago Press, 2011.

Lachapelle, Sofie. *Conjuring Science: A History of Scientific Entertainment and Stage Magic in Modern France*. New York: Palgrave Macmillan, 2015.

———. *Investigating the Supernatural: To Spiritism and Occultism to Psychical Research and Metapsychics in France, 1853–1931*. Baltimore, MD: Johns Hopkins University Press, 2011.

Lacqueur, Thomas. *The Work of the Dead: A Cultural History of Mortal Remains*. Princeton, NJ and Oxford: Princeton University Press, 2015.

Lamont, Peter. *Extraordinary Beliefs: A Historical Approach to A Psychological Problem*. Cambridge: Cambridge University Press, 2013.

———. 'Spiritualism and a Mid-Victorian Crisis of Evidence'. *The Historical Journal*, 47:4 (2004), 897–920.

Lause, Mark A. *Free Spirits: Spiritualism, Republicanism, and Radicalism in the Civil War Era*. Urbana, IL: University of Illinois Press, 2016.

Leaney, Jennifer. 'Ashes to Ashes: Cremation and the Celebration of Death in Nineteenth-Century Britain'. In Ralph Houlbrooke (ed.), *Death, Ritual, and Bereavement*, pp. 118–35. London and New York: Routledge, 1989.

Lee, Alan J. *The Origins of the Popular Press in England: 1855–1914*. London: Croom Helm, 1976.

Leed, Eric J. *No Man's Land: Combat and Identity in World War I*. Cambridge: Cambridge University Press, 1979.

Leese, Peter. *Shell Shock: Traumatic Neurosis and the British Soldiers of the First World War*. London: Palgrave Macmillan, 2002.

Lightman, Bernard. *Victorian Popularizers of Science: Designing Nature for New Audiences*. Chicago, IL: University of Chicago Press, 2007.

Lloyd, David W. *Battlefield Tourism: Pilgrimage and the Commemoration of the Great War in Britain, Australia and Canada*. Oxford: A&C Black, 1998.

Lloyd, Nick. *Passchendaele: A New History*. London: Viking, 2017.
Loez, André. 'Tears in the Trenches: A History of Emotions and the Experience of War'. In Jenny Macleod and Pierre Purseigle (eds), *Uncovered Fields: Perspectives in First World War Studies*, pp. 211–26. Leiden, Netherlands: Brill, 2004.
Lomas, Janis. '"Delicate Duties": Issues of Class and Respectability in Government Policy towards the Wives and Widows of British Soldiers in the Era of the Great War'. *Women's History Review*, 9:1 (2000), 123–47.
Lord, Peter (ed.). *Between Two Worlds: The Diary of Winifred Coombe Tennant*. Aberystwyth: The National Library of Wales, 2011.
Lowe, N. J. 'Gilbert Murray and Psychical Research'. In Christopher Stray (ed.), *Gilbert Murray Reassessed: Hellenism, Theatre, and International Politics*, pp. 349–70. Oxford: Oxford University Press, 2007.
Luckhurst, Roger. *The Invention of Telepathy, 1870–1901*. Oxford: Oxford University Press, 2002.
Lydon, Jane. *Imperial Emotions: The Politics of Empathy across the British Empire*. Cambridge: Cambridge University Press, 2019.
Lyons, Sherrie Lynne. *Species, Serpents, Spirits, and Skulls: Science at the Margins in the Victorian Age*. New York: State University of New York Press, 2009.
Macleod, Roy. 'Sight and Sound on the Western Front: Surveyors, Scientists, and the "Battlefield Laboratory", 1915–1918'. *War and Society*, 18:1 (2000), 21–46.
Macnaghten, Angus. *'Missing': An Account of the Efforts Made to Find an Officer of the Black Watch, Reported 'Missing' on 29th October, 1914, during the First Battle of Ypres*. Bala, North Wales: Dragon Books, 1970.
Madigan, Edward. *Faith under Fire: Anglican Army Chaplains and the Great War*. London: Palgrave Macmillan, 2011.
Mangan, Michael. *Performing Dark Arts: A Cultural History of Conjuring*. Chicago, IL: Intellect Books, 2007.
Manseau, Peter. *The Apparitionists: A Tale of Phantoms, Fraud, Photography and the Man Who Captured Lincoln's Ghost*. Boston, MA and New York: Houghton Mifflin Harcourt, 2017.
Marien, Mary Warner. *Photography: A Cultural History*, Third Edition. London: Prentice Hall, 2011.
Marshall, Peter 'Disenchantment and Re-Enchantment in Europe, 1240–1920'. *Historical Journal*, 54:2 (2011), 599–606.
Massicotte, Claudie. *Trance Speakers: Femininity and Authorship in Spiritual Séances, 1850–1930*. Montreal and Kingston, QC: McGill-Queen's University Press, 2017.
Matheson, Neil. 'The Ghost Stamp, the Detective and the Hospital for Boots: *Light* and the Post-War Battle Over Spirit-Photography'. *Early Popular Visual Culture*, 4:1 (2006), 35–51.

Mauskopf, Seymour H. and Michael R. McVaugh. *The Elusive Science: Origins of Experimental Psychical Research*. Baltimore, MD: Johns Hopkins University Press, 1980.

McCarthy, Helen. *The British People and the League of Nations: Democracy, Citizenship and Internationalism, c. 1918–1945*. Manchester: Manchester University Press, 2011.

McCorristine, Shane. *Spectres of the Self: Thinking about Ghosts and Ghost-Seeing in England, 1750–1920*. Cambridge: Cambridge University Press, 2010.

McDannell, Colleen and Bernhard Lang, *Heaven: A History*. New Haven, CT and London: Yale University Press, 1988.

McKay, Ian and Robert Bates. *The Province of History: The Making of the Public Past in Twentieth-Century Nova Scotia*. Montreal and Kingston, QC: McGill-Queen's University Press, 2010.

McKibbin, Ross. 'Why Was There No Marxism in Britain?' In *The Ideologies of Class: Social Relations in Britain 1880–1950*. Oxford: Clarendon Press, 1994.

McLeod, Hugh. *Religion and Society in England, 1850–1914*. London: Macmillan, 1996.

McMullin, Stan. *Anatomy of A Séance: A History of Spirit Communication in Central Canada*. Montreal and Kingston, QC: McGill-Queen's University Press, 2004.

Meyer, Jessica. *Men of War: Masculinity and the First World War in Britain*. New York: Palgrave Macmillan, 2009.

Miller, John. 'Going Unconscious'. In R. B. Silvers (ed.), *Hidden Histories of Science*, pp. 1–37. New York: New York Review, 1995.

Monroe, John Warne. *Laboratories of Faith: Mesmerism, Spiritism and Occultism in Modern France*. Ithaca, NY: Cornell University Press, 2008.

Natale, Simone. *Supernatural Entertainments: Victorian Spiritualism and the Rise of Modern Media Culture*. University Park, PA: The Pennsylvania State University Press, 2016.

Nelson, Geoffrey. *Spiritualism and Society*. London: Routledge & Kegan Paul, 1969.

Nickell, Joe. *The Science of Ghosts: Searching for Spirits of the Dead*. New York: Prometheus Books, 2012.

Noakes, Lucy. *Dying for the Nation: Death, Grief and Bereavement in Second World War Britain*. Manchester: Manchester University Press, 2020.

Noakes, Richard. *Physics and Psychics: The Occult and the Sciences in Modern Britain*. Cambridge: Cambridge University Press, 2019.

———. 'Telegraphy Is an Occult Art: Cromwell Fleetwood Varley and the Diffusion of Electricity to the Other World'. *The British Journal of the History of Science*, 32:4 (1999), 222–4.

———. 'Thoughts and Spirits by Wireless: Imagining and Building Psychic Telegraphs in America and Britain, circa 1900–1930'. *History and Technology*, 32:2 (2016), 137–58.

O'Hara, Gerald. *Dead Men's Embers*. York: Saturday Night Press, 2006.

Oppenheim, Janet. *The Other World: Spiritualism and Psychical Research in England, 1850–1914*. Cambridge: Cambridge University Press, 1988.

Owen, Alex. '"Borderland Forms": Arthur Conan Doyle, Albion's Daughters and the Politics of the Cottingley Fairies'. *History Workshop Journal*, 38:1 (1994), 48–85.

———. *The Darkened Room: Women, Power, and Spiritualism in Late Victorian England*. Chicago, IL: University of Chicago Press, 2004.

———. *The Place of Enchantment: British Occultism and the Culture of the Modern*. Chicago, IL: University of Chicago Press, 2004.

Pampler, Jan. *The History of Emotions*. Oxford: Oxford University Press, 2015.

Paris, Michael. *Over the Top: The Great War and Juvenile Literature in Britain*. Westport, CT: Praeger, 2004.

Partridge, Christopher (ed.). *UFO Religions*. London and New York: Routledge, 2003.

Paul, Lissa, Rosemary R. Johnston and Emma Short (eds). *Children's Literature and Culture of the First World War*. New York: Routledge, 2015.

Pick, Daniel. *Faces of Degeneration: A European Disorder, c. 1848–c.1918*. Cambridge: Cambridge University Press, 1989.

Price, Katy. *Loving Faster Than Light: Romance and Readers in Einstein's Universe*. Chicago, IL: University of Chicago Press, 2012.

Putkowski, J. *The Kinmel Park Riots 1919*. Hawarden: Flintshire Historical Society, 1989.

Raia, Courtenay. *The New Prometheans: Faith, Science and the Supernatural Mind in the Victorian Fin De Siècle*. Chicago, IL: University of Chicago Press, 2019.

Richards, Graham. *Mental Machinery: The Origins and Consequences of Psychological Ideas, Part 1: 1600–1850*. Baltimore, MD: Johns Hopkins University Press, 1992.

Rieger, Bernhard. *Technology and the Culture of Modernity in Britain and Germany, 1890–1945*. Cambridge: Cambridge University Press, 2005.

Robertson, Beth A. *Science of the Séance: Transnational Networks and Gendered Bodies in the Study of Psychic Phenomena, 1918–40*. Vancouver, BC: University of British Columbia Press, 2016.

Roper, Michael. *The Secret Battle: Emotional Survival in the Great War*. Manchester and New York: Manchester University Press, 2009.

Rosenblum, Naomi. *A World History of Photography*, Fourth Edition. New York and London: Abbeville Press, 2007.

Rothstein, Andrew. *The Soldiers' Strikes of 1919*. London and Basingstoke: Macmillan Press, 1980.

Ruickbie, Leo. *Angels in the Trenches: Spiritualism, Superstition and the Supernatural during the First World War*. London: Robinson, 2019.

Sagan, Carl. *The Demon Haunted World: Science as a Candle in the Dark*. New York: Random House, 1995.

Scates, Bruce. *Return To Gallipoli: Walking the Battlefields of the Great War*. Cambridge: Cambridge University Press, 2006.

Schweitzer, Jason. *The Cross and the Trenches: Religious Faith and Doubt among British and American Great War Soldiers*. London: Praeger, 2003.

Seale, Graham. *The Soldiers' Press: Trench Journals in the First World War*. London: Palgrave Macmillan, 2013.

Shamdasani, Sonu. *Jung and the Making of Modern Psychology*. Cambridge: Cambridge University Press, 2003.

Sheffield, Gary. *The Chief: Douglas Haig and the British Army*. London: Autumn Press, 2011.

———. *Forgotten Victory: The First World War Myths and Realities*. London: Headline, 2002.

Shorter, Edward. *A History of Psychiatry: From the Era of the Asylum to the Age of Prozac*. New York: John Wiley & Sons, 1997.

———. *From Paralysis to Fatigue: A History of Psychosomatic Illness in the Modern Era*. New York: The Free Press, 1992.

Smith, Justin E. H. *Irrationality: A History of the Dark Side of Reason*. Princeton, NJ and Oxford: Princeton University Press, 2019.

Smith, Susy. *The Mediumship of Mrs. Leonard*. New York: University Books, 1964.

Snape, Michael. *God and the British Soldier: Religion and the British Army in the First and Second World Wars*. New York: Routledge, 2005.

Stolow, Jeremy. 'Wired Religion: Spiritualism and Telegraphic Globalization in the Nineteenth Century'. In Stephen Streeter et al. (eds), *Empires and Autonomy: Moments in the History of Globalization*, pp. 79–92. Vancouver, BC: The University of British Columbia Press, 2009.

Stott, John R. W. *The Cross of Christ*. Downers Grove, IL: InterVarsity Press, 1986.

Straughan, Roger. 'Sir Arthur Conan Doyle: "The St. Paul of Spiritualism"'. In Christopher M. Moreman (ed.), *The Spiritualist Movement: Speaking with the Dead in America and around the World, Volume 1: American Origins and Global Proliferation*, pp. 116–27. Santa Barbara, CA: Praeger, 2013.

Swift, David. *For Class and Country: The Patriotic Left and the First World War.* Liverpool: Liverpool University Press, 2017.

Sylvest, Casper. *British Liberal Internationalism, 1880–1930: Making Progress?* Manchester: Manchester University Press, 2009.

Temple, Murphy. '"Death, Where Is Thy Sting?" British Spiritualism and the First World War', unpublished PhD dissertation. Stanford University, 2020.

Thane, Pat. 'The Impact of Mass Democracy on British Political Culture, 1918–1939'. In Julie V. Gottlieb and Richard Toye (eds), *The Aftermath of Suffrage: Women, Gender and Politics in Britain*, pp. 54–69. London: Palgrave Macmillan, 2013.

Thomas, Keith. *Religion and the Decline of Magic: Studies in Popular Beliefs in Sixteenth- and Seventeenth-Century England.* London: Weidenfeld and Nicolson, 1971.

Todman, Dan. *The Great War: Myth and Memory.* London: Hambledon & London, 2005.

Tucker, Jennifer. *Nature Exposed: Photography as Eyewitness in Victorian Science.* Baltimore, MD: Johns Hopkins University Press, 2005.

Turner, E. S. *Dear Old Blighty.* London: Michael Joseph, 1980.

Turner, Frank M. *Between Science and Religion: The Reaction to Scientific Naturalism in Late Victorian England.* New Haven, CT: Yale University Press, 1974.

Twaites, Peter. 'Circles of Confusion and Sharp Vision: British News Photography 1919–39'. In Peter Catterall, Colin Seymour-Ure and Adrian Smith (eds), *Northcliffe's Legacy: Aspects of the British Popular Press, 1896–1996*, pp. 97–120. London: Macmillan, 2000.

van Emden, Richard. *The Quick and the Dead: Fallen Soldiers and Their Families in the Great War.* London and New York: Bloomsbury, 2011.

Waites, Bernard. *A Class Society at War: England 1914–1918.* New York: Berg, 1987.

Waters, Thomas. *Cursed Britain: A History of Witchcraft and Black Magic in Modern Times.* New Haven, CT and London: Yale University Press, 2019.

Watson, Alexander. *Enduring the Great War: Combat, Morale and Collapse in the German and British Armies, 1914–1918.* Cambridge: Cambridge University Press, 2008.

Watson, Janet S. K. *Fighting Different Wars: Experience, Memory, and the First World War in Britain.* Cambridge: Cambridge University Press, 2007.

Watts, Michael R. *The Dissenters, Volume III: The Crisis and Conscience of Nonconformity*. Oxford: Oxford University Press, 2015.
Wessinger, Catherine. 'Millennialism With and Without the Mayhem'. In Thomas Robbins and Susan J. Palmer (eds), *Millennium, Messiahs, and Mayhem: Contemporary Apocalyptic Movements*, pp. 47–59. New York: Routledge, 1997.
——— (ed.). *The Oxford Handbook of Millennialism*. Oxford: Oxford University Press, 2011.
Wheeler-Barclay, Marjorie. *The Science of Religion in Britain, 1860–1915*. Charlottesville, VA: University of Virginia Press, 2010.
White, Christopher. *Other Worlds: Spirituality and the Search for Invisible Dimensions*. Cambridge, MA: Harvard University Press, 2018.
White, Jonathan W. *Midnight in America: Darkness, Sleep, and Dreams during the Civil War*. Chapel Hill, NC: University of North Carolina Press, 2017.
Wilkinson, Alan. *Dissent or Conform: War, Peace and the English Churches 1900–1945*. London: SCM Press, 1986.
Williams, S. C. *Religious Belief and Popular Culture in Southwark, c. 1800–1939*. Oxford: Oxford University Press, 1999.
Wilson, Trevor. *The Myriad Faces of War: Britain and the Great War, 1914–1918*. Cambridge: Polity Press, 1986.
Winter, Alison. *Memory: Fragments of a Modern History*. Chicago, IL: University of Chicago Press, 2012.
———. *Mesmerized: Powers of Mind in Victorian Britain*. Chicago, IL: University of Chicago Press, 2000.
Winter, Denis. *Death's Men: Soldiers of the Great War*. London: Penguin Books, 1979.
Winter, Jay. *Dreams of Peace and Freedom: Utopian Moments in the Twentieth Century*. New Haven, CT: Yale University Press, 2006.
———. *The Great War and the British People*. London: Macmillan, 1985.
———. 'Introduction'. In Paul Fussell, *The Great War and Modern Memory*, New Edition, pp. ix–xiv. Oxford: Oxford University Press, 2013.
———. *Remembering War: The Great War between Memory and History in the Twentieth Century*. New Haven, CT: Yale University Press, 2006.
———. *Sites of Memory, Sites of Mourning: The Great War in European Cultural History*, Canto Edition. Cambridge: Cambridge University Press, 1998.
———. *War beyond Words: Language of Remembrance from the Great War to the Present*. Cambridge: Cambridge University Press, 2017.
Wiseman, Richard. *Paranormality: Why We Believe the Impossible*. London: Macmillan, 2011.

Wittman, Laura. *The Tomb of the Unknown Soldier, Modern Mourning, and the Reinvention of the Mystical Body*. Toronto, ON: Toronto University Press, 2011.
Young, Derek. *Scottish Voices from the Great War*. Stroud: The History Press, 2008. Kindle.
Zaretsky, Eli. *Secrets of the Soul: A Social and Cultural History of Psychoanalysis*. New York: Alfred A. Knopf, 2004.
Ziino, Bart. *A Distant Grief: Australians, War Graves and the Great War*. Perth: University of Western Australia Press, 2007.

Index

Note: 'n.' after a page reference indicates the number of a note on that page

Adams, Wesley (Mrs) 178
Albert Hall 226, 242n.14,
  251n.177
American Civil War 140, 162n.76,
  213
American Society for Psychical
  Research 159n.38, 257
Anderson, David 252, 254–6
Angels of Mons 17–18, 81, 105,
  111
Anglican Church
  and *The Book of Common
    Prayer* 56, 181
  and the Communion of Saints 56
  and spiritualism 49, 55–6, 110
animal magnetism *see* mesmerism
apocalypse *see* millennialism,
  catastrophic millennialism
Armistice Day 210–12
  origins 225
  spiritualist services 59–60,
    62–3, 212, 223–9, 231,
    241, 241n.14, 247n.101,
    251n.177
  the two minutes of silence 212,
    216, 226
Asquith, Cynthia 178
Asquith, Herbert 14
atrocities in Belgium 42, 43
automatic writing 166–7, 173, 182,
  184–5
  amongst servicemen 108,
    200n.15

Bacon (Miss) 175, 178, 201n.17
Balfour, Gerald 39, 40
Bamber, L. Kelway 177, 187, 192
  Claude's Book 49, 177, 190
  Claude's Second Book 182
Barlow, Fred 217, 239–40,
  263–4
Barrett, William 6, 42, 59, 131,
  265
Battle of Gallipoli 112
  commemoration 272
Battle of Jutland 106
Battle of Loos 182
Battle of Second Ypres 145
Battle of the Somme 139, 145,
  169, 271
  commemoration 272
Battle of Third Ypres 48, 81, 82,
  93, 98
Battle of Vimy Ridge 80, 90–1
Begbie, Arthur 18
Bernheim, Hippolyte 130–1, 132
Berry, George F. 44, 59, 61
Bible on the battlefields, the 85, 86
Bird, Steve 80–1, 91–2
Bird, Will R. 20, 80–2, 90–2,
  113–16, 119n.58, 128, 256,
  274
  And We Go On 80–2, 92,
    113–16, 126n.176
  Ghosts Have Warm Hands
    113–15, 119n.60,
    126nn.175–6

Blake, Frank 33
Blavatsky, Helena Petrovna (Madam) 36–8
Bloody Sunday 37
Boer War 37
Borderland 230
Bowyer-Bower, Eldred Wolferston (Captain) 149–51, 155
Bowyer-Bower, Thomas (Captain) 149
Braid, James 130
Breuer, Joseph 132
British College of Psychic Science (BCPS) 214, 219, 220–2, 231
British Journal of Photography 216
Brittain, Annie 55, 149, 170, 177, 185
Brittain, Vera 143–5
Britten, Emma Hardinge 59
Brothers, Richard 35
Buguet, Edouard 215, 217
Buxton (Mrs) 214, 220
Buxton, Denis Bertram Sydney 98, 180–1

Cammell, Charles Richard 62
Canadian Expeditionary Force 30n.88, 80, 148
Cannock, Elizabeth 168, 178–80, 184, 189, 201n.25
Carnegie Hall 210
Carpenter, William Benjamin 130
Carrington, Hereward 112, 114
  Psychical Phenomena and the War 112, 114
Carrington, Whatley 176
cartes-de-visite 213–14
Casualty Clearing Stations 108–9, 117n.9
Catholicism
  on the battlefields 85, 96, 118nn.27–8
  and spiritualism 49
Cecil, Robert (Lord) 59
Cenotaph, the *see* war memorials
chaplains
  and fatalism 92–3, 94, 103
  and letters to loved ones back home 144, 156, 180
Charcot, Jean-Martin 15–16, 130–2, 267
children and the war 152–3
Christianity
  on the battlefields 7, 85–6, 96, 109–10, 123n.137
  in Britain 7–8, 26nn.32–3, 268
  on the home front 7–8
  and spiritualism 107, 109, 110–11, 196
class in Britain 254–5, 276n.14
  and the Society for Psychical Research 137, 150
  and spiritualism 9, 10, 188
Coates, Arthur 216
Colley, Christopher Clarence (Major) 101, 104
Colley, Thomas (Archdeacon) 110, 214
Commonwealth War Graves Commission (CWGC) 8, 267
  see also Imperial War Graves Commission (IWGC)
Comrade in White 111, 125n.165
conjuring 203n.51, 231–4, 237, 249n.134
  and gender 233–5, 240
Coombe Tenant, Winifred 39–41
Cottingley Fairies 214–15
COVID-19 pandemic 267
Crandon, Margery 240, 257
Creery Family 132, 137, 160n.52
Crewe Circle *see* Hope, William
crisis apparitions 20, 133, 137–8, 140, 141
  and Christianity 141
  and death rituals 140–1
  definition of 128
  and empire 128, 137–8, 140, 156
  and the First World War 128–9, 133–4, 138, 141–2, 146, 149–50
  and gender 146
crisis of faith 4, 6, 254

Index

Crookes (Sir) William 2, 5–6, 226, 234, 257
cross-correspondence 39, 58, 76n.141, 257
Crowley, Aleister 5, 121n.105
crystal balls 153, 173
Cummins, Geraldine 32, 64–5, 266, 269

Daily Sketch 211, 233, 235–8
Darwin, Charles
    natural selection, theory of 5, 36, 37–8, 253
    and spiritualism and psychical research 191, 255
    On the Origins of Species 37
Deane, Ada 201n.22, 210–13, 221, 232, 234–7, 239–41, 245n.70, 270
death 267
    burial traditions 14, 181
    cremation 181
    mourning 12, 186–7
    rates in Britain 12
    rituals 140, 168
De Brath, Stanley 56, 59
Dingwall, Eric J. 233, 234, 257, 258, 263–4
divination *see* prophecies
Doyle, Arthur Conan (Sir) 3, 12, 49, 53, 54, 60–1, 74n.102, 124n.147, 167, 181, 188, 226–8, 256, 257
    and Christianity 51, 268
    conversion to spiritualism 49–52, 152
    death 61, 199, 251n.177
    relationship with Harry Houdini 232, 240
    relationship with Oliver Lodge 57, 60, 169
    and spirit photography 60, 210–11, 214–15, 222, 231, 234, 240–1
dreams 156, 161n.67
    premonitory 91, 98–9, 127, 141–3, 144, 147, 266
    soldiers and their families 139–40

Dunne, J. W. 65, 265–6
    An Experiment with Time 266

Easter Rebellion 45
Eddington, Arthur Stanley 57, 265
Einstein, Albert 37, 43, 57, 264, 265, 271
Elliotson, John 129
Evans, William Henry 43, 66, 67
extrasensory perception (ESP) 258
    definition of 277n.23
    see also Rhine, J. B.

fatalism 92–4
    and chaplains 92–3, 94, 103
Fawcett, Percy (Colonel) 100
fortune telling 55, 86–7, 170, 182, 183–4, 189, 197
Freud, Sigmund 37, 131, 132
fugue states 15, 198
Fuller, Major J. F. C. 121n.105
Fussell, Paul 2

Garrett, Eileen 270
Garrison, William Lloyd 213
Geller, Uri 271
General Strike 255, 273
German spring offensive 127, 157n.1, 167
Ghost Club 101
Glenconner, Pamela 221
Gow, David 41–3, 47, 55, 65, 75n.122
Graves, Robert 2, 61
Greater World Christian Spiritualist League (GWCSL) 48
Gurney, Edmund 40, 131–3, 134, 137, 160n.55

Haig, Douglas (Field Marshall) 240–1, 273
Hall, Marshall 130, 158n.14
Hardy, Alister Clavering 252–6, 259, 263
Harris, Susannah 175
heaven 187–8, 191, 268
Heisenberg, Werner 57, 265

Index

Hermetic Order of the Golden Dawn 36
Hill, Arthur J. 170, 221
Hitler, Adolf 61
Holmes, Daniel Dunglus 6
Hope, William 219–21, 231, 234, 237
   and accusations of fraud 211, 233, 239–40
   and origins of the Crewe circle 214
   and the SPR 211
   success rate 221, 245n.68
Houdini, Harry 232, 234, 240, 249n.133, 271
Houghton, Georgina 214
Hudson, Frederick 214
Huxley, Thomas 230, 253
hypnotism 130, 135
hysteria 15, 16, 95, 130–1, 134, 151, 235

ideomotor phenomenon 130
Illustrated Sunday Herald, The 210
Imperial War Graves Commission (IWGC) 12, 182, 195
Innes, Taylor A. 137, 147

James, William 2, 159n.38, 176–7
   psychical research 2, 159n.38
   streams of consciousness 5, 134–5, 159n.38, 269
Janet, Pierre 131–2, 135, 175–7
Jephson, Ina 258
John Bull's investigations into spiritualism 232
Jung, Carl Gustav 176

Kelway-Bamber, Eliza 49
Khun, Thomas 57
Kinmel Park Mutiny 56
Kipling, Rudyard 15, 39, 182, 195, 197, 199
Kitchener's Army 143, 169

Labour Party 233, 234
   and the outbreak of the First World War 45

Lampeter, Wales 166, 193
Leadbeater, C. W. 46
Leaf, Horace 62, 231, 232
League of Nations 59–61, 228
League of Nations Union 59, 228
LeBon, Gustav 264
Leonard, Gladys Osborne 32–3, 124n.147, 166, 169, 174, 177, 180, 184, 189–90, 191–6, 201n.26, 220, 269
   and Feda 174, 177, 196, 220, 269
   and word association tests 176
   letters from soldiers and their families 138–9
Liberal Party 233, 234
Lincoln, Mary Todd and spirit photography 214
Little, Ellen 177, 254
Lodge, Mary 144, 174, 195
Lodge, Oliver 3, 8–9, 12, 14, 15, 39, 41–2, 47, 54, 57–8, 64, 103, 122nn.107, 146–7, 166, 169, 177
   death 199, 266
   and the ether 6, 57, 181, 264–6
   the ethereal body 181
   Raymond 23n.5, 49, 73n.97, 101, 102, 106, 174, 177, 190, 200n.15
   relationship with Conan Doyle 57, 60, 169
   spirit photography 235
Lodge, Raymond 47, 54, 144, 169, 174, 177, 185, 188, 206n.104
London Spiritualist Alliance (LSA) 11, 16, 55
Longstaff, Will 225
   Ghosts of Vimy Ridge 225
   Menin Gate at Midnight 225
lost generation
   myth of 14
Luther, Martin 110

MacDonald, Ramsay 45
MacDonell, Cameron (Lieutenant-General) 94

Index

McKenzie, Barbara 220–2, 240
McKenzie, James Hewat 220–1, 240, 245n.65
McKenzie, William (Second Lieutenant) 220–1, 240
Macnaghten, Angus and Hazel 183–4, 197–9
Magic Circle *see* Price, Harry
Margaret, Florence 150, 151
masculinity 168
  in the British Expeditionary Force 95, 106–7
  in letters home 152
  and spiritualism 11–12, 106–7, 173, 185, 194, 270
mesmerism 129–30, 131
  colonialism 148
  spiritualism 130
  telepathy 131
Mesopotamia battlefields 86
Methodism 45
Meurig-Morris, Louisa Ann 63, 65, 270
millennialism 34–5, 40–1, 54, 58, 194
  catastrophic millennialism 35, 46, 57, 60
  definition of 34
  progressive millennialism 35
  and the Second Coming 55–6
Montague, Charles Edward 1
Montgomery, Lucy Maud (L. M.) 145
  Rilla of Ingleside 145
Morse, James J. 9, 10, 42
Moses, William Stainton 37, 172
Moss, George 220, 239
mothers and spiritualism 186–7
Mulholland, Andrew Edward Somerset 186, 192
multiple personalities 15, 131–2, 135, 197–8, 259, 267–8
  and spiritualism 16, 175–6
  in the United States 15, 29n.75
Mumler, William 213–14, 215
Murray, Gilbert 59
Myers, Alfred 158n.20

Myers, Frederick W. H. 3, 39–40, 131–6, 138, 141, 150, 152–3, 158n.20, 193, 226, 266
  Human Personality and its Survival of Bodily Death 3, 134
  subliminal self 134–6, 159n.38, 266

Nash, Paul 81, 82
Northern Cyclist Battalion (NCB) 252–3, 255, 259
Nostradamus 46

Oaten, Ernest 227–8, 231, 239
occult revival
  in Britain 5
  on the Western Front 102
orientalism 148, 176
Ortner, Violet 170, 172, 189, 194, 195, 201n.26
Ouija boards 100, 173
Owen, Harold 2, 128, 129, 155
Owen, Wilfrid 2, 128, 129, 268

pacifism 58, 61, 67
  and spiritualism 43, 58, 100
paranormal 259
parapsychology 271
  origins of 257–9
Passchendaele *see* Battle of Third Ypres
Peirce, Charles S. 137, 141
Peters, Alfred Vout 170, 174, 177, 226
photography
  history of 213
  mechanical objectivity 214–15, 217
    definition of 243n.29
  technology 213
physics
  the ether 37, 264, 266
  and spiritualism 257, 265
Piddington, J. G. 11, 58, 256
Piper, Leonora 54, 172
Plumer, Herbert (General) 94

Podmore, Frank 133
prayer on the battlefields 96–7
premonitions 91, 94–6, 113
  false premonitions 95–6
Price, Harry 233, 234
progress 34, 43–4, 62, 273–4
prophecies 34, 47, 60, 66
  definition of 36
  of the First World War 46–7,
    57–8, 274
  of the Second World War 32–4
providence 97–8, 253–4
psychiatry 267–8
  and psychical research 6, 132,
    257
psychoanalysis 131, 156, 168
  in Britain 37, 159n.23, 267
Punch 146, 162n.81

Queen's Hall 228, 231, 241,
  242n.14

race riots of 1919 56
Randi, James 271
Red Cross 183–4
relativity 57, 65, 198, 265–6, 271,
  273
Rhine, J. B. 257–8, 263, 277nn.23,
  28
  Extrasensory Perception 258
Rhys-Davids, Arthur 182, 184,
  189, 192–3, 194
Rhys-Davids, Caroline 182, 184–5,
  186, 189, 192–3, 194, 197
Richet, Charles 2, 160n.55
Robinson, Henry Peach 215
Russo-Japanese War 228

St Leger, William Brett 98–9, 105
Saskatchewan 128
Sassoon, Siegfried 1, 61, 97, 268,
  275–6
  opinions on spiritualism 23n.5
science fiction 35
Scientific American 231, 240
Scientology 271
séances 21, 193, 255, 257
  on the battlefields 106–7,
    123n.138

  different varieties of 172
  mourning 168, 186–8, 190
  physical phenomena 172, 175,
    240
  as sources 169–72, 200n.16
  and technology 175
  and trance mediumship 172–4
Second World War 266–7
  fall of France 266
  outbreak of 32–4, 252
  and spiritualism 20, 32–4, 66–7,
    275–6
shell shock 15, 143, 168, 268,
  273
Sheridan, Claire 65–6
Sidgwick, Eleanor 40
Sidgwick, Henry 134
Sinclair, May 5, 269
Sinnett, Alfred Percy 46
Smith, Whatley *see* Carrington,
  Whatley
socialism 254
Society for Psychical Research
  (SPR) 6, 47, 137, 141,
  146–7, 149–51, 153–4,
  169, 230, 256, 263
  archives 21, 221
  and dynamic psychiatry 6, 156
  first generation of 40, 131–6
  hallucination census 128,
    157n.6
  *Journal of the Society for
    Psychical Research* 195
  on the Western Front 102
  membership 49
  origins of 6, 128, 131
  Phantasms of the Living 133,
    137
  criticisms of 137, 257
  *Proceedings of the Society
    for Psychical Research*
    132
  spirit photography 233
  William Hope *see* Hope,
    William
Society for the Study of
  Supernormal Pictures
  (SSSP) 214
Southcott, Joanna 35, 46

spirit photography 21, 212–13, 226, 271
  accusations of fraud 21–2, 215–16
  Armistice Day 210–11, 216–17, 229, 235–7, 239, 241
  class 234–5
  criticisms of 219–20, 235–6
  gender 234–5
  history of 213–17
  missing soldiers 220, 222
  mourning 217–21
  psychic photography 216
  recognition 218–22, 237–8, 239
spiritualist journals
  Banner of Light 213
  Light 41–7, 49, 56, 57, 65, 73n.99, 111, 212, 219, 220–2, 226, 230–1, 248n.124
    subscription numbers 55, 232
  Spiritual Magazine 214
  Two Worlds, The 10, 42–5, 48, 56–7, 63, 65, 102–3, 106, 111, 220, 226, 229, 232, 235, 237–9, 270
    on the battlefields 102–3
Spiritualist National Union (SNU) 33, 44, 55, 59, 67, 79n.201
  census numbers 48–9, 66, 67, 72n.94
  representation on the Western Front 102
Spital Tongues 252
Stead, Estelle 210–12, 229–31, 236–8
Stead, W. T. 148, 210, 216, 227–8, 230–1, 236–7, 239
  interest in spiritualism 230
Stravinsky, Igor
  Rite of Spring, The 37
Sudetenland crisis 32
Summerland *see* heaven
Sunday Express 231
supernormal, the 3, 17, 18, 82, 153, 258–9
  and children 153–5
  definition of 3

superstitions and soldiers 83–90, 111–12
Swaffer, Hannen 238, 250n.172

Talbot, Henry Fox 214
telegraphy
  and spiritualism 5, 6, 25n.23, 226, 274
telepathy 2, 135, 226, 227, 230, 257, 259
  acceptance of 2, 3, 257, 272
  definition of 133, 138, 157n.7
  and empire 137–8, 140, 147–9, 151, 156
  evidence for 132–3, 136–7, 145, 263
    criticisms of 137, 257–8
  and the First World War 128–9, 133–4, 146, 147, 153, 155–6
  origins of 128, 132–6
  reports of 127–8
  and spiritualism 129, 136, 151–4
theosophy 46, 271, 275
  criticisms of 37
  and divination 36
thin places 22, 226
thought-transference 132, 133
Thurston, Herbert 33
Times, The 157n.1, 189
Tomb of the Unknown Warrior, the *see* war memorials
Treaty of London 41
trench journals 83, 116n.7
  Listening Post, The 86–7
  R.M.R. Growler 101
  Shell Hole Advance, The 83
  Switchboard, The 95
Troubridge, Una 174, 269–70
Turner, E. S. 143
Tylor, Edward 36–7, 38

unidentified flying objects (UFOs) 271–2
Usborne Moore, William 43

Vango, J. J. 11, 182, 184
veterans 274

Walker, Damaris 166, 169, 173, 178, 192, 196, 203n.49
Walker, Elsi 22, 166–7, 169–72, 176–9, 185, 187, 188–99
Walker, Nea 122n.107, 166–7, 169–73, 175–80, 185, 188–9, 191–8, 269–70
  relationship with Oliver Lodge 166, 169
Wallace, Abraham 182
Wallace, Alfred Russell
  and spiritualism 2–3, 38–9
war memorials 13, 275
  Cenotaph, the 13, 21, 199, 210, 223–5
  Tomb of the Unknown Warrior, the 13, 198–9, 272
war profiteers 235–6
war telegrams 143–4
Watt, George 254

Wayte, Wilfrid 22, 166, 169–70, 173, 177–8, 180, 184–97, 198, 205n.91
Wayte family 139–40, 170, 179, 180, 184–6, 189, 191–3, 199
Weber, Max 3
Wells, H. G. 35–6, 45
Whig history 38
Wicca 271
widows 185–6
Wilhelm II (Kaiser) 43, 46
witchcraft 4–5
women and spiritualism 11–12, 185, 268–71
Woolf, Virginia 5, 269
Wundt, Wilhelm 132
Wynn, Walter (Reverend) 175, 178–9, 184

YMCA 92

EU authorised representative for GPSR:
Easy Access System Europe, Mustamäe tee 50,
10621 Tallinn, Estonia
gpsr.requests@easproject.com

www.ingramcontent.com/pod-product-compliance
Lightning Source LLC
Chambersburg PA
CBHW051558230426
43668CB00013B/1900